Elisha Calkins
&
Anna Dalrymple

Descendants

Compiled from

United States Federal

&

State Territorial Census Records

1850 – 1930

By **Donovan Hurst**

May 1, 2012

Cover Image – Wabasha County, Minnesota July 2006

ISBN: 098569680X
ISBN-13: 978-0-9856968-0-1

Dedication

This work is dedicated to all of those that came before us and shaped our lives

to make us the people that we are today.

"We are not famous, we are farmers."

Table of Contents

Introduction

This work focuses on the family of Mayflower descendant Elisha Calkins & Anna Dalrymple, who settled in the town of Otselic, in the county of Chenango, in the State of New York and their descendants with information compiled from United States Federal & State Territorial Census Records from the years of 1850 – 1930.

Elisha Calkins connection to the ship "Mayflower" is a s follows: Edward Fuller (Passenger on board the ship "Mayflower") married to Unknown, son Samuel Fuller married to Jane Lothrop, son John Fuller married to Mehitable Rowley, daughter Thankful Fuller married to Jabez Crippen, son Thomas Crippen married to Deborah Unknown, daughter Deborah Crippen married Joseph Calkins, and son Elisha Calkins married to Anna Dalrymple, the subject of this work.

Information gathered on the family of Elisha Calkins & Anna Dalrymple and each of their descendants regarding each individual's date of birth, death, and marriage were gathered through the LDS Family Search Website, which can be found at https://www.familysearch.org/. Additional information was gathered through researching newspapers, deed records, land records, vital records, church records, military records, books, and family correspondence. All of the information presented in this work is believed to be true and accurate based on the research conducted by the author.

To help guide the reader of this work, the format of this book is as follows:

- **Main Family Entry** (Husband and Wife) (Father and Mother) followed by birth date and location, death date and location – marriage date and location

  - **Child of Main Family Entry**, including Spouse(s) when available followed by birth date and location, death date and location – marriage date and location

    - **Grandchild of Main Family Entry**, including Spouse(s) when available followed by birth date and location, death date and location – marriage date and location

      - **Great-Grandchild of Main Family Entry**, including Spouse(s) when available followed by birth date and location, death date and location – marriage date and location

(**Bolded Text**) following any entry includes any additional information such as Residence(s), Occupation(s), Signature(s), etc. when available

Family Overview

- **Elisha Calkins**, b. 6 Feb 1777 in Sharon, Litchfield Co., Connecticut, d. 8 Aug 1861 in Otselic, Chenango Co., New York & **Anna Dalrymple**, b. 16 Jun 1778 in Northbridge, Worcester Co., Massachusetts, d. 22 Jan 1864 in Otselic, Chenango Co., New York – 31 Mar 1799 in Tinmouth, Rutland Co., Vermont

Signatures:

  o **Truman D. Calkins** – b. 1 Jun 1800 in Tinmouth, Rutland Co., Vermont, d. Before 1900 in Madison Co., New York

  o **Mary Calkins** – b. 16 Mar 1802 in Sudbury, Rutland Co., Vermont, d. 24 Jul 1883 Readmond, Emmet Co., Michigan

  o **Laura H. Calkins** – b. 11 Sep 1803 in Greenfield, Saratoga Co., New York, d. 18 Mar 1880 in Chenango Co., New York

  o **Almira Calkins** – b. 12 Sep 1805 in Greenfield, Saratoga Co., New York, d. 17 Mar 1887 in Columbus, Warren Co., Pennsylvania

  o **Freeman Calkins** – b. 9 Nov 1807 in Greenfield, Saratoga Co., New York, d. Between 1880 – 1885 in Minneiska, Wabasha Co., Minnesota

  o **Lyman Simon Calkins** – b. 16 May 1811 in Brookfield, Madison Co., New York, d. 30 Mar 1889 in Brodtville, Grant Co., Wisconsin

  o **Heman Calkins** – b. 13 Aug 1812 in Brookfield, Madison Co., New York, d. 5 Apr 1886 in Otselic, Chenango Co., New York

  o **Dorman Calkins** – b. 20 Jun 1816 in Brookfield, Madison Co., New York, d. 17 Dec 1883 in Otselic, Chenango Co., New York

1

○ **Harriet Calkins** – b. 9 Sep 1818 in Brookfield, Madison Co., New York, d. 31 Oct 1911 in Smyrna, Chenango Co., New York

○ **William Riley Calkins** – b. 7 Dec 1825 in Otselic, Chenango Co. New York, d. 16 Sep 1896 in Laurens, Otsego Co., New York

Elisha Calkins (father):

Residence – Tinmouth, Rutland Co., Vermont – 1800

Greenfield, Saratoga Co., New York – 1810

Otselic, Chenango Co., New York – 1820

1830

1840

August 5, 1850

June 27, 1860

Occupation – Farmer – August 5, 1850

June 27, 1860

Anna Dalrymple (mother):

Residence – Otselic, Chenango Co., New York – August 5, 1850

June 27, 1860

Occupation – None Listed – August 5, 1850

June 27, 1860

Elisha Calkins & Anna Dalrymple

Family Photo Album (Found at an Estate Sale near Medina, Ohio)

Date of Album – 1860s

Photographs – Tintypes

Photographs courtesy of The Hurst Family of Lake Elsinore, California

Elisha Calkins & Anna Dalrymple

Family Photo Album (Found at an Estate Sale near Medina, Ohio)

Date of Album – 1860s

Photographs courtesy of The Hurst Family of Lake Elsinore, California

Elisha Calkins & Anna Dalrymple

Photographs courtesy of The Hurst Family of Lake Elsinore, California

Children of Elisha Calkins & Anna Dalrymple

1st Row (Front): Lyman Simon & Mary

2nd Row: Heman, Laura H. & Dorman

3rd Row: Almira, Harriet & Possibly Sarah Ann Woods

4th Row (Back): Truman & Freeman

Photograph – Tintype

Photograph courtesy of The Hurst Family of Lake Elsinore, California

Chenango Union Thu Oct. 9, 1873

MR. EDITOR—On Wednesday, October 1st, there was one of those remarkable family reunions at the old homestead of the Calkins family, in Otselic, which in these days of small families, pampered children and dissipated living, bid fair to become a thing of the past. In the family are ten children, who grew up among the trials and toils of fifty years ago, to strong, robust manhood and fair yet active womanhood; then separated to enter upon the duties which devolve upon mankind at that age—one becoming a resident of Minnesota, one of Wisconsin, one of Pennsylvania, and the rest of different parts of New York. And now, when old age has frosted their locks, and diminished though not impaired their bodily vigor, they leave their distant homes and assemble around the old fireside, to talk over their childhood pranks, and recount the trials and successes of a well-spent life. The average age of the ten, as will be seen by the following list, is above 63 years, and they are all in comparatively good health. The following is a list of their names, ages, and places of residence:

T. D. Calkins, born June 1st, 1800; age 73 years and 4 months; residence, Peterboro, Madison County, N. Y.

Mary Calkins, born March 16th, 1802; age 71 years, 7 months and 14 days; residence, Smyrna, Chenango Co., N. Y.

Laura Calkins, born September 11th, 1803; age 70 years and 12 days; residence, Otselic, Chenango Co., N. Y.

Almira Calkins, born September 12th, 1805; age 68 years and 18 days; residence, Columbus, Warren Co., Pa.

Freeman Calkins, born November 9th, 1807; age 66 years, 11 months and 21 days; residence, Mt. Vernon, Minn.

Simon Calkins, born May 16th, 1811; age 62 years, 5 months and 14 days; residence, Wyalusing, Grant Co., Wis.

Heman Calkins, born August 13th, 1813; age 60 years, 2 months and 17 days; residence, Otselic, Chenango Co., N. Y.

Dorman Calkins, born June 20th, 1816; age 57 years, 5 months and 10 days; residence, Otselic, Chenango Co., N. Y.

Harriet Calkins, born September 9th, 1818; age 55 years and 21 days; residence, Smyrna, Chenango Co., N. Y.

W. R. Calkins, born December 7th, 1825; age 48 years, 10 months and 23 days; residence, Smyrna, Chenango Co., N. Y.

Total ages, 634 years, 1 month and 7 days.

E. W. S.

This remarkable family visited this village on Thursday last, and took dinner at the Spaulding House. They were also photographed by one of our artists.

The Chenango Union – Thursday, October 9, 1873 – Calkins Family Reunion

Calkins Family Reunion

1st Row (Front) (Left to Right):

Catharine Maria (Richard) Calkins, Laura H., Almira, Truman D., Mary & Harriet

2nd Row (Back) (Left to Right):

William Riley, Freeman, Dorman, Heman & Lyman Simon

Date – October 1, 1873

Photograph courtesy of The Hurst Family of Lake Elsinore, California

Calkins Family Reunion

October 1, 1873

Photograph courtesy of The Hurst Family of Lake Elsinore, California

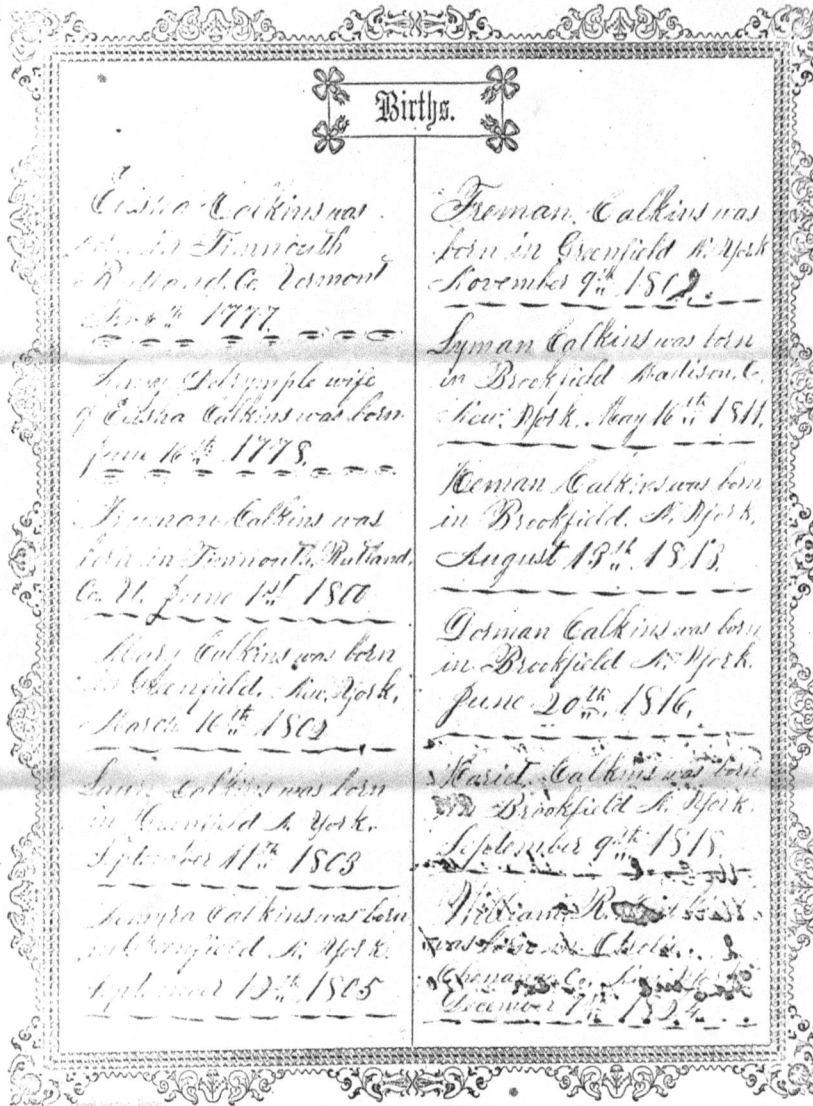

Births page of Family Bible belonging to

Mrs. Viola Calkins who donated a copy of four pages from the Calkins Family

Bible, July 12, 1980, to the Guernsey Memorial Library, Norwich, NY

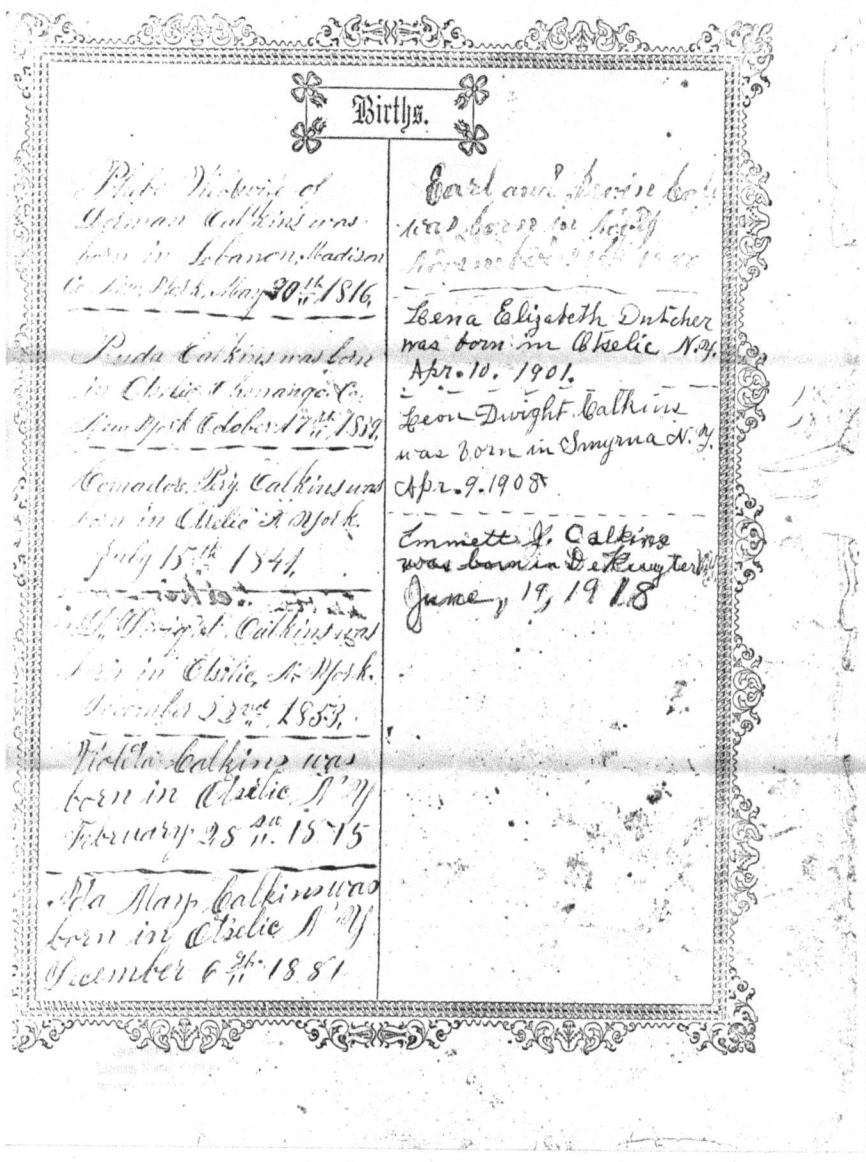

Births page of Family Bible belonging to

Mrs. Viola Calkins who donated a copy of four pages from the Calkins Family

Bible, July 12, 1980, to the Guernsey Memorial Library, Norwich, NY

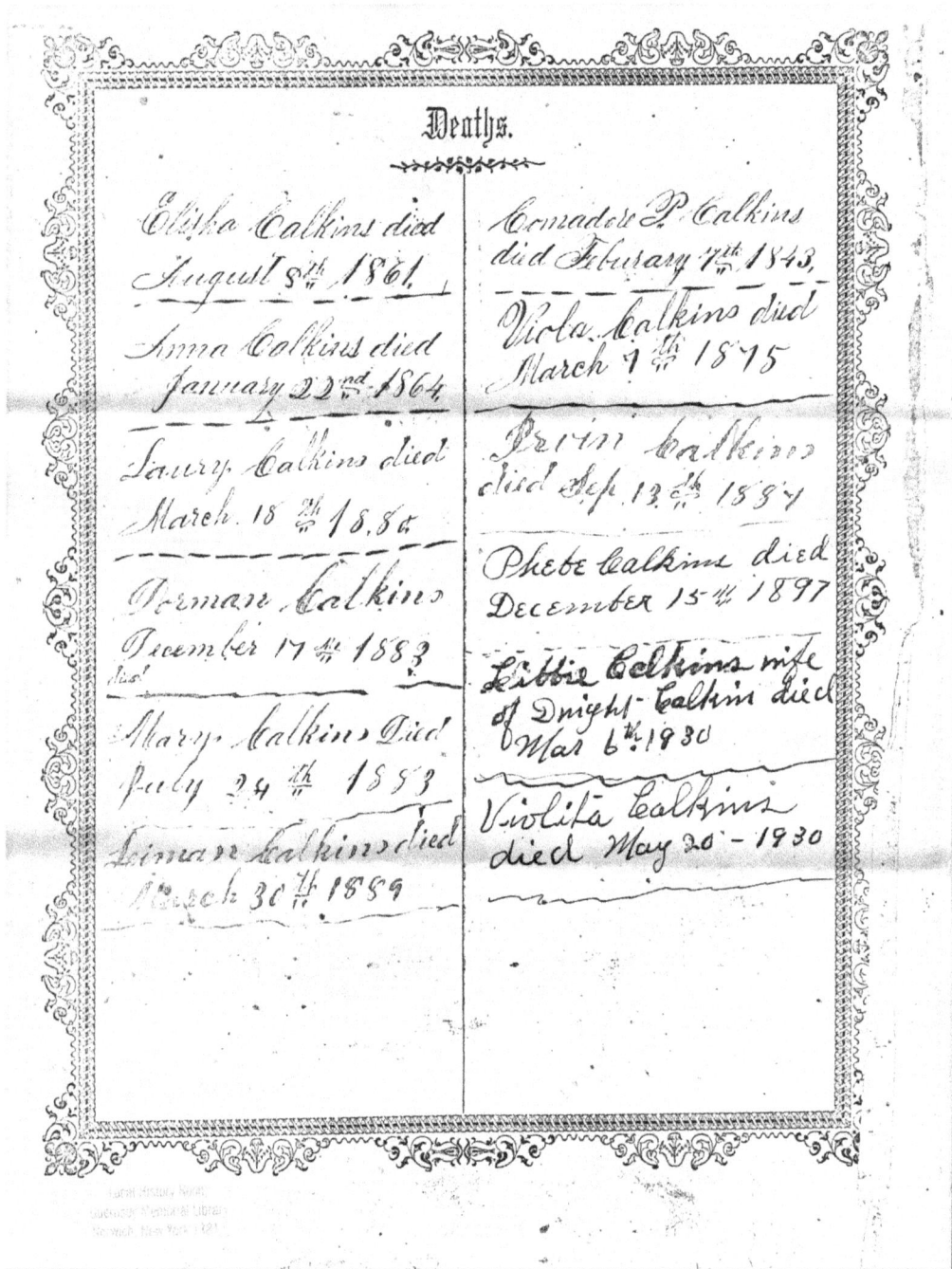

Deaths page of Family Bible belonging to

Mrs. Viola Calkins who donated a copy of four pages from the Calkins Family

Bible, July 12, 1980, to the Guernsey Memorial Library, Norwich, NY

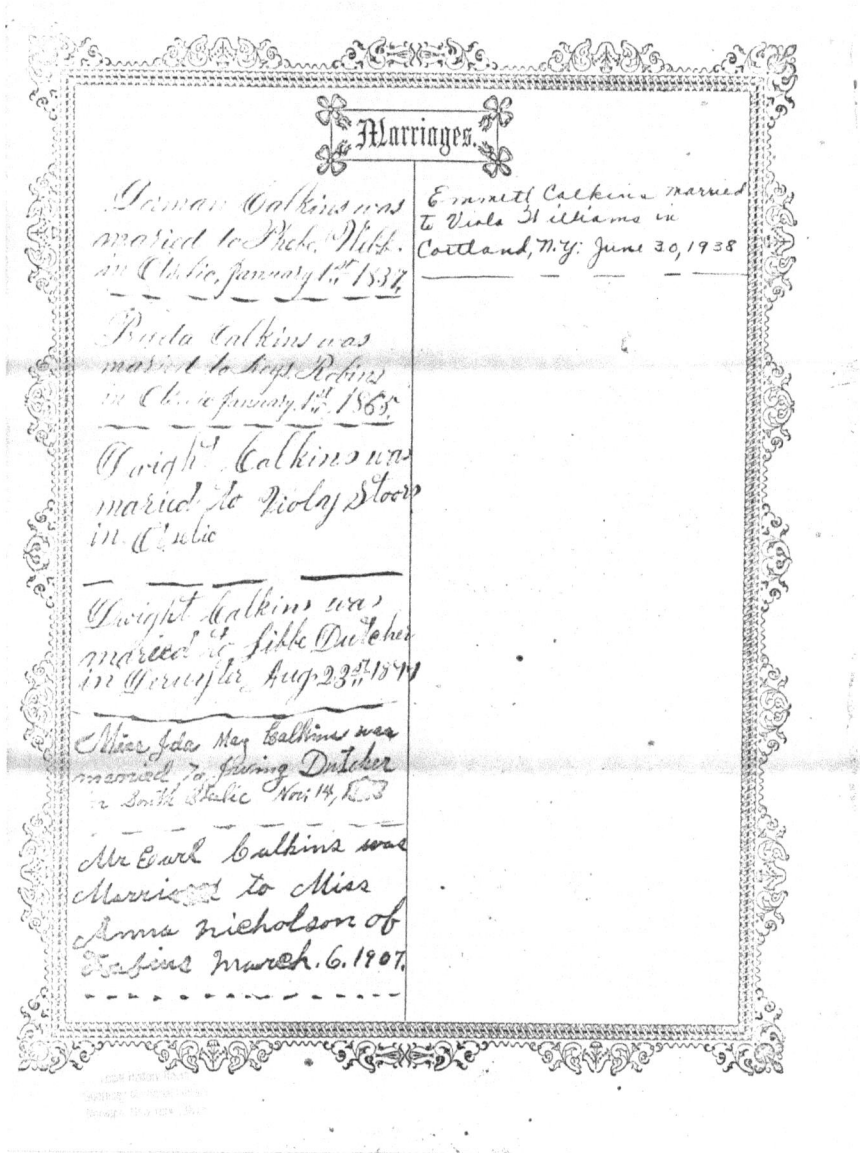

Marriages page of Family Bible belonging to

Mrs. Viola Calkins who donated a copy of four pages from the Calkins Family

Bible, July 12, 1980, to the Guernsey Memorial Library, Norwich, NY

Children Families

Truman D. Calkins & Descendants

- **Truman D. Calkins**, b. 1 Jun 1800 in Tinmouth, Rutland Co., Vermont, d. Before 1900 in New York & **Abigail P. Miles**, b. Between 1789 – 1790 in Maine, d. Before 1878 in New York – About 1818 in Vermont

Signatures:

- ○ **Rowena Calkins** – b. About 1815 in Chenango Co., New York, d. 1885 in Unadilla, Otsego Co., New York

Rowena Calkins (daughter):

Residence – Madison, Madison Co., New York – July 23, 1850

Lebanon, Madison Co., New York – July 24, 1860

Eaton, Madison Co., New York – June 7, 1880

Occupation – Keeping House – July 28, 1870

June 7, 1880

- ○ **Elisha Tracy Calkins**, b. 1 Feb 1824 in Otselic, Chenango Co., New York, d. 6 Aug 1904 in Hamilton, Madison Co., New York & **Celinda C. Ray**, b. 9 Nov 1829 in Otsego Co., New York, d. 18 Oct 1907 in Lebanon, Madison Co., New York – About 1847 in New York

  - ▪ **Unknown Calkins**

  - ▪ **Alice B. Calkins**, b. Aug 1861 in Madison Co., New York, d. 14 Dec 1915 in Lebanon, Madison Co., New York & **Clinton H. Stowell**, b. Dec 1855 in Georgetown, Madison Co., New York, d. 1922 in Madison, Madison Co., New York – 1 Sep 1897 in Randallsville, Madison Co., New York

14

• **George LaFayette Stowell** – b. 3 Feb 1900 in Madison, Madison Co., New York, d. Jan 1980 in

Marcy, Oneida Co., New York

Signature:

George LaFayette Stowell (son):

Residence – Lebanon, Madison Co., New York – June 12, 1900

April 30, 1910

June 1, 1915

September 13, 1918

January 2nd, 3rd, & 5th, 1920

Beacon City, Dutchess Co., New York – April 23, 1930

Occupation – School – June 1, 1915

Farmer – September 13, 1918

Laborer, Dairy Farm – January 2nd, 3rd, & 5th, 1920

Dining Room Worker (Manhattan State Hospital) – April 23, 1930

Alice B. Calkins (daughter):

Residence – Lebanon, Madison Co., New York – June 15, 1870

June 25, 1875

June 4, 1880

February 16, 1892

June 12, 1900

April 30, 1910

June 1, 1915

Occupation – None Listed – June 25, 1875

At School – June 4, 1880

Teacher – February 16, 1892

No Occupation – June 1, 1915

Obituary –

"Alice B. C. Stowell whose death occurred at her home in Lebanon Tuesday morning, Dec. 14, was the eldest daughter of Mr. and Mrs. E. Tracy Calkins, deceased of Hamilton. She was born in the town of Madison, Aug. 1, 1861, on the Carleton Rice place, but at that time owned by E. Tracy Calkins, who afterwards built a residence in Randallsville and lived there for a number of years, returning to Hamilton after the loss of the home by fire, and residing on Madison Street until his death. Alice B. C. Stowell received her early education in Hamilton Union school and the Randallsville school, and completed her course of study in Mrs. Hyde's Home school, Norwich Academy, Norwich. She was accomplished in art and a successful

15

Hurst

teacher for twenty years and taught eight years in Norwich high school, was married to Clinton H. Stowell, Sept. 1, 1897, at her home in Randallsville. She leaves her husband, C. H. Stowell, one son George L. Stowell, a student in Earlville High school; one sister, Minnie L. Calkins, and uncles, Judge G. W. Ray, Rev. J. L. Ray, D.D. of Norwich, and Rev. C. W. Ray, D.D. of Philadelphia." from The Madison County Times, Chittenango N.Y.

Clinton H. Stowell (son-in-law):

Residence – Lebanon, Madison Co., New York – June 12, 1900

April 30, 1910

June 1, 1915

September 13, 1918

January 2nd, 3rd, & 5th, 1920

Occupation – Farmer – June 12, 1900

September 13, 1918

Farmer, General Farm – April 30, 1910

General Farmer – June 1, 1915

Farmer, Dairy Farm – January 2nd, 3rd, & 5th, 1920

▪ **Minnie L. Calkins** – b. Jun 1864 in New York, d. Nov 1922 in Madison Co., New York

Minnie L. Calkins (daughter):

Residence – Lebanon, Madison Co., New York – June 15, 1870

June 25, 1875

June 4, 1880

February 16, 1892

June 3rd & 4th, 1900

April 30, 1910

June 1, 1915

January 2nd, 3rd, & 5th, 1920

Occupation – None Listed – June 25, 1875

At School – June 4, 1880

Music Teacher – June 3rd & 4th, 1900

June 1, 1915

January 2nd, 3rd, & 5th, 1920

Elisha Tracy Calkins (son):

Residence – Otselic, Chenango Co., New York – August 5, 1850

Madison, Madison Co., New York – August 14, 1860

Lebanon, Madison Co., New York – June 15, 1870

June 25, 1875

June 4, 1880

February 16, 1892

June 3rd & 4th, 1900

Occupation – Farmer – August 5, 1850

  Master Carpenter – August 14, 1860

  Carpenter – June 15, 1870

   June 25, 1875

   June 4, 1880

   February 16, 1892

Value of Real Estate – $ 1, 000 – August 14, 1860

Value of Personal Estate – $ 300 – August 14, 1860

   $ 500 – June 15, 1870

Home Data for 1875 – Framed, valued at $ 1,800

Obituary –

"E. Tracy Calkins died at his home on Madison Street at 6 o'clock this morning, aged 80 years. About fifteen years ago Mr. Calkins became broken in health and gradually worn away. He was a native of Hamilton and lived all his life here, except about twenty-two years, which he spent in Randallsville. He is survived by his wife and one daughter, Minnie L. Calkins." from The Utica Observer. Saturday, August 6, 1904

Celinda C. Ray (daughter-in-law):

Residence – Otselic, Chenango Co., New York – August 5, 1850

  Madison, Madison Co., New York – August 14, 1860

  Lebanon, Madison Co., New York – June 15, 1870

    June 25, 1875

    June 4, 1880

    February 16, 1892

    June 3rd & 4th, 1900

Occupation – Keeping House – June 15, 1870

   June 25, 1875

   June 4, 1880

  None Listed – February 16, 1892

Obituary –

"Norwich, Oct. 31 – Celinda C. Calkins of Hamilton, widow of E. T. Calkins of that place formerly, and oldest sister of Judge George W. Ray and the Rev. John L. Ray of this place, died at the home of her daughter in Lebanon October 18." From The Utica Herald Dispatch. Thursday Evening, October 31, 1907

o **Lydia Ann Calkins**, b. 4 Jun 1826 in Otselic, Chenango Co., New York, d. 15 Jun 1907 in Georgetown, Madison Co., New York & **Jacob Walradt** (also spelled **Walrod**), b. 14 May 1825 in Vermont, d. 2 Jun 1896 in Lebanon, Madison Co., New York – 2 Jul 1845 in New York

▪ **Abigail Delina Walradt**, b. 18 Mar 1847 in Madison Co., New York, d. May 10, 1896 in Madison Co., New York & **Edwin Humphrey**, b. 2 Sep 1847 in Smyrna, Chenango Co., New York, d. 18 Mar 1927 in Otselic, Chenango Co., New York – About 1870 in New York

• **Carrie A. Humphrey,** b. May 1875 in New York & **LaDurna A. Holmes**, b. Oct 1871 in Pennsylvania – About 1893 in New York

o **Nellie May Holmes**, b. 9 Sep 1900 in Georgetown, Madison Co. New York, d. 6 Jun 1993 in Norwich, Chenango Co., New York & **Bryan Jennings Stone** (1st Husband), b. 8 Nov 1899 in Georgetown, Madison Co., New York, d. 21 Jun 1965 in Georgetown, Madison Co. New York – 11 May 1918 in Smyrna, Chenango Co., New York

Signature:

▪ **Cecil H. Stone** – b. 14 Jun 1918 in Georgetown, Madison Co., New York, d. Nov 1964 in New York

Cecil H. Stone (son):

Residence – Georgetown, Madison Co., New York – January 6, 1920

Otselic, Chenango Co., New York – June 1, 1925

April 16, 1930

Occupation – None – January 6, 1920

June 1, 1925

April 16, 1930

    ○ **Nellie May Holmes**, b. 9 Sep 1900 in Georgetown, Madison Co. New York, d. 6 Jun 1993 in

        Norwich, Chenango Co., New York & **Unknown Cummings** (2nd Husband)

Nellie May Holmes (daughter):

Residence – Georgetown, Madison Co., New York – April 29, 1910

                                        June 1, 1915

                                        May 11, 1918

                                        September 12, 1918

                                        January 6, 1920

                                        June 1, 1925

            Otselic, Chenango Co., New York – April 14, 1930

Occupation – None Listed – April 29, 1910

            At School – June 1, 1915

            Domestic – May 11, 1918

            None – January 6, 1920

                    April 14, 1930

            Housewife – June 1, 1925

Bryan Jennings Stone (1st Husband) (son-in-law):

Residence – Smyrna, Chenango Co., New York – May 11, 1918

            Georgetown, Madison Co., New York – September 12, 1918

                                      January 6, 1920

                                      June 1, 1925

            Otselic, Chenango Co., New York – April 14, 1930

Occupation – Creamery Helper – May 11, 1918

            Laborer – September 12, 1918

            Farmer, General Farm – January 6, 1920

            County Road, Laborer – June 1, 1925

            Mechanic, Garage – April 14, 1930

Home Data for 1930 – Rental, $ 3 a month, no radio set, not on a farm

    ○ **Nina D. Holmes**, b. 5 Feb 1902 in Texas Hill, Madison Co., New York, d. 8 Mar 2000 in

        Cooperstown, Otsego Co., New York & **Lionell Mayne Kinney**, b. 13 Sep 1896 in

        Georgetown, Madison Co., New York, d. 1 Mar 1988 – 30 Mar 1918 in Sherburne, Chenango

        Co., New York

Signature:

■ **Melvin L. Kinney** – b. 5 Jul 1918 in Georgetown, Madison Co., New York, d. 7 May 2010 in Little Falls, Herkimer Co., New York

Melvin L. Kinney (son):

Residence – Georgetown, Madison Co., New York – January 6, 1920

Willet, Cortland Co., New York – June 1, 1925

Andes, Delaware Co., New York – April 11, 1930

Occupation – None – January 6, 1920

April 11, 1930

None Listed – June 1, 1925

■ **Hazel M. Kinney**, b. 5 Nov 1920 in Georgetown, Madison Co., New York, d. 17 Oct 2005 in Richfield Springs, Otsego Co., New York & **Raymond G. Smith**, b. 21 Jan 1919 in Van Hornesville, Herkimer Co., New York, d. 3 Mar 2000 in Richfield Springs, Otsego Co., New York

Hazel M. Kinney (daughter):

Residence – Willet, Cortland Co., New York – June 1, 1925

Andes, Delaware Co., New York – April 11, 1930

Occupation – None Listed – June 1, 1925

None – April 11, 1930

Nina D. Holmes (daughter):

Residence – Georgetown, Madison Co., New York – April 29, 1910

June 1, 1915

March 30, 1918

January 6, 1920

Willet, Cortland Co., New York – June 1, 1925

Andes, Delaware Co., New York – April 11, 1930

Occupation – None Listed – April 29, 1910

At School – June 1, 1915

Domestic – March 30, 1918

None – January 6, 1920

April 11, 1930

Housework – June 1, 1925

Lionell Mayne Kinney (son-in-law):

Residence – Georgetown, Madison Co., New York – March 30, 1918

June 5, 1918

January 6, 1920

Willet, Cortland Co., New York – June 1, 1925

Andes, Delaware Co., New York – April 11, 1930

Occupation – Laborer – March 30, 1918

? [Hard to Read] R. R. – June 5, 1918

Farmer, General Farm – January 6, 1920

Road Laborer – June 1, 1925

Foreman, Road Construction – April 11, 1930

Home Data for 1930 – Rental, $15 a month, has radio set, not on a farm

      o **Neta V. Holmes**, b. 5 Feb 1902 in Georgetown, Madison Co., New York, d. 24 Apr 1998 in Norwich, Chenango Co., New York & **Glenn Stone**, b. 4 Jul 1895 in Lyons, Wayne Co., New York, d. Dec 1971 in Georgetown, Madison Co., New York

Signature:

Neta V. Holmes (daughter):

Residence – Georgetown, Madison Co., New York – April 29, 1910

June 1, 1915

January 6, 1920

Otselic, Chenango Co., New York – June 1, 1925

April 16, 1930

Occupation – None Listed – April 29, 1910

At School – June 1, 1915

None – January 6, 1920

April 16, 1930

Housework – June 1, 1925

Glenn Stone (son-in-law):

Residence – Detroit, Wayne Co., Michigan – June 5, 1917

Otselic, Chenango Co., New York – June 1, 1925

April 16, 1930

Hurst

Occupation – Chauffer, Unemployed – June 5, 1917

    Farm Work – June 1, 1925

    Farmer, General Farm – April 16, 1930

Home Data for 1930 – Owns home, valued at $ 900, has radio set, not on a farm

Carrie A. Humphrey (daughter):

Residence – Georgetown, Madison Co., New York – June 3, 1880

        February 16, 1892

        June 5, 1900

        April 29, 1910

        June 1, 1915

        January 6, 1920

    Otselic, Chenango Co., New York – June 1, 1925

        April 16, 1930

Occupation – None Listed – June 3, 1880

    June 5, 1900

    Farmer – February 16, 1892

    None – April 29, 1910

    January 6, 1920

    April 16, 1930

    Housework – June 1, 1915

    June 1, 1925

LaDurna A. Holmes (son-in-law):

Residence – Georgetown, Madison Co., New York – June 5, 1900

    April 29, 1910

    June 1, 1915

    January 6, 1920

    Otselic, Chenango Co., New York – June 1, 1925

    April 16, 1930

Occupation – Farmer – June 5, 1900

    June 1, 1915

    Farmer, General Farm – April 29, 1910

    January 6, 1920

    April 16, 1930

    Farm Work – June 1, 1925

Home Data for 1930 – Owns home, valued at $ 700, no radio set, not on a farm

● **Fred Truman Humphrey** – b. 4 Sep 1878 in New York

Signature:

[He did not sign his name, he signed with a check]

Fred Truman Humphrey (son):

Residence – Georgetown, Madison Co., New York – June 3, 1880

February 16, 1892

June 1, 1905

Batavia, Genesee Co., New York – June 1, 1900

Nelson, Madison Co., New York – June 5, 1900

June 1, 1915

January 3, 1920

June 1, 1925

April 25, 1930

Erieville, Madison Co., New York – September 12, 1918

Occupation – None Listed – June 3, 1880

February 16, 1892

Pupil at the New York State School for the Blind – June 1, 1900

At School – June 5, 1900

Farm Laborer – June 1, 1905

June 1, 1915

Farming – September 12, 1918

Laborer, Farm – January 3, 1920

June 1, 1925

April 25, 1930

Abigail Delina Walradt (daughter):

Residence – Eaton, Madison Co., New York – July 17, 1850

Lebanon, Madison Co., New York – July 27, 1860

Georgetown, Madison Co., New York – August 10, 1870

June 3, 1880

February 16, 1892

Hurst

Occupation – None Listed – July 17, 1850

July 27, 1860

Keeps House – August 10, 1870

Keeping House – June 3, 1880

Farmer – February 16, 1892

Edwin Humphrey (son-in-law):

Residence – Georgetown, Madison Co., New York – August 10, 1870

June 3, 1880

February 16, 1892

Occupation – Farmer – August 10, 1870

June 3, 1880

February 16, 1892

Value of Real Estate – $ 3, 000 – August 10, 1870

Value of Personal Estate – $ 600 – August 10, 1870

- ▪ **Irving Jacob Walradt** – b. 13 Dec 1852 in Lebanon, Madison Co., New York, d. 9 Oct 1919 in Georgetown, Madison Co., New York & **Lodena L. Coye**, b. Aug 1857 in New York, d. 6 Apr 1907 in Otselic, Chenango Co., New York – 1877 in New York

  - ● **Frank Jacob Walradt**, b. 19 Sep 1878 in New York, d. 7 May 1939 in Georgetown, Madison Co., New York & **Nellie M. Robbins**, b. 19 Jun 1880 in New York, d. Jul 1968 in Georgetown, Madison Co., New York – About 1900 in New York

Signature:

    - ○ **Ivan J. Walradt**, b. 21 Feb 1901 in New York, d. 10 Jan 1956 in Hamilton, Madison Co., New York & **Joyce S. Carncross**, b. 1899 in New York, d. 1994 in New York – 15 Aug 1925 in New York

      - ▪ **Paul Richard Walradt** – b. 3 Sep 1926 in New York, d. 24 Apr 2004 in Banner Elk, Avery Co., North Carolina

Paul Richard Walradt (son):

Residence – Georgetown, Madison Co., New York – April 4th, 5th, & 7th, 1930

Occupation – None – April 4th, 5th, & 7th, 1930

Ivan J. Walradt (son):

    Residence – Georgetown, Madison Co., New York – April 19, 1910

                                        January 9, 1920

                                        June 1, 1925

                                        April 4th, 5th, & 7th, 1930

    Occupation – None Listed – April 19, 1910

        Farmer, At Home – January 9, 1920

        Cheese Factory, Laborer – June 1, 1925

        Farmer, Own Business – April 4th, 5th, & 7th, 1930

    Home Data for 1930 – Owns home, no radio set, on a farm

    Obituary –

"Ivan J. Walrod. Ivan J. Walrod, 54, passed away Jan. 10 at Hamilton, Memorial Hospital after a short illness. He was born Feb. 23, 1901, son of Frank and Nellie Robbins Walrod. He was a lifelong resident of Georgetown. At the time of his death, he was Postal Clerk at Georgetown Postoffice. He was a member of the Georgetown Baptist Church. On August 15, 1925, he was united in Marriage to Joyce Carncross of Plymouth. He is survived by his wife, Joyce Carncross Walrod; his mother, Mrs. Nellie Walrod of Sherrill; a son, Paul, of Otselic; a grandson and a granddaughter, also of Otselic; two sister, Mrs. Ila Utter of Erieville, and Mrs. Ona Coye of Georgetown. Funeral Services were held Friday, Jan. 13, at the Georgetown Baptist Church, with Rev. Ralph B. Davie officiating. Interment was in Hillside Cemetery, Georgetown." from The De Ruyter Gleaner. Page Seven. Thursday, January 19, 1956

Joyce S. Carncross (daughter-in-law):

    Residence – Georgetown, Madison Co., New York – April 4th, 5th, & 7th, 1930

    Occupation – None – April 4th, 5th, & 7th, 1930

        ○ **Ona H. Walradt,** b. 11 Dec 1906 in Earlville, Chenango Co., New York, d. 13 May 1995 in Georgetown, Madison Co., New York & **Archie E. Coye**, b. 25 Jul 1903 in New York, d. 28 Nov 1994 in Georgetown, Madison Co., New York – After 1924 in New York

            ■ **Gerald A. Coye** – b. About 1928 in Georgetown, Madison Co., New York

Gerald A. Coye (son):

    Residence – Georgetown, Madison Co., New York – April 7th – 11th, 1930

    Occupation – None – April 7th – 9th, 1930

Ona H. Walradt (daughter):

    Residence – Georgetown, Madison Co., New York – April 19, 1910

                                            January 9, 1920

                                          April 7th – 9th, 1930

Hurst

Occupation – None Listed – April 19, 1910

        None – January 9, 1920

        April 7ᵗʰ – 9ᵗʰ, 1930

Archie E. Coye (son-in-law):

    Residence – Georgetown, Madison Co., New York – April 7ᵗʰ – 9ᵗʰ, 1930

    Occupation – Farmer, Own Business – April 7ᵗʰ – 9ᵗʰ, 1930

    Home Data for 1930 – Rental, has radio set, on a farm

           ○ **Ila Marguerite Walradt,** b. 4 Feb 1909 in New York, d. 10 Sep 1997 in Cazenovia, Madison Co., New York & **Robert Corwin Utter,** b. 29 Oct 1906 in New York, d. 4 Jul 1988 in Cazenovia, Madison Co., New York

Ila Marguerite Walradt (daughter):

  Residence – Georgetown, Madison Co., New York – April 19, 1910

                        January 9, 1920

                        June 1, 1925

                        April 8ᵗʰ – 11ᵗʰ, 1930

    Occupation – None Listed – April 19, 1910

        None – January 9, 1920

           April 8ᵗʰ – 11ᵗʰ, 1930

      School – June 1, 1925

Frank Jacob Walradt (son):

  Residence – Smyrna, Chenango Co., New York – June 10, 1880

        Georgetown, Madison Co., New York – February 16, 1892

                    June 8, 1900

                    April 19, 1910

                    September 12, 1918

                    January 9, 1920

                    June 1, 1925

                    April 8ᵗʰ – 11ᵗʰ, 1930

    Occupation – None Listed – June 10, 1880

        Farmer – February 16, 1892

            June 8, 1900

            September 12, 1918

            June 1, 1925

      Farmer, General Farm – April 19, 1910

                January 9, 1920

    Farmer, Own Business – April 8ᵗʰ – 11ᵗʰ, 1930

Home Data for 1930 – Owns home, has radio set, on a farm

Obituary –

"May 9. – Funeral services for Frank Walrod, 60, who died suddenly Monday morning, were held at the home at 3 p. m. Thursday with Rev. J. I. Chapman, pastor of the Baptist church officiating with burial in Hillside Cemetery. Mr. Walrod was born in the town of Georgetown, September 19, 1878, son of Irving Jacob Walrod and Lodena Coye Walrod. He was married to Miss Nellie Robbins, 40 years ago. Their home was always in this vicinity where they operated a large farm which they sold a few months ago ad moved to Georgetown village. Surviving besides his wife are two daughters, Mrs. Robert C. Utter and Mrs. Archie Coye; one son Ivan Walrod; five grandchildren; two sisters, Mrs. May Foster and Mrs. Charles Waggoner; two brothers, Earl Walrod of Cazenovia and Olin Walrod of Erieville, besides nieces and nephews." from The De Ruyter Gleaner. Page Three. Thursday, May 11, 1939

Nellie M. Robbins (daughter-in-law):

Residence – Georgetown, Madison Co., New York – June 8, 1900

> *April 19, 1910*
> *September 12, 1918*
> *January 9, 1920*
> *June 1, 1925*
> *April 8th – 11th, 1930*

Occupation – None Listed – June 8, 1900

> *None – April 19, 1910*
> *January 9, 1920*
> *April 8th – 11th, 1930*
> *Housewife – June 1, 1925*

- **Earl Samuel Walradt**, b. 8 Mar 1881 in New York, d. Before 1946 in New York & **Bertha Sanderson** (1st Wife), b. 12 Jul 1881 in Otselic, Chenango Co., New York, d. Mar 1923 in Erieville, Madison Co., New York – 1902 in New York

Signature:

- **Earl Samuel Walradt**, b. 8 Mar 1881 in New York & **Grace M. Unknown** (2nd Wife), b. 9 Apr 1880 in Tully, Onondaga Co., New York, d. 20 Oct 1946 in New Woodstock, Madison Co., New York

Hurst

Earl Samuel Walradt (son):

Residence – Georgetown, Madison Co., New York – February 16, 1892

Pharsalia, Chenango Co., New York – June 2ⁿᵈ & 4ᵗʰ, 1900

Smyrna, Chenango Co., New York – June 1, 1905

Nelson, Madison Co., New York – April 25, 1910

June 1, 1915

January 3ʳᵈ – 5ᵗʰ, 1920

June 1, 1925

April 17ᵗʰ, 19ᵗʰ, & 21ˢᵗ, 1930

Erieville, Madison Co., New York –September 12, 1918

Occupation – None Listed – February 16, 1892

Farm Laborer – June 2ⁿᵈ & 4ᵗʰ, 1900

June 1, 1905

Farmer, Dairy Farm – April 25, 1910

Farmer – June 1, 1915

Farming – September 12, 1918

Operator, Farm – January 3ʳᵈ – 5ᵗʰ, 1920

Butter Maker – June 1, 1925

Foreman, Cheese Factory – April 17ᵗʰ, 19ᵗʰ, & 21ˢᵗ, 1930

Home Data for 1930 – Rental, $ 7 a month, has radio set, on a farm

Bertha Sanderson (1ˢᵗ Wife) (daughter-in-law):

Residence – Smyrna, Chenango Co., New York – June 1, 1905

Nelson, Madison Co., New York – April 25, 1910

June 1, 1915

January 3ʳᵈ – 5ᵗʰ, 1920

June 1, 1925

Occupation – Housework – June 1, 1905

June 1, 1915

June 1, 1925

None – April 25, 1910

January 3ʳᵈ – 5ᵗʰ, 1920

Obituary –

"Last Thursday morning, after an illness of only three days with pneumonia, Bertha Sanderson, wife of Earl Walrod, passed away. She was born in Otselic, the 12ᵗʰ of July, 1881. In her father's family were five children. Mr. and Mrs. Walrod were married about twenty-two years ago. Ten years ago this month a little motherless girl was taken into their home and two years later her little brother also came and Mrs. Walrod during these years has cared for them as a mother. Besides her husband, she leaves her parents, Mr. and Mrs. Fred Sanderson, and brother Lewis, of this place, a sister, Mrs. Merton Brown, of Canastota, the two children, Gertrude and Walter, and many more distant relatives by whom she will be greatly missed. The funeral was attended at the home Sunday afternoon, Rev. T. F. Harris, officiating. Friends were present at the funeral from Erieville, Georgetown, Canastota, and other places. Burial was made at Georgetown." from the De Ruyter Gleaner. Vol. 45. – No. 25. Thursday, March 8, 1923

Grace M. Unknown (2ⁿᵈ Wife) (daughter-in-law):

Residence – Nelson, Madison Co., New York – June 1, 1925

April 17ᵗʰ, 19ᵗʰ, & 21ˢᵗ, 1930

Occupation – Housework – June 1, 1925

None – April 17ᵗʰ, 19ᵗʰ, & 21ˢᵗ, 1930

Obituary –

"Mrs. Grace M. Walrod. Mrs. Grace M. Walrod, 66, widow of Earl Walrod of New Woodstock, died Monday at a convalescence home in New Woodstock after a long illness. Mrs. Walrod was born April 9, 1880, at Tully. She is survived by two sisters-in-law, Mrs. Max Miles of South Otselic and Mrs. Sarah Wagner of Erieville. Funeral services were held Wednesday at 2 p. m. in Smith's Home for Funerals, De Ruyter, The Rev. Clifford E. Webb officiating. Burial was made in Georgetown cemetery." from The De Ruyter Gleaner. Page Six. Thursday, October 24, 1946

- **Olin Irving Walradt**, b. 21 Aug 1884 in New York, d. 8 Jan 1947 in Skaneateles, Onondaga Co., New York & **Lula A. Damon**, b. About 1889 in New York – 1907 in New York

Signature:

  ○ **Alvin Joseph Walradt** – b. 8 Oct 1907 in New York, d. 24 Feb 1965

Alvin Joseph Walradt (son):

Residence – Eaton, Chenango Co., New York – April 20, 1910

Georgetown, Madison Co., New York – June 1, 1915

January 20, 1920

June 1, 1925

Nelson, Madison Co., New York – April 25, 1930

Occupation – None Listed – April 20, 1910

    At School – June 1, 1915

    None – January 20, 1920

    R. R. Section Laborer – June 1, 1925

    Laborer, Cheese Factory – April 25, 1930

o **Basil Olin Walradt**, b. 2 Jan 1917 in New York, d. 8 Jun 1989 in Zephyrhills, Pasco Co., Florida & **Anna Gertrude Isbell**, b. Apr 1920 in New York, d. Jun 1989

Basil Olin Walradt (son):

Residence – Georgetown, Madison Co., New York – January 20, 1920

        June 1, 1925

    Nelson, Madison Co., New York – April 25, 1930

Occupation – None – January 20, 1920

    April 25, 1930

    School – June 1, 1925

Obituary –

*"Basil Walrod, 72, who was born January 2, 1917 to Olin and Lula Walrod, died June 8 in Florida. Mr. Walrod was a graduate of Georgetown High School and farmed for many years in Erieville, Skaneateles, and Virginia before retiring to Zephyr Hills, Fla. He is survived by his wife Anna Isbell Walrod: two daughters, Linda Sutphen of Culpepper, Va., and Lory Payne of Warrenton, VA.; and six grandchildren. Mr. Walrod was buried from the Bealeton Baptist Church near Warrenton, Va. Attending the service from this area were the Rev. Norman Evans, who officiated; Florence Evans, the sister of Anna Walrod; Timothy Evans, who served as a pall bearer; Mr. and Mrs. Harold Foster, and Mr. and Mrs. Stanley Kellogg." **from the Press-Observer. Page A14. July 5, 1989***

Olin Irving Walradt (son):

Residence – Pharsalia, Chenango Co., New York – June 2nd & 4th, 1900

    Georgetown, Madison Co., New York – February 16, 1892

        June 1, 1905

        June 1, 1915

        September 12, 1918

        January 20, 1920

        June 1, 1925

    Eaton, Madison Co., New York – April 20, 1910

    Nelson, Madison Co., New York – April 25, 1930

Occupation – None Listed – February 16, 1892

> *April 20, 1910*

Farm Laborer – June 2ⁿᵈ & 4ᵗʰ, 1900

Farmer – June 1, 1905

> *June 1, 1915*

> *September 12, 1918*

Farmer, General Farm – January 20, 1920

Carpenter – June 1, 1925

> *April 25, 1930*

Obituary –

"*Olin Walrod. Funeral Services for Olin I. Walrod, 62, of Medina, and formerly of Georgetown were held Saturday at 3 p. m. at the Georgetown Baptist Church with the Rev. Augustus Peckham of the Chittenango Methodist Church and the Rev. Ralph Davie, pastor of the Georgetown Baptist Church, officiating. Mr. Walrod died suddenly Wednesday at the home of his son, Basil at Medina. He was born August 21, 1884, the son of Irving and Lodena Coye Walrod. He is survived by his wife, Lulu, two sons, Basil and Alvin; two sisters, Mrs. Charles Waggoner of Erieville and Mrs. Max Miles of South Otselic, and several nieces and nephews. Burial was in Hillside Cemetery.*" *from The De Ruyter Gleaner. Page Seven. Thursday, January 16, 1947*

Lula A. Damon (daughter-in-law):

Residence – Eaton, Madison Co., New York – April 20, 1910

> *Georgetown, Madison Co., New York – June 1, 1915*

> *September 12, 1918*

> *January 20, 1920*

> *June 1, 1925*

Nelson, Madison Co., New York – April 25, 1930

Occupation – None – April 20, 1910

> *January 20, 1920*

> *April 25, 1930*

Housework – June 1, 1915

Housewife – June 1, 1925

- **Euretta Walradt**, b. May 1887 in New York, d. Before 1915 in New York & **Windsor Charles Brown**, b. 23 Dec 1885 in New York, d. Dec 1967 in Erieville, Madison Co., New York – About 1906 in New York

Signature:

      ○ **Ethel Brown** – b. About 1907 in New York

Ethel Brown (daughter):

Residence – Georgetown, Madison Co., New York – April 19, 1910

June 1, 1915

June 1, 1925

Occupation – None Listed – April 19, 1910

At School – June 1, 1915

School – June 1, 1925

      ○ **Jerome W. Brown** – b. 30 Dec 1907 in New York, d. 7 Jun 1989 in New York

Jerome W. Brown (son):

Residence – Georgetown, Madison Co., New York – April 19, 1910

June 1, 1915

January 21, 1920

June 1, 1925

April 8th – 11th, 1930

Occupation – None Listed – April 19, 1910

At School – June 1, 1915

None – January 21, 1920

Farm Labor – June 1, 1925

Laborer, Farm – April 8th – 11th, 1930

      ○ **Lodena R. Brown** – b. About 1912 in New York

Lodena R. Brown (daughter):

Residence – Georgetown, Madison Co. , New York – June 1, 1915

January 21, 1920

June 1, 1925

April 8th – 11th, 1930

Occupation – No Occupation – June 1, 1915

None – January 21, 1920

April 8th – 11th, 1930

School – June 1, 1925

Elisha Calkins & Anna Dalrymple Descendants

○ **Aledah E. Brown,** b. 20 May 1913 in New York, d. 15 Aug 2003 in Manlius, Onondaga Co., New York & **Stanley B. Kellogg**, b. 6 Aug 1914 in New York, d. 27 Jan 2007 in Manlius, Onondaga Co., New York – Sept 1935 in Georgetown, Madison Co., New York

Aledah E. Brown (daughter):

Residence – Georgetown, Madison Co., New York – June 1, 1915

             January 21, 1920

             June 1, 1925

             April 8th – 11th, 1930

Occupation – No Occupation – June 1, 1915

        None – January 21, 1920

        April 8th – 11th, 1930

        School – June 1, 1925

Euretta Walradt (daughter):

Residence – Pharsalia, Chenango Co., New York – June 2nd & 4th, 1900

        Georgetown, Madison Co., New York – February 16, 1892

             June 1, 1905

             April 19, 1910

Occupation – None Listed – February 16, 1892

        At School – June 2nd & 4th, 1900

             June 1, 1905

        None – April 19, 1910

Windsor Charles Brown (son-in-law):

Residence – Georgetown, Madison Co., New York – April 19, 1910

             June 1, 1915

             September 12, 1918

             January 21, 1920

             June 1, 1925

             April 8th – 11th, 1930

Occupation – Farmer, Home Farm – April 19, 1910

        Farmer & Dealer – June 1, 1915

        Farmer – September 12, 1918

             June 1, 1925

        Partner, General Farm – January 21, 1920

        Farmer, Own Business – April 8th – 11th, 1930

Hurst

- **Elsie Sarah Walradt**, b. 9 Sep 1890 in Georgetown, Madison Co., New York, d. 23 Jul 1970 &

  Charles Arthur Waggoner, b. 24 Nov 1890 in Orwell, Oswego Co., New York, d. 15 Jun 1964

  in New York – 28 Nov 1912 in Hamilton, Madison Co., New York

Signature:

  ○ **Ruth Lillie Waggoner** – b. 14 Mar 1914 in New York, d. 14 Mar 1914 in New York

  ○ **Frieda M. Waggoner** – b. About 1921 in New York

Frieda M. Waggoner (daughter):

  Residence – Nelson, Madison Co., New York – April 25, 1930

  Occupation – None – April 25, 1930

Elsie Walradt (daughter):

  Residence – Georgetown, Madison Co., New York – February 16, 1892

  June 1, 1905

  Eaton, Madison Co., New York – April 20, 1910

  Munnsville, Madison Co., New York – November 28, 1912

  Georgetown, Madison Co., New York – June 1, 1915

  January 20, 1920

  Nelson, Madison Co., New York – April 25, 1930

  Occupation – None Listed – February 16, 1892

  November 28, 1912

  At School – June 1, 1905

  None – April 20, 1910

  January 20, 1920

  April 25, 1930

  Housework – June 1, 1915

Charles Arthur Waggoner (son-in-law):

  Residence – Munnsville, Madison Co., New York – November 28, 1912

  Georgetown, Madison Co., New York – June 1, 1915

  June 5, 1917

  January 20, 1920

  Nelson, Madison Co., New York – April 25, 1930

  Occupation – Farm Laborer – November 28, 1912

  Farmer – June 1, 1915

  June 5, 1917

Elisha Calkins & Anna Dalrymple Descendants

Farmer, General Farm – January 20, 1920

Famer, Dairy – April 25, 1930

Home Data for 1930 – Owns home, has radio set, on a farm

- **May Walradt** – b. About 1900 in New York

May Walradt (daughter):

Residence – Georgetown, Madison Co., New York – June 1, 1905

June 1, 1915

Eaton, Madison Co., New York – April 20, 1910

Occupation – None Listed – June 1, 1905

None – April 20, 1910

Housework – June 1, 1915

Irving Jacob Walradt (son):

Residence – Lebanon, Madison Co., New York – July 27, 1860

June 23, 1870

June 15, 1875

Smyrna, Chenango Co., New York – June 10, 1880

Georgetown, Madison Co., New York – February 16, 1892

June 1, 1915

Pharsalia, Chenango Co., New York – June 2nd & 4th, 1900

Eaton, Madison Co., New York – April 20, 1910

Occupation – Farm Labor – June 23, 1870

Farmer – June 15, 1875

June 10, 1880

February 16, 1892

June 2nd & 4th, 1900

June 1, 1915

Farmer, General Farm – April 20, 1910

Obituary –

"Georgetown. Oct 15. – Our community was pained to hear of the sudden death of Irving Walrod which occurred at his home Saturday morning. Mr. Walrod was able to be at his usual occupation Friday, and in the evening was in the village. Deceased leaves three sons, Frank, Earl, and Olin, and two daughters, Mrs. Elizabeth Wagner and Miss May Walrod, all of this town, who have the sincere sympathy of their many friends in their sudden bereavement. The funeral was held at his late home on Tuesday, Rev. Henry Buell officiating. Interment was made in Hillside cemetery beside his wife, who passed away several years ago." from the Madison County Leader and Observer. Morrisville, N. Y. Thursday Afternoon, October 16, 1919

Hurst

Lodena L. Coye (daughter-in-law):

Residence – Smyrna, Chenango Co., New York – June 10, 1880

    Georgetown, Madison Co., New York – February 16, 1892

    June 1, 1905

    Pharsalia, Chenango Co., June 2ⁿᵈ & 4ᵗʰ, 1900

Occupation – Keeping House – June 10, 1880

    Farmer – February 16, 1892

    None Listed – June 2ⁿᵈ & 4ᵗʰ, 1900

    Housework – June 1, 1905

Obituary –

"The sad news of the death of Mrs. Irving Walrod of pneumonia was received Sunday." from The De Ruyter Gleaner.

Page 2. Thursday, April 11, 1907

▪ **Truman Herbert Walradt**, b. 14 Aug 1858 in Lebanon, Madison Co., New York, d. 22 Apr 1912 in Lebanon, Madison Co., New York & **Lucy Arabelle Guiles**, b. 12 Jul 1861 in Union, Union Co., Illinois, d. 12 Feb 1942 in Norwich, Chenango Co., New York

● **Ella Mary Walradt**, b. 13 Aug 1882 in Lebanon, Madison Co., New York, d. 18 Feb 1966 & **Herbert Isaac Coye**, b. 18 Feb 1879 in New York, d. Jul 1956 in Pinellas Co., Florida – About 1899 in New York

Signature:

    ○ **Rena A. Coye** – b. About 1904 in New York

Rena A. Coye (daughter):

Residence – Smyrna, Chenango Co., New York – April 21, 1910

    January 16, 1920

Occupation – None – April 21, 1910

    January 16, 1920

    ○ **Alton H. Coye**, b. About 1909 in New York, d. 1939 in New York & **Florence Christine Anderson**, b. 14 Oct 1908 in Holmesville, Chenango Co., New York, d. 5 Apr 1985 in West Winfield, Herkimer Co., New York– 1919 in New York

      ▪ **Gladys C. Coye** – b. About 1930 in New York

Elisha Calkins & Anna Dalrymple Descendants

Gladys C. Coye (daughter):

   Residence – New Berlin, Chenango Co., New York – April 25, 1930

   Occupation – None – April 25, 1930

Alton H. Coye (son):

   Residence – Smyrna, Chenango Co., New York – April 21, 1910

                                        January 16, 1920

        New Berlin, Chenango Co., New York – April 25, 1930

   Occupation – None – April 21, 1910

                January 16, 1920

        Ass't Barber, Barber Shop – April 25, 1930

Florence Anderson (daughter-in-law):

   Residence – New Berlin, Chenango Co., New York – April 25, 1930

   Occupation – None – April 25, 1930

Ella Mary Walradt (daughter):

   Residence – Lebanon, Madison Co., New York – February 16, 1892

                                        June 26th & 27th, 1900

        Smyrna, Chenango Co., New York – April 21, 1910

                                        September 12, 1918

                                        January 16, 1920

                                        April 4, 1930

   Occupation – None Listed – February 16, 1892

                June 26th & 27th, 1900

        None – April 21, 1910

                January 16, 1920

        Matron, Boarding House – April 4, 1930

Herbert Isaac Coye (son-in-law):

   Residence – Lebanon, Madison Co., New York – June 26th & 27, 1900

        Smyrna, Chenango Co., New York – April 21, 1910

                                        September 12, 1918

                                        January 16, 1920

                                        April 4, 1930

   Occupation – Farmer – June 26th & 27th, 1900

        Farmer, General Farm – April 21, 1910

        Farming, By Himself – September 12, 1918

        Farmer, Diary Farm – January 16, 1920

        Operator, Portable saw-mill – April 4, 1930

37

Hurst

Home Data for 1930 – Rental, $ 8 a month, has radio set, not on a farm

- **Alma Belnett Walradt,** b. 30 Dec 1884 in Lebanon, Madison Co., New York, d. 25 May 1950 & **Clarence James Coye**, b. 5 Apr 1876 in Smyrna, Chenango Co., New York, d. 18 Sep 1952 in Sherburne, Chenango Co., New York – 16 Nov 1904 in New York
  - ○ **Franklin T. Coye** – b. 7 Jun 1909 in Sherburne, Chenango Co., New York, d. 31 Oct 2003 in Earlville, Chenango Co., New York

Franklin T. Coye (son):

Residence – Sherburne, Chenango Co., New York – May 13, 1910

January 2, 1920

June 1, 1925

Occupation – None – May 13, 1910

January 2, 1920

School – June 1, 1925

- ○ **Doris A. Coye** – b. About 1914 in New York

Doris A. Coye (daughter):

Residence – Sherburne, Chenango Co., New York – January 2, 1920

June 1, 1925

Occupation – None – January 2, 1920

School – June 1, 1925

- ○ **Gordon C. Coye** – b. 22 Apr 1915 in New York, d. 23 Oct 1996 in Syracuse, Onondaga Co., New York

Gordon C. Coye (son):

Residence – Sherburne, Chenango Co., New York – January 2, 1920

June 1, 1925

Occupation – None – January 2, 1920

School – June 1, 1925

Alma Belnett Walradt (daughter):

Residence – Lebanon, Madison Co., New York – February 16, 1892

June 5, 1900

Sherburne, Chenango Co., New York – May 13, 1910

January 2, 1920

June 1, 1925

Occupation – None Listed – February 16, 1892

June 5, 1900

None – May 13, 1910

January 2, 1920

Housework – June 1, 1925

Clarence James Coye (son-in-law):

Residence – Sherburne, Chenango Co., New York – May 13, 1910

January 2, 1920

June 1, 1925

Occupation – Farmer, General – May 13, 1910

Farmer, Diary Farm – January 2, 1920

Stenographer – June 1, 1925

- **Milton Adellon Walradt**, b. 1 Aug 1888 in Lebanon, Madison Co., New York, d. 24 Feb 1979 in Sherburne, Chenango Co., New York & **Mary Alta Reynolds**, b. About 1888 in Smyrna, Chenango Co., New York – 12 Aug 1908 in Chenango Co., New York

Signature:

○ **Mildred E. Walradt** – b. 1910 in New York

Mildred E. Walradt (daughter):

Residence – Smyrna, Chenango Co., New York – May 4, 1910

June 5, 1917

January 12, 1920

Sherburne, Chenango Co., New York – June 19, 1930

Occupation – None – May 4, 1910

January 12, 1920

Teacher, School – June 19, 1930

○ **Merle A. Walradt** – b. 10 Feb 1916 in New York, d. 10 Aug 1992 in New Hartford, Oneida Co., New York

Merle A. Walradt (son):

Residence – Smyrna, Chenango Co., New York – June 5, 1917

January 12, 1920

Sherburne, Chenango Co., New York – June 19, 1930

Occupation – None – January 12, 1920

June 19, 1930

Milton Adellon Walradt (son):

    Residence – Lebanon, Madison Co., New York – February 16, 1892

                      June 5, 1900

        Smyrna, Chenango Co., New York – August 12, 1908

                      May 4, 1910

                      June 5, 1917

                      January 12, 1920

        Sherburne, Chenango Co., New York – June 19, 1930

    Occupation – None Listed – February 16, 1892

                      June 5, 1900

        Farmer – August 12, 1908

                      June 5, 1917

        Farmer, General – May 4, 1910

        Farmer, Dairy, Farm – January 12, 1920

        Farmer, General Farm – June 19, 1930

    Home Data for 1930 – Owns home, has radio set, on a farm

Mary Alta Reynolds (daughter-in-law):

    Residence – Smyrna, Chenango Co., New York – August 12, 1908

                      May 4, 1910

                      June 5, 1917

                      January 12, 1920

        Sherburne, Chenango Co., New York – June 19, 1930

    Occupation – Teacher – August 12, 1908

        None – May 4, 1910

            January 12, 1920

            June 19, 1930

- **Nellie Daisy Walradt,** b. 23 Jan 1895 in Lebanon, Madison Co., New York, d. 15 Mar 1970 in Clearwater, Pinellas Co., Florida & **Howard Millard Greene**, b. 16 Jan 1893 in Rockland, Sullivan Co., New York, d. 25 Mar 1941 in Newburgh, Orange Co., New York – 1 Aug 1916 in Norwich, Chenango Co. New York

Signature:

40

Elisha Calkins & Anna Dalrymple Descendants

    ○ **Ardell Marie Greene**, b. 12 Feb 1922 in Orange Co., New York, d. 7 Feb 2003 in Palmyra, Fluvanna Co., Virginia & **Ernest Gould Peterson**, b. 9 Sep 1920 in Brooklyn, Kings Co., New York, d. 18 Nov 1995 in Palmyra, Fluvanna Co., Virginia

Ardell Marie Greene (daughter):

    Residence – Newburgh, Orange Co., New York – April 4, 1930

    Occupation – None – April 4, 1930

Nellie Daisy Walradt (daughter):

    Residence – Lebanon, Madison Co., New York – June 5, 1900

                                      April 26, 1910

        23 Rexford St. – August 1, 1916

        Norwich, Chenango Co., New York – June 5, 1917

        Middletown, Orange Co., New York – January 3, 1920

        Newburgh, Orange Co., New York – April 4, 1930

    Occupation – None Listed – June 5, 1900

        None – April 26, 1910

        April 4, 1930

        Teacher – August 1, 1916

        Teacher, School – January 3, 1920

Howard Millard Green (son-in-law):

    Residence – Norwich, Chenango Co., New York – August 1, 1916

                                 June 5, 1917

        Middletown, Orange Co., New York – January 3, 1920

        Newburgh, Orange Co., New York – April 4, 1930

    Occupation – Printer – August 1, 1916

        June 5, 1917

        Printer, Newspaper – January 3, 1920

        Vice President, Printing Co. – April 4, 1930

Home Data for 1930 – Owns home, valued at $ 10, 000, no radio set, not on farm

    • **Howard Guiles Walradt**, b. 1 Jul 1899 in Lebanon, Madison Co., New York, d. 19 Aug 1989 in Cary, Wake Co., North Carolina & **Dorothy Antoinette Burrows**, b. About 1900 – 10 Jun 1922 Norwich, Chenango Co., New York

        ○ **Elizabeth Walradt** – b. About 1925 in New York

Elizabeth Walradt (daughter):

    Residence – Wellsville, Allegany Co., New York – April 12, 1930

    Occupation – None Listed – April 12, 1930

Hurst

○ **Gordon Walradt** – b. Oct 1929 in New York

Gordon Walradt (son):

Residence – Wellsville, Allegany Co., New York – April 12, 1930

Occupation – None Listed – April 12, 1930

Howard Guiles Walradt (son):

Residence – Lebanon, Madison Co., New York – June 5, 1900

April 26, 1910

Norwich, Chenango Co., New York – January 6, 1920

June 10, 1922

Wellsville, Allegany Co., New York – April 12, 1930

Occupation – None Listed – June 5, 1900

None – April 26, 1910

Machinist, Rail Road Shop – January 6, 1920

Machinist – June 10, 1922

Machinist, ? [Hard to read] Heater – April 12, 1930

Home Data for 1930 – Rental, $ 20 a month, no radio set, not on a farm

Dorothy Antoinette Burrows (daughter-in-law):

Residence – Norwich, Chenango Co., New York – June 10, 1922

Wellsville, Allegany Co., New York – April 12, 1930

Occupation – Nurse – June 10, 1922

None – April 12, 1930

● **Lois Mildred Walradt**, b. 1 Jul 1902 in Lebanon, Madison Co., New York, d. May 1995 in Johnson, Broome Co., New York & **Daniel Hazard Burr**, b. 28 Sep 1898 in Norwich, Chenango Co., New York, d. May 1980 in Chenango Co., New York – 21 Mar 1919 in Norwich, Chenango Co., New York

○ **Donald H. Burr** – b. About 1920 in New York

Donald H. Burr (son):

Residence – Norwich, Chenango Co., New York – January 6, 1920

Occupation – None – January 6, 1920

○ **Doris Burr** – b. About 1922 in New York

Doris Burr (daughter):

Residence – Middletown, Orange Co., New York – April 5, 1930

Occupation – None – April 5, 1930

Elisha Calkins & Anna Dalrymple Descendants

o **Kenneth Burr** – b. About 1929 in New York

Kenneth Burr (son):

Residence – Middletown, Orange Co., New York – April 5, 1930

Occupation – None – April 5, 1930

Lois Mildred Walradt (daughter):

Residence – Lebanon, Madison Co., New York – April 26, 1910

Norwich, Chenango Co., New York – March 21, 1919

January 6, 1920

Middletown, Orange Co., New York – April 5, 1930

Occupation – None – April 26, 1910

January 6, 1920

April 5, 1930

Clerk – March 21, 1919

Daniel Hazard Burr (son-in-law):

Residence –Norwich, Chenango Co., New York – March 21, 1919

January 6, 1920

Middletown, Orange Co., New York – April 5, 1930

Occupation – Printer – March 21, 1919

Printer, Pharmacy – January 6, 1920

Printer ? [hard to read] – April 5, 1930

Home Data for 1930 – Rental, $ 40 a month, has radio set, not on a farm

Truman Herbert Walradt (son):

Residence – Lebanon, Madison Co., New York – July 27, 1860

June 23, 1870

June 15, 1875

June 12, 1880

February 16, 1892

June 5, 1900

April 26, 1910

Occupation – At School – June 23, 1870

Farmer – June 15, 1875

June 12, 1880

February 16, 1892

June 5, 1900

Farmer, General Farm – April 26, 1910

Home Data for 1875 – Framed, valued at $ 1,000

Hurst

Lucy Arabelle Guiles (daughter-in-law):

    Residence – Lebanon, Madison Co., New York – February 16, 1892

                                        June 5, 1900

                                        April 26, 1910

    Norwich, Chenango Co., New York – January 6, 1920

    Occupation – None Listed – February 16, 1892

                              June 5, 1900

                None – April 26, 1910

                      January 6, 1920

Lydia Ann Calkins (daughter):

    Residence – Eaton, Madison Co., New York – July 17, 1850

        Lebanon, Madison Co., New York – July 27, 1860

                                  June 23, 1870

                                  June 15, 1875

                                  June 12, 1880

                                February 16, 1892

                                June 5, 1900

    Occupation – Keeping House – June 12, 1880

            None Listed – June 15, 1875

                February 16, 1892

    Obituary –

*"Mrs. Jacob Walrod of Otselic, mother of Irving Walrod of this place, died very suddenly at his home June 15th while on a visit. Mr. Walrod has the sympathy of his friends in his double bereavement, having also lost his wife as late as April." **from the Madison County Leader and Observer. Morrisville, N. Y. 1907***

Jacob Walradt or Walrod (son-in-law):

    Residence – Eaton, Madison Co., New York – July 17, 1850

        Lebanon, Madison Co., New York – July 27, 1860

                                  June 23, 1870

                                  June 15, 1875

                                  June 12, 1880

                                  February 16, 1892

    Occupation – Farmer – July 17, 1850

                    June 23, 1870

                    June 15, 1875

                    June 12, 1880

February 16, 1892

Value of Real Estate – $ 1, 964 – July 27, 1860

$ 7, 500 – June 23, 1870

Value of Personal Estate – $1, 020 – July 27, 1860

$ 2, 500 – June 23, 1870

o **Abigail D. Calkins** – b. 1830 Chenango Co., New York, d. 9 Jan 1843 in Chenango Co., New York

o **Charlotte Melissa Calkins**, b. April 1837 in Otselic, Chenango Co., New York, d. 16 Jun 1901 in Unadilla, Otsego Co., New York & **Loren M. Tabor**, b. 23 Jun 1835 in Unadilla, Otsego Co., New York, d. 6 Sep 1914 in Wells Bridge, Otsego Co., New York

    ▪ **Hattie Lavantia Tabor**, b. May 1860 in Unadilla, Otsego Co., New York, d. 1931 in Afton, Chenango Co., New York & **George Washington Chapin**, b. 9 Dec 1840 in New York, d. 1922 Wells Bridge, Otsego Co., New York

Signature:

       • **Newell Ernest Chapin**, b. 24 May 1888 in Unadilla, Otsego Co. New York, d. 11 Dec 1972 in Afton, Chenango Co., New York & **Myrtle N. Root**, b. 6 Aug 1890 in Bainbridge, Chenango Co., New York, d. 3 Nov 1943 in Afton, Chenango Co., New York – 6 Aug 1913 in Wells Bridge, Otsego Co., New York

          o **Ernest Newell Chapin** – b. 23 Nov 1920 in Afton, Chenango Co., New York, d. 12 Oct 1979 in St. Petersburg, Pinellas Co., Florida

Ernest Newell Chapin (son):

Residence – Afton, Chenango Co., New York – June 1, 1925

April 4, 1930

Occupation – None Listed – June 1, 1925

None – April 4, 1930

Newell Ernest Chapin (son):

Residence – Unadilla, Otsego Co., New York – February 16, 1892

Sidney, Delaware Co., New York – June 22ⁿᵈ, 25ᵗʰ, & 27ᵗʰ, 1900

April 20, 1910

Afton, Chenango Co., New York – August 6, 1913

January 5, 1920

June 1, 1925

Hurst

April 4, 1930

Occupation – None Listed – February 16, 1892

At School – June 22nd, 25th, & 27th, 1900

Laborer, Creamery – April 20, 1910

Creamery – August 6, 1913

Laborer, Cheese Factory – January 5, 1920

Laborer, Feed Store – June 1, 1925

Laborer, Ice Business – April 4, 1930

Home Data for 1930 – no radio set, not on a farm

Myrtle N. Root (daughter-in-law):

Residence – Otsego, Otsego Co., New York – August 6, 1913

Afton, Chenango Co., New York – January 5, 1920

June 1, 1925

April 4, 1930

Occupation – Housework – August 6, 1913

June 1, 1925

None – January 5, 1920

April 4, 1930

- **Gladys Lucille Chapin**, b. Apr 1891 in Unadilla, Otsego Co., New York, d. 23 Jan 1967 in New York & **Jere Alton Jenks**, b. 7 Sep 1886 in Franklin, Delaware Co., New York, d. Oct 1966 in Afton, Chenango Co., New York – 18 Oct 1914 in Sidney, Delaware Co., New York

Signatures:

BRIDE

GROOM

- ○ **John Alton Jenks** – b. 23 Nov 1919 in Afton, Chenango Co., New York, d. 9 Nov 2009 in Afton, Chenango Co., New York

John Alton Jenks (son):

Residence – Afton, Chenango Co., New York – January 5, 1920

June 1, 1925

April 15, 1930

Occupation – None – January 5, 1920

April 15, 1930

Elisha Calkins & Anna Dalrymple Descendants

None Listed – June 1, 1925

      o **Lucille E. Jenks** – b. 1922 in New York

Lucille E. Jenks (daughter):

    Residence – Afton, Chenango Co., New York – June 1, 1925

                            April 15, 1930

    Occupation – None Listed – June 1, 1925

                    None – April 15, 1930

Gladys Lucille Chapin (daughter):

    Residence – Unadilla, Otsego Co., New York – February 16, 1892

        Sidney, Delaware Co., New York – June 22nd, 25th, & 27th, 1900

                          April 20, 1910

                          October 18, 1914

        Afton, Chenango Co., New York – June 1, 1915

                          January 5, 1920

                          June 1, 1925

                          April 15, 1930

    Occupation – None Listed – February 16, 1892

        At School – June 22nd, 25th, & 27th, 1900

        Teacher, District School – April 20, 1910

        School Teacher – October 18, 1914

        Teacher, School – January 5, 1920

        Housework – June 1, 1915

                    June 1, 1925

        None – April 15, 1930

Jere Alton Jenks (son-in-law):

    Residence – Afton, Chenango Co., New York – October 18, 1914

                            June 1, 1915

                            January 5, 1920

                            June 1, 1925

                            April 15, 1930

    Occupation – Clerk – October 18, 1914

        Salesman – June 1, 1915

        Merchant, Dry Goods Clerk – January 5, 1920

        Merchant – June 1, 1925

        Merchant, Retail Dry Goods – April 15, 1930

    Home Data for 1930 – Owns home, valued at $ 6, 000, has radio set, not on a farm

Hurst

Hattie Lavantia Tabor (daughter):

Residence – Unadilla, Otsego Co., New York – August 13, 1870

June 15, 1875

June 8, 1880

February 16, 1892

Sidney, Delaware Co., New York – June 22nd, 25th, & 27th, 1900

April 20, 1910

June 1, 1915

Afton, Chenango Co., New York – January 5, 1920

June 1, 1925

April 15, 1930

Occupation – None Listed – August 13, 1870

June 15, 1875

February 16, 1892

June 22nd, 25th, & 27th, 1900

Teaching School – June 8, 1880

None – April 20, 1910

January 5, 1920

April 15, 1930

Housework – June 1, 1915

No Occupation – June 1, 1925

George Washington Chapin (son-in-law):

Residence – Unadilla, Otsego Co., New York – February 16, 1892

Sidney, Delaware Co., New York – June 22nd, 25th, & 27th, 1900

April 20, 1910

June 1, 1915

Afton, Chenango Co., New York – January 5, 1920

Occupation – Farmer – February 16, 1892

June 22nd, 25th, & 27th, 1900

Own Income – April 20, 1910

No Occupation – June 1, 1915

Farmer, Retired – January 5, 1920

▪ **Carrie Edith Tabor**, b. 30 Jul 1865 in Unadilla, Otsego Co., New York, d. 10 Feb 1905 in Sidney, Delaware Co., New York & **Orle Brinton Jackson**, b. 28 Aug 1864 in Sidney, Delaware Co., New York, d. 16 Jun 1928 in Sidney, Delaware Co., New York – 1886 in Delaware Co., New York

Elisha Calkins & Anna Dalrymple Descendants

- **Nina Olive Jackson**, b. 14 May 1890 in Unadilla, Otsego Co., New York, d. 10 Mar 1983 in Cobleskill, Schoharie Co., New York & **Arthur Forest Earl**, b. 31 May 1870 in Unadilla, Otsego Co., New York, d. 25 Jan 1937 – 20 May 1908 in Sidney, Delaware Co., New York

Nina Olive Jackson (daughter):

Residence – Sidney, Delaware Co., New York – February 16, 1892

June 22, 1900

May 20, 1908

April 21, 1910

June 1, 1915

February 12, 1920

June 1, 1925

April 12, 1930

Occupation – None Listed – February 16, 1892

At School – June 22, 1900

Domestic – May 20, 1908

None – April 21, 1910

February 12, 1920

April 12, 1930

Housework – June 1, 1915

June 1, 1925

Arthur Forest Earl (son-in-law):

Residence – Sidney, Delaware Co., New York – May 20, 1908

April 21, 1910

June 1, 1915

February 12, 1920

June 1, 1925

April 12, 1930

Occupation – Farmer – May 20, 1908

June 1, 1915

June 1, 1925

Farmer, General Farm – April 21, 1910

Farmer, Diary Farm – February 12, 1920

Farmer, Own Farm – April 12, 1930

Home Data for 1930 – Owns home, has radio set, on a farm

- **Harvey L. Jackson** – b. 13 June 1895 in Unadilla, Otsego Co., New York

Signature:

Harvey L. Jackson (son):

> *Residence – Sidney, Delaware Co., New York – June 22, 1900*
>
> > *April 20, 1910*
> >
> > *June 1, 1915*
> >
> > *June 1, 1925*
>
> *Wells Bridge, Otsego Co., New York – June 4, 1917*
>
> *Oneonta, Otsego Co., New York – April 10, 1930*

> *Occupation – None Listed – June 22, 1900*
>
> > *Farm Laborer, Home Farm – April 20, 1910*
> >
> > *Farm Labor – June 1, 1915*
> >
> > *Locomotive Fireman – June 4, 1917*
> >
> > *Fireman, Rail Road – June 1, 1925*
> >
> > *Locomotive, Steam Rail Road – April 10, 1930*

- **Samuel Leroy Jackson**, b. 30 Dec 1898 in Unadilla, Otsego Co., New York, d. 6 Sep 1978 in Otsego, Otsego Co., New York & **Vera Marguerite Hulslander**, b. 26 Mar 1906 in Ithaca, Tompkins Co., New York, d. 11 May 1996 in Wells Bridge, Otsego Co., New York – 26 Jun 1933 in Candor, Tioga Co., New York

Signature:

Samuel Leroy Jackson (son):

> *Residence – Sidney, Delaware Co., New York – June 22, 1900*
>
> > *April 20, 1910*
> >
> > *June 1, 1915*
> >
> > *February 5, 1920*
> >
> > *June 1, 1925*
> >
> > *April 12, 1930*
>
> *Wells Bridge, Otsego Co., New York – September 12, 1918*

> *Occupation – None Listed – June 22, 1900*
>
> > *Farm Laborer, Home Farm – April 20, 1910*
> >
> > *Farm Labor – June 1, 1915*

50

June 1, 1925

Farmer – September 12, 1918

Laborer, farm – February 5, 1920

Farmer, Own Farm – April 12, 1930

Home Data for 1930 – Unclear if owned or rented, no radio set, on a farm

- **Paul Chester Jackson**, b. 3 Nov 1903 Unadilla, Otsego Co., New York, d. 1976 in New York &

  Gladys E. Unknown, b. 1910, d. 1978 in New York

Paul Chester Jackson (son):

Residence – Sidney, Delaware Co., New York – April 20, 1910

June 1, 1915

February 5, 1920

June 1, 1925

Occupation – None – April 20, 1910

School – June 1, 1915

Laborer, Home Farm – February 5, 1920

Mail Clerk, Rail Road – June 1, 1925

Carrie Edith Tabor (daughter):

Residence – Unadilla, Otsego Co., New York – August 13, 1870

June 15, 1875

June 8, 1880

Sidney, Delaware Co., New York – February 16, 1892

June 22, 1900

Occupation – None Listed – August 13, 1870

June 15, 1875

February 16, 1892

June 22, 1900

Attends School – June 8, 1880

Obituary –

"Mrs. Jackson [From our Wellsbridge Correspondent]. Mrs. O. B. Jackson died at her home on Friday morning at about 7:30 o'clock, the cause of death being pneumonia from which she was sick only about a week. The deceased was a daughter of Mr. and Mrs. Lorin Tabor and was a lady very much respected by everyone. Her death seemed the more sad when we think of her being taken down in the prime of her life, her age being 39 years 6 months and leaving four bright children, which so much need a mother's care, the youngest being only two years of age. Mrs. Jackson is survived by her husband, besides the four children, Nina, Harvey, Samuel, and Paul, her father Lorin Tabor, two brothers, Fred and Frank and one sister, Mrs. George Chapin. The funeral was held on Sunday from the house, the Rev. Charles Hubbell conducting the service, interment at Sand Hill cemetery." from February 10, 1905

Orle Brinton Jackson (son-in-law):

Residence – Sidney, Delaware Co., New York – February 16, 1892

June 22, 1900

April 20, 1910

June 1, 1915

February 5, 1920

June 1, 1925

Occupation – Farmer – February 16, 1892

June 22, 1900

June 1, 1915

June 1, 1925

Farmer, General Farm – April 20, 1910

Farmer, Diary Farm – February 5, 1920

▪ **Fred E. Tabor**, b. Mar 1869 in New York & **Elsie I. Benedict**, b. Jan 1864 in New York

Signatures:

● **Ernest Fred Tabor**, b. 11 May 1893 in Cannonsville, Delaware Co., New York & **Adelia R. Fowler**, b. Apr 1891 in Otsego, Otsego Co., New York – 17 Sep 1914 in East Worcester, Otsego Co., New York

Signature:

○ **Miriam E. Tabor** – b. 1919 in New York

Miriam E. Tabor (daughter):

Residence – Unadilla, Otsego Co., New York – January 2ⁿᵈ & 3ʳᵈ, 1920

June 1, 1925

Afton, Chenango Co., New York – April 12, 1930

Occupation – None – January 2ⁿᵈ & 3ʳᵈ, 1920

April 12, 1930

School – June 1, 1925

Elisha Calkins & Anna Dalrymple Descendants

Ernest Fred Tabor (son):

 Residence – Otsego, Otsego Co., New York – June 20, 1900

          June 1, 1905

          April 2nd & 3rd, 1910

          September 17, 1914

  Unadilla, Otsego Co., New York – June 5, 1917

          January 2nd & 3rd, 1920

          June 1, 1925

  Afton, Chenango Co., New York – April 12, 1930

 Occupation – At School – June 20, 1900

        June 1, 1905

  None – April 2nd & 3rd, 1910

  Embalmer – September 17, 1914

  Undertaker – June 5, 1917

        June 1, 1925

  Undertaker, Town & Vicinity – January 2nd & 3rd, 1920

  Director, Funerals – April 12, 1930

 Home Data for 1930 – Owns home, valued at $ 7, 000, has radio set, not on a farm

Adelia R. Fowler (daughter-in-law):

 Residence – Unadilla, Otsego Co., New York – September 17, 1914

          January 2nd & 3rd, 1920

          June 1, 1925

  Afton, Chenango Co., New York – April 12, 1930

 Occupation – Post Mistress – September 17, 1914

  None – January 2nd & 3rd, 1920

  Housework – June 1, 1925

  Saleswoman, Silk Shop – April 12, 1930

Fred E. Tabor (son):

 Residence – Unadilla, Otsego Co., New York – August 13, 1870

          June 15, 1875

          June 8, 1880

          January 2nd & 3rd, 1920

          June 1, 1925

          April 12, 1930

  Otsego, Otsego Co., New York – June 20, 1900

          June 1, 1905

April 2nd & 3rd, 1910

Occupation – None Listed – August 13, 1870

June 15, 1875

Attends School – June 8, 1880

Butter Maker – June 20, 1900

Creamery Man – June 1, 1905

Proprietor, Creamery – April 2nd & 3rd, 1910

Garage, Own Shop – January 2nd & 3rd, 1920

Garage Owner – June 1, 1925

Garage – April 12, 1930

Home Data for 1930 – Owns home, valued at $ 4, 000, has radio set, not on a farm

Elsie I. Benedict (daughter-in-law):

Residence – Otsego, Otsego Co., New York – June 20, 1900

June 1, 1905

April 2nd & 3rd, 1910

Unadilla, Otsego Co., New York – January 2nd & 3rd, 1920

June 1, 1925

April 12, 1930

Occupation – None Listed – June 20, 1900

June 1, 1925

April 12, 1930

Housework – June 1, 1905

None – April 2nd & 3rd, 1910

January 2nd & 3rd, 1920

- ▪ **Frank Irving Tabor**, b. Oct 1872 in New York, d. 25 Jun 1914 & **Alice Armstrong**, b. Nov 1877 in New York, d. 7 Jan 1953 in Deposit, Broome Co., New York – 1894 in New York

- • **Harold Irwin Tabor**, b. 19 Oct 1895 in Wells Bridge, Otsego Co., New York, d. 25 Mar 1931 in Arlington, Alexandria Co., Virginia & **Olive Kilbourn Lightfoot**, b. Nov 1893 in Tennessee – 30 Aug 1917 in Oneonta, Otsego Co., New York

Signature:

Harold Irwin Tabor (son):

Residence – Otsego, Otsego Co., New York – June 20, 1900

Sidney, Delaware Co., New York – June 22nd, 25th, & 27th, 1910

June 1, 1915

Oneonta, Otsego Co., New York – June 1917

August 30, 1917

Arlington, Alexandria Co., Virginia – January 27, 1920

Occupation – None Listed – June 20, 1900

None – June 22nd, 25th, & 27th, 1910

Window Trimmer – June 1, 1915

R. R. Trainman – June 1917

Trainman, D & H – August 30, 1917

Clerk, U. S. Government – January 27, 1920

Obituary –

"Harold Tabor died at Arlington, Va. March 25, after a long illness of tuberculosis. Aged 26 years. The body was brought here and the funeral was largely attended at the home of Mr. and Mrs. W. G. Pomeroy Tuesday afternoon. Rev. S. E. Carr, of Walton preached the sermon. Interment in the village cemetery. Mr. Tabor was a particular bright young man, having a responsible government position in Washington, D. C., which he was obliged to give up when his health failed. He is survived by his wife, also a government employee, his mother Mrs. Alice Tabor, three sisters, Edna, Florence and Charlotte Tabor, one brother, Chester, his grandfather, J. M. Armstrong." from 1931

Olive Kilbourn Lightfoot (daughter-in-law):

Residence – Oneonta, Otsego Co., New York – August 30, 1917

Arlington, Alexandria Co., Virginia – January 27, 1920

Occupation – Lady – August 30, 1917

Clerk, U. S. Government – January 27, 1920

- **Edna A. Tabor**, b. 10 Oct 1897 in Otsego, Otsego Co., New York, d. 13 Feb 1989 in Miami, Dade Co., Florida & **Willard Leigh Sudenga**, b. 13 Apr 1899 in Illinois, d. 8 Dec 1963 in Los Angeles Co., California – 16 Apr 1921 in Washington, District of Columbia

CERTIFIED ABOVE ANSWERS AND THAT THEY ARE TRUE

Willard L. Sudenga

6171 (Registrant's signature or mark) (OVER)

Signature:

Edna Tabor (daughter):

Residence – Otsego, Otsego Co., New York – June 20, 1900

Sidney, Delaware Co., New York – June 22nd, 25th, & 27th, 1910

June 1, 1915

Washington, Washington, District og Columbia – January 10th & 12th, 1920

Occupation – None Listed – June 20, 1900

None – June 22nd, 25th, & 27th, 1910

School – June 1, 1915

Clerk, Government – January 10ᵗʰ & 12ᵗʰ, 1920

Willard Leigh Sudenga (son-in-law):

Residence – Washington, Washington, District of Columbia – September 6, 1918

Occupation – Clerk, Auditor, War Dept. – September 6, 1918

- **Florence A. Tabor**, b. Jun 1901 in Otsego, Otsego Co., New York, d. 2 Mar 1972 & **Peter Edward Thimineur**, b. 22 May 1895 in Watervliet, Albany Co., New York, d. 8 Aug 1962 in Schenectady Co., New York

Signature:

  o **Marie A. Thimineur** – b. About 1926 in Niskayuna, Schenectady Co., New York

Marie A. Thimineur (daughter):

Residence – Niskayuna, Schenectady Co., New York – April 12ᵗʰ & 14ᵗʰ, 1930

Occupation – None – April 12ᵗʰ & 14ᵗʰ, 1930

Florence Tabor (daughter):

Residence – Sidney, Delaware Co., New York – June 22ⁿᵈ, 25ᵗʰ, & 27ᵗʰ, 1910

June 1, 1915

Binghamton, Broome Co., New York – January 2ⁿᵈ & 3ʳᵈ, 1920

Niskayuna, Schenectady Co., New York – June 1, 1925

April 12ᵗʰ & 14ᵗʰ, 1930

Occupation – None – June 22ⁿᵈ, 25ᵗʰ, & 27ᵗʰ, 1910

April 12ᵗʰ & 14ᵗʰ, 1930

School – June 1, 1915

Servant, Private Family – January 2ⁿᵈ & 3ʳᵈ, 1920

Housework – June 1, 1925

Obituary –

"Mrs. Thimineur, 71, Dies. Mrs. Florence A. Thimineur, 71, formerly of East Street in Alplaus, died yesterday at Glendale Home after a long illness. Born in Otsego, Mrs. Thimineur lived in the area most of her life. She was the widow of Peter Thimineur. Survivors include two daughters, Mrs. Marie Stohner of Seattle, Wash., Jennie Millington of Springfield, Ore.; a brother, Chester Tabor of Unadilla; two sisters Mrs. Edna Sudenga of Miami, Fla., and Mrs. Charlotte Dewent of Washington D.C.; six grandchildren, two great-grandchildren, several nieces and nephews. Private funeral services will be held at 8:15 a. m. Tuesday at Light's Funeral Home, 1428 State St., followed at 9 by the liturgy of Christian death and burial at St. Luke's Church. There will be no calling hours. Burial will be in Most Holy Redeemer Cemetery." from the Schenectady Gazette. Saturday, March 4, 1972

Peter Edward Thimineur (son-in-law):

  Residence – Manchester, Hartford Co., Connecticut – June 5, 1917

  Niskayuna, Schenectady Co., New York – June 1, 1925

  April 12ᵗʰ & 14ᵗʰ, 1930

  Occupation – Time Clerk – June 5, 1917

  Draftsman – June 1, 1925

  Draftsman, Electric Co., General Electric – April 12ᵗʰ & 14ᵗʰ, 1930

  Home Data for 1930 – Owns home, valued at $ 6, 500, has radio, not on a farm

  • **Charlotte Tabor**, b. 1 Dec 1905 in Sidney, Delaware Co., New York, d. 23 Apr 1982 in Fairfax, Fairfax Co., Virginia & **Allen John Derwent**, b. 24 Oct 1898 in Paducah, McCracken Co., Kentucky, d. 9 Dec 1970 in Arlington, Arlington Co., Virginia – 16 Jul 1923

  ○ **Betty Jean Derwent** – b. 7 Jan 1925 in Washington, District of Columbia, d. 12 Aug 2011 in Springfield, Fairfax Co., Virginia

Betty Jean Derwent (daughter):

  Residence – Washington, Washington, District of Columbia – April 11, 1930

  Occupation – None – April 11, 1930

  ○ **Allen John Derwent** – b. 10 Apr 1927 in Washington, District of Columbia, d. Dec 1988

Allen John Derwent (son):

  Residence – Washington, Washington, District of Columbia – April 11, 1930

  Occupation – None – April 11, 1930

  ○ **Robert I. Derwent** – b. 4 Jan 1929 in Washington, District of Columbia, d. 26 Dec 2011

Robert I. Derwent (son):

  Residence – Washington, Washington, District of Columbia – April 11, 1930

  Occupation – None – April 11, 1930

Charlotte Tabor (daughter):

  Residence – Sidney, Delaware Co., New York – June 1, 1915

  Washington, Washington, District of Columbia – April 11, 1930

  Occupation – School – June 1, 1915

  Telephone Operator, C & R Telephone Co. – April 11, 1930

Allen John Derwent (son-in-law):

  Residence – Washington, Washington, District of Columbia – April 11, 1930

  Occupation – Mail Carrier, U. S. Government – April 11, 1930

  Home Data for 1930 – Rental, $ 50 a month, no radio set, not on a farm

57

Hurst

- **Chester Tabor** – b. 1906 in New York

Chester Tabor (son):

Residence – Sidney, Delaware Co., New York – June 22nd, 25th, & 27th, 1910

June 1, 1915

Washington, Washington, District of Columbia – April 11, 1930

Occupation – None – June 22nd, 25th, & 27th, 1910

No Occupation – June 1, 1915

Waiter, Restaurant – April 11, 1930

Frank Irving Tabor (son):

Residence – Unadilla, Otsego Co., New York – June 15, 1875

June 8, 1880

February 16, 1892

Otsego, Otsego Co., New York – June 20, 1900

Sidney, Delaware Co., New York – June 22nd, 25th, & 27th, 1910

Occupation – None Listed – June 15, 1875

February 16, 1892

Attends School – June 8, 1880

Butter Maker – June 20, 1900

Electrician, Telephone – June 22nd, 25th, & 27th, 1910

Obituary –

"Frank Tabor died very suddenly at his home in our village last Thursday, June 25, of heart trouble. Deceased had been laboring during the day but complained of severe pains on returning home at night and passed away before a physician could reach him. He is surviced by a wife and five children. The funeral was held Saturday from the M. E. church. Interment at Sand Hill cemetery." *from 1914*

Alice Armstrong (daughter-in-law):

Residence – Otsego, Otsego Co., New York – June 20, 1900

Sidney, Delaware, Co., New York – June 22nd, 25th, & 27th, 1910

Occupation – None Listed – June 20, 1900

None – June 22nd, 25th, & 27th, 1910

Charlotte Melissa Calkins (daughter):

Residence – Madison, Madison Co., New York – July 23, 1850

Lebanon, Madison Co., New York – July 24, 1860

Unadilla, Otsego Co., New York – August 13, 1870

June 15, 1875

June 8, 1880

February 16, 1892

June 27, 1900

Occupation – None Listed – July 23, 1850

June 15, 1875

February 16, 1892

June 27, 1900

Domestic – July 24, 1860

Keeping House – August 13, 1870

June 8, 1880

Obituary –

"Sudden Death at Wells Bridge. Mrs. Lorin Tabor died very suddenly from heart disease at the home of her daughter, Mrs. George Chapin, on Sunday morning, June 16th, at the age of 63 years. Mrs. Tabor accompanied her husband to the milk station and then drove over to her daughter's to spend the day, where she passed away before she could be removed from the wagon. Besides her husband Mrs. Tabor is survived by two sons, Fred and Frank, and two daughters, Mrs. George Chapin and Mrs. O. B. Jackson. The funeral was held on Tuesday at Sand Hill, The Rev. N. B. Ripley of Otego conducting the services. Internment was given in the cemetery at that place." from 1901

Lorin M. Tabor (son-in-law):

Residence – Unadilla, Otsego Co., New York – August 13, 1870

June 15, 1875

June 8, 1880

February 16, 1892

June 27, 1900

Otsego, Otsego Co., New York – June 1, 1905

April 2nd & 3rd, 1910

Occupation – Farmer – August 13, 1870

June 15, 1875

June 8, 1880

February 16, 1892

June 27, 1900

None Listed – June 1, 1905

None – April 2nd & 3rd, 1910

Value of Real Estate – $ 3,000 – August 13, 1870

Value of Personal Estate – $ 1, 000 – August 13, 1870

Hurst

Obituary –

"Loren M. Tabor aged 79 years, died at the home of his son, Fred Tabor a Otego, shortly before 2 o'clock, Sunday afternoon of old age. The funeral services were held from the home of the son named, Tuesday afternoon at 2 o'clock and internment at Sand Hill. Mr. Tabor was born in the town of Unadilla June 23, 1835 and was a son of the late Jeremiah Tabor and Charlotte Fisher. He married Charlotte Hawkins, January 3, 1858, and most of his life has been passed in this locality. He leaves the son named, and one daughter, Mrs. Harriet Chapman of Wells Bridge. Another son, Frank Tabor, died recently." from Wells Bridge. September 6, 1914.

- o **Mariba D. Calkins**, b. 1842, d. 25 Mar 1867 & **Conrad M. Folts**, b. 9 Sep 1848 in New York, d. 1 Dec 1922 in Elm Creek, Buffalo Co., Nebraska
  - ▪ **Lottie A. Folts**, b. Nov 1865 in New York & **Unknown Northrup**, b. in Pennsylvania, d. Before 1900
    - • **Weaver Lamont Northrup**, b. 10 Aug 1895 in Seneca, Nemaha Co., Kansas, d. Oct 1980 in Elm Creek, Buffalo Co., Nebraska & **Hazel Icel Seel**, b. 13 Aug 1897 in Iowa, d. 15 Mar 1988 in Elm Creek, Buffalo Co., Nebraska

Signature:

- o **Levena A. Northrup** – b. 1918, d. 1930 in Elm Creek, Buffalo Co., Nebraska

Levena A. Northrup (daughter):

Residence – Elm Creek, Buffalo Co., Nebraska – January 5, 1920

April 16, 1930

Occupation – None – January 5, 1920

Student – April 16, 1930

- o **Merlin L. Northup** – b. 1919 in Elm Creek, Buffalo Co., Nebraska , d. 1919 in Elm Creek, Buffalo Co., Buffalo Co., Nebraska

Weaver Lamont Northrup (son):

Residence – Armada, Buffalo Co., Nebraska – June 1, 1900

April 16th & 18th, 1910

Elm Creek, Buffalo Co., Nebraska – June 5, 1917

January 5, 1920

April 16, 1930

Kearney, Nebraska – June 5, 1917

Occupation – None Listed – June 1, 1900

None – April 16th & 18th, 1910

Gunsmith & Metal Worker – June 5, 1917

Munition, Own Shop – January 5, 1920

Electrician, Electrical Engineer – April 16, 1930

Home Data for 1930 – Rental, no radio set, not on a farm

Hazel Icel Seel (daughter-in-law):

Residence – Elm Creek, Buffalo Co., Nebraska – January 5, 1920

April 16, 1930

Occupation – None – January 5, 1920

April 16, 1930

- Unknown Northrup

- Unknown Northrup

Lottie A. Folts (daughter):

Residence – Otselic, Chenango Co., New York – July 28, 1870

Armada, Buffalo Co., Nebraska – June 1, 1900

April 16th & 18th, 1910

Occupation – None Listed – June 1, 1900

None – April 16th & 18th, 1910

Mariba C. Calkins (daughter):

Residence – Madison, Madison Co., New York – July 23, 1850

Lebanon, Madison Co., New York – July 24, 1860

Occupation – None Listed – July 23, 1850

Domestic – July 24, 1860

Conrad M. Folts (son-in-law):

Residence – Lebanon, Madison Co., New York – July 24, 1860

Otselic, Chenango Co., New York – July 28, 1870

Armada, Buffalo Co., Nebraska – June 1, 1900

April 16th & 18th, 1910

Elm Creek, Buffalo Co., Nebraska – 1890

January 5, 1920

Occupation – Farm Labor – July 24, 1860

Farming – July 28, 1870

Bar Tender – June 1, 1900

Own Income – April 16th & 18th, 1910

None – January 5, 1920

61

Hurst

○ **Weaver Wilson Calkins**, b. 1 Oct 1844 in Otselic, Chenango Co., New York, d. 29 Aug 1921 in Unadilla, Otsego Co., New York & **Melissa Young** (1st Wife), b. Bet. 1843 – 1844 in New York, d. Before 1886 in Chenango Co., New York

■ **Adella Calkins**, b. 3 Jul 1865 in Unadilla, Otsego Co., New York, d. 28 Jul 1934 in New York & **James Duesler** (1st Husband), b. Aug 1859 in New York – 1883

● **Ada Blanche Duesler** – b. 9 Sep 1884 in Unadilla, Otsego Co., New York

Ada Blanche Duesler (daughter):

Residence – Caroga, Fulton Co., New York – June 18th & 19th, 1900

Occupation – Serving in making ? Gloves – June 18th & 19th, 1900

■ **Adella Calkins**, b. 3 Jul 1865 in Unadilla, Otsego Co., New York, d. 28 Jul 1934 in New York & **Gilbert Bradt** (2nd Husband), b. About 1863 in New York

Adella Calkins (daughter):

Residence – Otselic, Chenango Co., New York – July 28, 1870

Lenox, Madison Co., New York – June 1, 1875

Eaton, Madison Co., New York – June 7, 1880

Caroga, Fulton Co., New York – June 18th & 19th, 1900

April 23, 1910

January 12, 1920

April 21st & 22nd, 1930

Occupation – None Listed – June 1, 1875

June 18th & 19th, 1900

House Keeping – June 7, 1880

Glove Maker, At Home – April 23, 1910

Cook, Lumber Camp – January 12, 1920

Glover Maker, At Home – April 21st & 22nd, 1930

Obituary –

"Death Claims Mrs. G. Bradt – Town of Caroga Resident Passes Away Saturday After Illness: Mrs. Della Calkins Bradt, wife of Gilbert Bradt, former Town Superintendant of Highways of Caroga, passed away at her home in that town Saturday morning at 1:40. The deceased had been in poor health for some time. She was 69 years of age. Mrs. Bradt was born at Unadilla, July 3, 1865, the daughter of Mr. and Mrs. Weaver Calkins. She was a well known resident of Caroga, was a member of the Baptist church at Rockwood and was formerly superintendent of the Sunday school of that church. Besides her husband, she is survived by one daughter, Mrs. Ada Thompson, of Gloversville, and three grandchildren. The funeral will be held Monday afternoon at 2:30 at the home at Pine Lake. Rev. Harlow W. Parsons, pastor of the Johnstown Baptist church,

will officiate. Interment will be made in the North Bush Cemetery, where friends may view the remains." **from The**
Morning Herald, Gloversville and Johnstown, N. Y., Page Four, Monday, July 30, 1934

James Duesler (1st Husband) (son-in-law):

Residence – Caroga, Fulton Co., New York – June 18th & 19th, 1900

April 23, 1910

Occupation – Farmer – June 18th & 19th, 1900

Farmer, General Farm – April 23, 1910

Gilbert Bradt (2nd Husband) (son-in-law):

Residence – Caroga, Fulton Co., New York – January 12, 1920

April 21st & 22nd, 1930

Occupation – Superintendant, Highway – January 12, 1920

Superintendant, Town Highway – April 21st & 22nd, 1930

Home Value for 1930 – Owns home, valued at $ 2, 000, has radio set, not on a farm

▪ **Daisy Calkins** – b. About 1875 in Madison Co., New York, d. Before 1880

Daisy Calkins (daughter):

Residence – Lenox, Madison, Co., New York – June 1, 1875

Occupation – None Listed – June 1, 1875

Obituary/Death Notice –

"Charles Bassett's little boy of four years, and a little girl five years of age of Weaver Calkins, died of scarlet fever at Alderbrook, near Eaton, last week." **from the Brookfield Courier. Wednesday, September 3, 1879.**

○ **Weaver Wilson Calkins** (2nd Marriage), b. Oct 1844 in Otselic, Chenango Co., New York, d. 29 Aug 1921 in Unadilla, Otsego Co., New York & **Margaret A. Dumond** (2nd Wife), b. Nov 1846 in New York, d. 1923 in Unadilla, Otsego Co., New York – 1886

Weaver Wilson Calkins (son):

Residence – Madison, Madison Co., New York – July 23, 1850

Lebanon, Madison Co., New York – July 24, 1860

Otselic, Chenango Co., New York – June 1863

August 8, 1863

July 28, 1870

Lenox, Madison Co., New York – June 1, 1875

Eaton, Madison Co., New York – June 7, 1880

Unadilla, Otsego Co., New York – June 6th & 7th, 1900

June 1, 1905

Hurst

April 30, 1910

January 6th & 7th, 1920

Occupation – Farm Labor – July 24, 1860

June 1, 1875

Farmer – June 1863

July 28, 1870

Carpenter – June 7, 1880

June 6th & 7th, 1900

June 1, 1905

Janitor, School House – April 30, 1910

None – January 6th & 7th, 1920

Value of Real Estate – $ 1, 500 – July 28, 1870

Value of Personal Estate – $ 1, 500 – July 28, 1870

Melissa Young (1st Wife) (daughter-in-law):

Residence – Otselic, Chenango Co., New York – July 28, 1870

Lenox, Madison Co., New York – June 1, 1875

Occupation – Keeping House – July 28, 1870

None Listed – June 1, 1875

Margaret A. Dumond (2nd Wife) (daughter-in-law):

Residence – Unadilla, Otsego Co., New York – June 6th & 7th, 1900

June 1, 1905

April 30, 1910

January 6th & 7th, 1920

Occupation – None Listed – June 6th & 7th, 1900

Housework – June 1, 1905

At Home Laundress – April 30, 1910

None – January 6th & 7th, 1920

Truman D. Calkins (father):

Residence – Otselic, Chenango Co., New York – 1830

1840

July 28, 1870

Madison, Madison Co., New York – July 23, 1850

Lebanon, Madison Co., New York – Jul 24, 1860

Otselic, Chenango Co., New York – May 1865

Eaton, Madison Co., New York – June 7, 1880

Madison Co., New York – November 10, 1883

64

Occupation – Farmer – July 23, 1850

July 24, 1860

July 28, 1870

Retired Farmer – June 7, 1880

Insane living in Poorhouse – November 10, 1883

Value of Real Estate – $ 2, 500 – July 23, 1850

$ 2, 000 – July 24, 1860

Value of Personal Estate – $ 1, 260 – July 24, 1860

$ 4, 000 – July 28, 1870

Abigail P. Miles (mother):

Residence – Madison, Madison Co., New York – July 23, 1850

Lebanon, Madison Co., New York – July 24, 1860

Occupation – None Listed – July 23, 1850

July 24, 1860

Truman D. Calkins & Abigail P. Miles

Photographs – Tintypes

Photographs courtesy of The Jenks Family of Afton, New York

Truman D. Calkins

Photograph (Left) from Family Photo Album (Found at an Estate Sale near Medina, Ohio)

Date of Album – 1860s

Photographer Credit (Right): H. C. Brown – Norwich, New York

Photographs courtesy of The Hurst Family of Lake Elsinore, California

Elisha Tracy Calkins & Celinda C. Ray

Photograph (Left) from Family Photo Album (Found at an Estate Sale near Medina, Ohio)

Date of Album – 1860s

Photographer Credit (Right): E. D. Benjamin, De Ruyter, New York

Photographs courtesy of The Hurst Family of Lake Elsinore, California

Clinton H. Stowell & Alice B. Calkins

Photographer Credits: Wick – Norwich, New York

Photographs courtesy of The Hurst Family of Lake Elsinore, California

George LaFayette Stowell

Photographer Credits: Wick – Norwich, New York

Photographs courtesy of The Hurst Family of Lake Elsinore, California

Minnie L. Calkins

Photographer Credit: De Witt, Madison, New York

Photograph courtesy of The Hurst Family of Lake Elsinore, California

Lydia Ann Calkins

Photographer Credit (Left): Cornell & Wick – Norwich, New York

Photographer Credit (Right): Hotchkiss – Norwich, New York

Date – 1893

Photographs courtesy of The Hurst Family of Lake Elsinore, California

Jacob Walradt or Walrod

Photographer Credit: Cornell & Wick – Norwich New York

Photograph courtesy of The Hurst Family of Lake Elsinore, California

Abigail Delina Walradt or Walrod & Irving Jacob Walradt or Walrod

Photographer Credit (Left): Wick – Norwich, New York

Photographer Credit (Right): Cornell & Wick – Norwich, New York

Photographs courtesy of The Hurst Family of Lake Elsinore, California

Unknown Walradt or Walrod Children

Photographer Credit: Wick – Norwich, New York

Photographs courtesy of The Hurst Family of Lake Elsinore, California

Unknown Walradt or Walrod Children

Photographer Credit: Wick – Norwich, New York

Photographs courtesy of The Hurst Family of Lake Elsinore, California

Lucy Arabelle Guiles & Truman Herbert Walradt

Photograph courtesy of The Peterson Family of Chenango Bridge, New York

Truman Herbert and Lucy Arabelle (Guiles) Walradt Family

From Left to Right – Lucy Arabelle (Mother) holding Nellie Daisy, Alma Belnett, Ella Mary (Middle), Milton Adellon, and Truman Herbert (Father)

Photograph courtesy of The Peterson Family of Chenango Bridge, New York

Nellie Daisy Walradt Greene

Photograph courtesy of The Peterson Family of Chenango Bridge, New York

Charlotte Melissa Calkins

Photographer Credit: G. H. DeWitt – Madison, New York

Photograph courtesy of The Hurst Family of Lake Elsinore, California

Loren & Charlotte Melissa (Calkins) Tabor Family

With children & grand-children

Photograph courtesy of The Jenks Family of Afton, New York

Hattie Lavantia Tabor

Photograph courtesy of The Jenks Family of Afton, New York

Hattie Lavantia Tabor & George Washington Chapin

Photographs courtesy of The Jenks Family of Afton, New York

Lottie Folts Homestead in Elm Creek, Buffalo Co., Nebraska

Front of Postcard

Photograph courtesy of The Jenks Family of Afton, New York

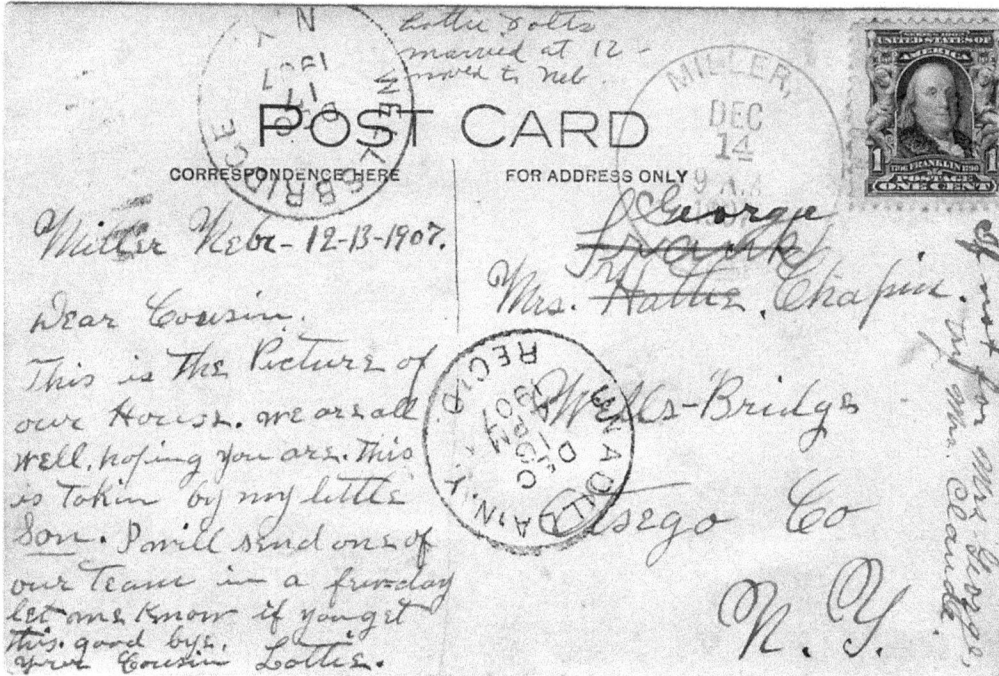

Postcard from Lottie Folts to Hattie Lavantia Tabor Chapin

December 13, 1907

Photograph courtesy of The Jenks Family of Afton, New York

Weaver Wilson Calkins

Photographer Credit (Left): Hotchkiss – Norwich, New York

Date – 1888

Photographer Credit (Right): E. D. Benjamin – De Ruyter, New York

Photographs courtesy of The Hurst Family of Lake Elsinore, California

Mary Calkins & Descendants

- **Mary Calkins**, b. 16 Mar 1802 in Sudbury, Rutland Co. Vermont, d. 24 Jul 1883 in Readmond, Emmet Co., Michigan & **John C. Miller**, b. Between 1796 – 1796 in New York, d. 30 Jun 1873 in Chenango Co., New York – Before 1829 in Chenango Co., New York

  o **Bethia W. Miller**, b. Aug 1829 in Chenango Co. New York, d. 25 Feb 1911 & **Ensign Briggs** (1st Husband), b. Between 1816 – 1817 in New York

    ▪ **Charles R. Briggs**, b. Sep 1842 in Smyrna, Chenango Co., New York & **Fanna Jane Depue**, b. About 1848 in New York, b. Before 1900 in New York – 28 Jul 1861 in Adrian, Monroe Co., Wisconsin

      • **Harry Banks Briggs** – b. 17 Nov 1872 in Binghamton, Broome Co., New York, d. After 1940 in New York

Signature:

Harry Banks Briggs (son):

    Residence – Bainbridge, Chenango Co., New York – June 24, 1880

                          June 14, 1900

                          May 14, 1910

    Binghamton, Broome Co., New York – June 1, 1915

                          September 12, 1917

                          1930

    Occupation – At School – June 24, 1880

        Hide Dealer – June 14, 1900

        Driver, Express Wagon – May 14, 1910

        Railroad Worker – June 1, 1915

        Motorman, Binghamton Railway Co. – September 12, 1917

      • **Mary L. Briggs** – b. Jul 1876 in New York

Mary L. Briggs (daughter):

    Residence – Bainbridge, Chenango Co., New York – June 24, 1880

                          June 14, 1900

    Occupation – None Listed – June 24, 1880

                          June 14, 1900

- **Olive A. Briggs** – b. Jun 1886 in New York

Olive A. Briggs (daughter):

    Residence – Bainbridge, Chenango Co., New York – June 14, 1900

                        May 14, 1910

    Occupation – None Listed – June 14, 1900

            School Teacher, High School – May 14, 1910

Charles R. Briggs (step-son):

    Residence – Smyrna, Chenango Co., New York – July 12, 1850

        Bainbridge, Chenango Co., New York – June 24, 1880

                    June 14, 1900

                    May 14, 1910

    Occupation – None Listed – July 12, 1850

        Telegraph Operator – June 24, 1880

            June 14, 1900

        Agent, Express Co. – May 14, 1910

Fanna Jane Depue (daughter-in-law):

    Residence – Bainbridge, Chenango Co., New York – June 24, 1880

    Occupation – At Home – June 24, 1880

- **Charlotte Briggs** – b. Between 1841 – 1842 in Smyrna, Chenango Co., New York

Charlotte Briggs (step-daughter):

    Residence – Smyrna, Chenango Co., New York – July 12, 1850

                July 13, 1860

    Occupation – School Teacher – July 12, 1850

            July 13, 1860

- **Martha Briggs** – b. About 1844 in Smyrna, Chenango Co., New York

Martha Briggs (step-daughter):

    Residence – Smyrna, Chenango Co., New York – July 12, 1850

                July 13, 1860

    Occupation – None Listed – July 12, 1850

            July 13, 1860

- **Joseph Plumb Briggs**, b. 31 Jan 1848 in Smyrna, Chenango Co., New York, d. Before April 7, 1930 in New York & **Ellen S. Fuller**, b. Jun 1849 in Delaware Co., New York, d. 11 Jan 1936 in Norwich, Chenango Co., New York – 1868 in New York

- **Frederick Plumb Briggs**, b. 20 Sep 1875 in New York & **Elizabeth E. Cochran**, b. June 1875 in New York, d. After 1936 – 1900 in New York

Signature:

- ○ **Theodore Gale Briggs** – b. About 1906 in New York

Theodore Gale Briggs (son):

Residence – Smyrna, Chenango Co., New York – May 3, 1910

June 1, 1915

January 28, 1920

Hamilton, Madison Co., New York – June 1, 1925

Norwich, Chenango Co., New York – April 7, 1930

Occupation – None – May 3, 1910

January 28, 1920

School – June 1, 1915

School (Navy) – June 1, 1925

Chef, Restaurant – April 7, 1930

- ○ **Truesdell C. Briggs** – b. About 1911 in New York, d. Jan 1961

Truesdell C. Briggs (son):

Residence – Smyrna, Chenango Co., New York – June 1, 1915

January 28, 1920

Hamilton, Madison Co., New York – June 1, 1925

Norwich, Chenango Co., New York – April 7, 1930

Occupation – No Occupation – June 1, 1915

None – January 28, 1920

School – June 1, 1925

Chef, Restaurant – April 7, 1930

- ○ **Theodosia R. Briggs** – About 1919 in New York

Theodosia Briggs (daughter):

Residence – Smyrna, Chenango Co., New York – January 28, 1920

Hamilton, Madison Co., New York – June 1, 1925

Norwich, Chenango Co., New York – April 7, 1930

Occupation – None – January 28, 1920

April 7, 1930

None Listed – June 1, 1925

89

Hurst

Frederick Plumb Briggs (son):

    Residence – Smyrna, Chenango Co., New York – June 8, 1880

                                June 23, 1900

                                May 3, 1910

                                June 1, 1915

                                September 12, 1918

                                January 28, 1920

        Hamilton, Madison Co., New York – June 1, 1925

        Norwich, Chenango Co., New York – April 7, 1930

    Occupation – None Listed – June 8, 1880

        Farmer – June 23, 1900

            June 1, 1915

        Farmer, General – May 3, 1910

        Farming – September 12, 1918

        Farmer, Diary Farm – January 28, 1920

        Carpenter – June 1, 1925

           April 7, 1930

    Home Data for 1930 – Owns home, valued at $ 4, 600, has radio set, not on a farm

Elizabeth E. Cochran (daughter-in-law):

    Residence – Smyrna, Chenango Co., New York – June 23, 1900

                                May 3, 1910

                                June 1, 1915

                                September 12, 1918

                                January 28, 1920

        Hamilton, Madison Co., New York – June 1, 1925

        Norwich, Chenango Co., New York – April 7, 1930

    Occupation – None Listed – June 23, 1900

        None – May 3, 1910

        January 28, 1920

        Housework – June 1, 1915

           June 1, 1925

        Laborer, Pharmacy – April 7, 1930

Joseph Plumb Briggs (step-son):

    Residence – Smyrna, Chenango Co., New York – July 12, 1850

                                July 13, 1860

                                June 8, 1880

June 23, 1900

May 3, 1910

June 1, 1915

January 28, 1920

Occupation – None Listed – July 12, 1850

July 13, 1860

Farmer – June 8, 1880

June 12, 1900

June 1, 1915

Farmer, General – May 3, 1910

Farmer, General Farm – January 28, 1920

Ellen S. Fuller (daughter-in-law):

Residence – Smyrna, Chenango Co., New York – June 8, 1880

June 23, 1900

May 3, 1910

June 1, 1915

January 28, 1920

Norwich, Chenango Co., New York – April 7, 1930

Occupation – Keeping House – June 8, 1880

None Listed – June 23, 1900

None – May 3, 1910

January 28, 1920

April 7, 1930

Housework – June 1, 1915

▪ **Elizur Briggs**, b. Oct 1851 in New York & **Martha Depew**, b. Jul 1861 in Wisconsin, d. Before 18 Apr 1910 in New York – 1877

● **Hubert Briggs** – b. 1879 in New York

Hubert Briggs (son):

Residence – Readmond, Emmet Co., Michigan – June 1ˢᵗ & 2ⁿᵈ, 1880

Occupation – None Listed – June 1ˢᵗ & 2ⁿᵈ, 1880

● **Lauren C. Briggs** – b. Nov 1883 in Michigan

Lauren C. Briggs (son):

Residence – Smyrna, Chenango Co., New York – June 4, 1900

Occupation – At School – June 4, 1900

- **Maud A. Briggs** – b. Sept 1885 in Michigan

Maud A. Briggs (daughter):

Residence – Smyrna, Chenango Co., New York – June 4, 1900

Occupation – At School – June 4, 1900

- **Grace E. Briggs**, b. 17 Mar 1887 in Athens, Calhoun Co., Michigan & **William Wallace Huntley**, b. 12 May 1886 in Pharsalia, Chenango Co., New York – 24 Aug 1910 in Chenango Co., New York

Signature:

Signatures (Marriage):

- **Neil E. Huntley** – b. About 1914 in New York, d. Before 2007

Neil E. Huntley (son):

Residence – Otselic, Chenango Co., New York – June 1, 1915

January 10, 1920

June 1, 1925

April 24, 1930

Occupation – No Occupation – June 1, 1925

None – January 10, 1920

April 24, 1930

School – June 1, 1925

- **Merle E. Huntley** – b. About 1917 in New York, d. May 31, 1956 in New York

Merle E. Huntley (son):

Residence – Otselic, Chenango Co., New York – January 10, 1920

June 1, 1925

April 24, 1930

Occupation – None – January 10, 1920

April 24, 1930

School – June 1, 1925

     o **William Earl Huntley** – b. 17 Mar 1920 in Otselic, Chenango Co., New York, d. 19 Mar 2007

in South Otselic, Chenango Co., New York

William Earl Huntley (son):

Residence – Otselic, Chenango Co., New York – June 1, 1925

April 24, 1930

Occupation – None Listed – June 1, 1925

None – April 24, 1930

Grace E. Briggs (daughter):

Residence – Smyrna, Chenango Co., New York – June 4, 1900

April 18, 1910

August 19, 1910

South Otselic, Chenango Co., New York – September 12, 1918

Otselic, Chenango Co., New York – June 1, 1915

January 10, 1920

June 1, 1925

April 24, 1930

Occupation – At School – June 4, 1900

Teacher, School – April 18, 1910

Teacher – August 19, 1910

Housework – June 1, 1915

None – January 10, 1920

April 24, 1930

Housewife – June 1, 1925

William Wallace Huntley (son-in-law):

Residence – South Otselic, Chenango Co., New York – August 19, 1910

September 12, 1918

Otselic, Chenango Co., New York – June 1, 1915

January 10, 1920

June 1, 1925

April 24, 1930

Hurst

Occupation – Farmer – August 19, 1910

June 1, 1915

September 12, 1918

June 1, 1925

Farmer, Diary Farm – January 10, 1920

Farmer, Own Diary Farm – April 24, 1930

Home Data for 1930 – Owns home, has radio set, on a farm

- **Donna B. Briggs** – b. Aug 1892 in Michigan

Donna B. Briggs (daughter):

Residence – Smyrna, Chenango Co., New York – June 4, 1900

April 18, 1910

Occupation – At School – June 4, 1900

None – April 18, 1910

Elizur Briggs (son):

Residence – Smyrna, Chenango Co., New York – July 13, 1860

June 23, 1870

June 23, 1875

June 4, 1900

1902

April 18, 1910

June 1, 1915

Readmond, Emmet Co., Michigan – June 1st & 2nd, 1880

Occupation – None Listed – July 13, 1860

At Home – June 23, 1870

Farm Laborer – June 23, 1875

June 1st & 2nd, 1880

June 1, 1915

Day Laborer – June 4, 1900

Laborer, Odd Jobs – April 18, 1900

Constable, Laborer – 1902

Martha Unknown (daughter-in-law):

Residence – Readmond, Emmet Co., Michigan – June 1st & 2nd, 1880

Smyrna, Chenango Co., New York – June 4, 1900

Occupation – Keeping House – June 1st & 2nd, 1880

None Listed – June 4, 1900

▪ **William Jerome Briggs**, b. Sep 1867 in Smyrna, Chenango Co., New York & **Margaret Unknown**, b. July 1872 in New York – 1892 in New York

- **Unknown Briggs** – b. After 1892, d. Before 1900

- **Jerome Francis Briggs** – b. 22 Jan 1894 in Albany, Albany, Co., New York, d. 22 May 1972 in Dalton, Berkshire Co., Massachusetts

Signatures:

Jerome Francis Briggs (son):

Residence – Dalton, Berkshire Co., Massachusetts – June 7, 1900

> *June 5, 1917*
>
> *January 15, 1920*
>
> *April 9, 1930*
>
> *1942*

Occupation – None Listed – June 7, 1900

> *Tool Machine Hand, General Electric Co. – June 5, 1917*
>
> *Tool Make, General Electric Plant – January 15, 1920*
>
> *Machine Trades, Paper mill – April 9, 1930*
>
> *Crane & Co., Pioneer Mill – 1942*

- **Irene M. Briggs** – b. Feb 1896 in Massachusetts

Irene M. Briggs (daughter):

Residence – Dalton, Berkshire Co., Massachusetts – June 7, 1900

Occupation – None Listed – June 7, 1900

- **Unknown Briggs** – b. After 1900 in Dalton, Berkshire Co., Massachusetts, d. Before 1910 in Dalton, Berkshire Co., Massachusetts

- **Unknown Briggs** – b. After 1900 in Dalton, Berkshire Co., Massachusetts, d. Before 1910 in Dalton, Berkshire Co., Massachusetts

Hurst

- **Unknown Briggs** – b. After 1900 in Dalton, Berkshire Co., Massachusetts, d. Before 1910 in Dalton, Berkshire Co., Massachusetts

- **Unknown Briggs** – b. After 1900 in Dalton, Berkshire Co., Massachusetts, d. Before 1910 in Dalton, Berkshire Co., Massachusetts

- **Unknown Briggs** – b. After 1900 in Dalton, Berkshire Co., Massachusetts, d. Before 1910 in Dalton, Berkshire Co., Massachusetts

- **Margaret Briggs** – b. 1902 in Dalton, Berkshire Co., Massachusetts

Margaret Briggs (daughter):

Residence – Dalton, Berkshire Co., Massachusetts – January 15, 1920

Occupation – None – January 15, 1920

- **Mary A. Briggs** – b. 1914 in Dalton, Berkshire Co., Massachusetts

Mary A. Briggs (daughter):

Residence – Dalton, Berkshire Co., Massachusetts – January 15, 1920

April 9, 1930

Occupation – None – January 15, 1920

April 9, 1930

William Jerome Briggs (son):

Residence – Smyrna, Chenango Co., New York – June 23, 1875

June 8, 1880

Dalton, Berkshire Co., Massachusetts – June 7, 1900

May 3, 1910

January 15, 1920

April 9, 1930

Occupation – None Listed – June 23, 1875

At School – June 8, 1880

Unclear – June 7, 1900

Odd Jobs, Paperwork – May 3, 1910

Papermaker, Paper Mill – January 15, 1920

Size Maker, Paper Mill – April 9, 1930

Home Data for 1930 – Owns home, valued at $ 7, 000, has radio set, not on a farm

Margaret Unknown (daughter-in-law):

Residence – Dalton, Berkshire Co., Massachusetts – June 7, 1930

May 3, 1910

January 15, 1920

Elisha Calkins & Anna Dalrymple Descendants

April 9, 1930

Occupation – None Listed – June 7, 1900

None – May 3, 1910

January 15, 1920

April 9, 1930

o **Bethia W. Miller**, b. Aug 1829 in Chenango Co. New York, d. 25 Feb 1911 & **Devalson A. Wilcox** (2nd Husband), b. 1833, d. 26 Aug 1891 in Smyrna, Chenango Co., New York

Bethia W. Miller (daughter):

Residence – Smyrna, Chenango Co., New York – July 23, 1850

July 13, 1860

June 23, 1870

June 23, 1875

June 8, 1880

June 5, 1900

April 18, 1910

Occupation – None Listed – July 23, 1850

July 13, 1860

Keeping House – June 23, 1870

June 8, 1880

House Keeping – June 23, 1875

None Listed [Relationship to head of House is Servant] – June 5, 1900

Own Income – April 18, 1910

Ensign Briggs (1st Husband) (son-in-law):

Residence – Smyrna, Chenango Co., New York – July 12, 1850

July 13, 1860

June 23, 1870

June 23, 1875

June 8, 1880

Occupation – Farmer – July 12, 1850

July 13, 1860

June 23, 1870

June 23, 1875

June 8, 1880

Value of Real Estate – $ 300 – July 12, 1850

$ 3, 500 – July 13, 1860

$ 4, 520 – June 23, 1870

Hurst

Value of Personal Estate – None Listed – July 12, 1850

$ 800 – July 13, 1860

$ 1, 500 – June 23, 1870

○ **Lyman Miller**, b. 31 Aug 1831 in Chenango Co., New York, d. 30 Jan 1920 in Emmet Co., Michigan & **Waitey A. Unknown** (1st Wife), b. Sep 1823 in Rhode Island or New York, d. 1903 in Readmond, Emmet Co., Michigan

▪ **Charles M. Miller** – b. 1854 in Chenango Co., New York, d. Before 1870 in New York

Charles M. Miller (son):

Residence – Otselic, Chenango Co., New York – June 27, 1860

Occupation – None Listed – June 27, 1860

▪ **Marybeth Nettie Miller** – b. About 1858 in Smyrna, Chenango Co., New York

Marybeth Nettie Miller (daughter):

Residence – Smyrna, Chenango Co., New York – June 13, 1870

June 11, 1875

Occupation – At School – June 13, 1870

Asst (House Keeping) – June 11, 1875

▪ **Charles E. Miller** – b. Between 1867 – 1869 in Chenango Co., New York

Charles E. Miller (son):

Residence – Smyrna, Chenango Co., New York – June 13, 1870

June 11, 1875

Readmond, Emmet Co., Michigan – June 1st & 2nd, 1880

Occupation – None Listed – June 13, 1870

June 11, 1875

Assisting on Farm – June 1st & 2nd 1880

○ **Lyman Miller**, b. 31 Aug 1831 in Chenango Co., New York, d. 30 Jan 1920 in Emmet Co., Michigan & **Emily Maria Gibson** (2nd Wife), b. 13 Apr 1842 in New York, d. 28 Jul 1928 in Harbor Springs, Emmet Co., Michigan

Lyman Miller (son):

Residence – Smyrna, Chenango Co., New York – July 23, 1850

June 13, 1870

June 11, 1875

Otselic, Chenango Co., New York – June 27, 1860

Readmond, Emmet Co., Michigan – June 1st & 2nd, 1880

1890

Elisha Calkins & Anna Dalrymple Descendants

June 15, 1900

April 25, 1910

Little Traverse, Emmet Co., Michigan – January 10, 1920

Occupation – Farmer – July 23, 1850

June 27, 1860

June 13, 1870

June 11, 1875

June 1st & 2nd, 1880

Farming – June 15, 1900

Farmer, General Farm – April 25, 1910

None – January 10, 1920

Value of Real Estate – None Listed – June 27, 1860

Value of Personal Estate – $ 150 – June 27, 1860

$ 600 – June 13, 1870

Waitey A. Unknown (1st Wife) (daughter-in-law):

Residence – Otselic, Chenango Co., New York – June 27, 1860

Smyrna, Chenango Co., New York – June 13, 1870

June 11, 1875

Readmond, Emmet Co., Michigan – June 1st & 2nd, 1880

June 15, 1900

Occupation – None Listed – June 27, 1860

June 15, 1900

Keeping House – June 13, 1870

June 1st & 2nd, 1880

House Keeping – June 11, 1875

Emily Maria Gibson (2nd Wife) (daughter-in-law):

Residence – Readmond, Emmet Co., Michigan – April 25, 1910

Little Traverse, Emmet Co., Michigan – January 10, 1920

Occupation – Carpet Weaver, at home – April 25, 1910

None – January 10, 1920

Mary Calkins (mother):

Residence – Smyrna, Chenango Co., New York – July 23, 1850

Columbus, Chenango Co., New York – July 27, 1870

Readmond, Emmet Co., Michigan – June 1st & 2nd, 1880

July 24, 1883

Occupation – None Listed – July 23, 1850

        Keeping House – July 27, 1870

        Assisting at House Keeping – June 1ˢᵗ & 2ⁿᵈ, 1880

        Housekeeper – July 24, 1883

John C. Miller (father):

    Residence – Otselic, Chenango Co., New York – 1830

                            1840

        Smyrna, Chenango Co., New York – July 23, 1850

        Columbus, Chenango Co., New York – July 27, 1870

Occupation – Farmer – July 23, 1850

        Retired Carpenter – July 27, 1870

Value of Real Estate – $ 1, 200 – July 23, 1850

        $ 300 – July 27, 1870

Value of Personal Estate – $ 200 – July 27, 1870

Mary Calkins & John C. Miller

Family Photo Album (Found at an Estate Sale near Medina, Ohio)

Date of Album – 1860s

Photographs courtesy of The Hurst Family of Lake Elsinore, California

Laura H. Calkins & Descendants

- **Laura H. Calkins**, b. 11 Sep 1803 in Greenfield, Saratoga Co., New York, d. 18 Mar 1880 in Chenango Co., New York & **Alexander Butts**, b. 1801 in Rhode Island, d. 10 Oct 1893 in Beaver Meadow, Chenango Co., New York – Before 1825 in Chenango Co., New York

  o **Samuel Calkins Butts**, b. 1825 in Otselic, Chenango Co., New York, d. Before 26 Mar 1884 in Chenango Co., New York & **Eliza M. McMinn**, b. Nov 1818 in New York, d. After 1900

    ▪ **Ransom Butts**, b. 5 Sep 1852 in Otselic, Chenango Co., New York, d. After June 1, 1925 in New York & **Flora E. Daily**, b. Feb 1855 in New York, d. Before 1920 – 20 Jun 1876 in Otselic, Chenango Co., New York

      • **Walter Niles Butts**, b. Jul 1878 in Beaver Meadows, Chenango Co., New York & **Mary G. Powell**, b. Dec 1879 in Plymouth, Chenango Co., New York – 1900 in New York

Signature:

Walter Niles Butts (son):

  Residence – Beaver Meadows, Chenango Co., New York – June 22, 1880

    Plymouth, Chenango Co., New York – June 19, 1900

    Waverly, Lackawanna Co., Pennsylvania – May 7, 1910

    Clark Summit, Lackawanna Co., Pennsylvania – September 12, 1918

                    April 9, 1930

    Los Angles, Los Angeles Co., California – January 12, 1920

  Occupation – None Listed – June 22, 1880

    Grocer – June 19, 1900

    Grocery Store, Retail – May 7, 1910

    Merchant – September 12, 1918

    Owner, General Store – January 12, 1920

    Proprietor, General Store – April 9, 1930

  Home Data for 1930 – Owns home, valued at $ 10, 000, has radio set, not on a farm

Mary G. Powell (daughter-in-law):

  Residence – Plymouth, Chenango Co., New York – June 19, 1900

    Los Angeles, Los Angeles Co., California – January 12, 1920

    Clark Summit, Lackawanna Co., Pennsylvania – September 12, 1918

                    April 9, 1930

Occupation – None Listed – June 19, 1900

None – January 12, 1920

April 9, 1930

- Unknown Butts

Ransom Butts (son):

Residence – Otselic, Chenango Co., New York – June 27, 1860

June 4, 1875

Plymouth, Chenango Co., New York – June 21, 1870

June 19, 1900

Beaver Meadows, Chenango Co., New York – June 22, 1880

Waverly, Lackawanna Co., Pennsylvania – May 7, 1910

Norwich, Chenango Co., New York – January 9, 1920

June 1, 1925

Occupation – None Listed – June 27, 1860

June 1, 1925

Farm Labor – June 21, 1870

Blacksmith – June 4, 1875

June 22, 1880

Grocer – June 19, 1900

None – May 7, 1910

January 9, 1920

Flora E. Daily (daughter-in-law):

Residence – Beaver Meadows, Chenango Co., New York – June 22, 1880

Plymouth, Chenango Co., New York – June 19, 1900

Waverly, Lackawanna Co., Pennsylvania – May 7, 1910

Occupation – Teaching School – June 22, 1880

None Listed – June 19, 1900

None – May 7, 1910

- **Nancy Butts** – b. 1853 in Chenango Co., New York

Nancy Butts (daughter):

Residence – Otselic, Chenango Co., New York – June 27, 1860

Occupation – None Listed – June 27, 1860

Hurst

- ▪ **William R. Butts**, b. Jun 1861 in Chenango Co., New York & **Flora M. Unknown**, b. Jul 1860 in New York – 1883

    - ● **Hubert William Butts** – b. 11 Jun 1895 in Plymouth, Chenango Co., New York

Signature:

Hubert William Butts (son):

 Residence – Plymouth, Chenango Co., New York – June 19, 1900

  Cazenovia, Madison Co., New York – April 18, 1910

   June 1, 1915

  New Woodstock, Ulster Co., New York – June 5, 1917

 Occupation – None Listed – June 19, 1900

  Clerk, General Store – April 18, 1910

  Laborer, Wagon Shop – June 1, 1915

  Clerk, Garage – June 5, 1917

William R. Butts (son):

 Residence – Plymouth, Chenango Co., New York – June 21, 1870

   June 19, 1900

  Otselic, Chenango Co., New York – June 4, 1875

  Beaver Meadows, Chenango Co., New York – June 22, 1880

  Cazenovia, Madison Co., New York – April 18, 1910

   June 1, 1915

   January 15, 1920

   June 1, 1925

   April 7, 1930

 Occupation – None Listed – June 21, 1870

   June 4, 1875

  Carpenter – June 22, 1880

  Blacksmith – June 19, 1900

   June 1, 1915

  Blacksmith, Own Shop – April 18, 1910

  General Repair Man, Own Shop – January 15, 1920

  Mechanic – June 1, 1925

  Blacksmith, Town Shop – April 7, 1930

Home Date for 1930 – Owns home, valued at $ 3, 000, no radio set, not on a farm

Flora M. Unknown (daughter-in-law):

    Residence – Plymouth, Chenango Co., New York – June 19, 1900

              Cazenovia, Madison Co., New York – April 18, 1910

                              June 1, 1915

                              January 15, 1920

                              June 1, 1925

                              April 7, 1930

    Occupation – None Listed – June 19, 1900

               None – April 18, 1910

                    January 15, 1920

                Housework – June 1, 1915

                        June 1, 1925

              Laundress, At Home – April 7, 1930

Samuel Calkins Butts (son):

    Residence – Otselic, Chenango Co., New York – August 5, 1850

                              June 27, 1860

                              August 11, 1862

                              June 4, 1875

              Plymouth, Chenango Co., New York – June 21, 1870

              Beaver Meadows, Chenango Co., New York – June 22, 1880

    Occupation – Farmer – August 5, 1850

                    June 27, 1860

                    August 11, 1862

               Blacksmith – June 21, 1870

                    June 4, 1875

                    June 22, 1880

    Value of Real Estate – $ 1, 500 – June 27, 1860

                    $ 5, 000 – June 21, 1870

    Value of Personal Estate – $ 500 – June 27, 1860

                      $ 690 – June 21, 1870

Eliza M. McMinn (daughter-in-law):

    Residence – Otselic, Chenango Co., New York – June 27, 1860

                              June 4, 1875

              Plymouth, Chenango Co., New York – June 21, 1870

                              June 19, 1900

              Beaver Meadows, Chenango Co., New York – June 22, 1880

Hurst

Occupation – None Listed – June 27, 1860

June 4, 1875

June 19, 1900

Keeping House – June 21, 1870

June 22, 1880

o   **Alexander Butts** – b. 1825 in Otselic, Chenango Co., New York, d. 21 Apr 1864 in Washington, Maryland

Alexander Butts (son):

Residence – Otselic, Chenango Co., New York – August 5, 1850

January 9, 1864

Occupation – Farmer – August 5, 1850

January 9, 1864

o   **Betsy Butts** – b. About 1835 in Otselic, Chenango Co., New York

Betsy Butts (daughter):

Residence – Otselic, Chenango Co., New York – August 5, 1850

Occupation – None Listed – August 5, 1850

o   **Lysander Butts** – b. About 1841 in Otselic, Chenango Co., New York, d. 18 Dec 1864 in Baltimore, Maryland

Lysander Butts (son):

Residence – Otselic, Chenango Co., New York – August 5, 1850

June 27, 1860

August 11, 1862

Occupation – None Listed – August 5, 1850

Farm Hand – June 27, 1860

Farmer – August 11, 1862

o   **Philander Butts**, b. Feb 1845 in Otselic, Chenango Co., New York, d. 28 Jul 1918 in Beaver Meadows, Chenango Co., New York & **Maria Hepsabeth Westcott**, b. 2 Nov 1845 in Oxford, Chenango Co., New York, d. 1919 in Beaver Meadows, Chenango Co., New York – 1 Jan 1866 in Oxford, Chenango Co., New York

Philander Butts (son):

Residence – Otselic, Chenango Co., New York – June 27, 1860

July 26, 1870

June 9, 1900

1902

June 1, 1905

May 4, 1910

Smyrna, Chenango Co., New York – June 14, 1880

Occupation – Farm Hand – June 27, 1860

Hotel Keeper – July 26, 1870

Laborer – June 14, 1880

Blacksmith – June 9, 1900

1902

June 1, 1905

Blacksmith, Own Shop – May 4, 1910

Justice of the Peace – 1902

Value of Real Estate – $ 5, 000 – July 26, 1870

Value of Personal Estate – $ 1, 685 – July 26, 1870

Obituary –

"Beaver Meadow. July 30 – Philander Butts died at his home in this place Sunday morning, July 28th. Mr. Butts had been in poor health for several years and had been confined to the house for about four months. He leaves a wife, and adopted daughter and two nephews and two nieces. Funeral services will be held Wednesday and interment in the old Baptist cemetery near Smyrna where his ancestors are buried." from the De Ruyter Gleaner. Page 8. Thursday, August 1, 1918

Maria Hepsabeth Westcott (daughter-in-law):

Residence – Otselic, Chenango Co., New York – July 26, 1870

June 9, 1900

June 1, 1905

May 4, 1910

Smyrna, Chenango Co., New York – June 14, 1880

Occupation – Keeping House – July 26, 1870

Servant – June 14, 1880

None Listed – June 9, 1900

Housework – June 1, 1905

None – May 4, 1910

Laura H. Calkins (mother):

Residence – Otselic, Chenango Co., New York – August 5, 1850

June 27, 1860

July 25, 1870

Occupation – None Listed – August 5, 1850

June 27, 1860

Hurst

Keeping House – July 25, 1870

Alexander Butts (father):

Residence – Otselic, Chenango Co., New York – 1830

1840

August 5, 1850

June 27, 1860

July 25, 1870

Beaver Meadows, Chenango Co., New York – June 22, 1880

Occupation – Blacksmith – August 5, 1850

July 25, 1870

June 22, 1880

Farmer – June 27, 1860

Value of Real Estate – $ 1, 800 – August 5, 1850

$ 1, 400 – June 27, 1860

$ 1, 200 – July 25, 1870

Value of Personal Estate – $ 500 – June 27, 1860

$ 300 – July 25, 1870

Obituary –

"Butts. – At Beaver Meadow, Oct 10 1893, Alexander Butts, aged 93 years." **from the Weekly Gleaner. Thursday**

October 26, 1893, De Ruyter, Madison Co., New York

Laura H. Calkins & Alexander Butts

Family Photo Album (Found at an Estate Sale near Medina, Ohio)

Date of Album – 1860s

Photographs courtesy of The Hurst Family of Lake Elsinore, California

Samuel Calkins Butts

Family Photo Album (Found at an Estate Sale near Medina, Ohio)

Date of Album – 1860s

Photographs – Tintypes

Photographs courtesy of The Hurst Family of Lake Elsinore, California

Eliza M. McMinn & children Nancy & Ransom Butts

Family Photo Album (Found at an Estate Sale near Medina, Ohio)

Date of Album – 1860s

Photographs courtesy of The Hurst Family of Lake Elsinore, California

Almira Calkins & Descendants

- **Almira Calkins**, b. 12 Sep 1805 in Greenfield, Saratoga Co., New York, d. 17 Mar 1887 in Columbus, Warren Co., Pennsylvania & **Lester A. Woods**, b. 11 Sep 1802 in Middlefield, Hampshire Co., Massachusetts, d. 11 Sep 1891 in Mina, Chautauqua Co., New York – 14 Jan 1823 in Madison Co., New York

  - **Viola Jane Woods** – b. 24 Apr 1826 in Madison Co., New York, d. 11 Sep 1872 in Columbus, Warren Co., Pennsylvania

  - **Dexter Florello Woods**, b. 28 Jun 1828 in Arkwright, Chautauqua Co., New York, d. 16 Dec 1893 in Goleta, Santa Barbara Valley, California & **Cordelia A. Baldwin**, b. 28 Nov 1829 in Sheridan, Chautauqua Co., New York – 14 Jun 1853 in Arkwright, Chautauqua Co., New York

    - **Clayton Forest Woods**, b. About 1855 in Arkwright, Chautauqua Co., New York & **Viola R. Newberry** (1st Wife), b. Jul 1864 New York – 13 Feb 1884 in Santa Barbara Co., California

    - **Clayton Forest Woods**, b. About 1855 in Arkwright, Chautauqua Co., New York & **Ann Helena Kyle Grammer** (2nd Wife), b. 21 Dec 1862 in Tennessee, d. 30 Dec 1950 in Riverside, Riverside Co., California – 4 Nov 1910 in Santa Barbara Co., California

Clayton Forest Woods (son):

Residence – Arkwright, Chautauqua Co., New York – August 16, 1860

Palmyra, Otoe Co., Nebraska – June 1, 1870

June 12, 1880

Dos Pueblos, Santa Barbara Co., California – 1890

1892

Pomona, Los Angles, California – July 6, 1896

Santa Barbara, Santa Barbra Co., California – 1910

January 6, 1920

Occupation – None Listed – August 16, 1860

At School – June 1, 1870

Horticulture – June 12, 1880

Farmer – 1890

1896

Solicitor, Periodicals – 1910

Gardener, Landscape – January 6, 1920

▪ **Lavinia R. Woods**, b. Feb 1856 in Arkwright, Chautauqua Co., New York & **Edgar J. Griswold**, b. About 1858 in Chautauqua Co., New York, d. Before 1910 – 11 Feb 1879 in Otoe, Co., Nebraska

Lavinia R. Woods (daughter):

    Residence – Arkwright, Chautauqua Co., New York – August 16, 1860

        Palmyra, Otoe Co., Nebraska – June 1, 1870

            June 12th & 14th, 1880

      Santa Barbra, Santa Barbara Co., California – June 3rd & 5th, 1900

      Colorado Springs, El Paso Co., Colorado – April 20, 1910

                January 3, 1920

    Occupation – None Listed – August 16, 1860

        June 3rd & 5th, 1900

      At School – June 1, 1870

      Keeping House – June 12th & 14th, 1880

      Own Income – April 20, 1910

      None – January 3, 1920

Edgar J. Griswold (son-in-law):

    Residence – Palmyra, Otoe Co., Nebraska – June 12th & 14th, 1880

    Occupation – Farm & Dairy – June 12th & 14th, 1880

▪ **Cora L. C. Woods**, b. 4 Jul 1865 in Erie, Erie Co., Pennsylvania, d. 11 Oct 1951 in Kern Co., California & **Nathaniel Jay Newman**, b. Jan 1863 in California, d. 30 Nov 1932 in Santa Barbara, Santa Barbara Co., California – 17 Mar 1887 in Santa Barbara Co., California

    ● **Victor Wayne Newman**, b. 21 Jan 1888 in California, d. 16 Oct 1953 in Los Angeles Co., California & **Charlotte E. Palmer**, b. 1898 in Massachusetts

Signature:

        ○ **Victor Wayne Newman** – b. 31 Dec 1919 in Massachusetts, d. 6 Jun 1985 in San Diego, San Diego Co., California

Victor W. Newman (son):

    Residence – Santa Barbara, Santa Barbara Co., California – April 15, 1930

      Ventura, Los Angele Co., California – 1942

    Occupation – None – April 15, 1930

        ○ **Ralph J. Newman** – b. 27 Nov 1920 in Massachusetts, d. 25 Jul 1991 in San Bernardino, San Bernardino Co., California

113

Ralph J. Newman (son):

    Residence – Santa Barbara, Santa Barbara Co., California – April 15, 1930

    Occupation – None – April 15, 1930

        ○ **Ruth A. Newman** – b. About 1922 in Massachusetts

Ruth A. Newman (daughter):

    Residence – Santa Barbara, Santa Barbara Co., California – April 15, 1930

    Occupation – None – April 15, 1930

Victor Wayne Newman (son):

    Residence – 3rd Township, Santa Barbara Co., California – June 14, 1900

        United States Navy Yard, Kitsap Co., Washington – April 22, 1910

        Boston, Suffolk Co., Massachusetts – January 5, 1920

        Santa Barbara, Santa Barbara Co., California – April 15, 1930

    Occupation – At School – June 14, 1900

        Private – April 22, 1910

        Watchman, Bank – January 5, 1920

        Mail Carrier, U.S. Postal Dept. – April 15, 1930

  Home Data for 1930 – Rental, $ 25 a month, has radio set, not on a farm

Charlotte E. Palmer (daughter-in-law):

    Residence – Boston, Suffolk Co., Massachusetts – 1920

        Santa Barbara, Santa Barbara Co., California – April 15, 1930

    Occupation – None – April 15, 1930

    • **Nellie Newman** – b. May 1897 in California

Nellie Newman (daughter):

    Residence – 3rd Township, Santa Barbara Co. California – June 14, 1900

        Santa Paul, Ventura Co., California – April 18, 1910

    Occupation – None Listed – June 14, 1900

        None – April 18, 1910

    • **Jay Lemar Newman**, b. 16 Feb 1899 in California, d. 23 Sep 1946 in Ventura Co., California &

      Catherine D. Clemmons, b. About 1900 in Missouri

Signature:

        ○ **Meredith W. Newman** – b. 25 Feb 1922 in Ventura, Ventura Co., California, d. 17 May 2012

        in Bennington, Bennington Co., Vermont

Elisha Calkins & Anna Dalrymple Descendants

Meredith W. Newman (son):

Residence – Ventura, Ventura Co., California – April 3, 1930

Occupation – None – April 3, 1930

    ○ **Kenneth Lee Newman** – b. 24 Jan 1926 in Ventura, Ventura Co., California, d. 23 Jul 1999 in Seal Beach, Orange Co., California

Kenneth Lee Newman (son):

Residence – Ventura, Ventura Co., California – April 3, 1930

Occupation – None – April 3, 1930

    ○ **Caroline Jean Newman**, b. 25 Apr 1927 in Ventura, Ventura Co., California, d. 2 Oct 2000 in Ventura, Ventura Co., California & **Clifford Noah Robertson**, b. 18 Feb 1923 in Excelsior Springs, Ray Co., Missouri, d. 18 Mar 2006 in Ventura, Ventura Co., California – 23 Dec 1968 in Ventura, Ventura Co., California

Caroline Jean Newman (daughter):

Residence – Ventura, Ventura Co., California – April 3, 1930

Occupation – None – April 3, 1930

Jay Lemar Newman (son):

Residence – 3ʳᵈ Township, Santa Barbara Co., California – June 14, 1900

    Santa Paul, Ventura Co., California – April 18, 1910

    Ventura, Ventura Co., California – September 12, 1918

                  January 29, 1920

                   April 3, 1930

Occupation – None Listed – June 14, 1900

    None – April 18, 1910

    Oil Work – September 12, 1918

    Tool Dresser, Oil Well – January 29, 1920

    Driller, Oil Field – April 3, 1930

Home Data for 1930 – Owns home, valued at $ 4, 500, has radio set, not on a farm

Catherine D. Clemmons (daughter-in-law):

Residence – Ventura, Ventura Co., California – April 3, 1930

Occupation – None – April 3, 1930

    • **Unknown Newman** – b. After 1900 in Santa Barbara Co., California, d. Before 1910 in Santa Barbara Co., California

Hurst

Cora L. C. Woods (daughter):

Residence – Palmyra, Otoe Co., Nebraska – June 1, 1870

June 12, 1880

3rd Township, Santa Barbara Co., California – June 14, 1900

Santa Paula, Ventura Co., California – April 18, 1910

Nordhoff, Ventura Co., California – February 5, 1920

Goleta, Santa Barbara Co., California – April 13, 1930

Ventura, Ventura Co., California – 1942

Occupation – None Listed – June 1, 1870

June 14, 1900

At School – June 12, 1880

None – April 18, 1910

February 5, 1920

April 13, 1930

Nathaniel Jay Newman (son-in-law):

Residence – 3rd Township, Santa Barbara Co., California – June 14, 1900

Santa Paula, Ventura Co., California – April 18, 1910

Nordhoff, Ventura Co., California – February 5, 1920

Goleta, Santa Barbara Co., California – April 13, 1930

Occupation – Farmer – June 14, 1900

Farmer, Walnut Farm – April 18, 1910

Farmer, Grain Farm – February 5, 1920

Caretaker, County Park – April 13, 1930

Home Data for 1930 – Rental, $ 25 a month, has radio set, not on a farm

Dexter Florello Woods (son):

Residence – Arkwright, Chautauqua Co., New York – August 28, 1850

August 16, 1860

July 1, 1863

Palmyra, Otoe Co., Nebraska – June 1, 1870

June 12, 1880

Santa Barbara, Santa Barbara Co., California – 1890 & 1892

Occupation – Farmer – August 28, 1850

August 16, 1860

July 1, 1863

June 1, 1870

June 12, 1880

1890

Value of Real Estate – $ 600 – August 28, 1850

$ 4, 475 – August 16, 1860

$ 4, 500 – June 1, 1870

Value of Personal Estate – $ 700 – August 16, 1860

$ 3, 900 – June 1, 1875

Cordelia A. Baldwin (daughter-in-law):

Residence – Arkwright, Chautauqua Co., New York – August 16, 1860

Palmyra, Otoe Co., Nebraska – June 1, 1870

June 12, 1880

Santa Barbara, Santa Barbra Co., California – June 3rd & 5th, 1900

Occupation – None Listed – August 16, 1860

June 3rd & 5th, 1900

Cheese Maker – June 1, 1875

Keeping House – June 12, 1880

○ **Clarinda S. Woods**, b. 1 Sep 1830 in Arkwright, Chautauqua Co., New York, d. After 1900 & **Curtis L. Smith**, b. About 1827 in New York, d. Before 1880 – 27 Oct 1853 in Chautauqua Co., New York

  ▪ **Flora E. Smith**, b. Sep 1854 in Pennsylvania, d. April 1910 in California & **Martin W. Brown**, b. Jul 1849 in Pennsylvania, d. Before 1920 in California – 1874 in Pennsylvania

    • **Embert Morelle Brown**, b. 3 Jan 1875 in Erie, Erie Co., Pennsylvania, d. 5 Oct 1974 in Santa Cruz, Santa Cruz Co., California & **Kate May Bauter**, b. 30 Apr 1871 in New York, d. 17 Feb 1929 In Los Angeles, Los Angeles Co., California

Signature:

    • **Morelle B. Brown** – b. 3 Oct 1907 in Santa Cruz, Santa Cruz Co., California

Morelle B. Brown (son):

Residence – Santa Cruz, Santa Cruz Co., California – April 23, 1910

Ventura, Ventura Co., California – January 10, 1920

Occupation – None – April 23, 1910

January 10, 1920

Hurst

- **Marjorie Brown**, b. 17 Jan 1910 in Santa Cruz, Santa Cruz Co., California, d. 1 Feb 2002 in Vista, San Diego Co., California & **Luther Garrett Bean**, b. 8 Mar 1905 in Ozona, Crockett Co., Texas, d. 8 Mar 1995 in Vista, San Diego Co., California

Signature:

Marjorie Brown (daughter):

    Residence – Santa Cruz, Santa Cruz Co., California – April 23, 1910

        Ventura, Ventura Co., California – January 10, 1920

    Occupation – None – April 23, 1910

        January 10, 1920

- **David Brown** – b. 1912 in California

David Brown (son):

    Residence – Ventura, Ventura Co., California – January 10, 1920

    Occupation – None – January 10, 1920

Embert Morelle Brown (son):

    Residence – Wayne Erie Co., Pennsylvania – June 19, 1880

        Long Beach, Los Angeles Co., California – September 12, 1918

        Ventura, Ventura Co., California – January 10, 1920

    Occupation – None Listed – June 19, 1880

        Real Estate – September 12, 1918

        Agent, Real Estate – January 10, 1920

Kate May Bauter (daughter-in-law):

    Residence – Santa Cruz, Santa Cruz Co., California – April 23, 1910

        Ventura, Ventura Co., California – January 10, 1920

    Occupation – Own Income – April 23, 1910

        None – January 10, 1920

- **Frances Brown** – b. 1877 in Pennsylvania

Frances Brown (daughter):

    Residence – Wayne, Erie Co., Pennsylvania – June 19, 1880

    Occupation – None Listed – June 19, 1880

Elisha Calkins & Anna Dalrymple Descendants

- **Cleo A. Brown**, b. Jun 1885 in California & **Alfred A. Green**, b. 12 Apr 1882 in California, d. 15 Feb 1944 in San Bernardino Co., California

   o **Glenn Merlin Green,** b. 15 May 1905 in Los Angeles Co., California, d. 13 Nov 1970 in Laguna Nigel, Orange Co., California & **Elizabeth F. Unknown**, b. About 1906 in California

Glenn Merlin Green (son):

Residence – Los Angeles, Los Angeles Co., California – April 28, 1910

January 1920

East Orange, Essex Co., New Jersey – April 2, 1930

Occupation – None – April 28, 1910

January 1920

Manager Telegram, Telephone Co. – April 2, 1930

Home Data for 1930 – Rental, $ 60 a month, has radio set, not on a farm

Elizabeth F. Unknown (daughter-in-law):

Residence – East Orange, Essex Co., New Jersey – April 2, 1930

Occupation – None – April 2, 1930

   o **Thelma Green** – b. 28 Feb 1910 in Los Angeles, Los Angeles Co., California

Thelma Green (daughter):

Residence – Los Angeles, Los Angeles Co., California – April 28, 1910

January 1920

Occupation – None – April 28, 1910

January 1920

Cleo A. Brown (daughter):

Residence – Santa Cruz, Santa Cruz Co., California – June 6, 1900

Los Angeles, Los Angeles Co., California – April 28, 1910

January 1920

Occupation – None Listed – June 6, 1900

None – April 28, 1910

January 1920

Alfred A. Green (son-in-law):

Residence – Los Angeles, Los Angeles Co., California – April 28, 1910

January 1920

Occupation – Police Officer, City – April 28, 1910

Policeman, City – January 1920

Hurst

Flora E. Smith (daughter):

Residence – Wayne, Erie Co. Pennsylvania – June 20, 1860

July 12, 1870

June 19, 1880

Santa Cruz, Santa Cruz Co., California – June 6, 1900

April 22, 1910

Occupation – None Listed – June 20, 1860

July 12, 1870

June 6, 1900

Keeping House – June 19, 1880

None – April 22, 1910

Martin W. Brown (son-in-law):

Residence – Wayne, Erie Co., Pennsylvania – June 19, 1880

Santa Cruz, Santa Cruz Co., California – June 6, 1900

April 22, 1910

Los Angeles, Los Angeles Co., California – April 28, 1910

Occupation – Laborer – June 19, 1880

Carpenter, Odd Jobs – June 6, 1900

April 22, 1910

Carpenter, House – April 28, 1910

- ▪ **Anna A. Smith** – b. About 1862 in Pennsylvania

Anna A. Smith (daughter):

Residence – Wayne, Erie Co. Pennsylvania – July 12, 1870

Chautauqua, Chautauqua Co., New York – June 14, 1880

Occupation – None Listed – July 12, 1870

Teacher – June 14, 1880

- ▪ **Alice May Smith**, b. Sep 1865, d. 4 Sep 1935 in Wildwood, Cape May Co., New Jersey & **Charles Brakiron**, b. 1857 in Pennsylvania – 1884

  - • **Ethel A. Brakiron** – b. Nov 1887 in Pennsylvania

Ethel A. Brakiron (daughter):

Residence – Meadville City, Crawford Co., Pennsylvania – June 8, 1900

1910

Occupation – At School – June 8, 1900

Teacher, Public School – 1910

Elisha Calkins & Anna Dalrymple Descendants

Alice May Smith (daughter):

   Residence – Wayne, Erie Co., Pennsylvania – July 12, 1870

       Chautauqua, Chautauqua Co., New York – June 14, 1880

       Meadville City, Crawford Co., Pennsylvania – June 8, 1900

                   1910

                   January 21, 1920

                   1930

   Occupation – None Listed – July 12, 1870

                   June 8, 1900

               1910

       Home – June 14, 1880

       None – January 21, 1920

           1930

Charles Brakiron (son-in-law):

   Residence – Meadville City, Crawford Co., Pennsylvania – June 8, 1900

                   1910

                   January 21, 1920

                   1930

   Occupation – Composition (book) – June 8, 1900

           Printer – 1910

           Clerk, County Courts – January 21, 1920

           Printer, Job Shop – 1930

   Home Data for 1930 – Owns home, valued at $ 9, 000, has radio set, not on a farm

       ▪ **Frances Smith** – b. About 1867 in Pennsylvania

Frances Smith (daughter):

   Residence – Wayne, Erie Co., Pennsylvania – July 12, 1870

   Occupation – None Listed – July 12, 1870

       ▪ **Corinda Smith** – b. Aug 1869 in Pennsylvania

Corinda Smith (daughter):

   Residence – Wayne, Erie Co., Pennsylvania – July 12, 1870

   Occupation – None Listed – July 12, 1870

       ▪ **Unknown Smith**

Clarinda S. Woods (daughter):

   Residence – Troy, Crawford Co., Pennsylvania – August 14, 1850

       Wayne, Erie Co., Pennsylvania – June 20, 1860

                   July 12, 1870

Hurst

Chautauqua, Chautauqua Co., New York – June 14, 1880

Meadville City, Crawford Co., Pennsylvania – June 8, 1900

Santa Cruz, Santa Cruz Co., California – April 22, 1910

Occupation – None Listed – August 14, 1850

June 20, 1860

June 8, 1900

Keeping House – July 12, 1870

June 14, 1880

None – April 22, 1910

Curtis Smith (son-in-law):

Residence – Wayne, Erie Co., Pennsylvania – June 20, 1860

July 12, 1870

Occupation – Farmer – June 20, 1860

July 12, 1870

Value of Real Estate – $ 1, 500 – June 20, 1860

$ 7, 000 – July 12, 1870

Value of Personal Estate – $ 200 – June 20, 1860

$ 1, 500 – July 12, 1870

○ **Arcelia M. Woods**, b. 18 Mar 1833 in Arkwright, Chautauqua Co., New York, d. After 1908 in Mina, Chautauqua Co., New York & **Zebulon Jones**, b. About 1827 in Genesee Co., New York, d. 23 Dec 1893 in Mina, Chautauqua Co., New York – 17 Apr 1849 in Chautauqua Co., New York

   ▪ **Delilah Jones**, b. 1852 in New York & **Caleb Aspinwall Eldred**, b. 9 Jan 1850 in Otsego, Otsego Co., New York, d. 23 May 1898 in New York – 1 Jun 1874 in New York

      • **Theron Eugene Eldred**, b. 9 Apr 1875 in New York, d. Oct 1968 in Dunkirk, Chautauqua Co., New York & **Theo Marie Taggart**, b. Nov 1880 in Pennsylvania

Signature:

      ○ **Roger Eldred** – b. May 1900 in Pennsylvania

Roger Eldred (son):

Residence – Rome, Crawford Co., Pennsylvania – June 2, 1900

Occupation – None Listed – June 2, 1900

○ **Inez Belle Eldred**, b. About 1906 in Mina, Chautauqua Co., New York & **William Henry Jackson**, b. About 1904 in Townville, Crawford Co., Pennsylvania – 23 Mar 1925 in Westfield, Chautauqua Co., New York

■ **William H. Jackson** – b. About 1927 in Pennsylvania

William H. Jackson (son):

Residence – Centerville, Crawford Co., Pennsylvania – April 2, 1930

Occupation – None – April 2, 1930

■ **Marjorie Jackson** – b. About 1929 in Pennsylvania

Marjorie Jackson (daughter):

Residence – Centerville, Crawford Co., Pennsylvania – April 2, 1930

Occupation – None – April 2, 1930

■ **Richard E. Jackson** – b. About 1930 in Pennsylvania

Richard E. Jackson (son):

Residence – Centerville, Crawford Co., Pennsylvania – April 2, 1930

Occupation – None – April 2, 1930

Inez Belle Eldred (daughter):

Residence – Westfield, Chautauqua Co., New York – April 26th & 27th, 1910

June 1, 1915

Centerville, Crawford Co., Pennsylvania – January 3, 1920

April 2, 1930

Sherman, Chautauqua Co., New York – March 23, 1925

Occupation – None – April 26th & 27th, 1910

January 3, 1920

April 2, 1930

School – June 1, 1915

Homemaker – March 23, 1925

William Henry Jackson (son-in-law):

Residence – Centerville, Crawford Co., Pennsylvania – March 23, 1925

April 2, 1930

Occupation – Laborer – March 23, 1925

Laborer, Milk Plant – April 2, 1930

Home Data for 1930 – Rental, $ 15 a month, no radio set, on a farm

Hurst

o **Irene Ethel Eldred** – b. About 1913 in New York

Irene Ethel Eldred (daughter):

> *Residence – Westfield, Chautauqua Co., New York – June 1, 1915*
>
> > > *June 1, 1925*
> > >
> > > *April 14, 1930*
> >
> > *Centerville, Crawford Co., Pennsylvania – January 3, 1920*
>
> *Occupation – No Occupation – June 1, 1915*
>
> > *None – January 3, 1920*
> >
> > *April 14, 1930*
> >
> > *School – June 1, 1925*

Theron Eldred (son):

> *Residence – Ripley, Chautauqua Co., New York – June 16th & 17th, 1880*
>
> > > *February 16, 1892*
> >
> > *Rome, Crawford Co., Pennsylvania – June 2, 1900*
> >
> > *Westfield, Chautauqua Co., New York – April 26th & 27th, 1910*
> >
> > > *June 1, 1915*
> > >
> > > *June 1, 1925*
> > >
> > > *April 14, 1930*
> >
> > *Allegany, Cattaraugus Co., New York – September 12, 1918*
> >
> > *Centerville, Crawford Co., Pennsylvania – January 3, 1920*
>
> *Occupation – None Listed – June 16th & 17th, 1880*
>
> > *February 16, 1892*
> >
> > *Butter Maker – June 2, 1900*
> >
> > *Farmer, General Farm – April 26th & 27th, 1910*
> >
> > *Farmer – June 1, 1915*
> >
> > *Creamery Plant – September 12, 1918*
> >
> > *Manager, Milk Plant – January 3, 1920*
> >
> > *Machinist – June 1, 1925*
> >
> > *Mechanic, Garage – April 14, 1930*
>
> *Home Data for 1930 – Owns home, valued at $ 4, 000, no radio set, not on a farm*

Theo Marie Taggart (daughter-in-law):

> *Residence – Rome, Crawford Co., Pennsylvania – June 2, 1900*
>
> > *Westfield, Chautauqua Co., New York – April 26th & 27th, 1910*
> >
> > > *June 1, 1915*
> > >
> > > *June 1, 1925*
> > >
> > > *April 14, 1930*

Elisha Calkins & Anna Dalrymple Descendants

Allegany, Cattaraugus Co., New York – September 12, 1918

Centerville, Crawford Co., Pennsylvania – January 3, 1920

Occupation – None Listed – June 2, 1900

None – April 26ᵗʰ & 27, 1910

January 3, 1920

Housework – June 1, 1915

June 1, 1925

Laborer, Grape Juice Factory – April 14, 1930

- Susie Eldred – b. Mar 1884 in New York

Susie Eldred (daughter):

Residence – Ripley, Chautauqua Co., New York – February 16, 1892

Mina, Chautauqua Co., New York – June 4, 1900

Occupation – None Listed – February 16, 1892

At School – June 4, 1900

- Addie M. Eldred, b. 24 Dec 1886 in Ripley, Chautauqua Co., New York, d. Aug 1982 in Westfield, Chautauqua Co., New York & Frank Edward Bellen, b. 19 Nov 1871 in Rome, Crawford Co., Pennsylvania, 23 Jan 1937 in Oil City, Venango Co., Pennsylvania – 24 Dec 1904 in Sherman, Chautauqua Co., New York

    o Everett E. Bellen – b. 15 May 1906 in Titusville, Crawford Co., Pennsylvania, d. 23 Jan 1957 in Oil City, Venango Co., Pennsylvania

Everett E. Bellen (son):

Residence – Rome, Crawford Co., Pennsylvania – April 22, 1910

January 30, 1920

Oil City, Venango Co., Pennsylvania – April 14, 1930

Occupation – None – April 22, 1910

January 30, 1920

Accounting, Crude Oil – April 14, 1930

    o Mildred M. Bellen – b. 3 Apr 1910 in Rome, Crawford Co., Pennsylvania

Mildred Bellen (daughter):

Residence – Rome, Crawford Co., Pennsylvania – April 22, 1910

January 30, 1920

Centerville, Crawford Co., Pennsylvania – April 9, 1930

Occupation – None – April 22, 1910

January 30, 1920

125

Hurst

April 9, 1930

Addie M. Eldred (daughter):

> *Residence – Ripley, Chautauqua Co., New York – February 16, 1892*
>
> > *Mina, Chautauqua Co., New York – June 4, 1900*
> >
> > *Rome, Crawford Co., Pennsylvania – April 22, 1910*
> >
> > > *January 30, 1920*
> >
> > *Centerville, Crawford Co., Pennsylvania – April 9, 1930*
>
> *Occupation – None Listed – February 16, 1892*
>
> > *June 4, 1900*
> >
> > *None – April 22, 1910*
> >
> > *January 30, 1920*
> >
> > *April 9, 1930*

Frank Edward Bellen (son-in-law):

> *Residence – Rome, Crawford Co., Pennsylvania – April 22, 1910*
>
> > *January 30, 1920*
> >
> > *Centerville, Crawford Co., Pennsylvania – April 9, 1930*
>
> *Occupation – Farmer, General Farm – April 22, 1910*
>
> > *January 30, 1920*
> >
> > *Farmer – Owns Farm – April 9, 1930*
>
> *Home Data for 1930 – Owns home, has radio set, on a farm*

Delilah Jones (daughter):

> *Residence – Mina, Chautauqua Co., New York – July 20, 1860*
>
> > *July 18, 1870*
> >
> > *June 4, 1900*
> >
> > *Ripley, Chautauqua Co., New York – June 16th & 17th, 1880*
> >
> > > *February 16, 1892*
> >
> > *Sherman, Chautauqua Co., New York – June 1, 1905*
>
> *Occupation – Child – July 20, 1860*
>
> > *At Home – July 18, 1870*
> >
> > *Keeping House – June 16th & 17th, 1880*
> >
> > *None Listed – February 16, 1892*
> >
> > > *June 4, 1900*
> >
> > *Housework – June 1, 1905*

Caleb Aspinwall Eldred (son-in-law):

> *Residence – Ripley, Chautauqua Co., New York – June 16th & 17th, 1880*
>
> > *February 16, 1892*

Occupation – Farmer – June 16th & 17th, 1880

February 16, 1892

▪ **Lester E. Jones**, b. About 1856 in Chautauqua Co., New York, d. 25 Jan 1906 in Mina, Chautauqua Co., New York & **Susan Ann Ottaway**, b. About 1862 in New York, d. 1923 in New York

• **Alvah Devillo Jones** – b. 14 Mar 1885 in Mina, Chautauqua Co., New York, d. Jun 1968 in Westfield, Chautauqua Co., New York

Signature:

Alvah Devillo Jones (son):

Residence – Mina, Chautauqua Co., New York – February 16, 1892

June 1, 1905

April 27, 1910

June 1, 1915

September 12, 1918

January 22, 1920

June 1, 1925

May 2, 1930

Occupation – None Listed – February 16, 1892

Farm Laborer – June 1, 1905

Farm Labor, Home Farm – April 27, 1910

Farmer – June 1, 1915

September 12, 1918

June 1, 1925

Laborer, Farm – January 22, 1920

Farmer, Diary Farm – May 2, 1930

• **Ray Ottaway Jones** – b. 28 Sep 1887 in Mina, Chautauqua Co., New York

Signature:

Ray Ottaway Jones (son):

Residence – Mina, Chautauqua Co., New York – February 16, 1892

June 1, 1905

April 27, 1910

Hurst

June 1, 1915

June 5, 1917

January 22, 1920

June 1, 1925

May 3, 1930

Occupation – None Listed – February 16, 1892

At School – June 1, 1905

Farm Labor, Home Farm – April 27, 1910

Farmer – June 1, 1915

June 5, 1917

June 1, 1925

Farmer, Farm – January 22, 1920

Farmer, Diary Farm – May 2, 1930

Home Data for 1930 – Owns home, has radio set, on a farm

Lester E. Jones (son):

Residence – Mina, Chautauqua Co., New York – July 20, 1860

July 18, 1870

June 22, 1880

February 16, 1892

June 1, 1905

Occupation – Child – July 20, 1860

At Home – July 18, 1870

Farm Laborer – June 22, 1880

Farmer – February 16, 1892

June 1, 1905

Susan Ann Ottaway (daughter-in-law):

Residence – Mina, Chautauqua Co., New York – February 16, 1892

June 1, 1905

April 27, 1910

June 1, 1915

January 22, 1920

June 1, 1925

Occupation – None Listed – February 16, 1892

Housework – June 1, 1905

June 1, 1915

June 1, 1925

Farmer, General Farm – April 27, 1910

None – January 22, 1920

▪ **Addie Marie Jones**, b. Aug 1857 in New York, d. 4 Mar 1920 in Titusville, Crawford Co., Pennsylvania & **Lafayette Jefferson Kerr**, b. 28 May 1850 in Oil Creek, Crawford Co., Pennsylvania, d. 17 Dec 1919 in Titusville, Crawford Co., Pennsylvania

• **Glenn Cora Kerr**, b. 17 Feb 1878 in Pennsylvania, d. 5 May 1963 & **James Law Alcorn**, b. 23 Dec 1869 in Cherry Tree, Venango Co., Pennsylvania, d. 1 Jul 1945 in Oil Creek, Crawford Co., Pennsylvania

○ **Roscoe Lafayette Alcorn** – b. 23 Apr 1914 in Pennsylvania, d. 14 Sep 1983 in Titusville, Crawford Co., Pennsylvania

Roscoe Layfayette Alcorn (son):

Residence – Titusville, Crawford Co., Pennsylvania – January 5, 1920

April 9, 1930

Occupation – None – January 5, 1920

April 9, 1930

○ **Sylvia M. Alcorn** – b. 3 Feb 1916 in Pennsylvania, d. 3 Nov 2002 in Titusville, Crawford Co., Pennsylvania

Sylvia M. Alcorn (daughter):

Residence – Titusville, Crawford Co., Pennsylvania – January 5, 1920

April 9, 1930

Occupation – None – January 5, 1920

April 9, 1930

Glenn Cora Kerr (daughter):

Residence – Oil Creek, Crawford Co., Pennsylvania – June 16, 1880

June 19, 1900

April 23, 1910

Titusville, Crawford Co., Pennsylvania – January 5, 1920

April 9, 1930

Occupation – At Home – June 16, 1880

School Teacher – June 19, 1900

Teacher, Public School – April 23, 1910

None – January 5, 1920

April 9, 1930

Hurst

James Law Alcorn (son-in-law):

    Residence – Titusville, Crawford Co., Pennsylvania – January 5, 1920

                                  April 9, 1930

    Occupation – Merchant, Coal Yard – January 5, 1920

        Merchant, Lumber Company – April 9, 1930

    Home Data For 1930 – Owns home, valued at $ 4, 500, has radio set, not on a farm

- **David Zacharias Kerr,** b. 20 Nov 1879 in Oil Creek, Crawford Co., Pennsylvania & **Gertrude Emma Preston**, b. 1879 in Pennsylvania – 1908

Signatures:

THAT THEY ARE TRUE.

David Kerr

(Registrant's signature)

David Zacharias Kerr (son):

    Residence – Oil Creek, Crawford Co., Pennsylvania – June 16, 1880

                          June 19, 1900

        Titusville, Crawford Co., Pennsylvania – April 19, 1910

                          1917 – 1918

                          January 9, 1920

                          April 5, 1930

                          1942

    Occupation – At Home – June 16, 1880

        Laborer – June 19, 1900

        Driller, Oil Wells – April 19, 1910

        Oil Contractor – 1917 – 1918

        Oil Producer, Lease – January 9, 1920

        Contractor, Oil Wells – April 5, 1930

    Home Data for 1930 – Rental, $ 25 a month, has radio set, not on a farm

Gertrude Emma Preston (daughter-in-law):

    Residence – Titusville, Crawford Co., Pennsylvania – April 19, 1910

                          January 9, 1920

                          April 5, 1930

    Occupation – None – April 19, 1910

        January 9, 1920

April 5, 1930

- **Unknown Kerr** – b. After 1880, d. Before 1900

- **Alpha Jefferson Kerr**, b. 18 Mar 1884 in Oil Creek, Crawford Co., Pennsylvania, d. 9 Jan 1944 &

  Julie Mae Carey, b. Oct 1887 in Troy Crawford Co., Pennsylvania

Signatures:

THEY ARE TRUE.

(Registrant's signa

   o **Ellen Marie Kerr** – b. About 1917 in Pennsylvania

Ellen Kerr (daughter):

   Residence – Troy, Crawford Co., Pennsylvania – January 29, 1920

   Titusville, Crawford Co., Pennsylvania – April 10, 1930

Occupation – None – January 29, 1920

   Saleslady, Woolworth Store – April 10, 1930

   o **Howard C. Kerr** – b. 10 Mar 1918 in Pennsylvania, d. 17 Nov 1980 in Columbus, Franklin

   Co., Ohio

Howard C. Kerr (son):

   Residence – Troy, Crawford Co., Pennsylvania – January 29, 1920

   Titusville, Crawford Co., Pennsylvania – April 10, 1930

Occupation – None – January 29, 1920

   April 10, 1930

Alpha Jefferson Kerr (son):

   Residence – Oil Creek, Crawford Co., Pennsylvania – June 16, 1900

   Troy, Crawford Co., Pennsylvania – April 18, 1910

   January 29, 1920

   Titusville, Crawford Co., Pennsylvania – September 12, 1918

   April 10, 1930

   1942

Occupation – Laborer – June 16, 1900

   Farmer – September 12, 1918

   Farmer, General Farm – April 18, 1910

131

January 29, 1920

Laborer, Odd Jobs – April 10, 1930

Home Date for 1930 – Rental, $ 25 a month, has radio set, not on a farm

Julie Mae Carey (daughter-in-law):

Residence – Troy, Crawford Co., Pennsylvania – April 18, 1910

January 29, 1920

Titusville, Crawford Co., Pennsylvania – September 12, 1918

April 10, 1930

Occupation – None – April 18, 1910

January 29, 1920

April 10, 1930

- **Leora Kerr** – b. May 1886 in Pennsylvania

Leora Kerr (daughter):

Residence – Oil Creek, Crawford Co., Pennsylvania – June 16, 1900

Occupation – Works at Home – June 16, 1900

- **Friend Ellsworth Kerr**, b. 26 June 1890 in Oil Creek, Crawford Co., Pennsylvania & **Bernice A.**

  Unknown, b. About 1889 in Pennsylvania – Before 1917 in Pennsylvania

Signatures:

Friend Ellsworth Kerr (son):

Residence – Oil Creek, Crawford Co., Pennsylvania – June 16, 1900

April 23, 1910

June 5, 1917

January 23, 1920

Titusville, Crawford Co., Pennsylvania – April 12, 1930

1942

Occupation – None Listed – June 16, 1900

Laborer, Farm Labor – April 23, 1910

Farmer & Dairy Man – June 5, 1917

Farmer, General Farm – January 23, 1920

Oil Producer, Oil Lease – April 12, 1930

Self-employed, Oil Leases – 1942

Home Data for 1930 – Rental, $ 25 a month, has radio set, not on a farm

Bernice A. Unknown (daughter-in-law):

> *Residence – Oil Creek, Crawford Co., Pennsylvania – June 5, 1917*
>
> *January 23, 1920*
>
> *Titusville, Crawford Co., Pennsylvania – April 12, 1930*
>
> *1942*
>
> *Occupation – None – January 23, 1920*
>
> *April 12, 1930*

- **Roscoe Kerr** – b. Oct 1892 In Pennsylvania

Roscoe Kerr (son):

> *Residence – Oil Creek, Crawford Co., Pennsylvania – June 16, 1900*
>
> *Occupation – None Listed – June 16, 1900*

- **Jessie Lynn Kerr**, b. 24 Sep 1895 in Bethel, Allegheny Co., Pennsylvania, d. 15 Jul 1970 in Titusville, Crawford Co., Pennsylvania & **Worth David Alcorn**, b. 28 Jun 1893 in Cherry Tree, Venango Co., Pennsylvania, d. 12 May 1960 in Lincolnville, Crawford Co., Pennsylvania

Signatures:

o **David L. Alcorn** – About 1918 in Pennsylvania

David L. Alcorn (son):

> *Residence – Cherry Tree, Venango Co., Pennsylvania – March 15, 1920*
>
> *April 25, 1930*
>
> *Occupation – None – March 15, 1920*
>
> *April 25, 1930*

o **Adalyn F. Alcorn** – b. About 1921 in Pennsylvania

Adalyn F. Alcorn (daughter):

> *Residence – Cherry Tree, Venango Co., Pennsylvania – April 25, 1930*
>
> *Occupation – None – April 25, 1930*

o **Eleanor J. Alcorn** – b. About 1922 in Pennsylvania

Eleanor J. Alcorn (daughter):

  Residence – Cherry Tree, Venango Co., Pennsylvania – April 25, 1930

  Occupation – None – April 25, 1930

o **Esther E. Alcorn** – b. About 1925 in Pennsylvania

Esther E. Alcorn (daughter):

  Residence – Cherry Tree, Venango Co., Pennsylvania – April 25, 1930

  Occupation – None – April 25, 1930

o **Betty J. Alcorn** – b. About 1928 in Pennsylvania

Betty J. Alcorn (daughter):

  Residence – Cherry Tree, Venango Co., Pennsylvania – April 25, 1930

  Occupation – None – April 25, 1930

Jessie Lynn Kerr (daughter):

  Residence – Oil Creek, Crawford Co., Pennsylvania – June 16, 1900

  April 23, 1910

  Cherry Tree, Venango Co., Pennsylvania – March 15, 1920

  April 25, 1930

  Occupation – None Listed – June 16, 1900

  None – April 23, 1910

  March 15, 1920

  April 25, 1930

Worth David Alcorn (son-in-law):

  Residence – Cherry Tree, Venango Co., New York – June 5, 1917

  March 15, 1920

  April 25, 1930

  Oil Creek, Crawford Co., Pennsylvania – 1942

  Occupation – Farmer – June 5, 1917

  Farmer, General Farm – March 15, 1920

  Pumper, Oil Lease – April 25, 1930

  Home Data for 1930 – Owns home, valued at $ 1, 500, no radio set, on a farm

Addie Marie Jones (daughter):

  Residence – Mina, Chautauqua Co., New York – July 20, 1860

  July 18, 1870

  Oil Creek, Crawford Co., Pennsylvania – June 16, 1880

  June 19, 1900

  April 23, 1910

Occupation – Child – July 20, 1860

Attending School – July 18, 1870

Keeping House – June 16, 1880

None Listed – June 19, 1900

None – April 23, 1910

Lafayette Jefferson Kerr (son-in-law):

Residence – Oil Creek, Crawford Co., Pennsylvania – June 16, 1880

June 19, 1900

April 23, 1910

Occupation – Farmer – June 16, 1880

June 19, 1900

Farmer, General Farm – April 23, 1910

- **Alta Susan Jones**, b. Sept 1861 in Chautauqua Co., New York & **William Harmelink**, b. Jan 1868 in Clymer, Chautauqua Co., New York – 1891 in New York

  - **La Fayette Harmelink** – b. May 1885 in New York

La Fayette Harmelink (son):

Residence – Mina, Chautauqua Co., New York – February 16, 1892

June 4, 1900

Occupation – None Listed – February 16, 1892

June 4, 1900

- **Iva B. Harmelink**, b. Nov 1893 in New York & **Vincent James Galloway**, b. 24 Jan 1895 in Westfield, Chautauqua Co., New York, d. Apr 1983 in Beamus Point, Chautauqua Co., New York – 17 Aug 1921 in Sherman, Chautauqua Co., New York

Signature:

Signatures (marriage):

○ **Bruce V. Galloway** – b. About 1925 in New York

Bruce V. Galloway (son):

Residence – Dewittville, Chautauqua Co., New York – April 8, 1930

Occupation – None – April 8, 1930

○ **Naomi S. Galloway** – b. About 1927 in New York

Naomi S. Galloway (daughter):

Residence – Dewittville, Chautauqua Co., New York – April 8, 1930

Occupation – None – April 8, 1930

Iva B. Harmelink (daughter):

Residence – Mina, Chautauqua Co., New York – June 4, 1900

> *April 21, 1910*

> *Sherman, Chautauqua Co., New York – January 20, 1920*

> *August 17, 1921*

> *Dewittville, Chautauqua Co., New York – April 8, 1930*

Occupation – At School – June 4, 1900

> *None – April 21, 1910*

> *April 8, 1930*

> *Teacher, Grade School – January 20, 1920*

> *School Teacher – August 17, 1921*

Vincent James Galloway (son-in-law):

Residence – Dewittville, Chautauqua Co., New York – June 5, 1917

> *August 17, 1921*

> *April 8, 1930*

Occupation – Grocery Business – June 5, 1917

> *Miller – August 17, 1921*

> *Milling, Feed Mill – April 8, 1930*

Home Data for 1930 – Owns home, valued at $ 2, 500, has radio set, not on a farm

- **Clifford Le Roy Harmelink**, b. 1 Mar 1897 in Mina, Chautauqua Co., New York, d. June 1968 in Sherman, Chautauqua Co., New York & **Alida M. Stebbins**, b. 2 Feb 1896 in Chautauqua, Chautauqua Co., New York – 5 Feb 1918 in Jamestown, Chautauqua Co., New York

Signature:

Signature (Marriage):

        ○ **Beth Harmelink** – b. About 1922 in Mina, Chautauqua Co., New York

Beth Harmelink (daughter):

    Residence – Mina, Chautauqua Co., New York – May 3, 1930

    Occupation – None – May 3, 1930

        ○ **Gerald Harmelink** – b. About 1926 in Mina, Chautauqua Co., New York

Gerald Harmelink (son):

    Residence – Mina, Chautauqua Co., New York – May 3, 1930

    Occupation – None – May 3, 1930

Clifford Le Roy Harmelink (son):

    Residence – Mina, Chautauqua Co., New York – June 4, 1900

                                 April 21, 1910

                                 February 5, 1918

                                 May 3, 1930

        Clymer, Chautauqua Co., New York – June 5, 1918

    Occupation – None Listed – June 4, 1900

        None – April 21, 1910

        Farming – February 5, 1918

        Self-employed – June 5, 1918

        Farmer, Dairy Farm – May 3, 1930

    Home Data for 1930 – Rental, has radio set, not on a farm

Alida M. Stebbins (daughter-in-law):

    Residence – Chautauqua, Chautauqua Co., New York – February 5, 1918

        Clymer, Chautauqua Co., New York – June 5, 1918

        Mina, Chautauqua Co., New York – May 3, 1930

    Occupation – None – February 5, 1918

        May 3, 1930

Alta Susan Jones (daughter):

    Residence – Mina, Chautauqua Co., New York – July 18, 1870

        June 22, 1880

Hurst

February 16, 1892

June 4, 1900

April 21, 1910

Sherman, Chautauqua Co., New York – January 20, 1920

Occupation – Attending School – July 18, 1870

No Occupation – June 22, 1880

None Listed – February 16, 1892

June 4, 1900

None – April 21, 1910

January 20, 1920

William Harmelink (son-in-law):

Residence – Mina Chautauqua Co., New York – February 16, 1892

June 4, 1900

April 21, 1910

Sherman, Chautauqua Co., New York – January 20, 1920

April 17th, 18th, & 22nd, 1930

Occupation – Farmer – February 16, 1892

June 4, 1900

Farmer, General Farm – April 21, 1910

Janitor, School Building – January 20, 1920

Janitor, School – April 17th, 18th, & 22nd, 1930

▪ **Chester L. Jones** – b. Jan 1864 in Chautauqua Co., New York, d. 1922 in Chautauqua Co., New York

Chester L. Jones (son):

Residence – Mina Chautauqua Co., New York – July 18, 1870

June 22, 1880

February 16, 1892

June 4, 1900

April 21, 1910

June 1, 1915

Sherman, Chautauqua Co., New York – June 1, 1905

January 20, 1920

Occupation – None Listed – July 18, 1870

June 4, 1900

June 1, 1905

Farm Laborer – June 22, 1880

June 1, 1915

Elisha Calkins & Anna Dalrymple Descendants

Unreadable – February 16, 1892

None – April 21, 1900

January 20, 1920

Arcelia M. Woods (daughter):

   Residence – Troy, Crawford Co., Pennsylvania – August 14, 1850

      Mina, Chautauqua Co., New York – July 20, 1860

                July 18, 1870

                June 22, 1880

                February 16, 1892

                June 4, 1900

      Sherman, Chautauqua Co., New York – June 1, 1905

   Occupation – None Listed – August 14, 1850

                July 20, 1860

                June 4, 1900

      Keeping House – July 18, 1870

                June 22, 1880

      Unreadable – February 16, 1892

      Housework – June 1, 1905

Zebulon Jones (son-in-law):

   Residence – Troy, Crawford Co., Pennsylvania – August 14, 1850

      Mina, Chautauqua Co., New York – July 20, 1860

                June 1863

                July 18, 1870

                June 22, 1880

                February 16, 1892

   Occupation – None Listed – August 14, 1850

      Farmer – July 20, 1860

      June 1863

      July 18, 1870

      June 22, 1880

   Unreadable – February 16, 1892

   Value of Real Estate – $ 2, 400 – July 20, 1860

      $ 3, 600 – July 18, 1870

   Value of Personal Estate – $ 900 – July 20, 1860

      $ 1, 450 – July 18, 1870

Hurst

○ **Elnora C. Woods**, b. 14 Jan 1835 in Chautauqua Co., New York, d. Before 1910 & **Job Barnett**, b. Dec 1824 in New York, d. After 1910 – 1854 in Arkwright, Chautauqua Co., New York

  ▪ **Eleanor De Dette Barnett**, b. Apr 1855, d. 6 Oct 1932 & **James Allen Aikens** (1ˢᵗ Husband), b. 17 Aug 1844 in New York, d. 27 Jun 1898 in Crawford Co., Pennsylvania – 1877 in Pennsylvania

   ● **Maud F. Aikens** – b. Apr 1878 in Crawford Co., Pennsylvania

Maud F. Aikens (daughter):

Residence – Sparta, Crawford Co., Pennsylvania – June 1880

June 16ᵗʰ & 18ᵗʰ, 1900

February 11, 1920

Occupation – None Listed – June 1880

June 16ᵗʰ & 18ᵗʰ, 1900

Teacher, Rural School – February 12, 1910

   ● **Cora D. Aikens**, b. 5 Feb 1880 in Crawford Co., Pennsylvania, d. Feb 1971 in Cory, Erie Co., Pennsylvania & **William John Reitz**, b. About 1870 in Pennsylvania – 10 Jul 1907 in Mahoning Co., Ohio

    ○ **George H. Reitz** – b. About 1911 in Pennsylvania

George H. Reitz (son):

Residence – Grays Landing, Fayette Co., Pennsylvania – January 19, 1920

Occupation – None – January 19, 1920

Cora D. Aikens (daughter):

Residence – Sparta, Crawford Co., Pennsylvania – June 1880

June 16ᵗʰ & 18ᵗʰ, 1900

Mt. Pleasant, Westmoreland Co., Pennsylvania – May 9, 1910

Grays Landing, Fayette Co., Pennsylvania – January 19, 1920

Masontown, Fayette Co., Pennsylvania – April 8, 1930

Occupation – None Listed – June 1880

June 16ᵗʰ & 18ᵗʰ, 1900

None – May 9, 1910

January 19, 1920

Teacher, Public School – April 8, 1930

William John Reitz (son-in-law):

Residence – Mt. Pleasant, Westmoreland Co., Pennsylvania – May 9, 1910

Grays Landing, Fayette Co., Pennsylvania – January 19, 1920

Masontown, Fayette Co., Pennsylvania – April 8, 1930

Occupation – Clerk, General Store – May 9, 1910

Manager, Store – January 19, 1920

Salesman, Grocery Store – April 8, 1930

Home Data for 1930 – Rental, $ 30 a month, has radio set, not on a farm

- **Jule P. Aikens**, b. 26 Feb 1884 in Sparta, Crawford Co., Pennsylvania, d. 18 May 1959 & **Hazel Jones**, b. 10 Jan 1889 in Pennsylvania, d. May 1982 in union City, Erie Co., Pennsylvania

Signatures:

○ **Allen D. Aikens** – b. About 1914 in Pennsylvania, d. Jan 1977 in Erie, Erie Co., Pennsylvania

Allen D. Aikens (son):

Residence – Sparta, Crawford Co., Pennsylvania – February 11, 1920

Union City, Erie Co., Pennsylvania – April 19, 1930

Occupation – None – February 11, 1920

April 19, 1930

○ **Earnestine Alexander Aikens** – b. 29 Jan 1916 in Pennsylvania, d. 20 Sep 1990 in Sebastian, Brevard Co., Florida

Earnestine Alexander Aikens (daughter):

Residence – Sparta, Crawford Co., Pennsylvania – February 11, 1920

Union City, Erie Co., Pennsylvania – April 19, 1930

Occupation – None – February 11, 1920

April 19, 1930

○ **Beatrice L. Aikens** – b. About 1918 in Pennsylvania

Beatrice L. Aikens (daughter):

Residence – Sparta, Crawford Co., Pennsylvania – February 11, 1920

Union City, Erie Co., Pennsylvania – April 19, 1930

Occupation – None – February 11, 1920

April 19, 1930

Jule P. Aikens (son):

Residence – Sparta, Crawford Co., Pennsylvania – June 16ᵗʰ & 18ᵗʰ, 1900

May 9, 1910

September 12, 1918

February 11, 1920

Union City, Erie Co., Pennsylvania – April 19, 1930

1942

Occupation – Laborer, Farm – June 16ᵗʰ & 18ᵗʰ, 1900

Farming – September 12, 1918

Farmer, General Farm – May 9, 1910

February 11, 1920

Laborer – April 19, 1930

Home Data for 1930 – Rental, $12 a month, no radio set, not on a farm

Hazel Jones (daughter-in-law):

Residence – Sparta, Crawford Co., Pennsylvania – September 12, 1918

February 11, 1920

Union City, Erie Co., Pennsylvania – April 19, 1930

1942

Occupation – None – February 11, 1920

April 19, 1930

- **Paul D. Aikens** – b. 22 Jul 1889 in Sparta, Crawford Co., Pennsylvania, d. Nov 1975 in Cory, Erie Co., Pennsylvania

Signatures:

Paul D. Aikens (son):

Residence – Sparta, Crawford Co., Pennsylvania – June 16ᵗʰ & 18ᵗʰ, 1900

May 9, 1910

June 5, 1917

February 11, 1920

Elgin, Erie Co., Pennsylvania – April 3, 1930

Concord, Erie Co., Pennsylvania – 1942

Occupation – None Listed – June 16ᵗʰ & 18ᵗʰ, 1900

> *Farmer, Home Farm – May 9, 1910*

> *Farmer – June 5, 1917*

> *Farmer, General Farm – February 11, 1920*

> *Truck Driver, Steel Plant – April 3, 1930*

Home Data for 1930 – Rental, $ 15 a month, no radio set, not on a farm

- **Adel Aikens** – b. Feb 1891 in Crawford Co., Pennsylvania

Adel Aikens (son):

Residence – Sparta, Crawford Co., Pennsylvania – June 16ᵗʰ & 18ᵗʰ, 1900

Occupation – None Listed – June 16ᵗʰ & 18ᵗʰ, 1900

- **Eleanor De Dette Barnett**, b. Apr 1855, d. After 1920 & **Clark Washburn** (2ⁿᵈ Husband), b. About 1841 in Vermont

Eleanor De Dette Barnett (daughter):

Residence – Clymer, Chautauqua Co., New York – July 31, 1860

> *Columbus, Warren Co., Pennsylvania – September 1, 1870*

> *Sparta, Crawford Co., Pennsylvania – June 1880*

>> *June 16ᵗʰ & 18ᵗʰ, 1900*

>> *May 9, 1910*

>> *February 11, 1920*

> *Elgin, Erie Co., Pennsylvania – April 3, 1930*

Occupation – Child – July 31, 1860

> *At Home – September 1, 1870*

> *Keeping House – June 1880*

> *Farmer – June 16ᵗʰ & 18ᵗʰ, 1900*

> *None – May 9, 1910*

>> *February 11, 1920*

>> *April 3, 1930*

James Allen Aikens (1ˢᵗ Husband) (son-in-law):

Residence – Sparta, Crawford Co., Pennsylvania – June 1880

Occupation – Farmer – June 1880

Clark Washburn (2ⁿᵈ Husband) (son-in-law):

Residence – Sparta, Crawford Co., Pennsylvania – May 9, 1910

Occupation – Own Income – May 9, 1910

Hurst

- **Saloe North Barnett** – b. About 1858 in New York

Saloe North Barnett (son):

Residence – Clymer, Chautauqua Co., New York – July 31, 1860

Columbus, Warren Co., Pennsylvania – September 1, 1870

Occupation – Child – July 31, 1860

At Home – September 1, 1870

- **Courtney K. Barnett**, b. Sep 1865 in Columbus, Warren Co., Pennsylvania & **Nellie Sarah Culver**, b. 1 Feb 1866 in Concord, Erie Co., Pennsylvania, d. 13 Nov 1954 in San Diego Co., California – 1885 Pennsylvania

Signatures:

- **Grace A. Barnett** – b. Oct 1886 in Pennsylvania

Grace Barnett (daughter):

Residence – Corry, Erie Co., Pennsylvania – June 13, 1900

Mayville, Chautauqua Co., New York – June 1, 1905

Occupation – At School – June 13, 1900

Housework – June 1, 1905

- **Merl E. Barnett**, b. Jan 1888 in Pennsylvania & **Bessie Unknown**, b. About 1889 in Pennsylvania – About 1908

Merl E. Barnett (son):

Residence – Corry, Erie Co., Pennsylvania – June 13, 1900

Mayville, Chautauqua Co., New York – June 1, 1905

Meadville, Crawford Co., Pennsylvania – April 15, 1910

Occupation – At School – June 13, 1900

At Home – June 1, 1905

Salesman, Furniture Store – April 15, 1910

Bessie Unknown (daughter-in-law):

Residence – Meadville, Crawford Co., Pennsylvania – April 15, 1910

Occupation – None – April 15, 1910

144

- **Luella A. Barnett**, b. Oct 1892 in Baker Hill, Warren Co., Pennsylvania & **Lawrence McElhney**, b. 1899 in Tryonville, Crawford Co., Pennsylvania – 24 Dec 1921 in Mayville, Chautauqua Co., New York

Signatures:

Luella Barnett (daughter):

    Residence – Corry, Erie Co., Pennsylvania – June 13, 1900

                                    December 24, 1921

             Mayville, Chautauqua Co., New York – June 1, 1905

                Concord, Erie Co., Pennsylvania – April 16, 1910

    Occupation – At School – June 13, 1900

                      June 1, 1905

            None Listed – April 16, 1910

            None – December 24, 1921

Lawrence McElhney (son-in-law):

    Residence – Tryonville, Pennsylvania – December 24, 1921

    Occupation – Teamster – December 24, 1921

- **Howard J. Barnett**, b. 5 Oct 1894 in Corry, Erie Co., Pennsylvania, d. 11 Nov 1941 & **Elsie Seamen**, b. About 1894 in Corry, Erie Co., Pennsylvania – 24 Oct 1924 in Chautauqua, Chautauqua Co., New York

Signatures:

Howard J. Barnett (son):

    Residence – Corry, Erie Co., Pennsylvania – June 13, 1900

                            October 24, 1924

             Mayville, Chautauqua Co., New York – June 1, 1905

                Concord, Erie Co., Pennsylvania – April 16, 1910

                    January 21, 1920

Occupation – None Listed – June 13, 1900

April 16, 1910

At School – June 1, 1905

Machinist, G. E. En. – January 21, 1920

Farmer – October 24, 1924

Elsie Seamen (daughter-in-law):

Residence – Corry, Erie Co., Pennsylvania – October 24, 1924

Occupation – None – October 24, 1924

- **Albert L. Barnett**, b. 1902 in Spring Creek, Warren Co., Pennsylvania & **Dorothy Viola Douglas** (1st Wife), b. About 1907 in Corry, Erie Co., Pennsylvania, d. 25 Feb 1940 – 8 Aug 1925 in Chautauqua, Chautauqua Co., New York

Signatures:

- **Albert L. Barnett**, b. 1902 in Spring Creek, Pennsylvania & **Margaret M. Rouen** (2nd Wife), b. About 1910 – 13 Jun 1942 in Erie, Erie Co., Pennsylvania

Signatures:

Albert L. Barnett (son):

Residence – Mayville, Chautauqua Co., New York – June 1, 1905

Concord, Erie Co., Pennsylvania – April 16, 1910

January 21, 1920

Corry, Erie Co., Pennsylvania – August 8, 1925

Erie, Erie Co., Pennsylvania – June 13, 1942

Occupation – At Home – June 1, 1905

None Listed – April, 16, 1910

None – January 21, 1920

Painter – August 8, 1925

Contractor – June 13, 1942

Elisha Calkins & Anna Dalrymple Descendants

Dorothy Viola Douglas (1st Wife) (daughter-in-law):

    Residence – Corry, Erie Co., Pennsylvania – August 8, 1925

    Occupation – None – August 8, 1925

Margaret M. Rouen (2nd Wife) (daughter-in-law):

    Residence – Erie, Erie Co., Pennsylvania – June 13, 1942

    Occupation – None – June 13, 1942

Courtney K. Barnett (son):

    Residence – Columbus, Warren Co., Pennsylvania – September 1, 1870

        Sparta, Crawford Co., Pennsylvania – June 1880

        Corry, Erie Co., Pennsylvania – June 13, 1900

        Mayville, Chautauqua Co., New York – June 1, 1905

        Concord, Erie Co., Pennsylvania – April 16, 1910

                January 21, 1920

                April 11, 1930

        Union City, Erie Co., Pennsylvania – June 13, 1942

    Occupation – At Home – September 1, 1870

        Farm Laborer – June 1880

        Salesman, Machines – June 13, 1900

        Traveling Salesman – June 1, 1905

        Farmer, General Farm – April 16, 1910

                January 21, 1920

        None – April 11, 1930

        Retired – June 13, 1942

    Home Data for 1930 – Rental, $ 5 a month, no radio set, not on a farm

Nellie E. Culver (daughter-in-law):

    Residence – Corry, Erie Co., Pennsylvania – June 13, 1900

        Mayville, Chautauqua Co., New York – June 1, 1905

        Concord, Erie Co., Pennsylvania – April 16, 1910

                January 21, 1920

                April 11, 1930

        Union City, Erie Co., Pennsylvania – June 13, 1942

    Occupation – None Listed – June 13, 1900

        April 16, 1910

        Housework – June 1, 1905

        None – January 21, 1920

        April 11, 1930

Hurst

Housewife – June 13, 1942

▪ **Purdy Grant Barnett**, b. 14 Oct 1870 in Pennsylvania & **Rose E. Pettis**, b. 27 Dec 1870 in Pennsylvania, d. Between 1910 – 1920 in Pennsylvania – 26 Nov 1892 in Crawford Co., Pennsylvania

Signatures:

- **Unknown Barnett** – b. After 1892 in Pennsylvania, d. Before 1900 in Pennsylvania

- **Wayne Waverly Barnett** – b. 7 Nov 1896 in Sparta, Crawford Co., Pennsylvania

Signature:

Wayne Waverly Barnett (son):

Residence – Union City, Erie Co., Pennsylvania – June 14, 1900

April 25, 1910

January 3, 1920

Erie, Erie Co., Pennsylvania – June 5, 1917

Corry, Erie Co., Pennsylvania – April 2, 1930

Occupation – None Listed – June 14, 1900

None – April 25, 1910

Clerk, U.S. Horse Shoe Co. – June 5, 1917

Chairmaker, Factory – January 3, 1920

Accounting Clerk, Spring Factory – April 2, 1930

- **Ruth M. Barnett** – b. April 1898 in Pennsylvania

Ruth Barnett (daughter):

Residence – Union City, Erie Co., Pennsylvania – June 14, 1900

April 25, 1910

January 3, 1920

Conewango, Warren Co., Pennsylvania – April 8, 1930

Occupation – None Listed – June 14, 1900

None – April 25, 1910

January 3, 1920

Patient, Warren State Hospital – April 8, 1930

- **Gerald Stanley Barnett** – b. 26 Sep 1908 in Pennsylvania, d. 30 Mar 1988 in Cayucos, San Luis Obispo Co., California

Gerald Stanley Barnett (son):

Residence – Union City, Erie Co., Pennsylvania – April 25, 1910

January 3, 1920

Portsmouth, Portsmouth Co., Virginia – April 23, 1930

Occupation – None – April 25, 1910

January 3, 1920

Student – April 23, 1930

Purdy Grant Barnett (son):

Residence – Columbus, Warren Co., Pennsylvania – September 1, 1870

Sparta, Crawford Co., Pennsylvania – June 1880

December 27, 1892

Union City, Erie Co., Pennsylvania – June 14, 1900

April 25, 1910

January 3, 1920

April 14, 1930

Occupation – At Home – September 1, 1870

At School – June 1880

Farmer – December 27, 1892

Chair ? Labor – June 14, 1900

Chair Maker, Chair Factory – April 25, 1910

Jobber, Chair Factory – January 3, 1920

Laborer, Chair Factory – April 14, 1930

Home Data for 1930 – Rental, $ 15 a month, has radio set, not on a farm

Rose E Pettis (daughter-in-law):

Residence – Bloomfield, Crawford Co., Pennsylvania – December 27, 1892

Union City, Erie Co., Pennsylvania – June 14, 1900

April 25, 1910

Occupation – Teacher – December 27, 1892

None Listed – June 14, 1900

None – April 25, 1910

Hurst

Elnora C. Woods (daughter):

> *Residence – Arkwright, Chautauqua Co., New York – August 28, 1850*
>
> > *Clymer, Chautauqua Co., New York – July 31, 1860*
> >
> > *Columbus, Warren Co., Pennsylvania – September 1, 1870*
> >
> > *Sparta, Crawford Co., Pennsylvania – 1880*
> >
> > > *June 14th & 15, 1900*
>
> *Occupation – None Listed – August 28, 1850*
>
> > *July 31, 1860*
> >
> > *June 14th & 15th, 1900*
> >
> > *Keeping House – September 1, 1870*
> >
> > *June 1880*

Job Barnett (son-in-law):

> *Residence – Clymer, Chautauqua Co., New York – July 31, 1860*
>
> > *Columbus, Warren Co., Pennsylvania – September 1, 1870*
> >
> > *Sparta, Crawford Co., Pennsylvania – June 1880*
> >
> > > *June 14th & 15th, 1900*
> > >
> > > *May 9, 1910*
>
> *Occupation – Peddler – July 31, 1860*
>
> > *Farmer – September 1, 1870*
> >
> > *June 1880*
> >
> > *June 14th & 15th, 1900*
> >
> > *None – May 9, 1910*
>
> *Value of Real Estate – None Listed – July 31, 1860*
>
> > *$ 9, 000 – September 1, 1870*
>
> *Value of Personal Estate – $ 1, 000 – July 31, 1860*
>
> > *$ 2, 500 – September 1, 1870*

o **Albert Davilla Woods**, b. 27 Apr 1839 in Arkwright, Chautauqua Co., New York, d. 16 Oct 1871 in Palmyra, Otoe Co., Nebraska & **Mary Etta Coon**, b. 10 Sep 1836 in Beaverdam, Erie Co., Pennsylvania, d. 18 May 1914 in Marshfield, Oregon – 27 Nov 1857

  ▪ **Linna Geneva Woods** – b. 27 Dec 1857 in Columbus, Warren Co., Pennsylvania, d. 27 Mar 1861 in Columbus, Warren Co., Pennsylvania

  ▪ **Ora Senica Woods**, b. 6 Feb 1861 in Columbus, Warren Co., Pennsylvania, d. 16 Sep 1940 in Ayr, Adams Co., Nebraska & **Anna Belle Dewey**, b. 15 Mar 1862 in Farnham, Surry, England, d. 18 Feb 1944 in Ayr, Adams Co., Nebraska – 14 Feb 1883 in Otoe Co., Nebraska

- **Charles Albert Woods**, b. 18 Jan 1884 in Douglas, Otoe Co., Nebraska, d. 4 Feb 1945 in Blue Hill, Webster Co., Nebraska & **Elva Madge Leetsch**, b. 13 Dec 1894 in Nebraska, d. 26 Nov 1984 in Nebraska

Signature:

Charles Albert Woods

  o **Dorothy E. Woods** – b. 1917 in Nebraska

Dorothy E. Woods (daughter):

  Residence – Blue Hill, Webster Co., Nebraska – January 8, 1920

  April 26, 1930

  Occupation – None Listed – January 8, 1920

  None – April 26, 1930

  o **Charles Lavern Woods** – b. 4 Nov 1920 in Blue Hill, Webster Co., Nebraska, d. 10 May 2005 in Bremerton, Kitsap Co., Washington

Charles Lavern Woods (son):

  Residence – Blue Hill, Webster Co., Nebraska – April 26, 1930

  Occupation – None – April 26, 1930

  o **Howard E. Woods** – b. About 1924 in Nebraska

Howard E. Woods (son):

  Residence – Blue Hill, Webster Co., Nebraska – April 26, 1930

  Occupation – None – April 26, 1930

Charles Albert Woods (son):

  Residence – Little Blue, Adams Co., Nebraska – June 13, 1900

  Panama, Lancaster Co., Nebraska – September 12, 1918

  Blue Hill, Webster Co., Nebraska – January 8, 1920

  April 26, 1930

  Occupation – At School – June 13, 1900

  Farmer – September 12, 1918

  Agent, Standard Oil – January 8, 1920

  Laborer, Odd Jobs – April 26, 1930

  Home Data for 1930 – Owns home, valued at $ 200, no radio set, not on a farm

Elva Madge Leetsch (daughter-in-law):

  Residence – Panama, Lancaster Co., Nebraska – September 12, 1918

  Blue Hill, Webster Co., Nebraska – January 8, 1920

  April 26, 1930

Occupation – None – January 8, 1920

    Seamstress, At Home – April 26, 1930

- **Lavannie R. Woods**, b. 30 Nov 1890 in Nebraska, d. 20 May 1983 in & **Ray J. Allen**, b. Aug 1885 in Frankville, Winneshiek Co., Iowa, d. 1961

Lavannie R. Woods (daughter):

 Residence – Little Blue, Adams Co., Nebraska – June 13, 1900

             April 20, 1910

             April 22, 1930

    Colome, Tripp Co., South Dakota – January 30, 1920

 Occupation – At School – June 13, 1900

   Teacher, Public School – April 20, 1910

   None – January 30, 1920

    April 22, 1930

Ray J. Allen (son-in-law):

 Residence – Colome, Tripp Co., South Dakota – January 30, 1920

  Little Blue, Adams Co., Nebraska – April 22, 1930

 Occupation – Farmer, General Farm – January 30, 1920

    April 22, 1930

Home Data for 1930 – Rental, no radio set, on a farm

- **Verna May Woods**, b. 25 Feb 1893 in Blue Hill, Webster Co., Nebraska, d. Jul 1973 in Guide Rock, Webster Co., Nebraska & **Alvin Hall James**, b. 4 May 1882 in Webster Co., Nebraska, d. 21 Apr 1963 in Nebraska – 18 Jun 1916 in Rosemont, Nebraska

E VERIFIED ABOVE ANSWERS AND THAT THEY ARE TRUE

Signature:

  o **Victor Hall James** – b. 3 Sep 1917 in Nebraska, d. 4 Jul 1997 in Guide Rock, Webster Co., Nebraska

Victor Hall James (son):

 Residence – Potsdam, Webster Co., Nebraska – January 28, 1920

    April 3, 1930

 Occupation – None Listed – January 28, 1920

   None – April 3, 1930

152

Elisha Calkins & Anna Dalrymple Descendants

Verna May Woods (daughter):

Residence – Little Blue, Adams Co., Nebraska – June 13, 1900

April 20, 1910

Potsdam, Webster Co., Nebraska – January 28, 1920

April 3, 1930

Occupation – None Listed – June 13, 1900

January 28, 1920

None – April 20, 1910

April 3, 1930

Alvin Hall James (son-in-law):

Residence – Blue Hill, Webster Co., Nebraska – September 12, 1918

Potsdam, Webster Co., Nebraska – January 28, 1920

April 3, 1930

Occupation – Farming – September 12, 1918

Farming, Farm – January 28, 1920

Farmer, General Farm – April 3, 1930

Home Data for 1930 – Rental, has radio set, on a farm

- **Mary Evelyn Woods** – b. 27 Feb 1895 in Blue Hill, Webster Co., Nebraska, d. 1976 in Lincoln, Webster Co., Nebraska

Mary Evelyn Woods (daughter):

Residence – Little Blue, Adams Co., Nebraska – June 13, 1900

April 20, 1910

Occupation – None Listed – June 13, 1900

None – April 20, 1920

- **Lester Dewey Woods**, b. 3 Jan 1901 in Pauline, Nebraska, d. 5 Dec 1990 in Blue Hill, Webster Co., Nebraska & **Catherine Unknown**, b. 1902 in Nebraska – 1926

  - **Lester Alan Woods**, b. 9 Oct 1937 in Nebraska, d. 16 Mar 2007 in Nebraska & **Marcia Brewster**

Lester Dewey Woods (son):

Residence – Little Blue, Adams Co., Nebraska – April 20, 1910

February 19th & 20th, 1920

Ayr, Adams Co., Nebraska – 1925 – 1926

Zero, Adams Co., Nebraska – April 10, 1930

Occupation – None – April 20, 1910

> *Farm Laborer, Home Farm – February 19ᵗʰ & 20ᵗʰ, 1920*

> *Filling Station – 1925 – 1926*

> *Farmer, General Farm – April 10, 1930*

Home Data for 1930 – Owns home, has radio set, on a farm

Catherine Unknown (daughter-in-law):

Residence – Zero, Adams Co., Nebraska – April 10, 1930

Occupation – Teacher, Public School – April 10, 1930

Ora Senica Woods (son):

Residence – Wayne, Erie Co., Pennsylvania – June 12, 1870

> *Little Blue, Adams Co., Nebraska – June 13, 1900*

> > *April 20, 1910*

> > *February 19ᵗʰ & 20ᵗʰ, 1920*

> *Ayr, Adams Co., Nebraska – 1925 – 1926*

Occupation – None Listed – June 12, 1870

> *June 13, 1900*

> *Farmer, General Farming – April 20, 1910*

> *Farmer, General Farm – February 19ᵗʰ & 20ᵗʰ, 1920*

> *Retired Farmer – 1925 – 1926*

Anna Belle Dewey (daughter-in-law):

Residence – Little Blue, Adams Co., Nebraska – June 13, 1900

> > *April 20, 1910*

> > *February 19ᵗʰ & 20ᵗʰ, 1920*

> *Ayr, Adams Co., Nebraska – 1925 – 1926*

Occupation – None Listed – June 13, 1900

> *None – April 20, 1910*

> *February 19ᵗʰ & 20ᵗʰ, 1920*

Immigration – 1866 – 1867 from England

Naturalization – 1872

- **Ray L. Woods**, b. 27 Nov 1862 in Columbus, Warren Co., Pennsylvania, d. 30 Mar 1954 in Hastings, Adams Co., Nebraska & **Martie Unknown** (1st Wife), b. Oct 1860 in England – 1882

- **Ray L. Woods**, b. 27 Nov 1862 in Columbus, Warren Co., Pennsylvania, d. 30 Mar 1954 in Hastings, Adams Co., Nebraska & **Reka Rodemacher** (2nd Wife), b. About 1885 in Nebraska – Sep 1907 in Nebraska

  - **Dexter D. Woods** – b. About 1910 in Nebraska

Dexter D. Woods (son):

Residence – Little Blue, Adams Co, Nebraska – April 29, 1910

May 3, 1930

Pleasant View, Holt Co., Nebraska – February 26, 1920

Occupation – None Listed – April 29, 1910

None – February 26, 1920

Laborer, General Farm – May 3, 1930

- **Chester H. Woods** – b. About 1913 in Nebraska

Chester H. Woods (son):

Residence – Pleasant View, Holt Co., Nebraska – February 26, 1920

Little Blue, Adams Co., Nebraska – May 3, 1930

Occupation – None – February 26, 1920

Laborer, General Farm – May 3, 1930

- **Cecil R. Woods** – b. Nov 1916 in Nebraska

Cecil R. Woods (son):

Residence – Pleasant View, Holt Co., Nebraska – February 26, 1920

Little Blue, Adams Co., Nebraska – May 3, 1930

Occupation – None – February 26, 1920

May 3, 1930

Ray L. Woods (son):

Residence – Wayne, Erie Co., Pennsylvania – June 12, 1870

Hanover, Adams Co., Nebraska – June 9, 1900

Little Blue, Adams Co., Nebraska – April 29, 1910

May 3, 1930

Pleasant View, Holt Co., Nebraska – February 26, 1920

Occupation – None Listed – June 12, 1870

Farmer – June 9, 1900

Merchant, Hardware & Implements – April 29, 1910

Farmer, General Farm – February 26, 1920

May 3, 1930

Home Data for 1930 – Rental, no radio set, on a farm

Martie Unknown (1st Wife) (daughter-in-law):

Residence – Hanover, Adams Co., Nebraska – June 9, 1900

Occupation – None Listed – June 9, 1900

Hurst

Reka Rodemacher (daughter-in-law):

Residence – Little Blue, Adams Co., Nebraska – April 29, 1910

          May 3, 1930

      Pleasant View, Holt Co., Nebraska – February 26, 1920

Occupation – None – April 29, 1910

        February 26, 1920

        May 3, 1930

- **Leland Owen Woods** – b. 5 Dec 1864 in Columbus, Warren Co., Pennsylvania, d. 29 Oct 1894 in Beaverdam, Erie Co., Pennsylvania

Leland Owen Woods (son):

Residence – Wayne, Erie Co., Pennsylvania – June 12, 1870

Occupation – None Listed – June 12, 1870

- **Clarence Albert Woods**, b. 24 Feb 1867 in Columbus, Warren Co., Pennsylvania, d. 4 Oct 1944 in Wauneta, Chase Co., Nebraska & **Charlotte Saunders**, b. 4 Aug 1870 in Douglas, Otoe Co., Nebraska, d. 23 May 1965 in Evans, Weld Co., Colorado – 1 Mar 1888 in Douglas, Otoe Co. Nebraska

  - **Bertha Adeline Woods** – b. 26 Mar 1890 in Blue Hill, Webster Co., Nebraska, d. 8 Feb 1931 in Oconto, Custer Co., Nebraska

Bertha Adeline Woods (daughter):

Residence – Glenwood, Webster Co., Nebraska – June 19, 1900

    Potsdam, Webster Co., Nebraska – April 26th & 28th, 1910

Occupation – At School – June 19, 1900

    Teacher, Common School – April 26th & 28th, 1910

- **Edith Woods** – b. Mar 1891 in Nebraska

Edith Woods (daughter):

Residence – Glenwood, Webster Co., Nebraska – June 19, 1900

    Potsdam, Webster Co., Nebraska – April 26th & 28th, 1910

Occupation – None Listed – June 19, 1900

    None – April 26th & 28th, 1910

- **Arthur James Woods**, b. 10 Jan 1893 in Douglas Co., Nebraska, d. 22 May 1982 in Holdrege, Phelps Co., Nebraska & **Caroline Zopf**, b. 1884, d. 1951

Arthur James Woods (son):

Residence – Glenwood, Webster Co., Nebraska – June 19, 1900

    Potsdam, Webster Co., Nebraska – April 26th & 28, 1910

Occupation – None Listed – June 19, 1900

None – April 26th & 28th, 1910

- **Gary Woods** – b. Dec 1894 in Nebraska

Gary Woods (son):

Residence – Glenwood, Webster Co., Nebraska – June 19, 1900

Potsdam, Webster Co., Nebraska – April 26th & 28th, 1910

Occupation – None Listed – June 19, 1900

None – April 26th & 28th, 1910

- **Carl Woods** – b. Nov 1898 in Nebraska

Carl Woods (son):

Residence – Glenwood, Webster Co., Nebraska – June 19, 1900

Potsdam, Webster Co., Nebraska – April 26th & 28th, 1910

Occupation – None Listed – June 19, 1900

None – April 26th & 28th, 1910

- **Lee Woods** – b. About 1901 in Nebraska

Lee Woods (son):

Residence – Potsdam, Webster Co., Nebraska – April 26th & 28th, 1910

January 27, 1920

Occupation – None – April 26th & 28th, 1910

None Listed – January 27, 1920

- **Charlotte Woods** – b. About 1907 in Nebraska

Charlotte Woods (daughter):

Residence – Potsdam, Webster Co., Nebraska – April 26th & 28th, 1910

January 27, 1920

Occupation – None – April 26th & 28th, 1910

None Listed – January 27, 1920

- **Glen Woods** – b. About 1911 in Nebraska

Glen Woods (son):

Residence – Potsdam, Webster Co., Nebraska – January 27, 1920

Occupation – None Listed – January 27, 1920

- **Marie Woods** – b. About 1914 in Nebraska

Marie Woods (daughter):

Residence –Potsdam, Webster Co., Nebraska – January 27, 1920

April 12, 1930

157

Occupation – None Listed – January 27, 1920

        None – April 12, 1930

Clarence Albert Woods (son):

Residence – Wayne, Erie Co., Pennsylvania – June 12, 1870

        Ripley, Chautauqua Co., New York – June 16ᵗʰ & 17ᵗʰ, 1880

        Glenwood, Webster Co., Nebraska – June 19, 1900

        Potsdam, Webster Co., Nebraska – April 26ᵗʰ & 28ᵗʰ, 1910

                January 27, 1920

                April 12, 1930

Occupation – None Listed – June 12, 1870

        Laborer – June 16ᵗʰ & 17ᵗʰ, 1880

        Farmer – June 19, 1900

        Farmer, General Farm – April 26ᵗʰ & 28ᵗʰ, 1910

                April 12, 1930

        Farming, Farm – January 27, 1920

Home Data for 1930 – Owns home, has radio set, on a farm

Charlotte Saunders (daughter-in-law):

Residence – Glenwood, Webster Co., Nebraska – June 19, 1900

        Potsdam, Webster Co., Nebraska – April 26ᵗʰ & 28ᵗʰ, 1910

                January 27, 1920

                April 12, 1930

Occupation – None Listed – June 19, 1900

        January 27, 1920

        None – April 26ᵗʰ & 28ᵗʰ, 1910

        April 12, 1930

▪ **Susie Bell Woods**, b. 24 Mar 1871 in Bowling Green, Pike Co., Missouri, d. About 1930 & **Joseph Nicholas Bayliss**, b. 29 Jan 1876 in Carlisle, Cumberland, England, d. 1918 – 1896

- **Unknown Bayliss** – b. After 1900, d. Before 1910

- **Unknown Bayliss** – b. After 1900, d. Before 1910

- **Unknown Bayliss** – b. After 1900, d. Before 1910

- **Leland Casley Bayliss**, b. 6 May 1901 in Pueblo, Pueblo Co., Colorado, d. Jan 1970 in Oxford, Warren Co., New Jersey & **Dorothy Wills Price**, b. 29 Dec 1900 in Norristown, Montgomery Co., Pennsylvania – 19 Jun 1926 in Norristown, Montgomery Co., Pennsylvania

Elisha Calkins & Anna Dalrymple Descendants

Leland Casley Bayliss
SIGNAT

We, who have subscribed our names below, were Witnes

Signatures (Marriage):

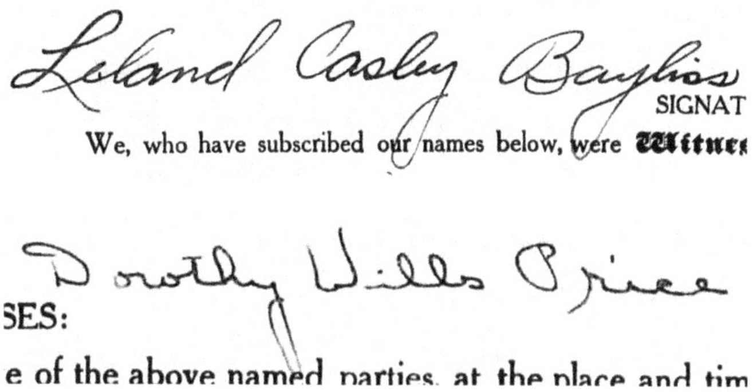

Dorothy Wills Price
SES:

e of the above named parties, at the place and tim

Leland Casley Bayliss (son):

Residence – Mt. Zion, Multnomah Co., Oregon – May 11th & 12th, 1910

Norristown, Montgomery Co., Pennsylvania – January 6, 1920

Oxford, Warren Co., New Jersey – April 9, 1930

Occupation – None – May 11th & 12th, 1910

Apprentice, Electric – January 6, 1920

Master Mechanic, Iron Ore Mine – April 9, 1930

Home Data for 1930 – Rental, $ 20 a month, no radio set, not on a farm

Dorothy Wills Price (daughter-in-law):

Residence – Oxford, Warren Co., New Jersey – April 9, 1930

Occupation – None – April 9, 1930

Susie Bell Woods (daughter):

Residence – Pueblo City, Pueblo Co., Colorado – June 5, 1900

Mt. Zion, Multnomah Co., Oregon – May 11th & 12th, 1910

Lincoln, Lancaster Co., Nebraska – 1916

Norristown, Montgomery Co., Pennsylvania – January 6, 1920

April 14, 1930

Occupation – None – June 5, 1900

May 11th & 12th, 1910

April 14, 1930

Packer, Cigars – January 6, 1920

Home Data for 1930 – Rental, $ 55 a month, has radio set, not on a farm

Joseph Nicholas Bayliss (son-in-law):

Residence – Pueblo City, Pueblo Co., Colorado – June 5, 1900

Mt. Zion, Multnomah Co., Oregon – May 11th & 12th, 1910

Lincoln, Nebraska – 1916

Occupation – Brick Mason – June 5, 1900

Bricklayer, Building – May 11th & 12th, 1910

Immigration – 1894 from England

Albert Davilla Woods (son):

Residence – Arkwright, Chautauqua Co., New York – August 28, 1850

Columbus, Warren Co., Pennsylvania – July 11, 1860

August 26, 1863

Wayne, Erie Co., Pennsylvania – June 12, 1870

Occupation – None Listed – August 28, 1850

Farmer – July 11, 1860

August 26, 1863

June 12, 1870

Value of Real Estate – $ 4, 300 – July 11, 1860

$ 5, 000 – June 12, 1870

Value of Personal Estate – $ 400 – July 11, 1860

$ 1, 000 – June 12, 1870

Mary Etta Coon (daughter-in-law):

Residence – Wayne, Erie Co., Pennsylvania – June 12, 1870

Pueblo City, Pueblo Co., Colorado – June 5, 1900

Mt. Zion, Multnomah Co., Oregon – May 11ᵗʰ & 12ᵗʰ, 1910

Occupation – Keeping House – June 12, 1870

None – June 5, 1900

May 11ᵗʰ & 12ᵗʰ, 1910

o **Ellen A. Woods**, b. 2 Jun 1844 in Chautauqua Co., New York, d. 17 Feb 1926 in Columbus, Warren Co., Pennsylvania & **Sears H. Raymond**, b. 19 Jun 1836 in Columbus, Warren Co., Pennsylvania, d. 14 Jan 1918 in Columbus, Warren Co., Pennsylvania – 14 Sep 1861 in Columbus, Warren Co., Pennsylvania

▪ **Bertha Ellen Raymond**, b. 13 Nov 1862 in Columbus, Warren Co., Pennsylvania, d. 27 Oct 1938 in Columbus, Warren Co., Pennsylvania & **Charles Nathan Dodd**, d. 8 Jan 1857 in Columbus, Warren Co., Pennsylvania, d. 19 Nov 1951 in Columbus, Warren Co., Pennsylvania – 9 Sep 1878 in Columbus, Warren Co., Pennsylvania

• **Leon Raymond Dodd**, b. 29 Mar 1880 in Columbus, Warren Co., Pennsylvania, d. 2 Aug 1962 in Jamestown, Chautauqua Co., New York & **Grace Flotilla Watson**, b. About 1880 in New York, d. Nov 1953 – 20 Nov 1901 in Corry, Erie Co., Pennsylvania

Signature:

160

    ○ **Marjorie Loleta Dodd** – b. 10 Oct 1902 in Pennsylvania, d. 29 Dec 1972 in Jamestown, Chautauqua Co., New York

Marjorie Loleta Dodd (daughter):

    Residence – Jamestown, Chautauqua Co., New York – April 21, 1910

        January 24, 1920

        April 7, 1930

    Occupation – None – April 21, 1910

        January 24, 1920

        Book Keeper, Insurance – April 7, 1930

    ○ **Benita Florence Dodd** – b. 15 Apr 1908 in Pennsylvania

Benita Florence Dodd (daughter):

    Residence – Jamestown, Chautauqua Co., New York – April 21, 1910

        January 24, 1920

    Occupation – None – April 21, 1910

        January 24, 1920

    ○ **Clare D. Dodd,** b. 15 Jun 1908 in Pennsylvania, d. 18 Jul 1988 in Jamestown, Chautauqua Co., New York & **Frances Steen**, b. 1 Feb 1908 in Jamestown, Chautauqua Co., New York, 1 May 1971 in Jamestown, Chautauqua Co., New York – 15 Jun 1934

Clare D. Dodd (son):

    Residence – Jamestown, Chautauqua Co., New York – April 21, 1910

        January 24, 1920

        April 7, 1930

    Occupation – None – April 21, 1910

        January 24, 1920

        Laborer, Cement Trade – April 7, 1930

Leon Raymond Dodd (son):

    Residence – Columbus, Warren Co., Pennsylvania – June 1880

        June 15, 1900

    Corry, Erie Co., Pennsylvania – November 20, 1901

    Jamestown, Chautauqua Co., New York – April 21, 1910

        September 12, 1918

        January 24, 1920

        April 7, 1930

Occupation – At Home – June 1880

> *Grocer, Salesman – June 15, 1900*

> *Commercial Traveller, Cigars – April 21, 1910*

> *Traveling Salesman – September 12, 1918*

> *Commercial Traveller, Dry Goods – January 24, 1920*

> *Salesman, Dry Goods – April 7, 1930*

Home Data for 1930 – Owns home, valued at $ 4,000, has radio set, not on a farm

Grace Flotilla Watson (daughter-in-law):

Residence – Corry, Erie Co., Pennsylvania – November 20, 1901

> *Jamestown, Chautauqua Co., New York – April 21, 1910*

> > *January 24, 1920*

> > *April 7, 1930*

Occupation – None – January 24, 1920

> *April 7, 1930*

- **Nathan Elton Dodd**, b. 14 Nov 1886 in Columbus, Warren Co., Pennsylvania, d. 26 Jun 1976 in Pueblo, Colorado & **Ava Laura Long** (1ˢᵗ Wife), b. 20 Dec 1884 in New York, d. 12 Apr 1940 in Columbus, Warren Co., Pennsylvania – 21 Aug 1907

Signature:

- ○ **Alice Marguerite Dodd**, b. 23 Nov 1910 in Columbus, Warren Co., Pennsylvania, d. 17 May 2005 in Denver, Denver Co., Colorado & **Arthur Leslie Page**, b. 15 Jun 1910 in Columbus, Warren Co., Pennsylvania, d. 28 Jun 1991 in Loveland, Larimer Co., Colorado – 4 Jun 1933

Alice Marguerite Dodd (daughter):

Residence – Columbus, Warren Co., Pennsylvania – January 29, 1920

> *April 12, 1930*

Occupation – None – January 29, 1920

> *April 12, 1930*

- ○ **Natalie Georgia Dodd**, b. 21 Nov 1916 in Boulder, Boulder Co., Colorado, d. 9 Feb 1965 in Columbus, Warren Co., Pennsylvania & **Russell C. Moore**, b. 29 Jan 1918 in Erie, Erie Co., Pennsylvania – 18 Jun 1942 in Columbus, Warren Co., Pennsylvania

Signatures:

Natalie Georgia Dodd (daughter):

> *Residence – Columbus, Warren Co., Pennsylvania – January 29, 1920*
>
>> *April 12, 1930*
>>
>> *June 18, 1942*
>
> *Occupation – None – January 29, 1920*
>
>> *April 12, 1930*
>>
>> *Teacher – June 18, 1942*

Russell C. Moore (son-in-law):

> *Residence – Corry, Erie Co., Pennsylvania – June 18, 1942*
>
> *Occupation – Sergeant U.S. Army, Newark Airport, Newark, New Jersey – June 18, 1942*

- **Nathan Elton Dodd**, b. 14 Nov 1886 in Columbus, Warren Co., Pennsylvania, d. 26 Jun 1976 in Pueblo, Colorado & **Mary Middleton** (2nd Wife), b. 16 Jul 1896 in Gosforth, Cumberland, England, d. Jan 1977 in Wattsburg, Erie Co., Pennsylvania – 2 Oct 1941 in Lake Haven, Clinton Co., Pennsylvania

Signatures:

Signatures (Marriage):

Nathan Elton Dodd (son):

> *Residence – Columbus, Warren Co., Pennsylvania – June 15, 1900*
>
>> *January 29, 1920*
>>
>> *April 12, 1930*
>>
>> *October 2, 1941*
>>
>> *1942*
>
> *Dry Fork, Randolph Co., West Virginia – April 20, 1910*
>
> *Boulder, Boulder Co., Colorado – June 5, 1917*

Occupation – At School – June 15, 1900

      Book Keeper, Lumber Company – April 20, 1910

      Farming – June 5, 1917

      Farmer, General Farm – January 29, 1920

      Farmer, Own Farm – April 12, 1930

      Farmer – October 2, 1941

          1942

Home Data for 1930 – Owns home, has radio set, on a farm

Ava Laura Long (1ˢᵗ Wife) (daughter-in-law):

Residence – Dry Fork, Randolph Co., West Virginia – April 20, 1910

      Columbus, Warren Co., Pennsylvania – January 29, 1920

          April 12, 1930

Occupation – None – April 30, 1910

      January 29, 1920

      Teacher, Public School – April 12, 1930

Mary Middleton (2ⁿᵈ Wife) (daughter-in-law):

Residence – Erie, Erie Co., Pennsylvania – October 2, 1941

      1942

Occupation – Nurse – October 2, 1941

- **Maud Lottie Dodd**, b. 24 Oct 1888 in Columbus, Warren Co., Pennsylvania, d. 13 Dec 1949 & **Nelson Wickwire Trisket**, b. 28 Oct 1887 in Columbus, Warren Co., Pennsylvania, d. 6 Apr 1977 in Corry, Erie Co., Pennsylvania – 13 May 1911 in Columbus, Warren Co., Pennsylvania

Signatures:

          o **Herbert Charles Trisket** – b. 22 Oct 1912 in Columbus, Warren Co., Pennsylvania, d. 22 Aug 1995 in Corry, Erie Co., Pennsylvania

Herbert Charles Trisket (son):

Residence – Columbus, Warren Co., Pennsylvania – February 2, 1920

          April 14, 1930

Occupation – None – February 2, 1920

      April 14, 1930

o   **Florence B. Trisket** – b. Nov 1916 in Pennsylvania

Florence B. Trisket (daughter):

   Residence – Columbus, Warren Co., Pennsylvania – February 2, 1920

                                                               April 14, 1930

   Occupation – None – February 2, 1920

                           April 14, 1930

o   **Vinora E. Trisket** – b. Jan 1920 in Pennsylvania

Vinora E. Trisket (daughter):

   Residence – Columbus, Warren Co., Pennsylvania – February 2, 1920

                                                               April 14, 1930

   Occupation – None – February 2, 1920

                           April 14, 1930

o   **Gladys L. Trisket** – b. About 1923 in Pennsylvania

Gladys L. Trisket (daughter):

   Residence – Columbus, Warren Co., Pennsylvania – April 14, 1930

   Occupation – None – April 14, 1930

Maud Lottie Dodd (daughter):

   Residence – Columbus, Warren Co., Pennsylvania – June 15, 1900

                                                               May 2, 1910

                                                               February 2, 1920

                                                               April 14, 1930

   Occupation – At School – June 15, 1900

                   Dress Maker, All Kinds – May 2, 1910

                   None – February 2, 1920

                           April 14, 1930

Nelson Wickwire Trisket (son-in-law):

   Residence – Columbus, Warren Co., Pennsylvania – June 5, 1917

                                                               February 2, 1920

                                                               April 14, 1930

   Occupation – Farmer – June 5, 1917

                   Farmer, General Farm – February 2, 1920

                   Truck Driver, Milk Route Independent – April 14, 1930

   Home Data for 1930 – Owns home, has radio set, on a farm

Hurst

- **Frank Leslie Dodd**, b. 23 Apr 1894 in Columbus, Warren Co., Pennsylvania, d. 20 May 1966 in Columbus, Warren Co., Pennsylvania & **Cora Luella Hall**, b. About 1891 in Pennsylvania – 5 Mar 1912 in Columbus, Warren Co., Pennsylvania

Signature:

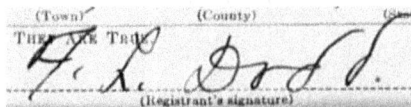

  - **Lester J. Dodd** – b. About 1915 in Pennsylvania

Lester J. Dodd (son):

  Residence – Columbus, Warren Co., Pennsylvania – February 2, 1920

  April 11, 1930

  Occupation – None – February 2, 1920

  April 11, 1930

  - **Merle E. Dodd** – b. Jan 1917 in Pennsylvania

Merle E. Dodd (son):

  Residence – Columbus, Warren Co., Pennsylvania – February 2, 1920

  April 11, 1930

  Occupation – None – February 2, 1920

  April 11, 1930

  - **Betty Jane Dodd** – b. 7 Mar 1929 in Columbus, Warren Co., Pennsylvania, d. 23 Apr 2007 in Prescott, Yavapai Co., Arizona

Betty Jane Dodd (daughter):

  Residence – Columbus, Warren Co., Pennsylvania – April 11, 1930

  Occupation – None – April 11, 1930

Frank Leslie Dodd (son):

  Residence – Columbus, Warren Co., Pennsylvania – June 15, 1900

  May 2, 1910

  February 2, 1920

  April 11, 1930

  1942

  Occupation – At School – June 15, 1900

  Farmer – May 2, 1910

  1942

  Farmer, General Farm – February 2, 1920

  Salesman, Silo & Farm Supplies – April 11, 1930

Home Data for 1930 – Owns home, valued at $ 3, 000, has radio set, not on a farm

Elisha Calkins & Anna Dalrymple Descendants

Cora Luella Hall (daughter-in-law):

> *Residence – Columbus, Warren Co., Pennsylvania – February 2, 1920*
>
> > > *April 11, 1930*
> > >
> > > *1942*

> *Occupation – None – February 2, 1920*
>
> > *April 11, 1930*

Bertha Ellen Raymond (daughter):

> *Residence – Columbus, Warren Co., Pennsylvania – August 25, 1870*
>
> > > *June 1880*
> > >
> > > *June 15, 1900*
> > >
> > > *May 2, 1910*
> > >
> > > *February 2, 1920*
> > >
> > > *April 12, 1930*

> *Occupation – At Home – August 25, 1870*
>
> > *Keeping House – June 1880*
> >
> > *None Listed – June 15, 1900*
> >
> > *None – May 2, 1910*
> >
> > > *February 2, 1920*
> > >
> > > *April 12, 1930*

Charles Nathan Dodd (son-in-law):

> *Residence – Columbus, Warren Co., Pennsylvania – June 1880*
>
> > > *June 15, 1900*
> > >
> > > *May 2, 1910*
> > >
> > > *February 2, 1920*
> > >
> > > *April 12, 1930*

> *Occupation – Farmer – June 1880*
>
> > *June 15, 1900*
> >
> > *Farmer, Dairy – May 2, 1910*
> >
> > *Farmer, General Farm – February 2, 1920*
> >
> > *Farmer, Own Farm – April 12, 1930*

Home Data for 1930 – Owns home, has radio set, on a farm

- ▪ **Adelaide Raymond**, b. 22 Jun 1865 in Columbus, Warren Co., Pennsylvania, d. 22 Jul 1944 in San Diego, San Diego Co., California & **Leonard Day**, d. Before 1900

  - ● **Raymond Edward Day**, b. 28 Jul 1883 in Columbus, Warren Co., Pennsylvania, d. 25 Jan 1947 in Kern Co., California & **Florence D. Unknown**, b. About 1889 in Pennsylvania

     ○ **Virginia Day** – b. 1909 in Ohio

Virginia Day (daughter):

  Residence – Painesville, Lake Co., Ohio – 1910

      Akron, Summit Co., Ohio – January 6, 1920

  Occupation – None – 1910

      January 6, 1920

Raymond Edward Day (son):

  Residence – Corry, Erie Co., Pennsylvania – June 6, 1900

      Painesville, Lake Co. Ohio – 1910

      Akron, Summit Co., Ohio – January 6, 1920

         April 2, 1930

  Occupation – Shipping Clerk, Factory – June 6, 1900

      None, Express Agent – 1910

      None – January 6, 1920

      April 2, 1930

Florence D. Unknown (daughter-in-law):

  Residence – Painesville, Lake Co., Ohio – 1910

  Occupation – None – 1910

     • **Merton Charles Day**, b. 14 May 1886 in Pennsylvania & **Marion A. Long**, b. About 1888 in Clymer, New York – 8 Jan 1914 Akron, Summit Co., Ohio

Signatures:

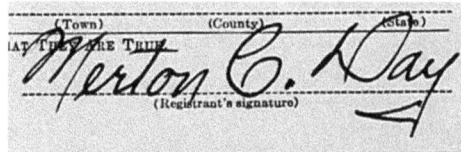

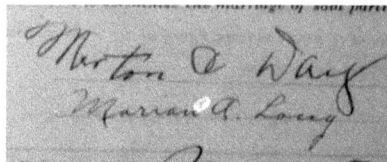

Signatures (Marriage):

     ○ **Merton Day** – b. About 1915 in Pennsylvania

Elisha Calkins & Anna Dalrymple Descendants

Merton Day (son):

   Residence – Corry, Erie Co., Pennsylvania – January 23, 1920

     Akron, Summit Co., Ohio – April 12, 1930

   Occupation – None – January 23, 1920

     April 12, 1930

     o **Dorothy Day** – b. About 1917 in Kansas

Dorothy Day (daughter):

   Residence – Corry, Erie Co., Pennsylvania – January 23, 1920

   Occupation – None – January 23, 1920

     o **Ellen Day** – About 1919 in Kansas

Ellen Day (daughter):

   Residence – Corry, Erie Co., Pennsylvania – January 23, 1920

     Akron, Summit Co., Ohio – April 12, 1930

   Occupation – None – January 23, 1920

     April 12, 1930

Merton Charles Day (son):

   Residence – Corry, Erie Co. Pennsylvania – June 6, 1900

     January 23, 1920

     Akron, Summit Co., Ohio – May 14, 1913

     April 12, 1930

     Wichita, Sedgwick Co., Kansas – September 12, 1918

     Alhambra, Los Angeles Co., California – 1942

   Occupation – At School – June 6, 1900

     Electrician – May 14, 1913

     Mechanic – September 12, 1918

     None – January 23, 1920

     Barber, Barbershop – April 12, 1930

     Unemployed – 1942

   Home Data for 1930 – Owns home, valued at $ 4, 000, has radio set, not on farm

Marion A. Long (daughter-in-law):

   Residence – Corry, Erie Co., Pennsylvania – January 23, 1920

     Akron, Summit Co., Ohio – May 9, 1913

     April 12, 1930

   Occupation – Nurse – May 9, 1913

     January 23, 1920

     Trained Nurse, Hospital – April 12, 1930

- **Sears Seth Day**, b. 3 Dec 1888 in Seattle, King Co., Washington, d. 8 Jan 1928 in Baltimore, Baltimore Co., Maryland & **Frances G. Trisch** (1st Wife), b. About 1889 in Akron, Summit Co., Ohio – 25 Apr 1908 in Akron, Summit Co., Ohio

Signature:

- **Sears Seth Day**, b. 3 Dec 1888 in Seattle, King Co., Washington, d. 8 Jan 1928 in Baltimore, Baltimore Co., Maryland & **Margaret White** (2nd Wife), b. About 1894 in Martin's Ferry, Belmont Co., Ohio – 16 February 1914 Jefferson Co., Ohio

Signatures (marriage):

- **Sears Seth Day**, b. 3 Dec 1888 in Seattle, King Co., Washington, d. 8 Jan 1928 in Baltimore, Baltimore Co., Maryland & **Luella G. Unknown** (3rd Wife), b. About 1891 in Ohio

Signature:

Sears Seth Day (son):

Residence – Corry, Erie Co., Pennsylvania – June 6, 1900

Akron, Summit Co., Ohio – December 3, 1907

June 5, 1917

January 10, 1920

Mt. Clemens, Macomb Co., Michigan – April 20, 1910

Rayland, Jefferson Co., Ohio – February 16, 1914

Occupation – At School – June 6, 1900

Merchant – December 3, 1907

Manager, Express Office – April 20, 1910

Salesman – February 16, 1914

Mechanical Engineer, Rubber Co. – June 5, 1917

January 10, 1920

Elisha Calkins & Anna Dalrymple Descendants

Frances G. Trisch (1ˢᵗ Wife) (daughter-in-law):

    Residence – Akron, Summit Co., Ohio – April 4, 1908

    Occupation – None – April 4, 1908

Margaret White (2ⁿᵈ Wife) (daughter-in-law):

    Residence – Rayland, Jefferson Co., Ohio – February 16, 1914

    Occupation – Housework – February 16, 1914

Luella G. Unknown (3ʳᵈ Wife) (daughter-in-law):

    Residence – Akron, Summit Co., Ohio – January 10, 1920

    Occupation – None – January 10, 1920

Adelaide Raymond, b. 22 Jun 1865 in Columbus, Warren Co., Pennsylvania, d. d. 22 Jul 1944 in San Diego, San Diego Co., California & **Unknown Aylsworth**, d. Before 1930

Adelaide Raymond (daughter):

    Residence – Columbus, Warren Co., Pennsylvania – August 25, 1870

                            June 1880

                            April 18, 1910

        Corry, Erie Co., Pennsylvania – June 6, 1900

        Akron, Summit Co., Ohio – January 6, 1920

                        April 2, 1930

    Occupation – None Listed – August 25, 1870

        At School – June 1880

        None – June 6, 1900

            April 2, 1930

        Post Mistress, U.S. Mail – April 18, 1910

        Tutoress – January 6, 1920

    Home Data for 1930 – Rental, $ 50 a month, has radio set, not on a farm

Maude Raymond – b. 25 May 1867 in Columbus, Warren Co., Pennsylvania, d. 26 Jun 1868 in Columbus, Warren Co., Pennsylvania

Ellen A. Woods (daughter):

    Residence – Arkwright, Chautauqua Co., New York – August 28, 1850

        Columbus, Warren Co., Pennsylvania – August 25, 1870

                        June 1880

                        June 15, 1900

                        April 18, 1910

                        February 2, 1920

171

Hurst

Occupation – None Listed – August 28, 1850

June 15, 1900

Keeping House – August 25, 1870

June 1880

June 15, 1900

None – April 18, 1910

February 2, 1920

Sears H. Raymond (son-in-law):

Residence – Columbus, Warren Co., Pennsylvania – August 25, 1870

June 1880

June 15, 1900

April 18, 1910

Occupation – Farmer – August 25, 1870

June 1880

June 15, 1900

Farmer, Retired – April 18, 1910

Value of Real Estate – $ 2, 800 – August 25, 1870

Value of Personal Estate – $ 200 – August 25, 1870

Almira Calkins (mother):

Residence – Arkwright, Chautauqua Co., New York – August 28, 1850

Columbus , Warren Co., Pennsylvania – August 26, 1870

June 1880

Occupation – None Listed – August 28, 1850

Keeping House – August 26, 1870

June 1880

Lester A. Woods (father):

Residence – Arkwright, Chautauqua Co., New York – August 28, 1850

Columbus, Warren Co., Pennsylvania – August 26 1870

June 1880

Occupation – Farmer – August 28, 1850

Farmer – August 26, 1870

Retired – June 1880

Value of Real Estate – $ 2, 000 – August 26, 1870

Value of Personal Estate – $ 1, 000 – August 26, 1870

Almira Calkins

Photograph – Tintype

Photograph courtesy of The Hurst Family of Lake Elsinore, California

Almira Calkins & Lester A. Woods

Family Photo Album (Found at an Estate Sale near Medina, Ohio)

Date of Album – 1860s

Photographs courtesy of The Hurst Family of Lake Elsinore, California

Almira Calkins & Lester A. Woods

Photographer Credits: H.C. Brown – Norwich, New York

Photographs courtesy of The Hurst Family of Lake Elsinore, California

Almira Calkins

Back of tintype was inscribed "Mother Almira Calkins"

Photograph – Tintype

Photograph courtesy of The Woods Family of Hastings, Nebraska

Lester A. Woods

Photograph – Tintype

Photograph courtesy of The Woods Family of Hastings, Nebraska

Verna, Charles, Mary, Ray Allen, Vinnie Wood Allen
Ora Senica Woods, Lester, Annie Belle Dewey

Photograph courtesy of The Butler Family of Dallas, Texas

Freeman Calkins & Descendants

- **Freeman Calkins**, b. 9 Nov 1807 in Greenfield, Saratoga Co., New York, d. Between 1880 – 1885 in Minneiska, Wabasha Co., Minnesota & **Sarah Ann Woods**, b. 31 Jan 1808 in Otsego Co., New York, d. Before 1 May 1875 in Minnesota – Between 1820 – 1830 in New York

Signatures:

- o **Fidelia Lossie Calkins**, b. 16 Jul 1830 in Arkwright, Chautauqua Co., New York, d. 15 May 1908 in Rothsay, Wilkin Co., Minnesota & **Carlton Washington Fuller**, d. 25 Apr 1826 in Arkwright, Chautauqua Co., New York, d. 18 Oct 1894 in Rothsay, Wilkin Co., Minnesota – 28 May 1846 in Arkwright, Chautauqua Co., New York

Signature:

  - ▪ **Unknown Fuller** – d. Before 1900

  - ▪ **Unknown Fuller** – d. Before 1900

  - ▪ **Unknown Fuller** – d. After 1900

  - ▪ **Frederick Deforest Fuller**, b. 28 Jul 1849 in Arkwright, Chautauqua Co., New York, d. 7 Dec 1934 in Minneapolis, Hennepin Co., Minnesota & **Anna Dorothy Nelson**, b. 9 Nov 1863 in Christianna, Norway, d. 11 Feb 1922 in Hubbard Co., Minnesota – 5 May 1886 in Marshall Co., Minnesota

- **Delia Maria Fuller**, b. 10 Apr 1887 in Nevis, Hubbard Co., Minnesota, d. 8 Dec 1942 in Nevis Hubbard Co., Minnesota & **Charles Clifton Smith**, b. 22 Jan 1889 in Iowa, d. 1947 in British Columbia, Canada – 22 Jul 1915 in Hubbard Co., Minnesota

Delia Maria Fuller (daughter):

Residence – Todd, Hubbard Co., Minnesota – June 15, 1895

June 27, 1900

June 1905

Nevis, Hubbard Co., Minnesota – April 18, 1910

Union, O'Brien Co., Iowa – January 7, 1920

Occupation – At School – June 27, 1900

Teacher, Public School – April 18, 1910

None – January 7, 1920

Charles Clifton Smith (son-in-law):

Residence – Union, O'Brien Co., Iowa – January 7, 1920

Occupation – Baker Shop – January 7, 1920

- **Lester Alvah Fuller** (1st Marriage), b. 19 Jan 1890 in Stephen, Marshall Co., Minnesota, d. 24 Aug 1969 in Sacramento, Sacramento Co., California & **Julia Mable Erikson** (1st Wife), b. 22 Sep 1889 in Aberdeen, Brown Co., South Dakota, d. May 1928 – 19 Jun 1912 in Aberdeen, Brown Co., South Dakota

  o **Marian Le Sette Fuller**, b. 10 Feb 1914 in South Dakota, d. 27 Apr 2008 in San Jose, Santa Clara Co., California & **Richard Green**, b. 2 May 1911

    - **Daniel Green** – b. 27 Jan 1939

    - **William David Green** – b. 16 Oct 1940

Marian Le Sette Fuller (daughter):

Residence – Aberdeen, Brown Co., South Dakota – January 10, 1920

April 3, 1930

Occupation – None – January 10, 1920

April 3, 1930

  o **Stella Orith Fuller**, b. 7 Dec 1915 in Aberdeen, Brown Co., South Dakota, d. 2 Jul 1986 in San Bernardino Co., California & **Harold Ralph Grohnke**, b. 28 Dec 1914 in Warner, Brown Co., South Dakota, d. Sep 1965 in Aberdeen, Brown Co., South Dakota

Elisha Calkins & Anna Dalrymple Descendants

Stella Orith Fuller (daughter):

Residence – Aberdeen, Brown Co., South Dakota – January 10, 1920

April 3, 1930

Occupation – None – April 10, 1920

April 3, 1930

o **Lucille M. Fuller**, b. 6 Sep 1917 in Aberdeen, Brown Co., South Dakota, d. 26 Dec 2011 in Kansas City, Clay Co., Missouri & **Arnold E. Heft**, b. 7 Aug 1913, d. 28 Dec 2000 in Kansas City, Clay Co., Missouri – 30 Apr 1939 in Anchorage, Anchorage Co., Alaska

Lucille M. Fuller (daughter):

Residence – Aberdeen, Brown Co., South Dakota – January 10, 1920

April 3, 1930

Occupation – None Listed – January 10, 1920

None – April 3, 1930

Obituary –

*"Lucille M. Heft passed away peacefully on December 26, 2011 at her home, where she had lived for nearly 60 years. She was 94. Lucille was energetic and full of life, and she lived by a creed of perseverance. She was a devoted wife and mother of four. She was married to Arnold Heft for 51 years and dedicated her life to fervently supporting all family members. Lucille was born on September 6, 1917 in Aberdeen, SD She graduated from Black Hills College in Spearfish, SD, and following WWII, moved to Alaska, where she met Arnold. They were married in a small ceremony on April 30, 1949, in Anchorage. Throughout her career, she taught various levels of school, finally retiring from Chouteau Elementary School in 1977, where she taught second grade for the previous seven years. She then pursued freelance writing, and she later served as the head of the local chapter of the National League of American Pen Women in the early 1990s. She encouraged scores of writers in the Kansas City area by offering a writing critique group, which met regularly at her home for 12 years. Lucille actively submitted short stories and cooking articles and was published in multiple publications, including the Kansas City Star food section. Lucille loved to travel, play accompaniments on piano at church events and try out new recipes. She had an infectious laugh and used the gift of encouragement. She was an active member of Avondale United Methodist Church for nearly 60 years. Lucille is survived by her four children: Kathy Gaskill, Warren Heft, Kim Heft, and Gordon Heft; her sister, Esther Roundy, in Los Angeles; six grandchildren and two great- grandchildren. Visitation will be Thursday, December 29th from 10:00-11:00 AM at Avondale United Methodist Church. Funeral service will follow at 11:00 AM. Burial will be at Mt. Moriah Terrace Park Cemetery. In lieu of flowers, contributions may be made to Crossroads Hospice or . (www.mcgilleyantiochchapel.com) McGilley Antioch Chapel, 3325 NE Vivion Rd, Kansas city, MO 64119, 816-453-7700." **Published in Kansas City Star on December 28, 2011**

o **Preston Kingsley Fuller**, b. 1 Nov 1919 in Aberdeen, Brown Co., South Dakota, d. 1 Sep 1982 in Eugene, Lane Co., Oregon & **Jeanne Unknown**

Preston Kingsley Fuller (son):

   Residence – Aberdeen, Brown Co., South Dakota – January 10, 1920

                                             April 3, 1930

   Occupation – None Listed – January 10, 1920

       None – April 3, 1930

o **Harriet E. Fuller**, b. 14 Oct 1922 in South Dakota, d. 12 Apr 2005 in Citrus Heights, Sacramento Co., California & **George Raymond Meyers**, b. 10 Apr 1920, d. 24 Mar 2000 in California

Harriet Fuller (daughter):

   Residence – Aberdeen, Brown Co., South Dakota – April 3, 1930

   Occupation – None – April 3, 1930

o **Wallace Fuller**, b. 22 Jan 1926 in South Dakota, d. Jul 1963 in California & **Bernice Hansen**

Wallace Fuller (son):

   Residence – Aberdeen, Brown Co., South Dakota – April 3, 1930

   Occupation – None – April 3, 1930

o **Esther Maurine Fuller**, b. 16 Apr 1927 in South Dakota & **Clayton Addison Roundy**, b. 27 Feb 1920 in Lincoln, Brown Co., South Dakota

Esther Maurine Fuller (daughter):

   Residence – Aberdeen, Brown Co., South Dakota – April 3, 1930

   Occupation – None – April 3, 1930

o **Viola Bernice Fuller** – b. May 1928 in South Dakota, d. 7 May 1928 in Brown Co., South Dakota

• **Lester Alvah Fuller** (2nd Marriage), b. 19 Jan 1890 in Nevis, Hubbard Co., Minnesota, d. 24 Aug 1969 in Sacramento, Sacramento Co., California & **Hazel Mawhinney Hanson** (2nd Wife), d. Mar 1969 – Aug 1946

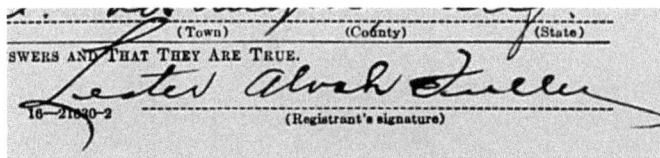

Signature:

182

Lester Alvah Fuller (son):

    Residence – Todd, Hubbard Co., Minnesota – June 15, 1895

        June 27, 1900

        June 1905

        Aberdeen, Brown Co., South Dakota – January 10, 1920

        April 3, 1930

        Tujunga, Los Angeles Co., California – 1942

    Occupation – At School – June 27, 1900

        Chief Clerk, Railroad Office – January 10, 1920

        Merchant, Grain Coal – April 3, 1930

        Employed by Los Angeles By-products Company – 1942

Julia Mabel Erikson (1st Wife) (daughter-in-law):

    Residence – Aberdeen, Brown Co., South Dakota – January 10, 1920

    Occupation – None – January 10, 1920

- **Clifford Alva Fuller**, b. 20 Jan 1893 in Grand Forks, North Dakota, d. 29 Nov 1964 in Park rapids, Hubbard Co., Minnesota & **Esther Edith Peyanske**, b. 22 Feb 1896 in Minnesota, d. 2 Apr 1970 in Park Rapids, Hubbard Co., Minnesota

Signature:

(Signature or mark)

- o **Frank Alvah Fuller** – b. 23 Feb 1923 in Park Rapids, Hubbard Co., Minnesota, d. 7 Sep 1997 in Webster, Harris Co., Texas

Frank Alvah Fuller (son):

    Residence – Park Rapids, Hubbard Co., Minnesota – April 16, 1930

    Occupation – None – April 16, 1930

- o **Charles Edward Fuller** – b. 9 Dec 1930 in Hubbard Co., Minnesota

Clifford Alva Fuller (son):

    Residence – Todd, Hubbard Co., Minnesota – June 15, 1895

        June 27, 1900

        June 1905

        Park Rapids, Hubbard Co., Minnesota – June 5, 1917

        January 20, 1920

        April 16, 1930

    Occupation – At School – June 27, 1900

        Book Keeper – June 5, 1917

Hurst

Book Keeper, Bank – January 20, 1920

Cashier, Bank – April 16, 1930

Home Data for 1930 – Owns home, valued at $ 2, 000, has radio set, not on a farm

Esther Edith Peyanske (daughter-in-law):

Residence – Park Rapids, Hubbard Co., Minnesota – January 20, 1920

April 16, 1930

Occupation – None – January 20, 1920

April 16, 1930

- **Leland Raymond Fuller** (1st Marriage), b. 7 Aug 1895 in Park Rapids, Hubbard Co., Minnesota, d. 8 Oct 1955 in Los Angeles, Los Angeles Co., California & **Mildred Olena Redfield** (1st Wife), b. 2 Feb 1899 in Riceville, Mitchell Co., Iowa, d. 7 May 1950 in Toledo, Lewis Co., Washington

  o **Milton Raymond Fuller**, b. 23 Jan 1916 in Aberdeen, Brown Co., South Dakota, d. 9 Jan 1951 in Santa Barbara, Santa Barbara Co., California & **Mary Jane Clinehens**, b. 1920 in Portland, Multnomah Co., Oregon – 7 Mar 1938 in Centralia, Lewis Co., Washington

Signatures (Marriage):

- Alice Marie Fuller – b. 7 Jan 1939 in Los Angeles Co., California

Milton Raymond Fuller (son):

Residence – Aberdeen, Brown Co., South Dakota – April 4, 1930

Occupation – None – April 4, 1930

  o Alice Fuller – b. 15 Aug 1917 in South Dakota

- **Leland Raymond Fuller**(2nd Marriage), b. 7 Aug 1895 in Park Rapids, Hubbard Co., Minnesota, d. 8 Oct 1955 in Los Angeles, Los Angeles Co., California & **Emma Harriet Tennant Plant** (2nd Wife), b. About 1897 in South Dakota – 21 Jun 1926 in Aberdeen, Brown Co., South Dakota

Signature:

Leland Ray Fuller (son):

Residence – Todd, Hubbard Co., Minnesota – June 27, 1900

June 1905

April 21, 1910

Aberdeen, Brown Co., South Dakota – June 21, 1926

April 4, 1930

Los Angeles, Los Angeles Co., California – 1942

Occupation – None Listed – June 27, 1900

None – April 21, 1910

Sales, Implements – April 4, 1930

Employed by Los Angeles By-Products – 1942

Home Data for 1930 – Rental, $ 25 a month, has radio set, not of a farm

Emma Harriet Tennant Plant (2ⁿᵈ Wife) (daughter-in-law):

Residence – Aberdeen, Brown Co., South Dakota – June 21, 1926

April 4, 1930

Los Angeles, Los Angeles Co., California – 1942

Occupation – None – April 4, 1930

- **Gladys Jeanette Fuller**, b. 12 Jun 1899 in Nevis, Hubbard Co., Minnesota, d. 2 Dec 1979 in Friendly, Anoka Co., Minnesota & **Otto Marcelius Johnson**, b. 3 Jun 1889 in Minneapolis, Hennepin Co., Minnesota, d. 12 Jul 1969 in Minneapolis, Hennepin Co., Minnesota – 2 Aug 1919

Signature:

  o **Quinlan Marcel Johnson** – b. 24 Oct 1920, d. 26 Jan 2003 in Minneapolis, Hennepin Co., Minnesota

Quinlan Marcel Johnson (son):

Residence – Minneapolis, Hennepin Co., Minnesota – April 7, 1930

Occupation – None – April 7, 1930

  o **Herbert Keith Johnson** – b. 20 Jul 1929 in Minneapolis, Hennepin Co., Minnesota, d. 22 Jul 1962 in San Diego, San Diego Co., California

Herbert Keith Johnson (son):

Residence – Minneapolis, Hennepin Co., Minnesota – April 7, 1930

Occupation – None – April 7, 1930

Hurst

Gladys Jeanette Fuller (daughter):

Residence – Todd, Hubbard Co., Minnesota – June 27, 1900

June 1905

April 21, 1910

Nevis, Hubbard Co., Minnesota – January 3, 1920

Minneapolis, Hennepin Co., Minnesota – April 7, 1930

Occupation – None Listed – June 27, 1900

None – April 21, 1910

January 3, 1920

April 7, 1930

Otto Marcelius Johnson (son-in-law):

Residence – Nevis, Hubbard Co., Minnesota – June 5, 1917

January 3, 1920

Minneapolis, Hennepin Co., Minnesota – April 7, 1930

Occupation – Drayman – June 5, 1917

Laborer, Farm – January 3, 1920

Truck Driver, Excelsior & Tow – April 7, 1930

Home Data for 1930 – Rental, $ 25 a month, has radio set, not on a farm

- **Freddie Fuller** – b. Feb 1902 in Nevis, Hubbard Co., Minnesota, d. 9 Feb 1902 in Nevis, Hubbard Co., Minnesota

- **Frankie Fuller** – b. Feb 1902 in Nevis, Hubbard Co., Minnesota, d. 11 Feb 1902 in Nevis, Hubbard Co., Minnesota

- **Freda Arvilla Fuller** – b. 24 Jun 1903 in Nevis, Hubbard Co., Minnesota, d. 11 Dec 1987 in Anoka Co., Minnesota

Freda Arvilla Fuller (daughter):

Residence – Todd, Hubbard Co., Minnesota – June 1905

April 21, 1910

Nevis, Hubbard Co., Minnesota – January 3, 1920

Minneapolis, Hennepin Co., Minnesota – April 7, 1930

Occupation – None – April 21, 1910

January 3, 1920

April 7, 1930

Frederick Deforest Fuller (son):

    Residence – Union, Johnson Co., Iowa – 1856

        Green, Iowa Co., Iowa – June 4, 1860

        Township 108 Range 12 (Elgin), Wabasha Co., Minnesota – October 31, 1857

        Minneapolis, Hennepin Co., Minnesota – May 1, 1875

        Perry, Lac Qui Parle Co., Minnesota – June 17, 1880

        Stephen, Marshall Co., Minnesota – June 17, 1885

        Todd, Hubbard Co., Minnesota – June 15, 1895

                June 27, 1900

                June 1905

                April 21, 1910

        Nevis, Hubbard Co., Minnesota – January 3, 1920

        Minneapolis, Hennepin Co., Minnesota – April 7, 1930

    Occupation – None Listed – 1856

                October 31, 1857

                June 4, 1860

        Farmer – June 17, 1880

                June 1905

        Carpenter – June 27, 1900

                April 21, 1910

        Carpenter, House – January 3, 1920

        None – April 7, 1930

Anna Dorothy Nelson (daughter-in-law):

    Residence – Todd, Hubbard Co., Minnesota – June 15, 1895

                June 27, 1900

                June 1905

                April 21, 1910

        Nevis, Hubbard Co., Minnesota – January 3, 1920

    Occupation – None Listed – June 27, 1900

        Housekeeper – April 21, 1910

        None – January 3, 1920

    Immigration – 1882 from Norway

- **Frank Alvah Fuller**, b. 30 Jan 1855 in Arkwright, Chautauqua Co., New York, d. 28 Jul 1915 in Park Rapids, Hubbard Co., Minnesota & **Johanna Elizabeth Sheehan**, b. 17 Jun 1856 in Galena, Illinois, d. 10 Nov 1912 in Hubbard Co., Minnesota – 10 Jan 1881 in Minneiska, Wabasha Co., Minnesota

  - **Carlton Lewis Fuller**, b. 5 Jan 1882 in Rothsay, Wilkin Co., Minnesota, d. Dec 1965 in Isabel, Dewey Co., South Dakota & **Mary Agnes Doerner**, b. 25 Dec 1884 in Minnesota, d. 1966 – 24 May 1914 in St. Cloud, Stearns Co., Minnesota

Signature:

  - ○ **Helen Agnes Fuller**, b. 20 Mar 1915 in Isabel, Dewey Co., South Dakota, d. 9 Mar 1981 in Portland, Multnomah Co., Oregon

Helen Agnes Fuller (daughter):

Residence – Isabel, Dewey Co., South Dakota – February 9ᵗʰ & 10ᵗʰ, 1920

April 11, 1930

Occupation – None – February 9ᵗʰ & 10ᵗʰ, 1920

April 11, 1930

  - ○ **Mary Ann Fuller**, b. 16 Jan 1917 in Isabel, Dewey Co., South Dakota, d. 14 Feb 2007 in Ilwaco, Pacific Co., Washington & **Ernest Richard Markham**, b. 25 Mar 1908 in Ilwaco, Pacific Co., Washington, d. 9 May 1965 in Ilwaco, Pacific Co., Washington – 1941 in Ilwaco, Pacific Co., Washington

Mary Ann Fuller (daughter):

Residence – Isabel, Dewey Co., South Dakota – February 9ᵗʰ & 10ᵗʰ, 1920

April 11, 1930

Occupation – None – February 9ᵗʰ & 10ᵗʰ, 1920

April 11, 1930

  - ○ **Carlton Edward Fuller** – b. 9 Oct 1918 in Isabel, Dewey Co., South Dakota, d. 27 Dec 2004 in Roseville, Placer Co., California

Carlton Edward Fuller (son):

Residence – Isabel, Dewey Co., South Dakota – February 9ᵗʰ & 10ᵗʰ, 1920

Occupation – None – February 9ᵗʰ & 10, 1920

  - ○ **Joan Fuller** – b. 26 Jan 1924 in Isabel, Dewey Co., South Dakota, d. 18 Sep 2009 in Portland, Multnomah Co., Oregon

Elisha Calkins & Anna Dalrymple Descendants

o **Frances Theresa Fuller** – b. 9 Oct 1925 in Isabel, Dewey Co., South Dakota, d. 17 Mar 2003

in Rapid City, Pennington Co., South Dakota

Carlton Lewis Fuller (son):

Residence – Rothsay, Wilkin Co., Minnesota – June 2, 1885

Park Rapids, Hubbard Co., Minnesota – June 10, 1895

June 1, 1900

Isabel, Dewey Co., South Dakota – September 17, 1918

February 9th & 10th, 1920

April 11, 1930

Occupation – None Listed – June 10, 1895

At School – June 1, 1900

Manager, Hardware – September 17, 1918

Proprietor, Hardware – February 9th & 10th, 1920

Dealer, Hardware – April 11, 1930

Home Data for 1930 – Owns home, valued at $ 2, 000, has radio set, not on a farm

Mary Agnes Doerner (daughter-in-law):

Residence – Isabel, Dewey Co., South Dakota – September 17, 1918

February 9th & 10th, 1920

April 11, 1930

Occupation – None – February 9th & 10th, 1920

April 11, 1930

• **Helen Georgeanna Fuller**, b. 20 Dec 1882 in Rothsay, Wilkin Co., Minnesota, d. 15 Jan 1980 in

Island & **Wilton John Lord**, b. 6 Sep 1877 in Detroit, Becker Co., Minnesota – 12 Jan 1909 in

Hubbard Co., Minnesota

Signatures:

189

Hurst

- **Unknown Lord** – b. After 1909, d. Before 1910 in Minnesota

- **Vincent Edward Lord** – b. 5 Apr 1911 in Aurora, St. Louis Co., Minnesota, d. 9 Aug 2002

Vincent Edward Lord (son):

  Residence – Straight River, Hubbard Co., Minnesota – January 26, 1920

  Nashwauk, Itasca Co., Minnesota – April 8, 1930

  Occupation – None – January 26, 1920

  Switch Tender, Iron Mine – April 8, 1930

- **Mary Irene Lord** – b. About 1919 in Minnesota

Mary Irene Lord (daughter):

  Residence – Straight River, Hubbard Co., Minnesota – January 26, 1920

  Nashwauk, Itasca Co., Minnesota – April 8, 1930

  Occupation – None – January 26, 1920

  April 8, 1930

- **Dorothy Ellen Lord** – b. 23 Aug 1920 in Itasca Co., Minnesota

Dorothy Ellen Lord (daughter):

  Residence – Nashwauk, Itasca Co., Minnesota – April 8, 1930

  Occupation – None – January 26, 1920

Helen Georgeanna Fuller (daughter):

  Residence – Rothsay, Wilkin Co., Minnesota – June 2, 1885

  Park Rapids, Hubbard Co., Minnesota – June 10, 1895

  June 1, 1900

  June 1905

  Aurora, St. Louis Co., Minnesota – April 26, 1910

  Chicago, Cook Co., Illinois – September 12, 1918

  Straight River, Hubbard Co., Minnesota – January 26, 1920

  Nashwauk, Itasca Co., Minnesota – April 8, 1930

  Occupation – None Listed – June 10, 1895

  At School – June 1, 1900

  Teacher – June 1905

  None – April 26, 1910

  January 26, 1920

  April 8, 1930

Wilton John Lord (son-in-law):

  Residence – Aurora, St. Louis Co., Minnesota – April 26, 1910

  Chicago, Cook Co., Illinois – September 12, 1918

Elisha Calkins & Anna Dalrymple Descendants

Straight River, Hubbard Co., Minnesota – January 26, 1920

Nashwauk, Itasca Co., Minnesota – April 8, 1930

Seattle, King Co., Washington – 1942

Occupation – Salesman, Hardware Store – April 26, 1910

Clerk – September 12, 1918

Clerk, Store – January 26, 1920

Pump Engineer, Iron Mine – April 8, 1930

Unemployed – 1942

Home Data for 1930 – Rental, $ 25 a month, no radio set, not on a farm

- **Mabel Mary Fuller** – b. 5 Jul 1884 in Rothsay, Wilkin Co., Minnesota, d. 5 Dec 1938 in Park Rapids, Hubbard Co., Minnesota

Mabel Mary Fuller (daughter):

Residence – Rothsay, Wilkin Co., Minnesota – June 2, 1885

Park Rapids, Hubbard Co., Minnesota – June 10, 1895

June 1, 1900

June 1905

April 23, 1910

January 3, 1920

Occupation – None Listed – June 10, 1895

At School – June 1, 1900

Teacher – June 1905

Teacher, School – April 23, 1910

Teacher, Public School – January 3, 1920

- **Francis Olive Fuller** – b. 4 Aug 1885 in Rothsay, Wilkin Co., Minnesota, d. 3 Dec 1936 in Seattle, King Co., Minnesota

Francis Olive Fuller (daughter):

Residence – Park Rapids, Hubbard Co., Minnesota – June 10, 1895

June 1, 1900

June 1905

April 23, 1910

January 3, 1920

Occupation – None Listed – June 10, 1895

At School – June 1, 1900

Teacher – June 1905

Teacher, School – April 23, 1910

Hurst

Teacher, Public School – January 3, 1920

- **Earl Vincent Fuller**, b. 18 Apr 1888 in Rothsay, Wilkin Co., Minnesota, d. 11 Oct 1971 in Park Rapids, Hubbard Co., Minnesota & **Eugenie Agnes Loiselle**, b. 3 Jan 1897 in New Canada, Ramsey Co., Minnesota, d. 6 Nov 1975 in Hubbard Co., Minnesota

Signature:

(Signature or mark)

- o **Mary Louise Fuller** – b. About 1927 in Hubbard Co., Minnesota, d. 2005

Mary Louise Fuller (daughter):

Residence – Park Rapids, Hubbard Co., Minnesota – April 9, 1930

Occupation – None – April 9, 1930

- o **Jerome Fuller** – b. About 1930 in Todd, Hubbard Co., Minnesota

Earl Vincent Fuller (son):

Residence – Park Rapids, Hubbard Co., Minnesota – June 10, 1895

June 1, 1900

June 1905

April 23, 1910

June 5, 1917

January 3, 1920

April 9, 1930

Occupation – None Listed – June 10, 1895

June 1905

At School – June 1, 1900

Salesman, On Road – April 23, 1910

Hardware Merchant – June 5, 1917

Salesman, Hardware – January 3, 1920

President, Fishing Tackle Shop – April 9, 1930

Home Data for 1930 – Rental, $ 40 a month, has radio set, not on a farm

Eugenie Agnes Loiselle (daughter-in-law):

Residence – Park Rapids, Hubbard Co., Minnesota – April 9, 1930

Occupation – None – April 9, 1930

● **Florence Irene Fuller**, b. 30 Dec 1890 in Park Rapids, Hubbard Co., Minnesota, d. 1 Dec 1972 in

Seattle, King Co., Washington & **Simon Stanley McMahon**, b. 27 Apr 1887 in White Bear Lake,

Ramsey or Washington Co., Minnesota, d. 16 Apr 1944 in Seattle, King Co., Washington – 7 Jun

1919 in Duluth, St. Louis Co., Minnesota

Signatures:

(Signature or mark)

(Registrant's signature)

   o   John Earl McMahon – b. 2 Jul 1920 in Itasca Co., Minnesota, d. 14 Dec 1997 in Washington

John Earl McMahon (son):

Residence – Bellevue, King Co.., Washington – April 14, 1930

Occupation – None – April 14, 1930

   o   Francis Jerome McMahon – b. 9 Mar 1922 in Itasca Co., Minnesota

Francis Jerome McMahon (son):

Residence – Bellevue, King Co., Washington – April 14, 1930

Occupation – None – April 14, 1930

   o   Carol McMahon

Florence Irene Fuller (daughter):

Residence – Park Rapids, Hubbard Co., Minnesota – June 10, 1895

June 1, 1900

June 1905

April 23, 1910

Grand Rapids, Itasca Co., Minnesota – January 23ʳᵈ & 24ᵗʰ, 1920

Bellevue, King Co., Washington – April 14, 1930

Occupation – None Listed – June 10, 1895

June 1905

At School – June 1, 1900

Teacher, School – April 23, 1910

None – January 23ʳᵈ & 24ᵗʰ, 1920

April 14, 1930

Simon Stanley McMahon (son-in-law):

    Residence – Grand Rapids, Itasca Co., Minnesota – June 5, 1917

                                January 23rd & 24th, 1920

        Bellevue, King Co., Washington – April 14, 1930

        Seattle, King Co., Washington – 1942

    Occupation – Assistant County Treasurer – June 5, 1917

        Insurance Agent, Life Insurance – January 23rd & 24th, 1920

        Retail Druggist, Drug Store – April 14, 1930

    Home Data for 1930 – Owns home, valued at $ 2, 500, has radio set, not on a farm

- **Paul Arnold Fuller** – b. 9 Feb 1896 in Park Rapids, Hubbard Co., Minnesota, d. 9 Feb 1896 in Park Rapids, Hubbard Co., Minnesota

- **Milton Jerome Fuller**, b. 30 Nov 1897 in Todd, Hubbard Co., Minnesota, d. 28 Oct 1963 in Los Angeles, Los Angles Co., California & **Winifred Klopfer**, b. 5 Mar 1901 in Staples, Minnesota, d. 9 Jul 1999 in Port Townsend, Washington

  - **Sally Ann Fuller** – b. About 1929 in Devil's Lake, Ramsey Co., North Dakota, d. 1978

Sally Ann Fuller (daughter):

    Residence – Devil's Lake, Ramsey Co., North Dakota – April 24, 1930

    Occupation – None – April 24, 1930

Milton Jerome Fuller (son):

    Residence – Park Rapids, Hubbard Co., Minnesota – June 1, 1900

                          June 1905

                          April 23, 1910

                          January 3, 1920

        Devil's Lake, Ramsey Co., North Dakota – April 24, 1930

    Occupation – None Listed – June 1, 1900

                      June 1905

        None – April 23, 1910

        Agent, Real Estate – January 3, 1920

        Travelling Salesman, Farm Machinery – April 24, 1930

    Home Date for 1930 – Rental, $ 60 a month, has radio set, not on a farm

Winifred Klopfer (daughter-in-law):

    Residence – Devil's Lake, Ramsey Co., North Dakota – April 24, 1930

    Occupation – None – April 24, 1930

Elisha Calkins & Anna Dalrymple Descendants

Frank Alvah Fuller (son):

Residence – Union, Johnson Co., Iowa – 1856

Township 108 Range 12 (Elgin), Wabasha Co., Minnesota – October 31, 1857

Minneiska, Wabasha Co., Minnesota – July 13, 1870

May 1, 1875

Rothsay, Wilkin Co., Minnesota – June 2, 1885

Park Rapids, Hubbard Co., Minnesota – June 10, 1895

June 1, 1900

June 1905

April 23, 1910

Occupation – None Listed – 1856

October 31, 1857

Community Laborer – July 13, 1870

Hardware Merchant – June 10, 1895

June 1, 1900

June 1905

April 23, 1910

Obituary –

"F. A. Fuller, Pioneer merchant called at Conclusion of a Life Well Spent He passed Quietly From the Home Scenes. F. A. Fuller died at his home in Park Rapids early Wednesday morning. For several days he had been in a serious condition and his death caused no surprise to those who knew what he had been suffering since he returned home from the west. Mr. Fuller went to the coast during the winter, remaining there until the severe part of the winter had passed, but while there was taken sick and had returned home. He received treatment in a city hospital for several weeks returning here, but the doctors were unable to give him any encouragement, and he gradually grew worse. He was able to be up and about in his home until just two or three days before he died. Early Wednesday morning he asked to be assisted to an easy chair where he could be more comfortable, and while lying there fell asleep. From this sleep he never awakened, but quietly and peacefully passed to the great beyond. F. A. Fuller was born January 30, 1855 in Chautauqua county, New York, near White Plains. He moved with his parents to Iowa, and later to Minnieski [Minneiska], Minnesota, where he spent his boyhood days and grew to young manhood. On January 10, 1881 he was married to Miss Joanna E. Sheehan, at Wabasha, and then moved to Rothsay, MN where he engaged in the grain and lumber business for about ten years. In June 1892, Mr. Fuller moved to Park Rapids, buying out Mr. Churchill, of the firm Churchill and Denning, and later bought out Mr. Denning. He continued in the hardware business until about three years ago, when he was succeeded by his son, Earl V. Fuller. He has been honored by being elected a member of the village council in past years, and for about 22 years was a member of the school board, of which he served as president for several years past, holding that office at the time of his death. He was a member of the M. W. A. and was sent by the local lodge as a delegate to the national convention at Little Rock, Arkansas, in 1911. Mr. Fuller was a man who enjoyed most happy home relation, in fact his home life and the relation between himself and the members of his household appeared

195

to be as near to ideal as is ever seen, and few can realize how he will be missed by members of his family. He is survived by seven children, four boys and five girls, also a brother, F. D. Fuller of Nevis and one sister, Mrs. G. M. Comie [Cowie], of Lovejoy, Montana. His wife died in 1912. The funeral services will be held on Friday morning at 9:30 o'clock, from St. Peter's Catholic Church and internment will be made in the Catholic cemetery." from The Enterprise.   July 29. 1915

Johanna Elizabeth Sheehan (daughter-in-law):

   Residence – Rothsay, Wilkin Co., Minnesota – June 3, 1885

      Park Rapids, Hubbard Co., Minnesota – June 10, 1895

                  June 1, 1900

                  June 1905

                  April 23, 1910

   Occupation – House Wife – June 10, 1895

      None Listed – June 1, 1900

         June 1905

     None – April 23, 1910

- **Sarah Jane Fuller**, b. 28 Mar 1865 in Iowa, d. 11 Jun 1939 in Great Falls, Cascade Co., Montana & **George M. Cowie**, b. 10 Nov 1856 in Glencoe, Buffalo Co., Wisconsin, d. Aug 1931 in Rothsay, Wilkin Co., Minnesota – 17 Jun 1885 in Marshall Co., Minnesota

  - **Leslie Donald Cowie**, b. 12 May 1886 in Minnesota, d. 4 Mar 1978 in Great Falls, Cascade Co., Montana & **Thelma Virginia Rennix**, b. 11 Jun 1894 in West Virginia, d. 12 Dec 1921 in Wilkin Co., Minnesota

I HAVE VERIFIED ABOVE ANSWERS AND THAT THEY ARE TRUE

Signature:

  - o **Alvis Donald Cowie**, b. 3 Nov 1912, d. 3 Sep 1966 in Great Falls, Cascade Co., Montana & **Bess Lund**

    - **Rex Cowie**

    - **Ronnie Cowie**

Alvis Donald Cowie (son):

   Residence – Rothsay, Wilkin Co., Minnesota – January 20, 1920

      Great Falls, Cascade Co., Montana – April 21, 1930

   Occupation – None – January 20, 1920

      April 21, 1930

Leslie Donald Cowie (son):

    Residence – Rothsay, Wilkin Co., Minnesota – June 2, 1900

                          June 6th & 7th, 1905

                          September 12, 1918

                          January 20, 1920

        Rutland, Sargent Co., North Dakota – April 16, 1910

    Occupation – At School – June 2, 1900

        Private School Teacher – June 6th & 7th, 1905

        Telegraph Operator, Railroad – April 16, 1910

        Assistant Postmaster, U.S. – September 12, 1918

        Station Agent, Railroad – January 20, 1920

Thelma Virginia Rennix (daughter-in-law):

    Residence – Rothsay, Wilkin Co., Minnesota – September 12, 1918

                          January 20, 1920

    Occupation – None – January 20, 1920

- **Ethel Beatrice Cowie**, b. 30 Apr 1888 in Minnesota, d. 6 Nov 1977 in Great Falls, Cascade Co., Montana & **Andrew Jackson Caldwell**, b. 8 Jun 1890 in Weiser, Washington Co., Idaho, d. 7 Jul 1963 in Great Falls, Cascade Co., Montana

Signature:

        o John B. Caldwell – b. 14 Oct 1921 in Montana

John B. Caldwell (son):

    Residence – Great Falls, Cascade Co., Montana – April 20, 1930

    Occupation – None – April 20, 1930

        o Doris Jane Caldwell – b. 22 Apr 1924 in Montana

Doris Jane Caldwell (daughter):

    Residence – Great Falls, Cascade Co., Montana – April 20, 1930

    Occupation – None – April 20, 1930

Ethel Beatrice Cowie (daughter):

    Residence – Rothsay, Wilkin Co., Minnesota – June 2, 1900

                          June 6th & 7th, 1905

                          April 20, 1910

        Great Falls, Cascade Co., Montana – April 20, 1930

    Occupation – At School – June 2, 1900

        School Teacher – June 6th & 7th, 1905

197

Hurst

Teacher, Public School – April 20, 1910

None – April 20, 1930

Andrew Jackson Caldwell (son-in-law):

Residence – Montana – June 5, 1917

Great Falls, Cascade Co., Montana – April 20, 1930

Occupation – Farmer – June 5, 1917

Agent, Insurance – April 20, 1930

Home Data for 1930 – Rental, $ 55 a month, has radio set, not on a farm

• **Robert Sheldon Cowie**, b. 4 Mar 1890 in Rothsay, Wilkin Co., Minnesota, d. 22 Jan 1964 in Rothsay, Wilkin Co., Minnesota & **Irene Theoline Skugrud**, b. 17 Sep 1898 in Akron, Wilkin Co., Minnesota, d. 31 May 1957 in Rothsay, Wilkin Co., Minnesota – 30 Jun 1920 in Wilkin Co., Minnesota

that I have verified above answers and that they are true.

Signature:

o **Robert Sheldon Cowie** – b. 14 Aug 1926 in Rothsay, Wilkin Co., Minnesota, d. 15 Aug 1980 in Rothsay, Wilkin Co., Minnesota

Robert Sheldon Cowie (son):

Residence – Rothsay, Wilkin Co., Minnesota – April 12, 1930

Occupation – None – April 12, 1930

Robert Sheldon Cowie (son):

Residence – Rothsay, Wilkin Co., Minnesota – June 2, 1900

June 6th & 7th, 1905

April 20, 1910

1917

January 21, 1920

April 12, 1930

Occupation – At School – June 2, 1900

None Listed – June 6th & 7th, 1905

None – April 20, 1910

Post Master – 1917

Post Master, Office – January 21, 1920

Editor, Newspaper – April 12, 1930

Home Data for 1930 – Owns home, valued at $ 3, 000, has radio set, not on a farm

Irene Theoline Skrugrud (daughter-in-law):

> *Residence – Rothsay, Wilkin Co., Minnesota – January 21, 1920*
>
> > *April 12, 1930*
>
> *Occupation – Clerk, Post Office – January 21, 1920*
>
> > *None – April 12, 1930*

- **George Carlton Cowie**, b. 5 Jan 1892 in Minnesota, d. 7 May 1973 in Great Falls, Cascade Co., Montana & **Mabel E. Laing**

Signature:

- ○ **Mabel Eldora Cowie**, b. 11 Sep 1918 in Seattle, King Co., Washington, d. 13 Apr 1974 in Spokane, Spokane Co., Washington & **Alfred Ray Tedrow**, b. 24 Jan 1904 in Benge, Adams Co., Washington, d. 19 Mar 1968 in Deer Park, Spokane Co., Washington

  - ▪ **Rodney Lee Peterson Tedrow** – b. 20 Sep 1938 in Great Falls, Cascade Co., Montana, d. 7 Aug 2001 in Coupeville, Island Co., Washington

Mabel Eldora Cowie (daughter):

> *Residence – Seattle, King Co., Washington – January 5, 1920*
>
> > *Malta, Phillips Co., Montana – April 4, 1930*
>
> *Occupation – None – January 5, 1920*
>
> > *April 4, 1930*

George Carlton Cowie (son):

> *Residence – Rothsay, Wilkin Co., Minnesota – June 2, 1900*
>
> > *June 6th & 7th, 1905*
> >
> > *April 20, 1910*
>
> *Malta, Phillips Co., Montana – June 5, 1917*
>
> > *April 4, 1930*
>
> *Seattle, King Co., Washington – January 5, 1920*
>
> *Occupation – At School – June 2, 1900*
>
> > *None Listed – June 6th & 7th, 1905*
> >
> > *None – April 20, 1910*
> >
> > *Farmer – June 5, 1917*
> >
> > *Store, Grocery Store – January 5, 1920*
> >
> > *Adjuster, Insurance – April 4, 1930*
>
> *Home Data for 1930 – Owns home, valued at $ 1, 200, no radio set, not on a farm*

Mabel E. Laing (daughter-in-law):

  Residence – Seattle, King Co., Washington – January 5, 1920

    Malta, Phillips Co., Montana – April 4, 1930

  Occupation – None – January 5, 1920

    Teacher, Public School – April 4, 1930

• **Doris Jane Cowie**, b. 4 Apr 1898 in Minnesota & **Albert Burr Morris**, b. 12 Sep 1900 in Montana, d. 25 Dec 1954 in Cascade Co., Montana

Signature:

  o **Betty Lou Morris** – b. 5 Mar 1934

  o **Garnet Lanell Morris** – b. 7 Jan 1937 in Great Falls, Cascade Co., Montana, d. 16 Feb 2004 in Big Sandy, Chouteau Co., Montana

Doris Jane Cowie (daughter):

  Residence – Rothsay, Wilkin Co., Minnesota – June 2, 1900

    June 6th & 7th, 1905

    April 20, 1910

  School District No. 22 & 35, Phillips Co., Montana – February 1920

  School District 171 (Danvers), Fergus Co., Montana – April 8, 1930

  Occupation – None Listed – June 2, 1900

    June 6th & 7th, 1905

  None – April 20, 1910

    February 1920

  Teacher, Graded School – April 8, 1930

  Home Data for 1930 – Rental, $ 8 a month, no radio set, not on a farm

Albert Burr Morris (son-in-law):

  Residence – Square Butte, Chouteau Co., Montana – September 12, 1918

  Occupation – Farm Laborer – September 12, 1918

Sarah Jane Fuller (daughter):

  Residence – Minneiska, Wabasha Co., Minnesota – July 13, 1870

    May 1, 1875

    June 16th & 17th, 1880

  Stephen, Marshall Co., Minnesota – June 17, 1885

  Rothsay, Wilkin Co., Minnesota – June 2, 1900

    June 6th & 7th, 1905

    April 20, 1910

School District No. 22 & 35, Phillips Co., Montana – February 1920

Great Falls, Cascade Co., Montana – April 10, 1930

Occupation – At School – June 16th & 17th, 1880

None Listed – June 2, 1900

June 6th & 7th, 1905

None – April 20, 1910

February 1920

April 10, 1930

Obituary –

"*Mrs. Cowie Dies in Montana. Prominent Pioneer Woman of Wilkin County Dies at Great Falls. Rothsay, June 12. – A message was received from Great Falls, Montana today stating that Mrs. Sarah Cowie, widow of the late Geo. M. Cowie had passed away. Her son, R. S. Cowie, the Rothsay editor and postmaster, was called to Montana a week ago and was with his mother when the end came. Mrs. Cowie is one of the pioneers of Wilkin county. Her husband was Judge of Probate at Breckenridge and later established and became editor of the Rothsay Enterprise. She leaves to mourn her death three sons and two daughters – Leslie of Ulm, Mont., R. S. Cowie of Rothsay; George, Mrs. A. J. Caldwell and Mrs. Burr Morris, all of Great Falls, Montana. The body will be brought here for burial beside her husband." from the Gazette Telegraph. Pg. 1, Col. 8. June 15, 1939*

George M. Cowie (son-in-law):

Residence – Rothsay, Wilkin Co., Minnesota – June 2, 1900

June 6th & 7th, 1905

April 20, 1910

School District No. 22 & 35, Phillips Co., Montana – February 1920

Great Falls, Cascade Co., Montana – April 10, 1930

Occupation – Grain Buyer – June 2, 1900

Editor – June 6th & 7th, 1905

None Listed – April 10, 1910

Farmer, Farm – February 1920

Proprietor, Rooming House – April 10, 1930

Home Data for 1930 – Owns home, valued at $ 3, 000, no radio set, not on a farm

Hurst

Fidelia Lossie Calkins (daughter):

Residence – Arkwright, Chautauqua Co.., New York – August 28, 1850

   Union, Johnson Co., Iowa – 1856

   Township 108 Range 12 (Elgin), Wabasha Co., Minnesota – October 31, 1857

   Minneiska, Wabasha Co., Minnesota – July 13, 1870

        1874

        May 1, 1875

        June 16th & 17th, 1880

        June 30, 1885

   Elgin, Wabasha Co., Minnesota – June 1, 1865

   Rothsay, Wilkin Co., Minnesota – July 13, 1895

        June 2, 1900

        June 6th & 7th, 1905

Occupation – None Listed – August 28, 1850

        1856

        October 31, 1857

        June 2, 1900

        June 6th & 7th, 1905

   Keeping House – July 13, 1870

        June 16th & 17th, 1880

   Warehouse Clerk – 1874

Obituary –

"In Memoriam. Mrs. Fidelia L. Fuller was born in Chitaqua [Chautauqua] county, New York in July 1830, her maiden name being Fidelia L. Calkins. She was married to Carlton W. Fuller in May, 1846. This union was blessed with three children, Fred D. and Frank A. Fuller, of Park Rapids, and Mrs. G. M. Cowie, of Rothsay. In 1858 they came west and settled at Minneiska, Wabasha county, thus being among the very early settlers of the state. In 1886 the deceased with her husband came to Rothsay in order to pass their declining years near their children, two of whom were married and residing here at that time. Since the death of her husband, which occurred in October 1894, she has made her home with her daughter, Mrs. G. M. Cowie, in this village, at whose home she peacefully passed away Friday, May 15, 1908 at 1:30 o'clock p. m. "Smooth the locks of silver hair, On our mother's brow with tenderest care, Gather the robe in final fold Around the form so still and cold; Lay on her bosom, pure as snow, The fairest, sweetest flowers that grow. Kiss her and leave her our heart's delight; Her pain is o'er, she sleeps tonight." After a long, busy and useful life she died as she lived – honored, trusted and loved. She reared her own monument while she lived in the hearts of all who knew her. Her life was completed if work all done and well done constitutes completion. Her Christian life was beautiful from its beginning to its close, and through all the trials and sorrows that she met in the way, her faith in God never wavered But she has left us to-day the sun shines upon another grave that hides from out sight all that is mortal of a true and noble woman. "So He giveth His beloved sleep." Her children and her

202

grandchildren shall rise up and call her blessed." Her son F. A. Fuller, arrives on Friday afternoon's local only a few hours after her death. Mrs. F. A. Fuller and Fred D. Fuller, arrived Saturday evening and all remained for the funeral, which took place Monday afternoon at 2 o'clock from the Methodist church, Rev. R. P. Hanaman, of Barnesville, officiating. The church was handsomely decorated with potted plants and the casket was covered with a profusion of wreaths and bouquets of beautiful cut flowers, the last sweet offerings of relatives and loving friends. Her remains was laid to rest in the South cemetery beside those of her long departed husband. Card of Thanks – To the dear friends and neighbors who so kindly assisted us in life's greatest trial, and those who deftly wove together the beautiful flowers, we tender our sincere thanks. Mrs. G. M. Cowie, F. A. Fuller, F. D. Fuller and families." from the Rothsay Enterprise. Pg. 2, Col. 2. May 23, 1908

Carlton Washington Fuller (son-in-law):

Residence – Arkwright, Chautauqua Co., New York – August 28, 1850

Union, Johnson Co., Iowa – 1856

Township 108 Range 12 (Elgin), Wabasha Co., Minnesota – October 31, 1857

Minneiska, Wabasha Co., Minnesota – July 13, 1870

1874

May 1, 1875

June 16th & 17th, 1880

June 30, 1885

Elgin, Wabasha Co., Minnesota – June 1, 1865

Occupation – Farmer – August 28, 1850

1856

October 31, 1857

Community Laborer – July 13, 1870

Warehouse Clerk – 1874

Laborer – June 16th & 17th, 1880

Value of Real Estate – $ 200 – July 13, 1870

Obituaries –

"Died. Fuller – at his home in this village, October 18th, 1894, of heart failure, Carlton W. Fuller, aged 68 years, 5 months and 23 days. The deceased was born in Arkwright, Chataqua [Chautauqua] county, N. Y., April 25th, 1826. On May 28th, 1846, he was married to Miss Fidelia L. Calkins, who with two sons, Frank A. and Fred D. Fuller, of Park Rapids, Minn., and one daughter, Mrs. G. M. Cowie, of this village, survive to mourn the loss of a devoted husband and loving father. Mr. Fuller spent the first thirty years of his life in his native state, coming west to Illinois in 1856, where he resided two years, then moved to Minneiska, Wabasha county, Minn., thus becoming one of the very early settlers of this state, within the limits of which he resided for more than 36 years. The last eight years of his life were spent here, in Rothsay, where he at all times commanded the highest respect and warmest of friendship among all ages and classes. Few men are constituted with a more sturdy character, or a higher appreciation of honor and courtesy in their dealings and intercourse with their fellows than were daily

exhibited in his life. A clear conscience, and a pure heart permitted him to meet death trustfully and in peace. The funeral occurred on Saturday, the 20ᵗʰ, from the house, Rev. W. V. Dunton of the M. E. church officiating, and was attended by a large concourse of relatives and friends, who followed the remains to the cemetery south of the village, where the burial occurred. Card of Thanks – To the many citizens of Rothsay who so generously lent assistance in our late days of trial, incident to the illness and death of our husband and father, we wish to extend our heartfelt gratitude and thanks. Mrs. C. W. Fuller. F. A. Fuller. Mrs. G. M. Cowie." from the Rothsay Enterprise. Pg 1, Col. 4. October 27, 1894 and from the Wilkin County Gazette. Pg. 1, Col. 5. November 2, 1894

○ **Lois Margaret Calkins**, b. About 1832 in Arkwright, Chautauqua Co., New York, d. After 1901 in North Dakota & **William Towne**, b. May 1829 in New York, d. 1904 in Fingal, Barnes Co., North Dakota – Between 1850 – 1857 in Arkwright, Chautauqua Co., New York

Signatures:

▪ **Lois Margaret Towne** – Between 1864 – 1866 in Elgin, Wabasha Co., Minnesota

▪ **Minnie Warren Wirt** (Adopted Child), b. 10 Jun 1877 in St. Paris, Ohio, d. 6 Dec 1942 in Fingal, Barnes Co., North Dakota & **Julius Oscar Thone**, b. 26 Feb 1874 in Iowa, d. 23 Nov 1954 in Fingal, Barnes Co., North Dakota – 1897 in North Dakota

Signature:

● **Unknown Thone** – b. After 1897 in North Dakota, d. Before 1910 in North Dakota

● **Evaline Thone**, b. Aug 1899 in North Dakota & **Art Carter**

Evaline Thone (daughter):

Residence – Clifton, Cass Co., North Dakota – June 14, 1900

Binghamton, Barnes Co., North Dakota – June 9, 1910

1915

February 2, 1920

Occupation – None Listed – June 14, 1900

None – June 9, 1910

February 2, 1920

- **Violet Thone**, b. 11 Jun 1903 in Fingal, Barnes Co., North Dakota, d. Apr 1974 in Aberdeen, Brown Co., South Dakota & **Jack Gallipo**

Violet Thone (daughter):

Residence – Binghamton, Barnes Co., North Dakota – June 9, 1910

1915

February 2, 1920

Occupation – None – June 9, 1910

February 2, 1920

- **Oscar Thone** – b. 21 Apr 1906 in Fingal, Barnes Co., North Dakota, d. 20 Oct 1963 in Dunseith, Rolette Co., North Dakota

Oscar Thone (son):

Residence – Binghamton, Barnes Co., North Dakota – June 9, 1910

1915

February 2, 1920

Fingal, Barnes Co., North Dakota – 1925

Occupation – None – June 9, 1910

February 2, 1920

- **Marjorie Thone**, b. 7 Nov 1911 in Fingal, Barnes Co., North Dakota, d. Jun 1985 in Roslyn, Day Co., South Dakota & **John Hanson**

Marjorie Thone (daughter):

Residence – Binghamton, Barnes Co., North Dakota – 1915

February 2, 1920

Fingal, Barnes Co., North Dakota – 1925

April 3, 1930

Occupation – None – February 2, 1920

April 3, 1930

- **Royal Francis Thone** – b. 1 Feb 1915 in Fingal, Barnes Co., North Dakota, d. 20 Dec 1964 in Flathead, Flathead Co., Montana

Royal Francis Thone (son):

Residence – Binghamton, Barnes Co., North Dakota – 1915

February 2, 1920

Fingal, Barnes Co., North Dakota – 1925

Hurst

April 3, 1930

Occupation – None – February 2, 1920

April 3, 1930

- **Muriel Thone**, b. 12 Dec 1917 in Fingal, Barnes Co., North Dakota, d. 14 Jun 1987 in Las Vegas, Clark Co., Nevada & **Bob Powell**

Muriel Thone (daughter):

    Residence – Binghamton, Barnes Co., North Dakota – February 2, 1920

        Fingal, Barnes Co., North Dakota – 1925

                April 3, 1930

    Occupation – None – February 2, 1920

        April 3, 1930

Minnie Warren Wirt (step-daughter):

    Residence – Clifton, Cass Co., North Dakota – June 14, 1900

        Binghamton, Barnes Co., North Dakota – June 9, 1910

                1915

                February 2, 1920

        Fingal, Barnes Co., North Dakota – September 12, 1918

                1925

                April 3, 1930

    Occupation – None Listed – June 14, 1900

        None – June 9, 1910

            February 2, 1920

        April 3, 1930

Julius Oscar Thone (son-in-law):

    Residence – Clifton, Cass Co., North Dakota – June 14, 1900

        Binghamton, Barnes Co., North Dakota – June 9, 1910

                1915

                February 2, 1920

        Fingal, Barnes Co., North Dakota – September 12, 1918

                1925

                April 3, 1930

    Occupation – Farmer – June 14, 1900

        Diary – June 9, 1910

        Manager, Standard Oil Co. – September 12, 1918

        Salesman, Standard Oil Company – February 2, 1920

        Agent, Standard Oil – April 3, 1930

206

Elisha Calkins & Anna Dalrymple Descendants

Home Date for 1930 – Owns home, valued at $ 1, 000, no radio set, not on a farm

Lois Margaret Calkins (daughter):

Residence – Arkwright, Chautauqua Co., New York – August 27, 1850

Township 108 Range 12 (Elgin), Wabasha Co., Minnesota – October 28, 1857

Elgin, Wabasha Co., Minnesota – June 21, 1860

June 1, 1865

July 7, 1870

May 1, 1875

Township 1387 Range 55 W, Cass Co., North Dakota – June 28, 1880

Occupation – None Listed – August 27, 1850

October 28, 1857

June 21, 1860

Keeping House – July 7, 1870

June 28, 1880

William Towne (son-in-law):

Residence – Township 108 Range 12 (Elgin), Wabasha Co., Minnesota – October 28, 1857

Elgin, Wabasha Co., Minnesota – June 21, 1860

July 1, 1863

June 1, 1865

July 7, 1870

1874

May 1, 1875

Township 1387 Range 55 W, Cass Co., North Dakota – June 28, 1880

Clifton, Cass Co., North Dakota – June 14, 1900

Occupation – Farmer – October 28, 1857

July 1, 1863

July 7, 1870

June 28, 1880

None Listed – June 21, 1860

Farmer & Stock Dealer – 1874

None Listed – June 14, 1900

Real of Real Estate – $ 1, 600 – June 21, 1860

$ 4, 500 – July 7, 1870

Value of Personal Estate – $ 500 – June 21, 1860

$ 1, 200 – July 7, 1870

o **William Riley Calkins**, b. 23 Jul 1834 in Arkwright, Chautauqua Co., New York, d. 12 Jan 1907 in Lone Rock, Moody Co., South Dakota & **Mary Etta Perry**, b. 16 Mar 1847 in Arkwright, Chautauqua Co., New York, d. 12 Oct 1912 in Pipestone, Pipestone Co., Minnesota – 1 Dec 1861 in Plainview, Wabasha Co., Minnesota

Signatures:

  ▪ **Ernest Nelson Calkins** – b. 12 Sep 1862 in Plainview, Wabasha Co., Minnesota, d. 1923 in Cherokee, Cherokee Co., Iowa

Signature:

Ernest Nelson Calkins (son):

Residence – Elgin, Wabasha Co., Minnesota – June 1, 1865

July 7, 1870

Pebble Precinct, Dodge Co., Nebraska – June 16, 1880

Scribner, Dodge Co., Nebraska – June 22, 1885

Spring Creek, Moody Co., South Dakota – June 4th & 4th, 1900

Flandreau, Moody Co., South Dakota – 1905

Ryder, Ward Co., North Dakota – May 7, 1910

January 19, 1920

Occupation – At Home – July 7, 1870

June 16, 1880

None Listed – June 22, 1885

Farmer – June 4th & 5th, 1900

Mechanic – 1905

Own Income – May 7, 1910

Farmer, General Farm – January 19, 1920

Obituary –

"Death of Ernest Calkins. Flandreau Enterprise: Ernest N. Calkins passed away last Wednesday at the hospital in Cherokee, Iowa, where he was operated on for a cancer of the throat. The remains were shipped here and internment took place Sunday afternoon at 2:30. Services were held at the M. E. church and were conducted by Rev. C. S. Lyles, pastor of the church. The

Elisha Calkins & Anna Dalrymple Descendants

Odd Fellows acted as an escort to Union Cemetery. Ernest Nelson Calkins was born in Plainview, Minnesota, Sept. 12, 1862. His parents were early settlers of Dodge County, Neb. Ernest came to Moody County in 1891, and farms in the Spring Creek neighborhood, until six years ago, when he bought a farm in North Dakota. He made his home while in Moody county with his sister Clara, the wife of L. E. Claflin. His parents came to Moody county in 1898. His father died on Jan. 12, 1907. His mother died Oct. 12, 1912. Ernest Calkins leaves the following brothers and sister: Lora Calkins of Neal, Neb.; Delbert Calkins of Friendship, Wisconsin; Clara, the wife of L. E. Claflin of Flandreau; Werdna Calkins of Flandreau; Floyd Calkins of Pipestone County, Minn.; and Arthur Calkins of Pipestone, Minn. He was a member of the I. O. O. F. of Flandreau. For some time he was superintendant of the Spring Creek Sunday school under the ministry of Rev. Arms." **from the Moody County Enterprise, 1923**

- **Lora Deloss Calkins**, b. 15 May 1864 in Plainview, Wabasha Co., Minnesota, d. 16 Feb 1930 in O'Neill, Holt Co., Nebraska & **Eva Estella Dickinson**, b. 10 Aug 1874 in Ironville, Boyd Co., Kentucky, d. 9 Nov 1928 in Liberty, Woodbury Co., Iowa – 27 Oct 1898 in Inman, Holt Co., Nebraska

  - **Walter Ozias Calkins**, b. 8 Sep 1899 in O'Neill, Holt Co., Nebraska, d. 27 Mar 1955 in O'Neill, Holt Co., Nebraska & **Lettie Mae Strong**, b. 31 Oct 1911 in Pierce, Pierce Co., Nebraska, d. 18 Jul 2001 in Fremont, Dodge Co., Nebraska – 17 Oct 1927 in Salix, Woodbury Co., Iowa

    - **Raymond O. Calkins** – b. 1 Jul 1928 in O'Neill, Holt Co., Nebraska, d. 12 Dec 2003 in Genoa, Nance Co., Nebraska

Raymond O. Calkins (son):

Residence – O'Neill, Holt Co., Nebraska – 1930

Occupation – None – 1930

    - Unknown Calkins

Walter Ozias Calkins (son):

Residence – Union, Moody Co., South Dakota – June 15, 1900

Spring Creek, Moody Co., South Dakota – 1905

Inman, Holt Co., Nebraska – April 28th & 29th, 1910

Gratton, Holt Co., Nebraska – January 19, 1920

O'Neill, Holt Co., Nebraska – 1930

Occupation – None Listed – June 15, 1900

1905

None – April 28th & 29th, 1910

Laborer, Teamster – January 19, 1920

Laborer, Railroad – 1930

Home Data for 1930 – Rental, $ 6 a month, no radio set, not on a farm

Hurst

Lettie Mae Strong (daughter-in-law):

   Residence – O'Neill, Holt Co., Nebraska – 1930

   Occupation – None – 1930

- **Chester Arthur Calkins**, b. 8 Dec 1900 in O'Neill, Holt Co., Nebraska, d. 7 Mar 1952 in O'Neill, Holt Co., Nebraska & **Hazel Frances Tarpenning**, b. 24 Sep 1903 in Bartlett, Wheeler Co., Nebraska, d. Aug 1971 in Cassville, Barry Co., Missouri – 19 Oct 1924 in Salix, Woodbury Co., Iowa

  - **Harold Lenard Calkins** – b. 24 Sep 1925 in Holt Co., Nebraska, d. 16 Nov 2008 in Gun Barrel City, Texas

  - **Ima Jean Calkins** – b. 6 Aug 1929 in O'Neill, Holt Co., Nebraska, d. 26 Jul 2009 in Cassville, Barry Co., Missouri

  - **Donald Lora Calkins** – b. 6 Feb 1934

Chester Arthur Calkins (son):

   Residence – Spring Creek, Moody Co., South Dakota – 1905

       Inman, Holt Co., Nebraska – April 28th & 29th, 1910

       Gratton, Holt Co., Nebraska – January 19, 1920

   Occupation – None Listed – 1905

       None – April 28th & 29th, 1910

       Cook, at Café – January 19, 1920

- **Mary Etta Calkins**, b. About 1902 in Nebraska & **David Robare**, b. 17 Mar 1901 in Iowa, d. Oct 1964 in Omaha, Douglas Co., Nebraska

  - **Edward Robare** – b. 1921 in Nebraska

Edward Robare (son):

   Residence – Salix, Woodbury Co., Iowa – April 2, 1930

   Occupation – None – April 2, 1930

Mary Etta Calkins (daughter):

   Residence – Inman, Holt Co., Nebraska – April 28th & 29th, 1910

       Gratton, Holt Co., Nebraska – January 19, 1920

       Salix, Woodbury Co., Iowa – April 2, 1930

   Occupation – None – April 28th & 29th, 1910

       January 19, 1920

       April 2, 1930

Elisha Calkins & Anna Dalrymple Descendants

David Robare (son-in-law):

Residence – Salix, Woodbury Co., Iowa – April 2, 1930

Occupation – Driver, Truck Driver – April 2, 1930

Home Data for 1930 – Rental, $ 8 a month, has radio set, not on a farm

- **Nellie Esther Calkins**, b. About 1903 in Holt Co., Nebraska & **James H. Harkins**, b. 25 Aug 1895 in Nebraska, d. 13 Feb 1960 in Los Angeles Co., California

  o **Robert James Harkins** – b. 25 Jun 1929 in Moville, Woodbury Co., Iowa, d. 27 Sep 2000 in Sioux City, Woodbury Co., Iowa

Robert James Harkins (son):

Residence – Moville, Woodbury Co., Iowa – April 5, 1930

Occupation – None – April 5, 1930

Nellie Calkins (daughter):

Residence – Inman, Holt Co., Nebraska – April 28th & 29th, 1910

Gratton, Holt Co., Nebraska – January 19, 1920

Moville, Woodbury Co., Iowa – April 5, 1930

Occupation – None – April 28th & 29th, 1910

January 19, 1920

April 5, 1930

James H. Harkins (son-in-law):

Residence – Moville, Woodbury Co., Iowa – April 5, 1930

Occupation – Harness Maker, Shop – April 5, 1930

Home Data for 1930 – Rental, $ 15 a month, no radio set, not on a farm

- **Lora Deloss Calkins**, b. 26 Jul 1906 in Arlie, Minnehaha Co., South Dakota, d. 10 Jan 1935 in O'Neill, Holt Co., Nebraska & **Lottie Mary Strong**, b. 31 Aug 1909 in Nebraska – 17 Dec 1927 in Holt Co., Nebraska

  o **Raymond O. Calkins** – b. 1 Jul 1928 in O'Neill, Holt Co., Nebraska, d. 12 Dec 2003 in Genoa, Nance Co., Nebraska

Raymond O. Calkins (son):

Residence – O'Neill, Holt Co., Nebraska – 1930

Occupation – None – 1930

  o **Joan Janet Calkins** – b. 2 Feb 1933 in O'Neill, Holt Co., Nebraska, d. 22 Nov 2007 in Ewing, Holt Co., Nebraska

  o **Donna Rae Calkins**

Lora Deloss Calkins (son):

    Residence – Inman, Holt Co., Nebraska – April 28th & 29th, 1910

        Gratton, Holt Co., Nebraska – January 19, 1920

        O'Neill, Holt Co., Nebraska – 1930

    Occupation – None – April 28th & 29th, 1910

        January 19, 1920

        Laborer, Railroad – 1930

    Home Data for 1930 – Rental, $ 6 a month, no radio set, not on a farm

Lottie Mary Strong (daughter-in-law):

    Residence –O'Neill, Holt Co., Nebraska – 1930

    Occupation – None – 1930

- **Frank Calkins** – b. 11 Nov 1908 in Holt Co., Nebraska, d. Before 1920 in Holt Co., Nebraska

Frank Calkins (son):

    Residence – Inman, Holt Co., Nebraska – April 28th & 29th, 1910

    Occupation – None – April 28th & 29th, 1910

- **Fred Har Calkins**, b. 9 Sep 1910 in Holt Co., Nebraska, d. 15 Oct 1985 in Portland, Multnomah Co., Oregon & **Lola M. Stauffer**, b. 1918 in Nebraska – 1 May 1937 in Union Co., South Dakota

  - Jane Calkins

  - Jack Calkins

  - Jim Calkins

Fred Har Calkins (son):

    Residence – Gratton, Holt Co., Nebraska – January 19, 1920

        Sioux City, Woodbury Co., Iowa – May 1, 1937

    Occupation – Laborer, with rounding horses – January 19, 1920

Lola M. Stauffer (daughter-in-law):

    Residence – Sioux City, Woodbury Co., Iowa – May 1, 1937

Lora Deloss Calkins (son):

    Residence – Elgin, Wabasha Co., Minnesota – June 1, 1865

        July 7, 1870

        Pebble Precinct, Dodge Co., Nebraska – June 16, 1880

        McClure Precinct, Holt Co., Nebraska – June 26, 1885

        Union, Moody Co., South Dakota – June 15, 1900

        Spring Creek, Moody Co., South Dakota – 1905

        Inman, Holt Co., Nebraska – April 28th & 29th, 1910

        Gratton, Holt Co., Nebraska – January 19, 1920

Occupation – At Home – July 7, 1870

June 16, 1880

None Listed – June 26, 1885

Farmer – June 15, 1900

1905

Carpenter, House – April 28th & 29th, 1910

None – January 19, 1920

Eva Estella Dickinson (daughter-in-law):

Residence – Union, Moody Co., South Dakota – June 15, 1900

Spring Creek, Moody Co., South Dakota – 1905

Inman, Holt Co., Nebraska – April 28th, 29th, 1910

Gratton, Holt Co., Nebraska – January 19, 1920

Occupation – None Listed – June 15, 1900

Housewife – 1905

None – April 28th & 29th, 1910

Laborer, Baling Hay – January 19, 1920

- **Martha M. Calkins** – b. 2 Jun 1867 in Wabasha Co., Minnesota, d. 8 Nov 1878 in Pebble, Dodge Co., Nebraska

Martha M. Calkins (daughter):

Residence – Elgin, Wabasha Co., Minnesota – July 7, 1870

Occupation – At Home – July 7, 1870

- **Delbert C. Calkins**, b. 19 Oct 1871 in Nebraska, d. 21 Aug 1938 in Big Flats, Adams Co., Wisconsin & **Maud P. Brott**, b. 28 Jul 1882 in Barren Co., Wisconsin, d. 28 Jul 1912 in Pipestone, Pipestone Co., Minnesota – Between 1901 – 1902 in South Dakota

  - **Grace L. Calkins**, b. 24 Mar 1903 in Brookings, Brookings Co., South Dakota, d. 22 Jan 1967 in Adams Co., Wisconsin & **Alfred William Maffett**, b. 23 Jun 1902 in Preston, Adams Co., Wisconsin, d. Between 1944 – 1945 in Preston, Adams Co., Wisconsin – 26 Feb 1923

    - **Robert Alfred Maffett** – b. 26 Apr 1923 in Preston, Adams Co., Wisconsin, d. 24 Jun 1998 in Preston, Adams Co., Wisconsin

Robert Alfred Maffett (son):

Residence – Preston, Adams Co., Wisconsin – April 23, 1930

Occupation – None – April 23, 1930

Hurst

○ **Ruby Maffett** – b. 1925 in Preston, Adams Co., Wisconsin

Ruby Maffett (daughter):

   Residence – Preston, Adams Co., Wisconsin – April 23, 1930

   Occupation – None – April 23, 1930

○ **Erwin W. Maffett** – b. 30 Dec 1931, d. 6 Jun 2005 in Sioux City, Woodbury Co., Iowa

Grace L. Calkins (daughter):

   Residence – Richfield, Adams Co., Wisconsin – June 1, 1905

                          January 12th, 13th & 15th, 1920

         Preston, Adams Co., Wisconsin – April 29, 1910

                          April 23, 1930

   Occupation – None Listed – June 1, 1905

         None – April 29, 1910

              January 12th, 13th, & 15th, 1920

         April 23, 1930

Alfred William Maffett (son-in-law):

   Residence – Preston, Adams Co., Wisconsin – April 23, 1930

   Occupation – Farmer, General Farm – April 12, 1930

   Home Data for 1930 – Rental, no radio set, not on a farm

● **Violet Mildred Calkins** – b. Between 1909 – 1910 in Preston, Adams Co., Wisconsin, d. 19 May 1910 in Adams Co., Wisconsin

Violet Mildred Calkins (daughter):

   Residence – Preston, Adams Co., Wisconsin – April 29, 1910

   Occupation – None – April 29, 1910

Delbert C. Calkins (son):

   Residence – Pebble Precinct, Dodge Co., Nebraska – June 16, 1880

         McClure Precinct, Holt Co., Nebraska – June 26, 1885

         Spring Creek, Moody Co., South Dakota – June 4th & 5th, 1900

         Richfield, Adams Co., Wisconsin – June 1, 1905

                          January 12th, 13th, & 15th, 1920

         Preston, Adams Co., Wisconsin – April 29, 1910

                          April 23, 1930

   Occupation – At Home – June 16, 1880

         None Listed – June 26, 1885

         Farm Laborer – June 4th & 5th, 1900

         Farming – June 1, 1905

Farmer, General Farm – April 29, 1910

January 12ᵗʰ, 13ᵗʰ, & 15ᵗʰ, 1920

Laborer, Farm Hand – April 23, 1930

Maud P. Brott (daughter-in-law):

Residence – Richfield, Adams Co., Wisconsin – June 1, 1905

Preston, Adams Co., Wisconsin – April 29, 1910

Occupation – Housekeeping – June 1, 1905

None – April 29, 1910

- ▪ **John C. Calkins** – b. 28 Mar 1874 in Pebble, Dodge Co., Nebraska, d. 4 Nov 1878 in Pebble, Dodge Co., Nebraska

- ▪ **Clara May Calkins**, b. 16 Feb 1878 in Scribner, Dodge Co., Nebraska, d. 13 Sep 1947 in Minnehaha Co., South Dakota & **Llwellyn Elwin Claflin**, b. 17 Jun 1870 in Woodstock, Windsor Co., Vermont, d. 7 Feb 1962 in Flandreau, Moody Co., South Dakota – Apr 1905 in Moody Co., South Dakota

Signature:

- • **James Claflin** – b. 10 Aug 1909 in Moody Co., South Dakota, d. in infancy

- • **Ernest E. Claflin** – b. 23 Jun 1913 in Flandreau, Moody Co., South Dakota, d. 9 Dec 1975 in Flandreau, Moody Co., South Dakota

Ernest E. Claflin (son):

Residence – Elkton, Brookings Co., South Dakota – January 6, 1920

Ryder, Ward Co., North Dakota – 1925

April 18, 1930

Occupation – None – January 6, 1920

April 18, 1930

- • **Unknown Claflin** (Daughter) – d. in infancy

- • **Unknown Claflin** (Daughter) – d. in infancy

Clara May Calkins (daughter):

Residence – Pebble Precinct, Dodge Co., Nebraska – June 16, 1880

McClure Precinct, Holt Co., Nebraska – June 26, 1885

Flandreau, Moody Co., South Dakota – April 21, 1910

Elkton, Brookings Co., South Dakota – January 6, 1920

Ryder, Ward Co., North Dakota – 1925

April 18, 1930

Occupation – At Home – June 16, 1880

> *None Listed – June 26, 1885*

> *Cook, Restaurant – April 21, 1910*

> *None – January 6, 1920*

> *April 18, 1930*

Llwellyn Elwin Claflin (son-in-law):

Residence – Flandreau, Moody Co., South Dakota – April 21, 1910

> *Elkton, Brooking Co., South Dakota – January 6, 1920*

> *Ryder, Ward Co., North Dakota – 1925*

> *April 18, 1930*

Occupation – Restaurant Keeper – April 21, 1910

> *Manager Candy Store – January 6, 1920*

> *Farmer, Farm – April 18, 1930*

Home Data for 1930 – Rental, has radio set, on a farm

- **James Werdna Calkins**, b. 13 Apr 1880 in Scribner, Dodge Co., Nebraska, d. 24 Aug 1970 in Flandreau, moody Co., South Dakota & **Alice Nettie Richardson**, b. 23 Feb 1891 in Flandreau, Moody Co., South Dakota, d. 17 Jun 1959 in Brookings Co., South Dakota – 18 Jun 1913 in Arlie, Pipestone Co., Minnesota

Signature:

- **Mildred Belle Calkins** – b. 8 Oct 1914 in Flandreau, Moody Co., South Dakota, d. 13 Jul 2001 in Pipestone, Pipestone Co., Minnesota

Mildred Belle Calkins (daughter):

Residence – Sweet, Pipestone Co., Minnesota – January 17, 1920

> *April 12, 1930*

Occupation – None – January 17, 1920

> *April 12, 1930*

- **Ethel N. Calkins** – b. 3 Jun 1923 in South Dakota, d. 17 Sep 2003 in Flandreau, Moody Co., South Dakota

Ethel N. Calkins (daughter):

Residence – Sweet, Pipestone Co., Minnesota – April 12, 1930

Occupation – None – April 12, 1930

Elisha Calkins & Anna Dalrymple Descendants

- **Violet E. Calkins** – b. About 1925 in Flandreau, Moody Co., South Dakota

Violet E. Calkins (daughter):

Residence – Sweet, Pipestone Co., Minnesota – April 12, 1930

Occupation – None – April 12, 1930

- **James J. Calkins** – b. 20 Aug 1928 in Flandreau, Moody Co., South Dakota, d. 12 Nov 1978 in Flandreau, Moody Co., South Dakota

James J. Calkins (son):

Residence – Sweet, Pipestone Co., Minnesota – April 12, 1930

Occupation – None – April 12, 1930

Obituary –

"Jim Calkins was born Aug. 20, 1928 on a farm north of Flandreau to James W. and Alice Richardson Calkins. As an infant he moved with his parents to Minnesota where he started his education. When he was 10 years old they returned to Moody county and he completed his education. He and his father then worked for various farmers in the area. He was married on April 4, 1961 to Dorothy Meeuw Smid at Flandreau and since then has farmed 6 miles southwest of Trent. He was active in the United Methodist Church in Flandreau." from Funeral Program

James Werdna Calkins (son):

Residence – Pebble Precinct, Dodge Co., Nebraska – June 16, 1880

McClure Precinct, Holt Co., Nebraska – June 26, 1885

Union, Moody Co., South Dakota – June 15, 1900

Sprig Creek, Moody Co., South Dakota – 1905

Sweet, Pipestone Co., Minnesota – January 17, 1920

April 12, 1930

Flandreau, Moody Co., South Dakota – September 12, 1918

1925

Occupation – None Listed – June 16, 1880

June 26, 1885

June 15, 1900

Farmer – 1905

1925

Farming – September 12, 1918

Farmer, General Farm – January 17, 1920

April 12, 1930

Home Data for 1930 – Rental, no radio set, on a farm

Obituary –

"James W. Calkins, Sr., son of William and Mary Etta Perry Calkins was born on April 13, 1881 near Ewing, Neb. He received his education there and in 1896 moved to Moody County. He was married to Alice Richardson on June 18, 1913. He worked on farms and farmed most of his life in Moody County. For the past several years he lived east of Trent on a farm. He was a member of the Methodist Church." from Funeral Program

Alice Nettie Richardson (daughter-in-law):

   Residence – Flandreau, Moody Co., South Dakota – 1905

                         September 12, 1918

          Sweet, Pipestone Co., Minnesota – January 17, 1920

                         April 12, 1930

   Occupation – Farmer & School – 1905

             None – January 17, 1920

                  April 12, 1930

Obituary –

"Alice N. Richardson was born in Moody county South Dakota, and was raised and educated in this county. She lived with her parents on a farm three miles north of Flandreau until her marriage on June 18, 1913, to James W. Calkins. With the exception of 10 years spent in Minnesota, she has lived in this vicinity all of her life. In 1952 she moved to a farm in Brookings county, and has resided there since." from Funeral Program

    ■ **Floyd Elisha Calkins**, b. 15 Aug 1885 in Ewing, Holt Co., Nebraska, d. 4 Feb 1958 in Pipestone, Pipestone Co., Minnesota & **Minnie Thompson** (2nd Marriage), b. 21 Dec 1878 in Lone Rock, Moody Co., South Dakota, d. 31 May 1969 in Sweet Township, Pipestone Co., Minnesota – 14 Jan 1914 in Sioux Falls, Minnehaha Co., South Dakota

Signature:

     • **Florence Thompson Calkins** – b. 29 Nov 1914, d. 15 Oct 2001 in Madelia, Watonwan Co., Minnesota

Florence Thompson Calkins (daughter):

   Residence – Sweet, Pipestone Co., Minnesota – January 17, 1920

                         April 9, 1930

   Occupation – None – January 17, 1920

                   April 9, 1930

Elisha Calkins & Anna Dalrymple Descendants

- **Minerva Perry Calkins**, b. 2 Jul 1916 in Minnesota & **William Andrew Smith**, b. 27 Aug 1907 in Alba Township, Jackson Co., Minnesota, d. 5 Jan 1999 in Nobles Co., Minnesota – 20 Jun 1938 in Worthington, Minnesota

Minerva Perry Calkins (daughter):

Residence – Sweet, Pipestone Co., Minnesota – January 17, 1920

April 9, 1930

Occupation – None – January 17, 1920

April 9, 1930

- **Shirll Riley Calkins** – b. 11 Jan 1918 in Pipestone Co., Minnesota, d. 6 Jul 1985 in Pipestone, Pipestone Co., Minnesota

Shirll Riley Calkins (son):

Residence – Sweet, Pipestone Co., Minnesota – January 17, 1920

April 9, 1930

Occupation – None – January 17, 1920

April 9, 1930

- **Angeline Anne Calkins** – b. 8 Nov 1919 in Sweet, Pipestone Co., Minnesota, d. 21 Aug 2002 in Red Wing, Goodhue Co., Minnesota

Angeline Anne Calkins (daughter):

Residence – Sweet, Pipestone Co., Minnesota – January 17, 1920

April 9, 1930

Occupation – None – January 17, 1920

April 9, 1930

- **Alex Brown Calkins** – b. 19 Apr 1924 in Pipestone, Pipestone Co., Minnesota, d. 11 Sep 1997 in Pipestone, Pipestone Co., Minnesota

Alex Brown Calkins (son):

Residence – Sweet, Pipestone Co., Minnesota – April 9, 1930

Occupation – None – April 9, 1930

Floyd Elisha Calkins (son):

Residence – Union, Moody Co., South Dakota – June 15, 1900

Lone Rock, Moody Co., South Dakota – 1905

April 22, 1910

Pipestone, Pipestone Co., Minnesota – September 12, 1918

Sweet, Pipestone Co., Minnesota – January 17, 1920

April 9, 1930

Hurst

Occupation – None Listed – June 15, 1900

Laborer, Home Farm – April 22, 1910

Farming – 1905

September 12, 1918

Farmer, General Farm – January 17, 1920

April 9, 1930

Home Data for 1930 – Owns home, no radio set, on a farm

Obituary –

"Floyd E. Calkins Dies Here Tuesday. Floyd Elisha Calkins, a well known farmer in Sweet township, Pipestone county, passed away at the Ashton hospital on Tuesday evening, February 4, at the age of seventy-two years. Funeral Services will be held on Friday, February 7, at 2 p. m., at the Walz & Geise Funeral Chapel in Pipestone, with Rev. Johnson officiating. Interment will be in the Lone Rock cemetery in Moody County. Floyd Elisha Calkins was born on August 15, 1885, at Ewing, Neb., to the late William and Marietta Calkins. He made his home at Ewing until 1909, at which time he moved to Moody county in South Dakota. He was united in marriage with Minnie Nelson on January 14, 1914, in Sioux Falls. In 1919 they moved to a farm located in Sweet township, Pipestone county, and had resided there since that time. Surviving relatives include his widow; three daughters, Mrs. Marvin Joramo (Florence), of Madelia, Minn., Mrs. Wm Smith (Minerva), of Brewster, Minn., and Angeline Calkins, of Pipestone; two sons, Shirll and Alex Calkins, of Pipestone; one brother, J. W. Calkins, of Brookings, S.D.,; and five grandchildren. He was preceded in death by his parents, two sisters and six brothers."

from the Pipestone County Star 1958

Minnie Thompson (daughter-in-law):

Residence – Pipestone, Pipestone Co., Minnesota – September 12, 1918

Sweet, Pipestone Co., Minnesota – January 17, 1920

April 9, 1930

Occupation – None – January 17, 1920

April 9, 1930

Obituary –

"Mrs. Minnie Calkins. Minnie Thompson, age 89 years, was born to Seivert & Sarah Thompson on December 11, 1879 in Moody Co., So. Dak. At an early age she was baptized & confirmed in the Lone Rock Lutheran Church. In 1896 she was united in marriage to Nels Nelson & to this union 3 children were born. She was united in marriage to Floyd E. Calkins, Jan. 14, 1913, & they farmed in the Moody Co. Area where she lived the remainder of her life. She is lovingly remembered by two sons, Alex & Shirll of Pipestone, 4 daughters, Florence, Mrs. Marvin Joramo of Madelia, Minn., Minerva, Mrs. Wm. Smith of Brewster, Minn., Angeline, Mrs. John Landeck of Redwing, Minn. & Sadie Calkins of Bellflower, Calif. Also, Helen, Mrs. Richard Reynolds of Rochester, Minn., Marlene, Mrs. James Assimes & Miss Oda Thomas of Mpls., the 3 children of her sister, who she took into her home & raised after the passing of their mother. 9 grandchildren and 14 great-grandchildren. She was preceded in death by her husband in 1958, 2 sons, 2 brothers, and 3 sisters." from Funeral Program

▪ **William Arthur Calkins**, b. 26 Jul 1887 in Inman, Holt Co., Nebraska, d. 19 Oct 1956 in Bellflower, Los Angeles Co., California & **Sadie Anita Cecelia Nelson** (daughter of Minnie Thompson, wife of Floyd Elisha Calkins), b. 10 Apr 1900 in Lake Benton, Lincoln Co., Minnesota, d. 30 Dec 1989 in Bellflower, Los Angles Co., California – 15 Sep 1920 in Pipestone, Pipestone Co., Minnesota

Signature:

- **Daisy Ann Calkins** – b. 31 Mar 1922 in Sweet Township, Pipestone Co., Minnesota, d. 24 Jun 2010 in Mission Viejo, California

Daisy Ann Calkins (daughter):

    Residence – Sweet, Pipestone Co., Minnesota – April 10, 1930

    Occupation – None – April 10, 1930

- **Donna Zoe Calkins** – b. 28 Apr 1924 in Sweet Township, Pipestone Co., Minnesota, d. 9 May 2007 in Moreno Valley, Riverside Co., California

Donna Zoe Calkins (daughter):

    Residence – Sweet, Pipestone Co., Minnesota – April 10, 1930

    Occupation – None – April 10, 1930

- **William Richard Calkins** – b. 15 Jan 1927 in Sweet Township, Pipestone Co., Minnesota, d. 21 Jul 2001 in Long Beach, California

William Richard Calkins (son):

    Residence – Sweet, Pipestone Co., Minnesota – April 10, 1930

    Occupation – None – April 10, 1930

- **Doris Jane Calkins** – b. About 1930 in Sweet Township, Pipestone Co., Minnesota

William Arthur Calkins (son):

    Residence – Union, Moody Co., South Dakota – June 15, 1900

        Lone Rock, Moody Co., South Dakota – 1905

                April 22, 1910

        Flandreau, Moody Co., South Dakota – June 5, 1917

        Sweet, Pipestone Co., Minnesota – January 17, 1920

                April 10, 1930

    Occupation – At School – June 15, 1900

        Farming – 1905

        Laborer, Home Farm – April 22, 1910

Hurst

Farmer – June 5, 1917

Farmer, General farm – January 17, 1920

April 10, 1930

Home Data for 1930 – Rental, has Radio Set, not on farm

Obituary –

"Calkins (Bellflower) – William Arthur, 69, of 9852 Walnut Ave., died Friday. Survivors are wife, Sadie; son, William: daughters, Mrs. Daisy Ann Harmsen, Mrs. Donna Radinzel and Mrs. Doris Smith; brothers, Floyd and Werdna: and six grandchildren. Service Thursday, 11 a.m. in Veterans Administration Chapel, West Los Angeles, with Mottell's & Peek directing. Friends may call Tuesday evening at Motell's & Peek Mortuary, 3rd St. and Alamitos Ave." **from the Independent Press Telegram – C-3. Long Beach, Calif., Sunday, Oct. 21, 1956**

Sadie Anita Cecelia Nelson (daughter-in-law):

Residence – Sweet, Pipestone Co., Minnesota – April 10, 1930

Occupation – None – April 10, 1930

Obituary –

"Sadie Calkins. Sadie N. Calkins, beloved mother of Daisy Ann Harmsen, Donna Radinzel, William R. Calkins, and Doris Smith; sister of Alex B. Calkins, Florence Joramo, Minerva Smith and Angeline Landeck, died on December 30, 1989, In California where she had lived for many years. Sadie was born on April 10, 1900 in Lake Benton, Minn. Services for Mrs. Calkins were conducted by Rev. Harold Schultz at the Church of Our Fathers. Burial was in Forest Lawn Memorial Park, Cypress, Calif. On Jan. 3, 1990. Sadie was preceded in death by her mother, Minnie Calkins and step-father Floyd, husband, Arthur, and two brothers, Erwin and Palmer. She has nine grandchildren, 14 great-grandchildren, and three great-great-grandchildren surviving her. Funeral arrangements were made by Forest Lawn Mortuary, Cypress, Calif." **from Bellflower or Long Beach Area Newspaper**

- **Mabel Effie Calkins**, b. Jan 1892 in Holt Co., Nebraska, d. 10 Nov 1918 in Rockwell City, Calhoun Co., Iowa & **George Leland Morgan**, b. Oct 1895 in Pixley, Clay Co., Illinois – 10 Apr 1916 in Pipestone, Pipestone Co., Minnesota

Signature:

George L Morgan

(Signature or mark)

- **Everett Edgar Morgan** – b. 6 Feb 1917 in Rockwell City, Calhoun Co., Iowa

Everett Edgar Morgan (son):

Residence – Rockwell City, Calhoun Co., Iowa – January 14, 1920

April 10, 1930

Occupation – None – January 14, 1920

April 10, 1930

Mabel Effie Calkins (daughter):

Residence – Union, Moody Co., South Dakota – June 15, 1900

Lone Rock, Moody Co., South Dakota – April 22, 1910

1915

Occupation – At School – June 15, 1900

None – April 22, 1910

None Listed – 1915

Obituary –

"Mrs. Geo Morgan Dies of Influenza. Mrs. George L. Morgan of Rockwell City died at her home in the north-west part of town last Sunday morning. Death was due to heart trouble, following an attack of influenza. Mrs. Morgan is survived by her husband and one child. Funeral services were conducted at the home Monday afternoon at 2 o'clock, Rev. M. L. Dilley officiating. Interment in Rose Hill cemetery." **from the Advocate, Rockwell City, Calhoun Co., Iowa. Thursday.** Nov 14, 1918

George Leland Morgan (son-in-law):

Residence – Rockwell City, Calhoun Co., Iowa – June 5, 1917

January 14, 1920

April 10, 1930

Occupation – Farming – June 5, 1917

Laborer, General Farm – January 14, 1920

Laborer, Carpenter – April 10, 1930

Home Data for 1930 – Owns home, valued at $ 700, no radio set, not on a farm

William Riley Calkins (son):

Residence – Arkwright, Chautauqua Co., New York – August 28, 1850

1855

Union, Johnson Co., Iowa – 1856

Green, Iowa Co., Iowa – June 4, 1860

Elgin, Wabasha Co., Minnesota – July 1, 1863

June 1, 1865

July 7, 1870

Pebble Precinct, Dodge Co., Nebraska – June 16, 1880

McClure Precinct, Holt Co., Nebraska – June 26, 1885

Union, Moody Co., South Dakota – June 15, 1900

Lone Rock, Moody Co., South Dakota – 1905

Hurst

Occupation – Laborer – August 28, 1850

Farmer – 1855

July 1, 1863

July 7, 1870

June 16, 1880

June 26, 1885

June 15, 1900

Carpenter – 1856

None Listed – June 4, 1860

Farming – 1905

Value of Real Estate – $ 1, 600 – June 4, 1860

$ 2, 500 – July 7, 1870

Value of Personal Estate – $ 400 – June 4, 1860

$ 800 – July 7, 1870

Obituary –

"Obituary of W. R. Calkins. William Riley Calkins was born in Arkwright, Chautauqua County, N. Y., July 23rd, 1834 and was married to Miss Mary Etta Perry Dec. 1st, 1861 at Plainview, Minn. After living in Wabasha County, Minnesota, for a number of years, he and his family moved to Dodge County, Neb., and were among the earliest settlers there. In 1885 the family moved to Ewing, Holt County, Neb., and resided there until the spring of 1898 when he and his wife came to Moody County, most of his family having preceded him here, and has made his home in this county ever since. In 1881 he united with the Congregational church, and a few years later with the M. E. church. His death occurred at his home in Lone Rock township, Saturday Jan. 12, 1907. The funeral took place from the home at 2 o'clock Sunday afternoon and the remains brought to Flandreau and laid at rest in the Union cemetery east of town, Rev. D. C. Arms conducting the services. He leaves to mourn his death, his wife, six sons, Ernest, Lora, Delbert, Werdna, Floyd, Arthur, and two daughters, Mrs. L. E. Claflin, of Flandreau, and Mabel Calkins, all of this county, excepting one brother in Wisconsin. Mr. Calkins was a kind and loving husband and father, a consistent Christian, well liked and highly respected by friends and neighbors, and will be greatly missed by all." from the Moody County Enterprise. Thursday, January 17, 1907

Mary Etta Perry (daughter-in-law):

Residence – Elgin, Wabasha Co., Minnesota – June 1, 1865

July 7, 1870

Pebble Precinct, Dodge Co., Nebraska – June 16, 1880

McClure Precinct, Holt Co., Nebraska – June 26, 1885

Union, Moody Co., South Dakota – June 15, 1900

Lone Rock, Moody Co., South Dakota – 1905

April 22, 1910

Elisha Calkins & Anna Dalrymple Descendants

Occupation – Keeping House – July 7, 1870

June 16, 1880

June 26, 1885

None Listed – June 15, 1900

Farming – 1905

Farmer, General Farm – April, 22, 1910

Obituary –

"Written in Memory of Mrs. Mary Etta Calkins - Dearest Mother, thou hast left us, Gone to join the Heavenly throng, There with Jesus and the loved ones, Where all is happiness and song. Oh! How we miss that gentle foot step, How we miss that loving voice. In our home a chair is vacant In our home a voice is stilled And the lonely chair that's vacant Never more can be refilled. Oh! Her dying words a message, To her children one and all, "Meet me in that Heavenly Mansion," Was our dying Mother's call. "Oh! 'Tis sweet to trust in Jesus," Were some words she sweetly said, And "I am not afraid to die, for Jesus is right near by." Oh me thinks I hear her loving voice, Calling to us one and all, "Be ye ready to join the Heavenly circle, When the Master comes to call." C. M. C. [Poem written by Clara May Calkins before the Obituary] Miss Mary Etta Perry was born in Arkwright, Chautauqua County, New York, on March 16, 1842. She was married to Wm. Riley Calkins at Plainview, Minn., Dec. 1, 1861. After living in Wabasha county a number of years they moved with their family to Dodge county, Nebraska, and were among the earliest settlers there. In 1885 the family moved to Ewing, Holt county, Nebraska, and resided there until the spring of 1898, when they moved to Moody county. January 12, 1907, the father was called to the Great Beyond and the mother has since made her home with her two youngest sons, who reside in Pipestone county, Minnesota, until October 12, 1912, the mother too was called to join her husband on the other shore. In 1881 Mr. and Mrs. Calkins both united with the Congregational church at Scribner, Nebraska, and when they moved to Ewing, Nebraska, were transferred to the Methodist church and they were both members of the M. E. church in Flandreau. She was a kind and loving mother, a true Christian, and a friend to everyone. She had been a sufferer for many months, yet she bore her pains with patience. She was conscious nearly all the time to the last. About an hour before she died she called all her children to her bedside and bade then all a dying farewell and begged them all to meet her in Heaven. She said Jesus was right there to take her and she was not afraid to die. She leaves to mourn her loss six sons, Ernest, Lora, Delbert, Werdna, Floyd and Arthur, and two daughters, Miss Mable Calkins and Mrs. L. E. Claflin, besides an aged mother, Mrs. B. E. Perry of Surrey, N. D., and three brothers, Wilton Perry of North Dakota, Ed Perry of Norfolk, Nebraska, Forest Perry of Stanton, Nebraska, and two sisters, Mrs. J. W. Pearson of Surrey, North Dakota, and Mrs. Helen Barkdull of Lucas, South Dakota. Ed. And Forest Perry were present at the funeral. The funeral took place at the M. E. church, Rev. Arms having charge of the services. Interment was made in the Union cemetery." ***from the Moody County Enterprise 1912***

Hurst

Freeman Calkins (father):

Residence – Arkwright, Chautauqua Co., New York – 1840

August 27, 1850

1855

Union, Johnson Co., Iowa – 1856

Green, Iowa Co., Iowa – June 4, 1860

Minneiska, Wabasha Co., Minnesota – May 1, 1875

June 16th & 17th, 1880

Occupation – Carpenter & Joiner – August 27, 1850

Farmer – 1855

June 4, 1860

Carpenter – 1856

At Home – June 16th & 17th, 1880

Value of Real Estate – $ 1, 000 – August 27, 1850

Value of Personal Estate – $ 50 – June 4, 1860

Home Data for 1855 – framed, valued at $ 300

Sarah Ann Woods (mother):

Residence – Arkwright, Chautauqua Co., New York – August 27, 1850

1855

Union, Johnson Co., Iowa – 1856

Green, Iowa Co., Iowa – June 4, 1860

Occupation – None Listed – August 27, 1850

1855

1856

June 4, 1860

Freeman Calkins & Sarah Ann Woods

Family Photo Album (Found at an Estate Sale near Medina, Ohio)

Date of Album – 1860s

Photographs courtesy of The Hurst Family of Lake Elsinore, California

Freeman Calkins & Sarah Ann Woods

Photograph courtesy of The Hurst Family of Lake Elsinore, California

Sarah Ann (Woods) Calkins

Photographer Credit (Left): L.H. Phillips – Wabasha, Minnesota

Date – March 1865

Photographer Credit (Right): C.D. Taylor – Cresco, Iowa

Date – Circa 1870 – 1875

Photographs courtesy of The Hurst Family of Lake Elsinore, California

Carlton Washington Fuller & Fidelia Lossie Calkins

Photograph courtesy of Mr. & Mrs. Carl Fuller and Family

Fred Fuller Family -- 1905
Back row -- Leland, Lester, Delia, Clifford
Front row -- Mother Anna, Freda, Father Fred, Gladys

From the work entitled:

Record of the "Fullers and Relatives"

Compiled by Gladys J. Johnson

December – 1976

Frank Alvah Fuller & Johanna Elizabeth Sheehan

Photographs courtesy of Mr. & Mrs. Carl Fuller and Family

Frank Alvah & Johanna Elizabeth (Sheehan) Fuller's Family

From Left to Right (Back Row) – Carlton Lewis, Florence Irene, Helen Georgeanna,

Francis Olive, Earl Vincent, Mabel Mary

From Left to Right (Front Row) – Johanna Elizabeth (Mother), Frank Alvah (Father),

Milton Jerome

Photograph courtesy of Mr. & Mrs. Carl Fuller and Family

J.J. Prescott,   MELROSE, MINN.

George M. & Sarah Jane (Fuller) Cowie's Family

Date – Before 1898 in Melrose, Minnesota

Photograph courtesy of the Cowie-Caldwell Family of

Glencoe, Wisconsin & Madesto, California

William Riley Calkins

Circa 1854 – 1860

Photograph courtesy of The Hurst Family of Lake Elsinore, California

William Riley Calkins holding William Arthur Calkins

Mary Etta Perry holding Mabel Effie Calkins

Circa 1892

Photographer Credits: Corbett – O'Neill, Nebraska

Photograph courtesy of The Hurst Family of Lake Elsinore, California

Lora Deloss Calkins & Eva Estella Dickinson

Date – October 27, 1898

Photograph courtesy of The Hurst Family of Lake Elsinore, California

Delbert C. Calkins & wife Maud P. Brott

Photographer Credits: C. F. Martin & Co. – Stevens Point, Wisconsin

Photograph courtesy of The Hurst Family of Lake Elsinore, California

Clara May Calkins

Photographer Credits: Lincoln Studio – Pipestone, Minnesota

Photograph courtesy of The Hurst Family of Lake Elsinore, California

Llwellyn Elwin Claflin & Clara May Calkins

Date – April 1905

Photograph courtesy of The Hurst Family of Lake Elsinore, California

Llwellyn Elwin Claflin's Store

Llwellyn Elwin Claflin is on the right side in a black suit

Photograph courtesy of The Hurst Family of Lake Elsinore, California

James Werdna Calkins

Photograph courtesy of The Hurst Family of Lake Elsinore, California

James Werdna Calkins & Alice Nettie Richardson

Date – June 18, 1913

Photograph courtesy of The Hurst Family of Lake Elsinore, California

Floyd Elisha Calkins & Minnie Thompson

Photographer Credits: Hawks – Elton, South Dakota

Photograph courtesy of The Hurst Family of Lake Elsinore, California

Minnie Thompson

wife of Floyd Elisha Calkins

Photograph courtesy of The Hurst Family of Lake Elsinore, California

Floyd Elisha & Minnie Calkins Home

Circa 1916 – 1917

Pipestone, Minnesota

Photograph courtesy of The Hurst Family of Lake Elsinore, California

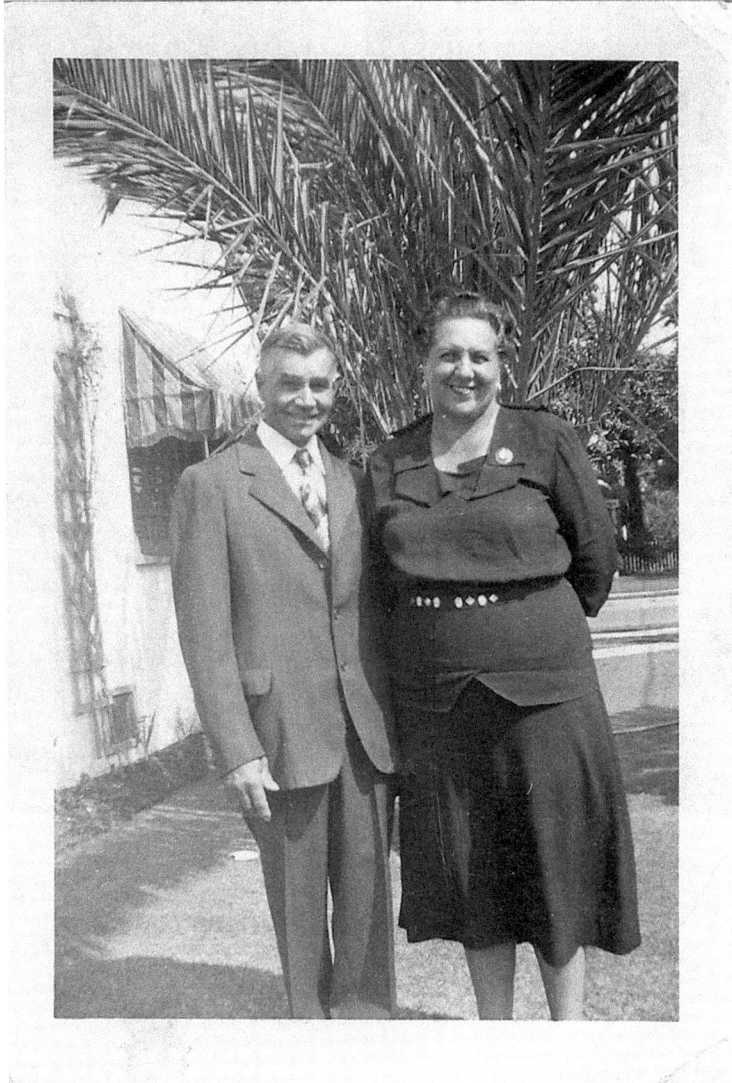

William Arthur Calkins

&

Sadie Anita Cecelia Nelson

Date – 1951

Photograph courtesy of The Hurst Family of Lake Elsinore, California

Mabel Effie Calkins & George Leland Morgan

Date – April 10, 1916

Photographs courtesy of The Hurst Family of Lake Elsinore, California

Lyman Simon Calkins & Descendants

- **Lyman Simon Calkins**, b. 16 May 1811 in Brookfield, Madison Co., New York, d. 30 Mar 1889 in Brodtville, Grant Co., Wisconsin & **Amy Albee**, b. 7 Apr 1811 in New York, d. 6 Jun 1885 in Brodtville, Grant Co., Wisconsin – 23 Oct 1832 in Otselic, Chenango Co., New York

Signatures:

- o **Arcelia Calkins**, b. 9 Nov 1834 in Chenango Co., New York, d. 26 Apr 1903 in Westmoreland, Pottawatomie Co., Kansas & **Curtis Badgley** (1st Husband), b. About 1830 in Chautauqua Co., New York, d. 1854 in Wisconsin

  - ▪ **Levant L. Badgley**, b. 8 May 1851 in Lake Chautauqua, Chautauqua Co., New York, d. Before 1930 & **Henrietta Warner**, b. 23 May 1847 in Pennsylvania – 18 May 1874 in Sugar Grove, Warren Co., Pennsylvania

    - **Guy Badgley** – b. 1876 in Pennsylvania, d. 18 Sep 1882

Guy Badgley (son):

Residence – Louisville, Pottawatomie Co., Kansas – June 22, 1880

Occupation – None Listed – June 22, 1880

- **Vera Mabel Badgley** – b. 4 Jan 1879 in Pennsylvania, d. 24 Jun 1944 in San Diego, San Diego Co., California

Vera Mabel Badgley (daughter):

Residence – Louisville, Pottawatomie Co., Kansas – June 22, 1880

March 1, 1885

Westmoreland, Pottawatomie Co., Kansas – March 1, 1895

Rock Creek, Pottawatomie Co., Kansas – June 4, 1900

Topeka, Shawnee Co., Kansas – April 21, 1910

Occupation – None Listed – June 22, 1880

March 1, 1885

Stenographer – June 4, 1900

Stenographer, Federal Court – April 21, 1910

Hurst

- **Rena Badgley** – b. Feb 1880 in Pennsylvania, d. 4 Oct 1882

Rena Badgley (daughter):

  Residence – Louisville, Pottawatomie Co., Kansas – June 22, 1880

  Occupation – None Listed – June 22, 1880

- **Lena A. Badgley** – b. 11 Mar 1885 in Pottawatomie Co., Kansas, d. 28 Mar 1971 in San Diego, San Diego Co., California

Lena A. Badgley (daughter):

  Residence – Westmoreland, Pottawatomie Co., Kansas – March 1, 1895

  Rock Creek, Pottawatomie Co., Kansas – June 4, 1900

  Topeka, Shawnee Co., Kansas – April 21, 1910

  Occupation – At School – June 4, 1900

  Stenographer, Railway – April 21, 1910

Levant L. Badgley (son):

  Residence – Harmony, Chautauqua Co., New York – June 29, 1860

  Louisville, Pottawatomie Co., Kansas – June 22, 1880

  March 1, 1885

  Westmoreland, Pottawatomie Co., Kansa – March 1, 1895

  Rock Creek, Pottawatomie Co., Kansas – June 4, 1900

  Topeka, Shawnee Co., Kansas – April 21, 1910

  Occupation – None Listed – June 29, 1860

  Dry Goods Clerk – June 22, 1880

  Clerk & Book Keeper – March 1, 1885

  County Attorney – June 4, 1900

  Lawyer, General Practice – April 21, 1910

Henrietta Warner (daughter-in-law):

  Residence – Louisville, Pottawatomie Co., Kansas – June 22, 1880

  March 1, 1885

  Westmoreland, Pottawatomie Co., Kansas – March 1, 1895

  Rock Creek, Pottawatomie Co., Kansas – June 4, 1900

  Topeka, Shawnee Co., Kansas – April 21, 1910

  Occupation – At Home – June 22, 1880

  None Listed – March 1, 1885

  June 4, 1900

  None – April 21, 1910

Elisha Calkins & Anna Dalrymple Descendants

- **John P. Badgley**, b. Jan 1854 in Wisconsin & **Alta Marion Hoag**, b. 13 Aug 1856 in Wisconsin, d. 10 Sep 1940 in Los Angeles Co., California – 1875

  - **Leon Curtis Badgley**, b. 2 Jul 1876 in New York, d. 19 Dec 1955 in Los Angeles Co., California & **Gertrude Casnor**, b. About 1878 in Iowa – 1897

    - ○ **Erma Lareta Badgley** – b. Aug 1898 in Nebraska

Erma Lareta Badgley (daughter):

    Residence – Lincoln, Lancaster Co., Nebraska – June 5, 1900

        Santa Monica, Los Angeles Co., California – April 21, 1910

    Occupation – None Listed – June 5, 1900

        None – April 21, 1910

    ○ **Loran A. Badgley** – b. About 1902 in California

Loran A. Badgley (son):

    Residence – Santa Monica, Los Angeles Co., California – April 21, 1910

    Occupation – None – April 21, 1910

    ○ **Alma Badgley** – b. About 1904 in California

Alma Badgley (daughter):

    Residence – Santa Monica, Los Angeles Co., California – April 21, 1910

    Occupation – None – April 21, 1910

    ○ **Alice Badgley** – b. About 1904 in California

Alice Badgley (daughter):

    Residence – Santa Monica, Los Angeles Co., California – April 21, 1910

    Occupation – None – April 21, 1910

    ○ **Gertrude Doris Badgley** – b. 16 Nov 1909 in Los Angeles Co., California

Gertrude Doris Badgley (daughter):

    Residence – Santa Monica, Los Angeles Co., California – April 21, 1910

    Occupation – None –April 21, 1910

Leon Curtis Badgley (son):

    Residence – Lincoln, Lancaster Co., Nebraska – June 5, 1900

        Santa Monica, Los Angeles Co., California – April 21, 1910

    Occupation – Street Car Conductor – June 5, 1900

        Motorman – Stunt Car – April 21, 1910

Gertrude Casnor (daughter-in-law):

    Residence – Lincoln, Lancaster Co., Nebraska – June 5, 1900

        Santa Monica, Los Angeles Co., California – April 21, 1910

Hurst

Occupation – None Listed – June 5, 1900

> *None – April 21, 1910*

- **Lyle Hurst Badgley,** b. 7 June 1881 in Bolo, Kansas & **Luella Davis**, b. About 1885 in Nebraska – 16 Jul 1905 in Crete, Saline Co., Nebraska

Lyle Hurst Badgley (son):

Residence – Lancaster, Lancaster Co., Nebraska – June 9, 1900

> *Los Angles Co., California – 1942*

Occupation – Clerk Grocery – June 9, 1900

> *Unemployed – 1942*

John P. Badgley (son):

Residence – Harmony, Chautauqua Co., New York – June 29, 1860

> *Auburn, Fayette Co., Iowa – August 3, 1870*
>
> *Harmony, Chautauqua Co., New York – June 1, 1875*
>
> *Lancaster, Lancaster Co., Nebraska – June 9, 1900*
>
> *Santa Monica, Los Angeles Co., California – April 21, 1910*
>
> > *1920*
> >
> > *April 4, 1930*

Occupation – None Listed – June 29, 1860

> *Farm Laborer – August 3, 1870*
>
> *Farmer – June 1, 1875*
>
> *Minister – June 9, 1900*
>
> *Florist, Nursery – April 21, 1910*
>
> *None, retired – April 4, 1930*

Home Data for 1930 – Owns home, valued at $ 4, 500, has radio set, not on a farm

Alta Marion Hoag (daughter-in-law):

Residence – Harmony, Chautauqua Co., New York – June 1, 1875

> *Lancaster, Lancaster Co., Nebraska – June 9, 1900*
>
> *Santa Monica, Los Angeles Co., California – April 21, 1910*
>
> > *1920*
> >
> > *April 4, 1930*

Occupation – None Listed – June 1, 1875

> *None – June 9, 1900*
>
> *April 21, 1910*
>
> *April 4, 1930*

○ **Arcelia Calkins**, b. 9 Nov 1834 in Chenango Co., New York, d. 26 Apr 1903 in Westmoreland, Pottawatomie Co., Kansas & **Donald McDonald** (2nd Husband), b. Apr 1829 in Scotland, d. Aug 1903 in Lottsville, Warren Co., Pennsylvania

■ **Nathan Peter McDonald**, b. 6 Nov 1862 in Columbus, Warren Co., Pennsylvania, d. 1937 & **Ella Nora Upton**, b. Oct 1861 in Illinois, d. 1945 - 1888

● **Archie Lamont McDonald**, b. 22 Jan 1889 in Elm Creek, Buffalo Co., Nebraska, d. 6 Feb 1936 in Kearney, Buffalo Co., Nebraska & **Josephine Robb**, b. 1891 in Pennsylvania, d. 22 Jan 1955 in Kearney, Buffalo Co., Nebraska – 6 May 1911 in Lexington, Dawson Co., Nebraska

Signature:

(Signature or mark)

○ **Margaret Ella McDonald** – b. About 1912 in Nebraska

Margaret Ella McDonald (daughter):

Residence – Gering, Scotts Bluff Co., Nebraska – January 2, 1920

Kearney, Buffalo Co., Nebraska – April 12, 1930

Occupation – None – January 2, 1920

April 12, 1930

○ **N. Robert McDonald** – b. 1 May 1914 in Everett, Snohomish Co., Washington

N. Robert McDonald (son):

Residence – Gering, Scotts Bluff Co., Nebraska – January 2, 1920

Kearney, Buffalo Co., Nebraska – April 12, 1930

Occupation – None – January 2, 1920

April 12, 1930

○ **Dale McDonald** – b. About 1924 in Nebraska

Dale McDonald (son):

Residence – Kearney, Buffalo Co., Nebraska – April 12, 1930

Occupation – None – April 12, 1930

Archie Lamont McDonald (son):

Residence – Kearney, Buffalo Co., Nebraska – June 2, 1900

April 19, 1910

June 5, 1917

April 12, 1930

Gering, Scotts Bluff Co., Nebraska – January 2, 1920

Occupation – At School – June 2, 1900

        Laborer, Implements – April 19, 1910

        Machinist – June 5, 1917

        Mechanic, Garage – January 2, 1920

        Welding & Machine Worker, Machine Shop – April 12, 1930

Home Data for 1930 – Rental, $ 25 a month, no radio set, not on a farm

Josephine Robb (daughter-in-law):

    Residence – Gering, Scotts Bluff Co., Nebraska – January 2, 1920

        Kearney, Buffalo Co., Nebraska – April 12, 1930

    Occupation – None – January 2, 1920

        Laundry, Own Home – April 12, 1930

Nathan Peter McDonald (son):

    Residence – Harmony, Chautauqua Co., New York – June 23, 1880

        Kearney, Buffalo Co., Nebraska – June 2, 1900

                April 19, 1910

                January 9, 1920

                April 15, 1930

    Occupation – None Listed – June 23, 1880

        Lawyer – June 2, 1900

        January 9, 1920

        Lawyer, Practicing Attorney – April 19, 1910

        Lawyer, General Practice – April 15, 1930

Home Data for 1930 – Rental, $ 50 a month, no radio set, not on a farm

Ella Nora Upton (daughter-in-law):

    Residence – Kearney, Buffalo Co., Nebraska – June 2, 1900

                April 19, 1910

                January 9, 1920

    Occupation – None Listed – June 2, 1900

        None – April 19, 1910

        January 9, 1920

Elisha Calkins & Anna Dalrymple Descendants

- **Lamont McDonald**, b. Sep 1864 in Columbus, Warren Co., Pennsylvania & **Ella L. Demmon**, b. Jan 1865 in Pennsylvania – 1889

  - **James Donald McDonald**, b. 4 Aug 1892 in Overton, Dawson Co., Nebraska & **Edith Louise Adams**, b. About 1888 in Williamson, New York – 3 Jul 1924 in Ontario, Wayne Co., New York

Signature:

  - ○ **Jean M. McDonald** – b. About 1926 in New York

Jean M. McDonald (daughter):

  Residence – Williamsville, Erie Co., New York – April 22, 1930

  Occupation – None – April 22, 1930

  - ○ **Robert D. McDonald** – b. About 1929 in New York

Robert D. McDonald (son):

  Residence – Williamsville, Erie Co., New York – April 22, 1930

  Occupation – None – April 22, 1930

James Donald McDonald (son):

  Residence – Harmony, Chautauqua Co., New York – June 26, 1900

  Hillside, Dawson Co., Nebraska – May 9, 1910

  Spring Creek, Erie Co., Pennsylvania – June 5, 1917

  Gerry, Chautauqua Co., New York – January 28, 1920

  Hamburg, Erie Co., New York – July 3, 1924

  Williamsville, Erie Co., New York – April 22, 1930

  Occupation – At School – June 26, 1900

  Laborer, Home Farm – May 9, 1910

  Farmer – June 5, 1917

  Carpenter, House – January 28, 1920

  July 3, 1924

  Carpenter, General Work – April 22, 1930

  Home Data for 1930 – Rental, $40 a month, no radio set, not on a farm

Edith Louise Adams (daughter-in-law):

  Residence – Ontario, Wayne Co., New York – July 3, 1924

  Williamsville, Erie Co., New York – April 22, 1930

  Occupation – School Teacher – July 3, 1924

  Teacher, High School – April 22, 1930

Hurst

- **Gerald John McDonald**, b. 2 Sep 1897 in Harmony, Chautauqua Co., New York & **Gladys Florelle Herrick**, b. About 1894 in Gerry, Chautauqua Co., New York – 6 Sep 1921 in Gerry, Chautauqua Co., New York

Signature:

Gerald John McDonald (son):

Residence – Harmony, Chautauqua Co., New York – June 26, 1900

Hillside, Dawson Co., Nebraska –May 9, 1910

Gerry, Chautauqua Co., New York – June 5, 1918

January 28, 1920

September 6, 1921

Occupation – None Listed – June 26, 1900

Laborer, Home Farm – May 9, 1910

Farming – June 5, 1918

Farming, Home Farm – January 28, 1920

Farmer – September 6, 1921

Gladys Florelle Herrick (daughter-in-law):

Residence – Gerry, Chautauqua Co., New York – September 6, 1921

Occupation – Teacher – September 6, 1921

- **Unknown McDonald** – b. After 1900, d. Before 1910

- **Irene Mary McDonald**, b. About 1917 in Lexington, Nebraska & **Luman Vincent Bentley**, b. About 1902 in Gerry, Chautauqua Co., New York – 8 Jun 1927 in Chautauqua Co., New York

Irene Mary McDonald (daughter):

Residence – Hillside, Dawson Co., Nebraska – May 9, 1910

Gerry, Chautauqua Co., New York – January 28, 1920

June 8, 1927

Cambridge, White Creek Co., Washington – April 24, 1930

Occupation – None Listed – May 9, 1910

None – January 28, 1920

Stenographer – June 8, 1827

Stenographer, Seed – April 24, 1930

Luman Vincent Bentley (son-in-law):

Residence – Gerry, Chautauqua Co., New York – June 8, 1927

Cambridge, White Creek Co., Washington – April 24, 1930

Elisha Calkins & Anna Dalrymple Descendants

Occupation – Salesman – June 8, 1927

Stenographer, Seed – April 24, 1930

Home Data for 1930 – Rental, $ 30 a month, has radio set, not on a farm

Lamont McDonald (son):

Residence – Harmony, Chautauqua Co., New York – June 23, 1880

June 26, 1900

Hillside, Dawson Co., Nebraska – May 9, 1910

Gerry, Chautauqua Co., New York – January 28, 1920

Occupation – None Listed – June 23, 1880

Farmer – June 26, 1900

Farmer, General Farm – May 9, 1910

Farmer, Diary Farm – January 28, 1920

Ella L. Demmon (daughter-in-law):

Residence – Harmony, Chautauqua Co., New York – June 26, 1900

Hillside, Dawson Co., Nebraska – May 9, 1910

Gerry, Chautauqua Co., New York – January 28, 1920

Cambridge, White Creek Co., Washington – April 24, 1930

Occupation – None Listed – June 26, 1900

None – May 9, 1910

January 28, 1920

April 24, 1930

Arcelia Calkins (daughter):

Residence – Harmony, Chautauqua Co., New York – June 29, 1860

June 23, 1880

Occupation – None Listed – June 29, 1860

Keeping House – June 23, 1880

Values of Real Estate – None Listed – June 29, 1860

Value of Personal Estate – $ 400 – June 29, 1860

Donald McDonald (2nd Husband) (son-in-law):

Residence – Harmony, Chautauqua Co., New York June 26, 1900

Occupation – Farm Laborer – June 26, 1900

o **Arcus Riley Calkins**, b. 5 Mar 1836 in Columbus, Warren Co., Pennsylvania, d. 6 Dec 1906 in Bagley, Grant Co., Wisconsin & **Mary E. Patch**, b. 3 Jan 1842 in Danby, Vermont, d. 22 Apr 1919 in Bagley, Grant Co., Wisconsin – 8 Sep 1859 in Grant Co., Wisconsin

Hurst

- **Edward Mason Calkins**, b. 12 Jun 1861 in Brodtville, Grant Co., Wisconsin, d. 11 Jun 1918 in Hemet, Riverside Co., California & **Etta Twining** (1st Wife), b. 28 Jul 1866 in Crawford Co., Wisconsin, d. 20 Jul 1889 – 13 Sep 1888 in Crawford Co., Wisconsin

- **Edward Mason Calkins**, b. 12 Jun 1861 in Brodtville, Grant Co., Wisconsin, d. 11 Jun 1918 in Hemet, Riverside Co., California & **Ardella Brokaw** (2nd Wife), b. 7 Feb 1866, d. 6 Feb 1952 in Los Angles Co., California – 30 Jun 1895 in La Crosse, La Crosse Co., Wisconsin

Signature:

Edward Mason Calkins (son):

   Residence – Wyalusing, Grant Co., Wisconsin – June 22, 1870

                                      June 15, 1880

         La Crosse, La Crosse Co., Wisconsin – June 8, 1900

         Inglewood, Los Angeles Co., California – April 25, 1910

   Occupation – At Home – June 22, 1870

         Assists on Farm – June 15, 1880

         Editor – June 8, 1900

         Superintendant, Paper Route – April 25, 1910

Ardella Brokaw (2nd Wife) (daughter-in-law):

   Residence – La Crosse, La Crosse Co., Wisconsin – June 8, 1900

         Inglewood, Los Angeles Co., California – April 25, 1910

         Redlands, San Bernardino Co., California – January 7, 1920

   Occupation – None Listed – June 8, 1900

         None – April 25, 1910

         Teacher, Grammar School – January 7, 1920

- **Riley Calkins** – b. 19 Mar 1864 in Brodtville, Grant Co., Wisconsin, d. 20 May 1864 in Brodtville, Grant Co., Wisconsin

- **Bertie Calkins** – b. Jun 1865 in Brodtville, Grant Co., Wisconsin, d. 16 Apr 1866 in Brodtville, Grant Co., Wisconsin

- **Charles Denton Calkins**, b. 16 Oct 1867 in Brodtville, Grant Co., Wisconsin, d. 1948 in Bagley, Grant Co., Wisconsin & **Mary Jane Day**, b. 9 Sep 1875 in Wisconsin – 15 Jul 1894 in Patch Grove, Grant Co., Wisconsin

Signature:

- **Earle Denton Calkins**, b. 14 Mar 1895 in Bagley, Grant Co., Wisconsin, d. 14 May 1975 in Racine, Racine Co., Wisconsin & **Alice Unknown**, b. About 1901 in Wisconsin – about 1926

Signatures:

- o **Willard Calkins** – b. About 1927 in Wisconsin

Willard Calkins (son):

   Residence – Racine, Racine Co., Wisconsin – 1930

   Occupation – None – 1930

Earle Denton Calkins (son):

   Residence – Wyalusing, Grant Co., Wisconsin – June 23, 1900

                           May 6, 1910

            Bagley, Grant Co., Wisconsin – June 3, 1917

            Racine, Racine Co., Wisconsin – January 13, 1920

                           1930

                           1942

   Occupation – None Listed – June 23, 1900

                    June 1, 1905

     None – May 6, 1910

     Student, Dentist – June 3, 1917

     Dentist, Office Work – January 13, 1920

     Dentist – 1930

     Self Employed – 1942

   Home Data for 1930 – Rental, $ 50 a month, has radio set, not on a farm

Hurst

Alice Unknown (daughter-in-law):

    Residence – Racine, Racine Co., Wisconsin – 1930

                        1942

    Occupation – None – 1930

- **Arcus Riley Calkins**, b. Oct 1896 in Grant Co., Wisconsin & **Mary Mills Gifford**, b. 26 Nov 1895 in Fennimore, Grant Co., Wisconsin – 1922

Signature:

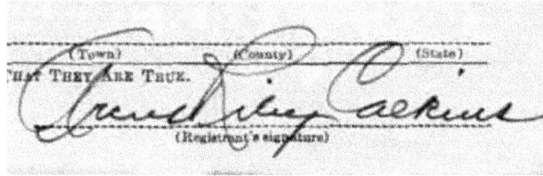

        ○ **Samuel Gifford Calkins**, b. 2 May 1925 in Bagley, Grant Co., Wisconsin, d. 21 Jun 2009 in Cincinnati, Hamilton Co., Ohio & **Mary Louise Ruka**, b. 1924 in Boscobel, Grant Co., Wisconsin, d. 6 Jun 1986 in Cincinnati, Hamilton Co., Ohio

Samuel Gifford Calkins (son):

    Residence – Janesville, Rock Co., Wisconsin – April 7, 1930

    Occupation – None – April 7, 1930

Arcus Riley Calkins (son):

    Residence – Wyalusing, Grant Co., Wisconsin – June 23, 1900

                        June 1, 1905

                        May 6, 1910

        Bagley, Grant Co., Wisconsin – March 6, 1920

                        1942

        Janesville, Rock Co., Wisconsin – April 7, 1930

    Occupation – None Listed – June 23, 1900

                        June 1, 1905

        None – May 6, 1910

        Agent, Life Insurance – March 6, 1920

        Salesman, Bond Company – April 7, 1930

        Unemployed – 1942

    Home Data for 1930 – Rental, $ 75 a month, has radio set, not on a farm

Mary Unknown (daughter-in-law):

    Residence – Janesville, Rock Co., Wisconsin – April 7, 1930

    Occupation – None – April 7, 1930

Elisha Calkins & Anna Dalrymple Descendants

- **Ralph Mason Calkins**, b. Dec 1898 in Grant Co., Wisconsin & **Evelyn A. Unknown**, b. About 1909 in Minnesota

Signature:

Ralph Mason Calkins (son):

    Residence – Wyalusing, Grant Co., Wisconsin – June 23, 1900

                                June 1, 1905

                                May 6, 1910

    Bagley, Grant Co., Wisconsin – September 9, 1918

                                March 6, 1920

    Belgrade, Gallatin Co., Montana – April 2, 1930

    Occupation – None – June 23, 1900

                                May 6, 1910

    None Listed – June 1, 1905

    Student – September 9, 1920

    Student, Normal – March 6, 1920

    Teacher, Public School – April 2, 1930

    Home Data for 1930 – Rental, $ 35 a month, no radio set, not on a farm

Evelyn A. Unknown (daughter-in-law):

    Residence – Belgrade, Gallatin Co., Montana – April 2, 1930

    Occupation – None – April 2, 1930

- **Sophie Glee Calkins** – b. About 1904 in Grant Co., Wisconsin

Sophie Glee Calkins (daughter):

    Residence – Wyalusing, Grant Co., Wisconsin – June 1, 1905

                                May 6, 1910

    Bagley, Grant Co., Wisconsin – March 6, 1920

    Occupation – None Listed – June 1, 1905

              None – May 6, 1910

              Student, High School – March 6, 1920

Charles Denton Calkins (son):

    Residence – Wyalusing, Grant Co., Wisconsin – June 22, 1870

                                June 15, 1880

                                June 23, 1900

                                June 1, 1905

261

Hurst

May 6, 1910

Bagley, Grant Co., Wisconsin – March 6, 1920

April 21, 1930

Occupation – At Home – June 22, 1870

Attends School – June 15, 1880

Salesman – June 23, 1900

General Merchant – June 1, 1905

Retail Merchant – May 6, 1910

Merchant, General Store – March 6, 1920

Retail, Own Store – April 21, 1930

Home Data for 1930 – Owns home, valued at $ 4, 000, has radio set, not on a farm

Mary Jane Day (daughter-in-law):

Residence – Wyalusing, Grant Co., Wisconsin – June 23, 1900

June 1, 1905

May 6, 1910

Bagley, Grant Co., Wisconsin – March 6, 1920

April 21, 1930

Occupation – None Listed – June 23, 1900

June 1, 1905

None – May 6, 1910

April 21, 1930

Milliner – March 6, 1920

■ **William Leslie Calkins**, b. 12 Jul 1871 in Brodtville, Grant Co., Wisconsin, d. 22 Apr 1956 in Winona, Winona Co., Minnesota & **Dorilla Dorcus Bagley**, b. 28 Oct 1872 in Bagley, Grant Co., Wisconsin, d. 18 Mar 1934 in Winona, Winona Co., Minnesota – 20 Sep 1893 in Bagley, Grant Co., Wisconsin

• **Juanita Mary Calkins** – b. 29 May 1895 in Bagley, Grant Co., Wisconsin, d. 17 Aug 1981 in Winona, Winona Co., Minnesota

Juanita Mary Calkins (daughter):

Residence – Wyalusing, Grant Co., Wisconsin – June 21, 1900

June 1, 1905

Dubuque, Dubuque Co., Iowa – April 20th & 21st, 1910

Winona, Winona Co., Minnesota – April 11, 1930

Occupation – None Listed – June 21, 1900

June 1, 1905

None – April 20th & 21st, 1910

Clerk, Dry Goods – April 11, 1930

- **Marie Celeste Calkins**, b. 25 Feb 1903 in Grant Co., Wisconsin & **George R. Allen** – 22 Jan 1923

  in Winona, Winona Co., Minnesota

Marie Celeste Calkins (daughter):

  Residence – Wyalusing, Grant Co., Wisconsin – June 1, 1905

  Dubuque, Dubuque Co., Iowa – April 20th & 21st, 1910

  Occupation – None Listed – June 1, 1905

  None – April 20th & 21st, 1910

William Leslie Calkins (son):

  Residence – Wyalusing, Grant Co., Wisconsin – June 15, 1880

  June 21, 1900

  June 1, 1905

  Dubuque, Dubuque Co., Iowa – April 20th & 21st, 1910

  Winona, Winona Co., Minnesota – April 11, 1930

  Occupation – None Listed – June 15, 1880

  Hotel Keeper – June 21, 1900

  Hotel – June 1, 1905

  Laborer, Odd Jobs – April 20th & 21st, 1910

  Deliveryman, Dry Goods – April 11, 1930

Home Data for 1930 – Owns home, valued at $ 5, 000, has radio set, not on a farm

Dorilla Dorcus Bagley (daughter-in-law):

  Residence – Wyalusing, Grant Co., Wisconsin – June 21, 1900

  June 1, 1905

  Dubuque, Dubuque Co., Iowa – April 20th & 21st, 1910

  Winona, Winona Co., Minnesota – April 11, 1930

  Occupation – None Listed – June 21, 1900

  June 1, 1905

  Dressmaker, At Home – April 20th & 21st, 1910

  None – April 11, 1930

- **Arthur Riley Calkins**, b. 24 Sep 1877 in Brodtville, Grant Co., Wisconsin, d. Jul 1934 in Bagley, Grant

  Co., Wisconsin & **Elva Aurelia Bailey**, b. 26 Sep 1875 in Bloomington, Grant Co., Wisconsin, d. 20

  Jul 1938 – 25 Sep 1901

VERIFIED ABOVE ANSWERS AND THAT THEY ARE TRUE.

Arthur Riley Calkins

Signature:

- **Donald Bailey Calkins** – b. 6 Jul 1906 in Minnesota, d. 14 Jul 1910

Donald Bailey Calkins (son):

Residence – Wyalusing, Grant Co., Wisconsin – May 7, 1910

Occupation – None – May 7, 1910

- **Edward Ira Calkins** – b. 24 Oct 1913 in Portland, Multnomah Co., Oregon, d. 24 Apr 1976 in Portland, Multnomah Co., Oregon

Edward Ira Calkins (son):

Residence – Portland, Multnomah Co., Oregon – January 5, 1920

April 4, 1930

Occupation – None – January 5, 1920

April 4, 1930

- **Greta Mary Calkins**, b. 5 Oct 1917 in Portland, Multnomah Co., Oregon, d. 22 Nov 1989 in Riverside Co., California & **Unknown Symms**

Greta Mary Calkins (son):

Residence – Portland, Multnomah Co., Oregon – January 5, 1920

April 4, 1930

Occupation – None – January 5, 1920

April 4, 1930

Arthur Riley Calkins (son):

Residence – Wyalusing, Grant Co.,, Wisconsin – June 15, 1880

June 23, 1900

June 1, 1905

May 7, 1910

Portland, Multnomah Co., Oregon – September 12, 1918

January 5, 1920

April 4, 1930

Occupation – None Listed – June 15, 1900

Salesman – June 23, 1900

? Dry Goods - June 1, 1905

Retail Merchant, General Store – May 7, 1910

Carman – September 12, 1918

Order Clerk, Drug Department – January 5, 1920

Clerk, Wholesale Drug Store – April 4, 1930

Home Data for 1930 – Owns home, valued at $ 2, 500, has radio set, not on a farm

Elisha Calkins & Anna Dalrymple Descendants

Elva Aurelia Bailey (daughter-in-law):

Residence – Wyalusing, Grant Co., Wisconsin – June 1, 1905

May 7, 1910

Portland, Multnomah Co., Oregon – September 12, 1918

January 5, 1920

April 4, 1930

Occupation – None Listed – June 1, 1905

None – May 7, 1910

January 5, 1920

April 4, 1930

Arcus Riley Calkins (son):

Residence –Wyalusing, Grant Co., Wisconsin – June 13, 1860

June 1863

June 22, 1870

June 15, 1880

June 23, 1900

June 1, 1905

Occupation – Farmer – June 13, 1860

June 22, 1870

June 15, 1880

Dealer, General Merchandise – June 23, 1900

General Store – June 23, 1900

Value of Real Estate – $ 1, 500 – June 13, 1860

$ 4, 000 – June 22, 1870

Value of Personal Estate – $ 200 – June 13, 1860

$ 900 – June 22, 1870

Mary E. Patch (daughter-in-law):

Residence – Wyalusing, Grant Co., Wisconsin – June 13, 1860

June 22, 1870

June 15, 1880

June 23, 1900

June 1, 1905

Occupation – None Listed – June 13, 1860

June 23, 1900

June 1, 1900

Keeping House – June 22, 1870

Hurst

○ **Anna Calkins** – b. 30 Jun 1837, d. Nov 1865

○ **Harriet A. Calkins**, b. 17 Aug 1839, d. 5 Feb 1915 in Topeka, Shawnee Co., Kansas & **Asa Peter Smith** (1st Husband) – 22 Mar 1859 in Grant Co., Wisconsin

○ **Harriet A. Calkins**, b. 17 Aug 1839, d. 5 Feb 1915 in Topeka, Shawnee Co., Kansas & **Joseph M. Scott** (2nd Husband), b. Aug 1837 in New York, d. Before 1920 in New York – 1858

▪ **Cassius M. Scott**, b. Mar 1864 in New York & **Clara M. Unknown**, b. Sep 1866 in New York – 1887

● **Unknown Scott** – b. Before 1900, d. Before 1900

● **Flora Belle Scott**, b. 14 Feb 1884 in Otsego , Otsego Co., New York, d. 3 Dec 1973 Fort Pierce, St. Lucie Co., Florida & **Albert Stanley Persons**, b. 22 Jun 1880 in Prattsville, Greene Co., New York, d. 22 Oct 1950 Mt, Vision, Otsego Co., New York – 1895 in New York

Signature:

○ **Unknown Persons** – b. Before 1900, d. Before 1900

○ **Gilbert J. Persons** – b. About 1906 in New York

Gilbert J. Persons (son):

Residence – Laurens, Otsego Co., New York – May 5, 1910

January 12th & 13th, 1920

April 4, 1930

Occupation – None – May 5, 1910

January 12th & 13th, 1920

Laborer, Freight Train – April 4, 1930

○ **Lynn Randolph Persons**, b. 16 Oct 1910 in Laurens, Otsego Co., New York, d. 23 Mar 1982 in Cooperstown, Otsego Co., New York & **Pearl Vuletta MacKey**, b. 27 Sep 1910 in Grand Gorge, Delaware Co., New York, d. 14 Sep 1978 in Hartwick, Otsego Co., New York – 1930

Lynn Randolph Persons (son):

Residence – Laurens, Otsego Co., New York – January 12th & 13th, 1920

April 4, 1930

Occupation – None – January 12th & 13th, 1920

Automobile Mechanic, Garage – April 4, 1930

Elisha Calkins & Anna Dalrymple Descendants

Pearl Vuletta MacKey (daughter-in-law):

    Residence – Laurens, Otsego Co., New York – April 4, 1930

    Occupation – Telephone Operator, Telephone Office – April 4, 1930

    Home Date for 1930 – Owns home, valued at $ 3, 000, no radio set, not on a farm

Flora Belle Scott (daughter):

    Residence – Laurens, Otsego Co., New York – June 14, 1900

                             May 5, 1910

                             January 12th & 13th, 1920

                             April 4, 1930

        Mt. Vision, Otsego Co., New York – September 12, 1918

    Occupation – At School – June 14, 1900

        None – May 5, 1910

                January 12th & 13th, 1920

                April 4, 1930

Albert Stanley Persons (son-in-law):

    Residence – Laurens, Otsego Co., New York – May 5, 1910

                             January 12th & 13th, 1920

                             April 4, 1930

        Mt. Vision, Otsego Co., New York – September 12, 1918

    Occupation – Laborer, Saw Mill – May 5, 1910

        Farmer – September 12, 1918

        Farmer, General Farm – January 12th & 13th, 1920

        Farmer, Farm – April 4, 1930

    Home Data for 1930 – Owns home valued at $ 3, 500, has radio set, on a farm

Cassius M. Scott (son):

    Residence – Otsego, Otsego Co., New York – June 1, 1880

        New Lisbon, Otsego Co., New York – June 13th & 14th, 1900

    Occupation – Farmer – June 1, 1880

        Carpenter – June 13th & 14th, 1900

Clara M. Unknown (daughter-in-law):

    Residence –New Lisbon, Otsego Co., New York – June 13th & 14th, 1900

    Occupation – None Listed – June 13th & 14th, 1900

Harriet A. Calkins (daughter):

    Residence – Milford, Otsego Co., New York – August 5, 1860

        Otsego, Otsego Co., New York – June 1, 1880

        Laurens, Otsego Co., New York – June 14, 1900

Hurst

May 5, 1910

January 12ᵗʰ & 13ᵗʰ, 1920

Occupation – None Listed – August 5, 1860

June 14, 1900

Keeping House – June 1, 1880

None – May 5, 1910

January 12ᵗʰ & 13ᵗʰ, 1920

Joseph M. Scott (2ⁿᵈ Husband) (son-in-law):

Residence – Milford, Otsego Co., New York – August 5, 1860

June 1863

Otsego, Otsego Co., New York – June 1, 1880

Laurens, Otsego Co., New York – June 14, 1900

May 5, 1910

Occupation – Farming – August 5, 1860

Laborer – June 1863

Farmer – June 1, 1880

June 14, 1900

Farm Laborer, Working Out – June 14, 1910

Value of Real Estate – $ 6, 500 – August 5, 1860

Value of Personal Estate – $ 200 – August 5, 1860

o **Nathan Orson Calkins**, b. 24 Apr 1841 in Columbus, Warren Co., Pennsylvania, d. 9 Jun 1903 in Inglewood, Los Angles Co., California & **Caroline E. Carpenter** (1ˢᵗ Wife), b. 22 Nov 1835 in Mentor, Lake Co., Ohio, d. 29 Dec 1866 in Monona, Clayton Co., Iowa – 26 Aug 1863

  ▪ **Asa Benton Calkins** – b. 7 Nov 1866 in Monona, Clayton Co., Iowa, d. 1877

o **Nathan Orson Calkins**, b. 24 Apr 1841 in Columbus, Warren Co., Pennsylvania, d. 9 Jun 1903 in Inglewood, Los Angles Co., California & **Emily S. Coe** (2ⁿᵈ Wife), b. Jun 1847 in Toledo, Lucas Co., Ohio or in Illinois – 28 Jan 1868

  ▪ **Amy Belle Calkins** – b. 8 Dec 1868 in Eden, Marshall Co., Iowa

Amy Belle Calkins (daughter):

Residence – Auburn, Fayette Co., Iowa – August 3, 1870

Western, Buffalo Co., Nebraska – June 11, 1880

Elm Creek, Buffalo Co., Nebraska – June 29, 1885

Hyde Park, Los Angeles Co., California – June 12, 1900

Inglewood, Los Angeles Co., California – April 22, 1910

1922

April 5, 1930

Occupation – None Listed – August 3, 1870

June 11, 1880

June 29, 1885

House Keeper – June 12, 1900

P. O. [Post Office] Mistress – April 22, 1910

Book Keeper – 1922

None – April 5, 1930

- ▪ **Charles D. Calkins** – b. 18 Aug 1871, d. 1872

- ○ **Nathan Orson Calkins**, b. 24 Apr 1841 in Columbus, Warren Co., Pennsylvania, d. 9 Jun 1903 in Inglewood, Los Angles Co., California & **Jane Cornelia Eastman** (3rd Wife), b. 26 Apr 1856 in Eden, Fayette Co., Iowa, d. 18 Aug 1941 in Inglewood, Los Angles Co., California – 24 Sep 1873 in Fredericks, Chickasaw Co., Iowa

  - ▪ **Mary Olive Calkins**, b. 2 Apr 1876 in Brodtville, Grant Co., Wisconsin & **Nathan D. Smith**, b. About 1899 in Nebraska – 26 Aug 1896 in Inglewood, Los Angeles Co., California

    - ● **Stewart Smith** – b. About 1927 in California

Stewart Smith (son):

Residence – Torrance, Los Angeles Co., California – April 5th – 11th, 1930

Occupation – None – April 5th – 11th, 1930

Mary Olive Calkins (daughter):

Residence – Western, Buffalo Co., Nebraska – June 11, 1880

Elm Creek, Buffalo Co., Nebraska – June 29, 1885

Torrance, Los Angeles Co., California – April 5th – 11th, 1930

Occupation – None Listed – June 11, 1880

June 29, 1885

None – April 5th – 11th, 1930

Nathan D. Smith (son-in-law):

Residence – Torrance, Los Angeles Co., California – April 5th – 11th, 1930

Occupation – News Agent, Street – April 5th – 11th, 1930

Home Data for 1930 – Rental, $ 28.75 a month, has radio set, not on a farm

Hurst

▪ **Lyman Oral Calkins**, b. 5 Aug 1877 in Wyalusing, Grant Co., Wisconsin & **Edith Alminia Kelso**, b. 2 Apr 1879 in Marion Center, Pennsylvania – 21 Mar 1911 in Inglewood, California

Signature:

- **William Kelso Calkins** – b. 1914 in Los Angles Co., California

William Kelso Calkins (son):

   Residence – Inglewood, Los Angeles Co., California – January 12, 1920

                                    April 2, 1930

   Occupation – None – January 12, 1920

                   April 2, 1930

- **Lyman Oral Calkins** – b. Jun 1917 in Los Angeles Co., California

Lyman Oral Calkins (son):

   Residence – Inglewood, Los Angeles Co., California – January 12, 1920

                                      April 2, 1930

   Occupation – None – January 12, 1920

                   April 2, 1930

- **Alminia Calkins** – b. About 1922 in California

Alminia Calkins (daughter):

   Residence – Inglewood, Los Angeles Co., California – April 2, 1930

   Occupation – None – April 2, 1930

- **Elizabeth Calkins** – b. About 1925 in California

Elizabeth Calkins (daughter):

   Residence – Inglewood, Los Angeles Co., California – April 2, 1930

   Occupation – None – April 2, 1930

Lyman Oral Calkins (son):

   Residence – Western, Buffalo Co., Nebraska – June 11, 1880

                Elm Creek, Buffalo Co., Nebraska – June 29, 1885

                Hyde Park, Los Angeles Co., California – June 29, 1900

                Inglewood, Los Angles Co., California – April 22, 1910

                                        1916

                                        September 12, 1918

                                        January 12, 1920

                                        1922

                                        April 2, 1930

Occupation – None Listed – June 11, 1880

June 29, 1885

Farm Laborer – June 29, 1900

Proprietor & P.M., Grocery Store – April 22, 1910

Merchant – 1916

September 12, 1918

1922

President, Mercantile Company – January 12, 1920

Merchant, Hardware – April 2, 1930

Home Data for 1930 – Owns home, valued at $ 15, 000, has radio set, not on a farm

Edith Almina Kelso (daughter-in-law):

Residence – Inglewood, Los Angles Co., California – 1916

September 12, 1918

January 12, 1920

April 2, 1930

Occupation – Housewife – 1916

1922

None – January 12, 1920

April 2, 1930

- **Reuben Roy Calkins**, b. 25 Jul 1880 in Elm Creek, Buffalo Co., Nebraska, d. 24 Apr 1953 in San Diego Co., California & **Inez Mabel Slawson**, b. May 1882 in North Dakota – 24 May 1904

Signature:

- **Jennie Leola Calkins** – b. 27 Nov 1911 in Los Angeles Co., California

Jennie Leola Calkins (daughter):

Residence – Los Angeles, Los Angeles Co., California – 1920

Occupation – None – 1920

- **Elmer Leroy Calkins** – b. 10 Sep 1913 in National City, San Diego Co., California, d. 24 Jun 2001 in Colfax, Placer Co., California

Elmer Leroy Calkins (son):

Residence – Los Angeles, Los Angeles Co., California – 1920

National City, San Diego Co., California – April 21, 1930

Occupation – None – 1920

April 21, 1930

Reuben Roy Calkins (son):

Residence – Elm Creek, Buffalo Co., Nebraska – June 29, 1885

Hyde Park, Los Angeles Co., California – June 29, 1900

San Diego, San Diego Co., California – May 4, 1910

Los Angeles, Los Angeles Co., California – September 12, 1918

1920

National City, san Diego Co., California – April 21, 1930

Occupation – None Listed – June 29, 1885

Farm Laborer – June 29, 1900

Reporter, Newspaper – May 4, 1910

Mech. Teacher – September 12, 1918

Pattern Maker, Foundry – 1920

Salesman, Electric Appliances – April 21, 1930

Home Data for 1930 – Owns home, valued at $ 7, 000, has radio set, not on a farm

Inez Mabel Slawson (daughter-in-law):

Residence – San Diego, San Diego Co., California – May 4, 1910

Los Angeles, Los Angeles Co., California – September 12, 1918

1920

National City, San Diego Co., California – April 21, 1930

Occupation – None – May 4, 1910

1920

April 21, 1930

■ **Oel Leo Calkins**, b. 5 Dec 1882 in Elm Creek, Buffalo Co., Nebraska, d. 17 Jul 1946 in Inglewood, Los Angeles Co., California & **Ava Lucy Spaulding**, b. 17 Feb 1883 in Hartford, Van Buren Co., Michigan, d. 12 Feb 1959 in Inglewood, Los Angeles Co., California – 2 May 1906 in Inglewood, Los Angeles Co., California

Signature:

● **Amy Winifred Calkins** – b. 3 May 1907 in Los Angeles Co., California

Amy Winifred Calkins (daughter):

Residence – Inglewood, Los Angeles Co., California – January 9ᵗʰ – 15ᵗʰ, 1920

April 2, 1930

Occupation – None – January 9ᵗʰ – 15ᵗʰ, 1920

Seamstress, Dress Shop – April 2, 1930

- **Myron Leo Calkins**, b. 20 May 1910 in California, d. 11 May 1990 in California & **Mildred Virginia Moses**, b. 29 Mar 1910 in Lordsburg, Grant Co., New Mexico, d. 16 Feb 1984 in Atascadera, San Luis Obispo Co., California

  o **Gary Calkins**

  o **Sandra Calkins**

Myron Leo Calkins (son):

   Residence – Inglewood, Los Angeles Co., California – January 9th – 15th, 1920

   April 2, 1930

   Occupation – None – January 9th – 15th, 1920

   Salesman, Hardware Store – April 2, 1930

Oel Leo Calkins (son):

   Residence – Elm Creek, Buffalo Co., Nebraska – June 29, 1885

   Hyde Park, Los Angeles Co., California – June 29, 1900

   Inglewood, Los Angles Co., California – September 12, 1918

   January 9th – 15th, 1920

   April 2, 1930

   Occupation – None Listed – June 29, 1885

   At School – June 29, 1900

   Merchant – September 12, 1918

   Salesman, Hardware – January 9th – 15th, 1920

   Merchant, Hardware – April 2, 1930

   Home Data for 1930 – Owns home, valued at $ 12, 000, has radio set, not on a farm

Ava Lucy Spaulding (daughter-in-law):

   Residence – Inglewood, Los Angles Co., California – September 12, 1918

   January 9th – 15th, 1920

   April 2, 1930

   Occupation – None – January 9th – 15th, 1920

   April 2, 1930

- **Ansil Basil Calkins**, b. 15 Mar 1885 in Elm Creek, Buffalo Co., Nebraska, d. 11 Jan 1966 in Los Angeles, Los Angeles Co., California & **Louise Youngworth Riggs**, b. About 1888 in Austria – 29 Jun 1916 in San Francisco, San Mateo Co., California

Signature:

Hurst

- **Ansil Basil Calkins** – b. 9 Dec 1918 in Los Angeles Co., California, d. 16 Apr 2012 in Mesa, Maricopa Co., Arizona

Ansil Basil Calkins (son):

   Residence – Inglewood, Los Angeles Co., California – January 7, 1920

   April 3, 1930

   Occupation – None – January 7, 1920

   April 3, 1930

- Anna Belle Calkins – b. About 1921 in Los Angles Co., California

Anna Belle Calkins (daughter):

   Residence – Inglewood, Los Angeles Co., California – April 3, 1930

   Occupation – None – April 3, 1930

Ansil Basil Calkins (son):

   Residence – Elm Creek, Buffalo Co., Nebraska – June 29, 1885

   Inglewood, Los Angeles Co., California – April 22, 1910

   September 12, 1918

   January 7, 1920

   April 3, 1930

   Occupation – None Listed – June 29, 1885

   Carpenter, House – April 22, 1910

   January 7, 1920

   Clerk, Inglewood Mer. Co. – September 12, 1918

   Carpenter, Building – April 3, 1930

Home Data for 1930 – Owns home, valued at $ 5, 000, has radio set, not on a farm

Louise Youngworth Riggs (daughter-in-law):

   Residence – Inglewood, Los Angeles Co., California – January 7, 1920

   April 3, 1930

   Occupation – None – January 7, 1920

   April 3, 1930

- Hazel Glenn Calkins – b. 27 Dec 1887 in Kimball, Kimball Co., Nebraska

Hazel Glenn Calkins (daughter):

   Residence – Inglewood, Los Angeles Co., California – April 22, 1910

   San Diego, San Diego Co., California – May 4, 1910

   Occupation – None – April 22, 1910

   May 4, 1910

274

Elisha Calkins & Anna Dalrymple Descendants

Nathan Orson Calkins (son):

    Residence – Wyalusing, Grant Co., Wisconsin – June 13, 1860

        Auburn, Fayette Co., Iowa – August 2, 1870

        Western, Buffalo Co., Nebraska – June 11, 1880

        Elm Creek, Buffalo Co., Nebraska – June 29, 1885

        Kimball, Kimball Co., Nebraska – June 1890

        Hyde Park, Los Angeles Co., California – July 1, 1896

                June 12, 1900

    Occupation – Farm Laborer – June 13, 1860

        Farmer – August 2, 1870

        June 11, 1880

        June 12, 1900

        Wheel Wright – June 29, 1885

        Furniture – June 1890

        Blacksmith – July 1, 1896

    Value of Real Estate – $ 4,000 – August 2, 1870

    Value of Personal Estate – $ 1, 000 – August 2, 1870

Emily S. Coe (2ⁿᵈ Wife) (daughter-in-law):

    Residence – Auburn, Fayette Co., Iowa – August 3, 1870

    Occupation – Keeping House – August 3, 1870

Jane Cornelia Eastman (3ʳᵈ Wife) (daughter-in-law):

    Residence – Western, Buffalo Co.., Nebraska – June 11, 1880

        Elm Creek, Buffalo Co., Nebraska – June 29, 1885

        Hyde Park, Los Angeles Co., California – June 12, 1900

        Inglewood, Los Angeles Co., California – April 22, 1910

                1922

                April 5, 1930

    Occupation – Keeping House – June 11, 1880

        June 29, 1885

        None Listed – June 12, 1900

        None – April 22, 1910

        April 5, 1930

        Housewife – 1922

    Home Data for 1930 – Owns home, valued at $ 8, 000, has radio set, not on a farm

o **Victor M. Calkins**, b. 27 Jul 1853 in Brodtville, Grant Co., Wisconsin, d. 18 Jul 1926 in Minneapolis, Hennepin Co., Minnesota & **Eleanor C. Van Dusen**, b. 24 Aug 1858 in Ellenburgh, Clinton Co., New York, d. 1 May 1953 in Minneapolis, Hennepin Co., Minnesota – 23 Jan 1879 in Prairie du Chien, Crawford Co., Wisconsin

  ▪ **Mildred Beth Calkins**, b. 27 Nov 1879 in Wyalusing, Grant Co., Wisconsin, d. 20 Jan 1955 in Lyon Co., Minnesota & **Bert Eugene Ingalls**, b. About 1883 in Austin, Mower Co., Minnesota – 15 Oct 1903 in La Crosse, La Crosse Co., Wisconsin

Signature:

  • **Lance Laverne Ingalls** – b. 24 Jan 1910 in Iowa, d. 12 Apr 1962 in Lyon Co., Minnesota

Lance Laverne Ingalls (son):

   Residence – Huron, Beadle Co., South Dakota – May 17, 1910

       Tracy, Lyon Co., Minnesota – January 2, 1920

   Occupation – None – May 17, 1910

       January 2, 1920

Mildred Beth Calkins (daughter):

   Residence – Wyalusing, Grant Co., Wisconsin – June 5th & 7th, 1880

       Huron, Beadle Co., South Dakota – May 17, 1910

       Tracy, Lyon Co., Minnesota – January 2, 1920

   Occupation – None – May 17, 1910

       January 2, 1920

Bert Eugene Ingalls (son-in-law):

   Residence – Huron, Beadle Co., South Dakota – May 17, 1910

                  September 9, 1918

       Tracy, Lyon Co., Minnesota – January 2, 1920

   Occupation – Engineer, Steam Rail Road – May 17, 1910

       Conductor, C. N. W. Railway – September 9, 1918

       Conductor, Rail Road – January 2, 1920

▪ **Randall Branch Calkins**, b. 14 Nov 1881 in Wyalusing, Grant Co., Wisconsin, d. 24 Feb 1921 in St. Paul Ramsey Co., Minnesota & **Lovina P. Bainter**, b. About 1888 in Michigan – 4 Dec 1911 in St. Paul, Ramsey Co., Minnesota

Signature:

• **Unknown Calkins** (Baby Girl) – b. Before 12 Feb 1916 in St. Paul, Ramsey Co., Minnesota, d. 12 Feb 1916 in St. Paul, Ramsey Co., Minnesota

Randall Branch Calkins (son):

Residence – Minneapolis, Hennepin Co., Minnesota – April 25, 1910

St. Paul, Ramsey Co., Minnesota – September 12, 1918

Occupation – Painter – April 25, 1925

Decorator – September 12, 1918

Lovina P. Bainter (daughter-in-law):

Residence – St. Paul, Ramsey Co., Minnesota – September 12, 1918

Minneapolis, Hennepin Co., Minnesota – April 14, 1930

Occupation – Draper, Furniture – April 14, 1930

▪ **Ida May Calkins**, b. 2 Jan 1885 in Wyalusing, Grant Co., Wisconsin, d. 17 Oct 1975 in Watsonville, Santa Cruz Co., California & **William Luther Shepard**, b. 20 Nov 1876

Signature:

• **Virginia Lee Shepard** – b. 20 Feb 1915 Hennepin Co., Minnesota

Virginia Lee Shepard (daughter):

Residence – Huron, Beadle Co., South Dakota – September 12, 1918

January 17, 1920

April 24, 1930

Occupation – None – January 17, 1920

April 24, 1930

Ida May Calkins (daughter):

Residence – Huron, Beadle Co., South Dakota – January 17, 1920

April 24, 1930

Occupation – None – January 17, 1920

Nurse Practical, Private Family – April 24, 1930

Hurst

William Luther Shepard (son-in-law):

    Residence – Huron, Beadle Co., South Dakota – September 12, 1918

                                       January 17, 1920

                                       April 24, 1930

    Occupation – Layer, Floor Finisher – September 12, 1918

        Floor Finishing, General – January 17, 1920

        Janitor, Rail Road Station – April 24, 1930

    Home Data for 1930 – Owns home, valued at $ 4, 700, no radio set, not on a farm

- **Harriet Adele Calkins**, b. 17 Jul 1886 in Wyalusing, Grant Co., Wisconsin, d. 7 Jul 1970 in Fresno, Fresno Co., California & **Frank Vernon Randall**, b. 16 Jan 1885 in Minnesota, d. 4 Nov 1957 in Fresno Co., California – 4 Jun 1913 in Beadle Co., South Dakota

Signature:

- **Ardath Randall** – b. About 1916 in Beadle Co., South Dakota

Ardath Randall (daughter):

    Residence – Huron, Beadle Co., South Dakota – May 27, 1920

        Minneapolis, Hennepin Co., Minnesota – April 14, 1930

    Occupation – None – May 27, 1920

        April 14, 1930

Harriet Adele Calkins (daughter):

    Residence – Minneapolis, Hennepin Co., Minnesota – April 25, 1910

        April 14, 1930

        Huron, Beadle Co., South Dakota – September 5, 1918

        May 27, 1920

    Occupation – None – April 25, 1910

        May 27, 1920

        April 14, 1930

Frank Vernon Randall (son-in-law):

    Residence – Huron, Beadle Co., South Dakota – September 5, 1918

        May 27, 1920

        Minneapolis, Hennepin Co., Minnesota – April 14, 1930

    Occupation – Conductor, C. & N.W. Railway – September 5, 1918

        Conductor, Steam Rail Road – May 27, 1920

        City Weigher [hard to read], City Minneapolis – April 14, 1930

    Home Data for 1930 – Owns home, valued at $ 5, 000, has radio set, not on a farm

▪ **Caraetta Calkins**, b. 1 Feb 1893 in Brodtville, Grant Co., Wisconsin, d. 21 Feb 1980 in Fresno, Fresno Co., California & **George McKinley Fosdick**, b. 24 May 1892 in Knoxville, Marion Co., Iowa, d. 9 Aug 1971 in Fresno, Fresno Co., California – 10 Jul 1915 in Minneapolis, Hennepin Co., Minnesota

Signature:

• **Betty Gail Fosdick** – b. 26 May 1916 in Hennepin Co., Minnesota

Betty Gail Fosdick (daughter):

　　Residence – Minneapolis, Hennepin Co., Minnesota – June 5, 1917

　　　　　　　　　　　　　　　　　　　　　　January 12, 1920

　　　　　　　　　　　　　　　　　　　　　　April 12, 1930

　　Occupation – None Listed – January 12, 1920

　　　　None – April 12, 1930

• **Robert Lee Fosdick** – b. 5 Oct 1918 in Hennepin Co., Minnesota

Robert Lee Fosdick (son):

　　Residence – Minneapolis, Hennepin Co., Minnesota – January 12, 1920

　　　　　　　　　　　　　　　　　　　　　　April 12, 1930

　　Occupation – None Listed – January 12, 1920

　　　　None – April 12, 1930

• **Phyllis Eleanor Fosdick** – b. 26 Jan 1920 in Hennepin Co., Minnesota

Phyllis Eleanor Fosdick (daughter):

　　Residence – Minneapolis, Hennepin Co., Minnesota – April 12, 1930

　　Occupation – None – April 12, 1930

• **Lois Marie Fosdick** – b. 29 Dec 1921 in Hennepin Co., Minnesota

Lois Marie Fosdick (daughter):

　　Residence – Minneapolis, Hennepin Co., Minnesota – April 12, 1930

　　Occupation – None – April 12, 1930

• **Jean Ann Fosdick** – b. 2 Oct 1926 in Hennepin Co., Minnesota

Jean Ann Fosdick (daughter):

　　Residence – Minneapolis, Hennepin Co., Minnesota – April 12, 1930

　　Occupation – None – April 12, 1930

Hurst

Caraetta Calkins (daughter):

    Residence – Windom, Mower Co., Minnesota – June 14, 1905

        Minneapolis, Hennepin Co., Minnesota – June 5, 1917

                      January 12, 1920

                      April 12, 1930

    Occupation – None Listed – June 14, 1905

        None – January 12, 1920

          April 12, 1930

George McKinley Fosdick (son-in-law):

    Residence – Minneapolis, Hennepin Co., Minnesota – June 5, 1917

                      January 12, 1920

                      April 12, 1930

    Occupation – Booking Clerk – June 5, 1917

        Booker, Film Company – January 12, 1920

        Assets Manager, Film Exchange – April 12, 1930

    Home Data for 1930 – Owns home, valued at $ 5, 000, has radio set, not on a farm

Victor M. Calkins (son):

    Residence – Wyalusing, Grant Co., Wisconsin – June 13, 1860

                      June 18, 1870

                      June 5th & 7th, 1880

        Windom, Mower Co., Minnesota – June 14, 1905

        Minneapolis, Hennepin Co., Minnesota – April 25, 1910

        Huron, Beadle Co., South Dakota – January 17, 1920

    Occupation – None Listed – June 13, 1860

        At Home – June 18, 1870

        Works on farm – June 5th & 7th, 1880

        Farm Laborer – June 14, 1905

        Manager, Hotel – April 25, 1910

        Clerk, Round House – January 17, 1920

Eleanor C. Van Dusen (daughter-in-law):

    Residence – Wyalusing, Grant Co., Wisconsin – June 5th & 7th, 1880

        Windom, Mower Co., Minnesota – June 14, 1905

        Minneapolis, Hennepin Co., Minnesota – April 25, 1910

        Huron, Beadle Co., South Dakota – January 17, 1920

                      April 24, 1930

Occupation – Assists Keeping House – June 5ᵗʰ & 7ᵗʰ, 1880

None Listed – June 14, 1905

None – April 25, 1910

January 17, 1920

April 24, 1930

Lyman Simon Calkins (father):

Residence – Otselic, Chenango Co., New York – October 23, 1832

Columbus, Warren Co., Pennsylvania – 1840

Wyalusing, Grant Co., Wisconsin – 1855

June 13, 1860

June 18, 1870

June 5ᵗʰ & 7ᵗʰ, 1880

Occupation – Farmer – June 13, 1860

June 18, 1870

June 5ᵗʰ & 7ᵗʰ, 1880

Value of Real Estate – $ 1, 600 – June 13, 1860

$ 4, 000 – June 18, 1870

Value of Personal Estate – $ 420 – June 13, 1860

$ 1, 000 – June 18, 1870

Amy Albee (mother):

Residence – Otselic, Chenango Co., New York – October 23, 1832

Wyalusing, Grant Co., Wisconsin – June 13, 1860

June 18, 1870

June 5ᵗʰ & 7ᵗʰ, 1880

Occupation – None Listed – June 13, 1860

Keeping House – June 18, 1870

Keeps House – June 5ᵗʰ & 7ᵗʰ, 1880

Lyman Simon Calkins & Amy Albee

Family Photo Album (Found at an Estate Sale near Medina, Ohio)

Date of Album – 1860s

Photographs courtesy of The Hurst Family of Lake Elsinore, California

Carliste, Photo., Stevens Point, Wis.

N. O. CALKINS.

Arcus Riley Calkins & Nathan Orson Calkins

Photograph (Right) from <u>The Calkins memorial military roster</u>

Photographs courtesy of The Hurst Family of Lake Elsinore, California

Heman Calkins & Descendants

- **Heman Calkins**, b. 13 Aug 1812 in Brookfield, Madison Co., New York, d. 5 Apr 1886 in Otselic, Chenango Co., New York & **Almira Webb**, b. About 1814 in Madison Co., New York, d. 23 Aug 1889 in Otselic, Chenango Co., New York – 1 Jan 1834 in Otselic, Chenango Co., New York

  o **Sidney M. Calkins**, b. 26 Oct 1836 in Otselic, Chenango Co., New York, d. 20 Jan 1900 in Chenango Co., New York & **Sarah Abby Curtis**, b. Aug 1841 in Otselic, Chenango Co., New York, d. 1902 in New York – 1853 in Chenango Co., New York

    ▪ **Emma Retta Calkins**, b. 9 May 1862 in New York, d. 9 Jan 1915 in New York & **William Brooks**, b. About 1860 in New York, d. Before 1900 in New York

      • **Ernest S. Brooks**, b. Mar 1882 in New York, d. Bef. 1920 in New York & **Mina A. Watters**, b. 1882 in New York

        o **Sylvia E. Brooks**, b. 28 Oct 1902 in Otselic, Chenango Co., New York, d. 8 Sep 1982 in Syracuse, Onondaga Co. New York & **George William Swayze**, b. 14 Oct 1901 in Smyrna, Chenango Co., New York, d. 26 Aug 1998 in Syracuse, Onondaga Co., New York – 25 Oct 1922 in Otselic, Chenango Co., New York

Sylvia E. Brooks (daughter):

Residence – Otselic, Chenango Co., New York – May 2, 1910

June 1, 1915

January 3, 1920

October 25, 1922

Occupation – None – May 2, 1910

January 3, 1920

School – June 1, 1915

Teacher – October 25, 1922

George William Swayze (son-in-law):

Residence – Otselic, Chenango Co., New York – October 25, 1922

Occupation – Farmer – October 25, 1922

        o **Susie E. Brooks**, b. 1907 in New York & **Daniel Robert Swayze**, b. 12 Apr 1903 in New York, d. 19 Jul 1989

Susie E. Brooks (daughter):

Residence – Otselic, Chenango Co., New York – May 2, 1910

June 1, 1915

January 3, 1920

April 14, 1930

Occupation – None – May 2, 1910

January 3, 1920

April 14, 1930

School – June 1, 1915

Daniel R. Swayze (son-in-law):

Residence – Otselic, Chenango Co., New York – April 14, 1930

Occupation – Chauffeur, ? [Hard to read] – April 14, 1930

Home Data for 1930 – Rental, $ 8 a month, no radio set, not on a farm

○ Goldie M. Brooks – b. 1908 in New York

Goldie M. Brooks (daughter):

Residence – Otselic, Chenango Co., New York – May 2, 1910

June 1, 1915

January 3, 1920

Occupation – None – May 2, 1910

January 3, 1920

School – June 1, 1915

○ Jessie I. Brooks – b. 1912 in New York

Jessie I. Brooks (daughter):

Residence – Otselic, Chenango Co., New York – June 1, 1915

January 3, 1920

April 14, 1930

Occupation – None Listed – June 1, 1915

None – January 3, 1920

Teacher, Grade School – April 14, 1930

Ernest S. Brooks (son):

Residence – Otselic, Chenango Co., New York – June 1, 1900

May 2, 1910

June 1, 1915

Occupation – Farmer – June 1, 1900

June 1, 1915

Farmer, Own Farm – May 2, 1910

Mina A. Watters (daughter-in-law):

   Residence – Otselic, Chenango Co., New York – May 2, 1910

                    June 1, 1915

                    January 3, 1920

   Occupation – None – May 2, 1910

                 January 3, 1920

      Housekeeper – June 1, 1915

- **Verna L. Brooks**, b. May 1888 in Otselic, Chenango Co., New York, d. Before 1930 in Smyrna, Chenango Co., New York & **Charles Abner Tucker**, b. 21 Apr 1889 in Otselic, Chenango Co., New York – 10 Sep 1912 in Cincinnatus, Chenango Co., New York

Signature:

Signatures (Marriage):

BRIDE

GROOM

    o **Andley B. Tucker** – b. About 1915 in New York

Andley B. Tucker (son):

   Residence – Smyrna, Chenango Co., New York – January 13, 1920

                  April 11, 1930

   Occupation – None – January 13, 1920

      Laborer, Farm – April 11, 1930

    o **Eleanor E. Tucker** – b. About 1917 in New York

Eleanor E. Tucker (daughter):

   Residence – Smyrna, Chenango Co., New York – January 13, 1920

                  April 11, 1930

   Occupation – None – January 13, 1920

           April 11, 1930

Elisha Calkins & Anna Dalrymple Descendants

○ **Stanley E. Tucker** – b. About 1923 in New York

Stanley E. Tucker (son):

    Residence – Smyrna, Chenango Co., New York – April 11, 1930

    Occupation – None – April 11, 1930

Verna L. Brooks (daughter):

    Residence – Otselic, Chenango Co., New York – June 1, 1900

                            May 2, 1910

                            September 10, 1912

        Smyrna, Chenango Co., New York – January 13, 1920

    Occupation – At School – June 1, 1900

        Domestic – September 10, 1912

        None – January 13, 1920

Charles Abner Tucker (son-in-law):

    Residence – North Pharsalia, Chenango Co., New York – September 10, 1912

        Smyrna, Chenango Co., New York – June 5, 1917

                            January 13, 1920

                            April 11, 1930

    Occupation – Farmer – September 10, 1912

                  June 5, 1917

        Farmer, Diary Farm – January 13, 1920

        Farmer, General Farm – April 11, 1930

    Home Data for 1930 – Owns home, no radio set, on a farm

Emma Retta Calkins (daughter):

    Residence – Otselic, Chenango Co., New York – June 2, 1875

                            1880

                            June 1, 1900

                            May 2, 1910

    Occupation – None Listed – June 2, 1875

                            June 1, 1900

        At Home – 1880

        None – May 2, 1910

Obituary –

*"Mrs. Emma Brooks died Friday at her son's. She was a daughter of Sidney Calkins and a widow of Wm. Brooks. She leaves a son, Ernest, and a daughter, Vern. The funeral is held today at the home; Burial at Cole Hill." **from The De Ruyter Gleaner. Page 2. Thursday, January 14, 1915***

Hurst

▪ **Myrtle E. Calkins**, b. 15 May 1866 in New York, d. 27 Jan 1938 in Georgetown, Madison Co., New York & **Lafayette F. Sherwood**, b. Sep 1855 in New York – Between 1882 – 1883

- **Claude S. Sherwood** – b. 14 Nov 1883 in New York, d. 21 Mar 1947 in Norwich, Chenango Co., New York

Claude S. Sherwood (son):

Residence – Otselic, Chenango Co., New York – June 2, 1900

June 1, 1905

January 28, 1920

Beaver Meadow, Chenango Co., New York – April 22, 1930

Occupation – None Listed – June 2, 1900

Farm Laborer – June 1, 1905

Farmer, General Farm – January 28, 1920

Laborer, Farm Dairy – April 22, 1930

Home Data for 1930 – Owns home valued at $ 500, no radio set, not on a farm

Obituary –

"Claude S. Sherwood. Claude S. Sherwood, 62, of Beaver Meadow, died Friday, March 21, 1947, in Norwich Hospital. The son of the late Mr. and Mrs. LaFayette Sherwood, he was born Nov. 18, 1884. He is survived by two brothers, Leon Sherwood and Myrl Sherwood, both of Beaver Meadow. Funeral services were held Monday at 2 p. m. in the Christian Church at Beaver Meadow, the Rev. Ralph Davis officiating. Burial was made in Otselic Cemetery." from Page Four, The De Ruyter Gleaner. Thursday, March 27, 1947

- Leon Wallace Sherwood – b. 18 Apr 1886 in New York

Signature:

Leon Wallace Sherwood (son):

Residence – Otselic, Chenango Co., New York – June 2, 1900

June 1, 1905

May 4, 1910

January 28, 1920

Beaver Meadow, Chenango Co., New York – September 12, 1918

April 22, 1930

Occupation – At School – June 2, 1900

Farm Laborer – June 1, 1905

Farmer, Home Farm – May 4, 1910

Farmer – September 12, 1918

Farmer, Dairy Farm – January 28, 1920

Farmer, General Farm – April 22, 1930

- **Myrl La Fayette Sherwood**, b. 12 Nov 1898 in New York & **Nettie Unknown**, b. About 1897 in Michigan – 1904

Signature:

Myrl La Fayette Sherwood (son):

Residence – Otselic, Chenango Co., New York – June 2, 1900

June 1, 1905

May 4, 1910

Beaver Meadow, Chenango Co., New York – September 12, 1918

April 22, 1930

Occupation – None Listed – June 2, 1900

At School – June 1, 1905

None – May 4, 1910

Farmer – September 12, 1918

Farmer, Home Farm Dairy – April 22, 1930

Home Data for 1930 – Owns home, has radio set, on a farm

Nettie Unknown (daughter-in-law):

Residence – Beaver Meadow, Chenango Co., New York – April 22, 1930

Occupation – None – April 22, 1930

Myrtle E. Calkins (daughter):

Residence – Otselic, Chenango Co., New York – June 2, 1875

1880

June 2, 1900

June 1, 1905

May 4, 1910

January 28, 1920

Beaver Meadow, Chenango Co., New York – April 22, 1930

Occupation – None Listed – June 2, 1875

June 2, 1900

At School – 1880

Housework – June 1, 1905

None – May 4, 1910

January 28, 1920

Hurst

April 22, 1930

Lafayette F. Sherwood (son-in-law):

Residence – Otselic, Chenango Co., New York – June 2, 1900

June 1, 1905

May 4, 1910

January 28, 1920

Beaver Meadow, Chenango Co., New York – September 12, 1918

April 22, 1930

Occupation – Farmer – June 2, 1900

June 1, 1905

Farmer, Own Farm – May 4, 1910

None – January 28, 1920

April 22, 1930

Home Data for 1930 – Owns home, has radio set, on a farm

Sidney M. Calkins (son):

Residence – Otselic, Chenango Co., New York – August 5, 1850

June 27, 1860

June 2, 1875

1880

Occupation – None Listed – August 5, 1850

Farm Hand – June 27, 1860

Farmer – June 2, 1875

1880

Obituary –

"Sidney Calkins, who has been in poor health for sometime, died Sunday afternoon." **from The De Ruyter Gleaner.**

Page 2. Thursday, January 25, 1900

Sarah Abby Curtis (daughter-in-law):

Residence – Otselic, Chenango Co., New York – June 2, 1875

1880

June 1, 1900

Occupation – Keeping House – June 8, 1870

1880

None Listed – June 2, 1875

June 1, 1900

○ **Leman Calkins**, b. 1838 in Otselic, Chenango Co., New York, d. 1901 & **Mary Ann Griffin** (1st Wife), b. About 1836 in New York, d. 7 Feb 1864 in Chenango Co., New York

▪ **Charles D. Calkins** – b. 1856 in Chenango Co., New York, d. 5 Sep 1877 in Chenango Co., New York

Charles D. Calkins (son):

Residence – Otselic, Chenango Co., New York – June 4, 1875

Occupation – Farm Laborer – June 4, 1875

○ **Leman Calkins**, b. 1838 in Otselic, Chenango Co., New York, d. 1901 & **Louisa Bellinger** (2nd Wife), b. 1848 in New York, d. 16 Oct 1877 in Chenango Co., New York

▪ **James H. Calkins** – b. About 1870 in Chenango Co., New York

James H. Calkins (son):

Residence – Otselic, Chenango Co., New York – June 4, 1875

Occupation – None Listed – June 4, 1875

Leman Calkins (son):

Residence – Otselic, Chenango Co., New York – August 5, 1850

June 27, 1860

June 4, 1875

Smyrna, Chenango Co., New York – June 24, 1870

Truxton, Cortland Co., New York – June 1, 1880

February 16, 1892

Occupation – None Listed – August 5, 1850

Farm Hand – June 27, 1860

Lumber Dealer – June 24, 1870

Lumbering – June 1, 1875

Lumberman – June 1, 1880

None Listed – February 16, 1892

Value of Real Estate – $ 12, 550 – June 24, 1870

Value of Personal Estate – $ 2, 200 – June 24, 1870

Obituary –

"Nov. 19 – Leman Calkins, who lived at Crain's Mills, one mile east of this village and is known from his dealings in lumber for many years in this vicinity, died at his late residence last evening. He has been in poor health for a long time and the end, though it finally came suddenly, had been expected by many. He will be buried in Beaver Meadow." **from the De Ruyter Gleaner. Thursday, November 21, 1901**

Hurst

Louisa Bellinger (2nd Wife) (daughter-in-law):

    Residence – Smyrna, Chenango Co., New York – June 24, 1870

        Otselic, Chenango Co., New York – June 4, 1875

    Occupation – Keeping House – June 24, 1870

        None Listed – June 4, 1875

    o   **Louisa Calkins**, b. 4 Jul 1842 in Otselic, Chenango Co., New York, d. 5 Apr 1919 in Chenango Co., New York & **Daniel B. Rider**, b. Jan 1834 in Madison Co., New York, d. 26 Mar 1909 in Chenango Co., New York – 1865 in Otselic, Chenango Co., New York

        ▪ **Sarah Jennie Rider** – b. About 1869 in Otselic, Chenango Co., New York

Sarah Jennie Rider (daughter):

    Residence – Otselic, Chenango Co., New York – July 27, 1870

                            June 3, 1875

                            June 5, 1880

    Occupation – None Listed – July 27, 1870

                      June 3, 1875

                      June 5, 1880

        ▪ **Charles A. Rider** – b. About 1872 in Otselic, Chenango Co., New York

Charles A. Rider (son):

    Residence – Otselic, Chenango Co., New York – June 3, 1875

    Occupation – None Listed – June 3, 1875

Louisa Calkins (daughter):

    Residence – Otselic, Chenango Co., New York – August 5, 1850

                            June 27, 1860

                            July 27, 1870

                            June 3, 1875

                            June 5, 1880

                            June 1, 1900

                            June 1, 1905

                            May 2, 1910

    Occupation – None Listed – New York – August 5, 1850

                        June 27, 1860

                        June 1, 1900

       Keeping House – July 27, 1870

                      June 5, 1880

       Housework – June 1, 1905

None – May 2, 1910

Obituary –

"The funeral of Louisa Rider was held Wednesday at the Christian Church. Rev. Stokum of Sherburne officiated and Undertaker Benedict also of Sherburne had charge of the burial in Cole Hill Cemetery. Mrs. Rider had always lived in this community. She was the daughter of the late Herman and Almira Calkins and wife of the late Daniel Rider. Since the death of her husband, she has been away doing housework in various families and at the time of her death was working near Sherburne. She was sick only a few days with pneumonia. She had a trained nurse and all was done for her that friends could do. The day was very stormy and only a few of her relatives were present. She leaves one brother and one sister and 3 grandchildren to mourn her loss. She was about 70 years old." **from The De Ruyter Gleaner. Thursday, April 16, 1914**

Daniel B. Rider (son-in-law):

Residence – Otselic, Chenango Co., New York – July 27, 1870

> *June 3, 1875*
>
> *June 5, 1880*
>
> *June 1, 1900*
>
> *June 1, 1905*

Occupation – Farmer – July 27, 1870

> *June 3, 1875*
>
> *June 5, 1880*
>
> *June 1, 1900*
>
> *June 1, 1905*

Value of Real Estate – $ 1, 100 – July 27, 1870

Value of Personal Estate – $ 200 – July 27, 1870

Obituary/Death Notice –

"Funeral Director Woodley conducted the burial of Daniel Rider at Beaver Meadow on Monday. He was a brother of B. Z. Rider." **from the De Ruyter Gleaner. Vol. 39 – No. 29. De Ruyter, N.Y., Thursday, April 1, 1909**

- **William Henry Calkins** – b. 12 Jan 1842 in Otselic, Chenango Co. New York, d. 16 Aug 1863 in Thibodeaux, Lafourche Parish, Louisiana

William Henry Calkins (son):

Residence – Otselic, Chenango Co., New York – August 5, 1850

> *June 27, 1860*

> *August 11, 1862*

Occupation – None Listed – August 5, 1850

> *June 27, 1860*

> *Farmer – August 11, 1862*

Cause of Death – Typhoid Fever

- **Sally Ann Calkins** – b. 1844 in Otselic, Chenango Co., New York

Sally Ann Calkins (daughter):

Residence – Otselic, Chenango Co., New York – August 5, 1850

> *June 27, 1860*

> *July 25, 1870*

> *June 3, 1875*

> *June 22, 1880*

Occupation – None Listed – August 5, 1850

> *June 27, 1860*

> *House Keeper – June 3, 1875*

> *At Home – June 22, 1880*

- Francis Adelbart Calkins – b. 8 Jun 1847 in Otselic, Chenango Co., New York, d. 15 Sep 1863

Francis Adelbart Calkins (son):

Residence – Otselic, Chenango Co., New York – August 5, 1850

> *June 27, 1860*

Occupation – None Listed – August 5, 1850

> *June 27, 1860*

- **Morrell Calkins**, b. 18 Jan 1849 in Otselic, Chenango Co., New York, d. 25 Sep 1936 in Taylor, Cortland Co., New York & **Lydia A. O'Hare** (1st Wife), b. About 1846, d. 5 Apr 1896 in Cortland Co., New York

  - **Charles Calkins**, b. Apr 1879 in New York, d. 1946 in Taylor, Cortland Co., New York & **Minnie Louise Thorington**, b. 12 Oct 1872 in Taylor, Cortland Co., New York, d. 10 Jan 1942 in Taylor, Cortland Co., New York – 19 Jan 1897 in Taylor, Cortland Co., New York

Signature:

294

- **Clyde Calkins**, b. 1892 in New York & **Maud Unknown**, b. 1892 in New York

Signature:

o **Francis Calkins** – b. 7 Feb 1918 in New York, d. 17 Aug 1998 in Willet, Cortland Co., New York

Francis Calkins (son):

    Residence – Willet, Cortland Co., New York – April 18, 1930

    Occupation – None – April 18, 1930

Clyde Calkins (son):

    Residence – Taylor, Cortland Co., New York – May 2, 1910

        Willet, Cortland Co., New York – June 5, 1917

                January 3, 1920

                April 18, 1930

    Occupation – Farmer, Farm – May 2, 1910

        Laborer – June 5, 1917

        Stage Driver, Star Route – January 3, 1920

        Tin Smith, Hardware Store – January 18, 1930

    Home Data for 1930 – Owns home, valued at $ 1, 000, no radio set, not on a farm

Maud Unknown (daughter-in-law):

    Residence – Willet, Cortland Co., New York – June 5, 1917

                January 3, 1920

                April 18, 1930

    Occupation – None – January 3, 1920

        April 18, 1930

Charles Calkins (son):

    Residence – Taylor, Cortland Co., New York – June 6, 1900

                May 2, 1910

                September 12, 1918

                January 17, 1920

                1930

    Occupation – Farmer – June 6, 1900

        Farmer, Farm – May 2, 1910

        Farming – September 12, 1918

        Farmer, Dairy Farm – January 17, 1920

Hurst

Laborer Roofing – 1930

Home Data for 1930 – Owns home, valued at $ 800, has radio set, not on a farm

Obituary –

"Charles Calkins Died in the Cortland Hospital. Charles Calkins, son of the late Morrell Calkins, died in the Cortland Hospital Saturday afternoon at the age of 67 years. He had been in failing health for some time and lived in the Bert Oliver home. With the exception of a short time in Willet, he spent his entire life in Taylor, having operated a farm for many years in Taylor Valley. Mr. Calkins was married to Minnie Thorington, who died about four years ago. They brought up Clyde Calkins of Willet. There are no surviving relatives. Funeral services were held Tuesday at 1 p. m. in the Bush Funeral Parlors in Cincinnatus with Rev. G. C. LaCelle officiating. Burial was in Taylor Cemetery." From The De Ruyter Gleaner. Thursday, November 27, 1946

Minnie Louise Thorington (daughter-in-law):

Residence – Taylor, Cortland Co., New York – June 6, 1900

> *May 2, 1910*
> *September 12, 1918*
> *January 17, 1920*

Occupation – None Listed – June 6, 1900

> *None – May 2, 1910*
> *January 17, 1920*

Obituary –

"Mrs. Charles Calkins – This community was sadden by the death of Mrs. Charles Calkins at 5 o'clock Saturday morning at her home in this village. After an illness of one week, Minnie Louise Thorington was the daughter of the late Lorenzo Thorington and Selina Smith was born, October 12, 1872, in the town of Taylor. She was married on January 19, 1897, to Charles Calkins of Taylor. They lived on a farm in Taylor Center until about 20 years ago, when they came to Taylor village to make their home. Mrs. Calkins leaves to mourn her loss, her husband, an adopted son, Clyde Calkins; a grand-son Francis Calkins and a great grand-daughter Nancy Jeanine Calkins, all of Willet; four sisters, Mrs. Nina Stewart of De Ruyter, Mrs. Myra Potter of Cincinnatus; Mrs. Ella Baker of Cortland and Mrs. Estella Brenchley of Syracuse; besides nieces, nephews, cousins and many friends. The funeral was held on Tuesday, January 13, at 2 o'clock, in the Wesleyan Methodist church in Taylor cemetery." from The De Ruyter Gleaner. Page 7. Thursday, January 15, 1942

○ **Morrell Calkins**, b. 18 Jan 1849 in Otselic, Chenango Co., New York, d. 25 Sep 1936 in Taylor, Cortland

Co., New York & **Gertrude A. Unknown** (2nd Wife), d. 27 Oct 1917 in Cortland Co., New York

▪ **Nina L. Calkins** – b. Mar 1884 in New York

Nina L. Calkins (daughter):

Residence – Truxton, Cortland Co., New York – February 16, 1892

June 13, 1900

June 1, 1905

Occupation – None Listed – June 4, 1875

At School – June 13, 1900

House Work – June 1, 1905

○ **Morrell Calkins**, b. 18 Jan 1849 in Otselic, Chenango Co., New York, d. 25 Sep 1936 in Taylor, Cortland

Co., New York & **Minnie P. Gilbert** (3rd Wife), b. Aug 1867 in New York – About 1897

Morrell Calkins (son):

Residence – Otselic Chenango Co., New York – August 5, 1850

June 27, 1860

July 25, 1870

June 2, 1875

Taylor, Cortland Co., New York – June 16th & 18th, 1900

May 2, 1910

January 30, 1920

1930

Occupation – None Listed – August 5, 1850

June 27, 1860

Farmer – June 2, 1875

June 16th & 18th, 1900

Farmer, Farm – May 2, 1910

Farmer Retired, None – January 30, 1920

None – 1930

Home Data for 1930 – Owns home, valued at $ 1, 000, no radio set, not on a farm

Obituary –

"Morrell Calkins – Morrell Calkins died at his late home here Friday evening, September 25th, at the age of eighty-seven. He had been active until a few weeks ago when his health began to fail but not until the last three weeks had he taken his bed and then not all the time. For three days before he died he lay in a coma for fifty-nine hours. He leaves one son, Charles of this place. The funeral was held at the late home Monday afternoon with burial in the Truxton Cemetery." from The De Ruyter Gleaner. Thursday, October 1, 1936

Hurst

Gertrude A. Unknown (2nd Wife) (daughter-in-law):

Residence – Truxton, Cortland Co., New York – February 16, 1892

June 13, 1900

June 1, 1905

1910

Occupation – None Listed – February 16, 1892

Dress Maker – June 13, 1900

June 1, 1905

Minnie P. Gilbert (3rd Wife) (daughter-in-law):

Residence – Taylor, Cortland Co., New York – June 16th & 18th, 1900

May 2, 1910

January 30, 1920

1930

Occupation – None Listed – June 16th & 18th, 1900

None – May 2, 1910

January 30, 1920

1930

○ **Phebe R. Calkins** – b. 1851 in Otselic, Chenango Co., New York, d. 8 Mar 1875 in Otselic, Chenango Co., New York

Phebe R. Calkins (daughter):

Residence – Otselic, Chenango Co., New York – June 27, 1860

July 25, 1870

March 8, 1875

Occupation – None Listed – June 27, 1860

None – March 8, 1875

Cause of Death – Epileptic Fits

○ **Emmoretta Calkins** – b. 1857 in Otselic, Chenango Co., New York, d. 7 Jun 1862 in Chenango Co., New York

Emmoretta Calkins (daughter):

Residence – Otselic, Chenango Co., New York – June 27, 1860

Occupation – None Listed – June 27, 1860

Elisha Calkins & Anna Dalrymple Descendants

Heman Calkins (father):

Residence – Otselic, Chenango Co., New York – 1840

August 5, 1850

June 27, 1860

July 25, 1870

June 2, 1875

June 22, 1880

Occupation – Farmer – August 5, 1850

June 27, 1860

July 25, 1870

June 22, 1880

Retired Farmer – June 2, 1875

Value of Real Estate – $ 1, 200 – August 5, 1850

$ 3, 000 – June 27, 1860

$ 4, 500 – July 25, 1870

Value of Personal Estate – $ 780 – June 27, 1860

$ 1, 500 – July 25, 1870

Almira Webb (mother):

Residence – Otselic, Chenango Co., New York – August 5, 1850

June 27, 1860

July 25, 1870

June 2, 1875

June 22, 1880

Occupation – None Listed – August 5, 1850

June 27, 1860

House Keeper – June 2, 1875

Keeping House – June 22, 1880

Transcription of Will –

"In the name of God, Amen, I, Almira Calkins of the town of Otselic in the County of Chenango and State of New York of the age of seventy-five years and being of sound mind and memory do make, publish and declare this my last Will and Testament in manner following the is to say: <u>First</u>: I give, devise and bequeath to my daughter Sally Ann Calkins the use of all my property of every manner and nature both real estate and personal property for and during her natural life under the following condition that is the property that I shall have and own at the time of my decease and after all my lawful debts are paid and my burial expenses are paid and a set of grave stones are erected at my grave suitable to my condition and standing in life. And I hereby authorize and empower my Executor hereinafter named at the time of my decease to take possession of all my said property and have the care, custody and control thereof and invest and [word scribbled out] rent the same as in his

judgment he shall think best and use the avails thereof for the support and maintenance of my said daughter Sally Ann Calkins as he shall think most prudent and proper except when shall be required to pay my said property and expenses and in case the use of my said property and all the parties thereof shall not be sufficient to furnish my said daughter Sally Ann Calkins a comfortable support and maintenance then and in such case I hereby authorize and empower my said Executor to use any of my said personal property for the support and maintenance of my said daughter Sally Ann Calkins, and if in the judgment of my said Executor he shall think is necessary and proper to sell any or all of the real estate which I may own at the time of my decease, I hereby authorize and empower my said Executor to sell the same, and to take all lawful and necessary steps to sell and convey the same and use so much of the avails thereof as may be necessary to support my said daughter Sally Ann Calkins a comfortable manner. <u>Second</u>: At the time of the decease of my said daughter Sally Ann Calkins, I order and direct my said Executor to pay all funeral and burial expenses of said Sally Ann Calkins and erect at her grave a set of grave stones suitable to her condition and standing in Society and pay all expenses of the same out of and funds in his hands belonging to my said estate. <u>Third</u>: After the death and burial of my said daughter Sally Ann Calkins and the erection of grave stones at her grave as above provided and my Executor shall be paid a fair and legal compensation for his services and expenses then all the rest and residue of my estate and property whether realty or personal which shall be left remain in the hands of my said Executor, I give devise and bequeath to my remaining children viz; Sidney M. Calkins, Louisa Rider, Leeman Calkins and Morrell Calkins to be divided equally share and share alike between them, and if either of any said children above named shall not be living at the time of the death of said Sally Ann Calkins, then their individual share is to be paid to their heirs and next of kin and if any of my said children shall be owing or indebted to my estate by more or otherwise, then such indebtedness is to apply as a payment on their individual share whether the same is paid to them or their heirs or next of kin. <u>Fourth</u>: and lastly I hereby appoint Warren A. Webb, Executor of this my last will and testament hereby revoking all former wills by me made. In witness whereof I have hereunto set my hand and seal this 14th day of June in the year 1889. Almira Calkins [Her Mark]. The above instrument consisting of one sheet of paper and a part of another was as the date thereof signed by the said Almira Calkins by her making her mark, sealed published and declared by the said Almira Calkins as and for her last Will and Testament in presence of us who at her request and in her presence, and in the presence of each other have subscribed our names as witnesses thereto Wallace E. Webb of Beaver Meadow Chenango Co. N.Y. Deloss A. Campbell of the town of Otselic Chenango Co. N.Y. Chenango County, S.S.: - I hereby certify that the foregoing is a correct record of the last Will and Testament of Almira Calkins, deceased, and of the proofs [?] thereof and that said Will and Proofs [?] have been duly recorded this 16th day of Sept. 1889. W. F. Jenks Surrogate." **Made June 14, 1889**

Heman Calkins

Photograph from Family Photo Album (Found at an Estate Sale near Medina, Ohio)

Date of Album – 1860s

Photograph courtesy of The Hurst Family of Lake Elsinore, California

Heman Calkins & Almira Webb

Family Photo Album (Found at an Estate Sale near Medina, Ohio)

Date of Album – 1860s

Photographs courtesy of The Hurst Family of Lake Elsinore, California

Sidney M. Calkins

Photographer Credit: G. H. DeWitt – Madison, New York

Photograph courtesy of The Hurst Family of Lake Elsinore, California

Leman Calkins & Louisa Bellinger

Photographer Credit (Left): G. J. Pruden – Cortland, New York

Photographer Credit (Right): E. D. Benjamin – De Ruyter, New York

Photographs courtesy of The Hurst Family of Lake Elsinore, California

James H. Calkins

Photographer Credit: Pruden & Jones – Cortland, New York

Photograph courtesy of The Hurst Family of Lake Elsinore, California

Louisa Calkins & Daniel B. Rider

Photographer Credit (Left): Hotchkiss – Norwich, New York

Date – 1889

Photographer Credit (Right): Hotchkiss – Norwich, New York

Date – 1891

Photographs courtesy of The Hurst Family of Lake Elsinore, California

Charles A. Rider

Photographer Credit: Hotchkiss – Norwich, New York

Date – 1889

Photograph courtesy of The Hurst Family of Lake Elsinore, California

William Henry Calkins & Sally Ann Calkins

Photograph (Left) – Tintype

Photographer Credit (Right): Hotchkiss – Norwich, New York

Date – 1891

Photographs courtesy of The Hurst Family of Lake Elsinore, California

Morrell Calkins

Photographer Credit: Hotchkiss – Norwich, New York

Date – 1887

Photograph courtesy of The Hurst Family of Lake Elsinore, California

Dorman Calkins & Descendants

- **Dorman Calkins**, b. 20 Jun 1816 in Brookfield, Madison Co., New York, d. 17 Dec 1883 in Otselic, Chenango Co., New York & **Phebe Webb**, b. 30 May 1816 in Lebanon, Madison Co., New York, d. 15 Dec 1897 in Chenango Co., New York – 1 Jan 1837 in Otselic, Chenango Co., New York

Signatures:

  o **Parmelia Calkins** – b. 1838 in Otselic, Chenango Co., New York, d. 1839

  o **Peruda Calkins**, b. 17 Oct 1839 in Otselic, Chenango Co., New York, d. Jun 1911 in Beaver Meadow, Chenango Co., New York & **Noyes Robbins**, b. Aug 1843 in New York, d. 10 Sep 1917 in Beaver Meadow, Chenango Co., New York – 1 Jan 1865 in Otselic, Chenango Co., New York

   ▪ **Frank Robbins** – b. About 1859 in Otselic, Chenango Co., New York

Frank Robbins (son):

Residence – Otselic, Chenango Co., New York – July 27, 1870

Occupation – At Home – July 27, 1870

   ▪ **Mary A. Robbins** – b. About 1865 in New York

Mary A. Robbins (adopted-daughter):

Residence – Otselic, Chenango Co., New York – June 30, 1880

Occupation – At School – June 30, 1880

Peruda Calkins (daughter):

Residence – Otselic, Chenango Co., New York – August 5, 1850

June 27, 1860

July 27, 1870

June 30, 1880

June 1, 1900

May 2, 1910

Occupation – None Listed – August 5, 1850

Farm Hand – June 27, 1860

Keeping House – July 27, 1870

June 30, 1880

None Listed – June 1, 1900

None – May 2, 1910

Obituary –

"Beaver Meadow. June 26. – The funeral of Mrs. Noyes Robbins was largely attended at her late home on Sunday last. Rev. Mr. Meyers of Georgetown officiated and Undertaker Newcomb of Pitcher had charge of the burial which was made in Cole Hill cemetery. Mrs. Robbins has lived all her life in this vicinity and was well and favorably known to a large circle of friends. She suffered a shock about 3 years ago and has since been gradually failing till death came to her relief. She leaves her husband, who has cared for her with untiring devotion through her long illness and one brother, Dwight Calkins, of Sherburne, besides many more distant relatives. She was a daughter of Dorman and Phoebe Calkins and will be remembered by some of the older residents as a teacher in her youth. Mrs. R. was about 70 years of age. Among those present from a distance were Mr. and Mrs. Charles Smith and daughter, Helen, of Cobleskill, Mr. and Mrs. Dwight Calkings [Calkins] and wife and daughter, Lettie, of Sherburne, Mr. and Mrs. I. W. Duthcer, wife and daughter, Lena, of Smyrna, Mrs. Alice Crandall of West Eaton, Mrs. Frank Hitchcock and daughter of Earlville and many from Bonney, Otselic and South Otselic ." from The De Ruyter Gleaner. Thursday, June 29, 1911

Noyes Robbins (son-in-law):

    Residence – Otselic, Chenango Co., New York – July 27, 1870

                                        June 30, 1880

                                        June 1, 1900

                                        May 2, 1910

    Occupation – Farmer – July 27, 1870

                                June 30, 1880

                                June 1, 1900

                          Farmer, Own Farm – May 2, 1910

    Value of Real Estate – $ 6, 550 in July 27, 1870

    Value of Personal Estate – $ 1, 300 – July 27, 1870

    Obituary –

    "The funeral of Noyes Robbins was held at the house Wednesday. Rev. E. J. Yesdon officiated and Chas. Woodley had charge of the burial. Those from a distance who attended were: Van Gray and John Gray of Brookfield and Mr. and Mrs. Bever Bellinger of Earlville." from The De Ruyter Gleaner. Thursday, September 20, 1917

○   **Comadore Perry Calkins** – b. 15 Jul 1841 in Otselic, Chenango Co., New York, d. 7 Feb 1843 in Otselic, Chenango Co., New York

o **Dorman Dwight Calkins**, b. 22 Dec 1853 in Otselic, Chenango Co., New York, d. 1930 in Smyrna, Chenango Co., New York & **Sarah Viola Storrs** (1st Wife), b. About 1854 in Worcester, Otsego Co., New York, d. 6 Mar 1875 in Otselic, Chenango Co., New York – About 1874 in Otselic, Chenango Co., New York

   ▪ **Violetta Calkins** – b. 28 Feb 1875 in Otselic, Chenango Co., New York, d. 20 May 1930 Binghamton, Broome Co., New York

Violetta Calkins (daughter):

Residence – Otselic, Chenango Co., New York – June 3, 1875

June 17, 1880

June 1, 1900

Sherburne, Chenango Co., New York – May 23, 1910

Smyrna, Chenango Co., New York – January 6, 1920

Occupation – None Listed – June 3, 1875

June 17, 1880

June 1, 1900

None – May 23, 1910

January 6, 1920

Obituary –

"Lettie Calkins – Miss Lettie Calkins passed away at the Binghamton Stat Hospital, where she had been just one week, on Tuesday evening, May 20, 1930. She was the daughter of Dwight and Viola Storrs Calkins and was born in the town of Otselic on February 28, 1875. She had been a resident of this section all her life and of Smyrna Village for many years, where she has many friends who will learn of her death with sorrow. Besides her father she is survived by a sister, Mrs. I. W. Dutcher of this place, and a brother, Earl Calkins of Syracuse. Funeral services will be held from the Baptist church Sunday at 2 p. m., Rev. Arhtur Lacy officiating, with internment in the Wilcox cemetery. – Smyrna cor." from The De Ruyter Gleaner. Page 5. Thursday, May 29, 1930

o **Dorman Dwight Calkins**, b. 22 Dec 1853 in Otselic, Chenango Co., New York, d. Jun 1930 in Smyrna, Chenango Co., New York & **Elizabeth Dutcher** (2nd Wife), b. 12 Aug 1855 in Union, Broome Co., New York, d. 6 Mar 1930 in Smyrna, Chenango Co., New York – 23 Aug 1877 in De Ruyter, Madison Co., New York

   ▪ **Ida May Calkins**, b. 6 Dec 1881 in Otselic, Chenango Co., New York & **Irving Washington Dutcher**, b. 18 Jan 1879 in South Otselic, Chenango Co., New York – About 1900

Signature:

- **Lena Elizabeth Dutcher** – b. 10 Apr 1901 in Otselic, Chenango Co., New York

Lena Elizabeth Dutcher (daughter):

    Residence – Smyrna, Chenango Co. New York – April 21, 1910

                                    January 6, 1920

    Occupation – None – April 21, 1910

                            January 6, 1920

- **Lawrence E. Dutcher** – b. About 1916 in New York

Lawrence E. Dutcher (adopted-son):

    Residence – Smyrna, Chenango Co. New York – January 6, 1920

                                    April 4, 1930

    Occupation – None – January 6, 1920

                            April 4, 1930

Ida May Calkins (daughter):

    Residence – Otselic, Chenango Co., New York – June 1, 1900

        Smyrna, Chenango Co., New York – April 21, 1910

                                    September 12, 1918

                                    January 6, 1920

                                    April 4, 1930

    Occupation – None Listed – June 1, 1900

               None – April 21, 1910

                        January 6, 1920

                        April 4, 1930

Irving Washington Dutcher (son-in-law):

    Residence – Smyrna, Chenango Co., New York – April 21, 1910

                                    September 12, 1918

                                    January 6, 1920

                                    April 4, 1930

    Occupation – Farmer, General Farm – April 21, 1910

                                  April 4, 1930

        Farmer – September 12, 1918

        Farmer, Diary Farm – January 6, 1920

    Home Data for 1930 – Owns home, has radio set, on a farm

Hurst

- **Earl Calkins**, b. 21 Nov 1886 in Smyrna, Chenango Co., New York, d. 20 Apr 1943 in Cortland, Cortland Co., New York & **Anna Nicholson**, b. 24 Nov 1882 in Solon, Cortland Co., New York, d. 23 Feb 1950 in Cortland, Cortland Co., New York – 6 Mar 1907 in Fabius, Onondaga Co., New York

  - **Leon Dwight Calkins**, b. 9 Apr 1908 in Smyrna, Chenango Co., New York, d. Mar 1968 & **Rose Holcomb**, b. 9 Apr 1909 in New York, d. Jan 1980 in Phoenix, Oswego Co., New York

Leon Dwight Calkins (son):

Residence – Cuyler, Cortland Co., New York – May 5, 1910

De Ruyter, Madison Co., New York – February 9, 1920

Syracuse, Onondaga Co., New York – April 11, 1930

Occupation – None – May 5, 1910

February 9, 1920

April 11, 1930

  - **Emmett Joseph Calkins**, b. 19 Jun 1918 in De Ruyter, Madison Co., New York, d. 30 Oct 1989 in Sodus, New York & **Viola Lena Williams** – 30 Jun 1938 in Cortland, Cortland Co., New York

Emmett Joseph Calkins (son):

Residence – De Ruyter, Madison Co., New York – February 9, 1920

Syracuse, Onondaga Co., New York – April 11, 1930

Occupation – None – February 9, 1920

April 11, 1930

Earl Calkins (son):

Residence – Otselic, Chenango Co., New York – June 1, 1900

Cuyler, Cortland Co., New York – May 5, 1910

De Ruyter, Madison Co., New York – February 9, 1920

Syracuse, Onondaga Co., New York – April 11, 1930

Occupation – At School – June 1, 1900

Farmer, General Farm – May 5, 1910

February 9, 1920

Laborer, Foundry – April 11, 1930

Home Data for 1930 – Rental, $ 25 a month, has radio set, not on a farm

Anna Nicholson (daughter-in-law):

Residence – Cuyler, Cortland Co., New York – May 5, 1910

De Ruyter, Madison Co., New York – February 9, 1920

Syracuse, Onondaga Co., New York – April 11, 1930

Occupation – None – May 5, 1910

February 9, 1920

April 11, 1930

▪ **Irvin Calkins** – b. 21 Nov 1886 in Smyrna, Chenango Co., New York, d. 13 Sep 1887 in Chenango Co.,

New York

Dorman Dwight Calkins (son):

Residence – Otselic, Chenango Co., New York – June 27, 1860

July 26, 1870

June 3, 1875

June 17, 1880

June 1, 1900

Sherburne, Chenango Co., New York – May 23, 1910

Smyrna, Chenango Co., New York – January 6, 1920

Occupation – None Listed – June 27, 1860

At Home – July 26, 1870

Farm Laborer – June 3, 1875

June 17, 1880

Farmer – June 1 1900

Farmer, General – May 23, 1910

None – January 6, 1920

Obituary –

"Dwight Calkins. Dwight Calkins who went to Syracuse on May 25 to visit his son Earl, returned Sunday afternoon critically ill. Dr. William Little of Sherburne was called and pronounced pneumonia the cause of his trouble and he passed away on Monday morning about eight o'clock. The funeral will be held Thursday at 1 p. m. in the Baptist Church in this village with burial in the Wilcox Cemetery. It will be remembered that Mrs. Calkins died March 5 and his daughter, Lettie, died May 20, 1930, thus removing the family within three months. He was 76 years of age. – Smyrna cor. Norwich Sun." **from Page Four, The De Ruyter Gleaner. Thursday, June 5, 1930**

Sarah Viola Storrs (1ˢᵗ Wife) (daughter-in-law):

Residence – Otselic, Chenango Co., New York – March 6, 1875

Occupation – House Keeper – March 6, 1875

Cause of Death – Plura Pneumonia

Hurst

Elizabeth Dutcher (2nd Wife) (daughter-in-law):

Residence – Otselic, Chenango Co., New York – June 17, 1880

June 1, 1900

Sherburne, Chenango Co., New York – May 23, 1910

Smyrna, Chenango Co., New York – January 6, 1920

Occupation – At Home – June 17, 1880

None Listed – June 1, 1900

None – May 23, 1910

January 6, 1920

Obituary –

"Mrs. Dwight Calkins (Smyrna cor. Norwich Sun.) – Mrs. Dwight Calkins one of the oldest residents of the town, passed away at her home in this village on Thursday, March 6, after a serious illness of several weeks. Although a partial invalid for many years she kept as active as her physical handicap would permit in taking an active part in the making and keeping of her home, where she always displayed a most friendly and optimistic nature toward everyone and everything, and it was a source of much pleasure visit her in her home. Elizabeth Dutcher Calkins, daughter of the late Milton and Mary Gager Dutcher, was born in the town of Union, N. Y., August 12, 1844, and 53 years age was married to Dwight Calkins, who, with two daughters, Miss Lettie Calkins and Mrs. Irving Dutcher of Smyrna; a son, Earl Calkins of Syracuse, and a brother, Bert Dutcher of Cincinnatus, survives. Funeral services were held on Sunday afternoon, a prayer at the home at 2 and from the Baptist church at 2:30, Rev. Mr. Lacey, pastor, officiating, with interment in the Wilcox Cemetery. A true and devoted wife, mother, and friend, whose trust was in God, has passed from her earthly troubles to a fuller life and to her reward." from The De Ruyter Gleaner. Page Eight, Thursday, March 12, 1930

o **Willie Calkins** – b. About 1861 in Cayuga Co., New York

Willie Calkins (adopted-son):

Residence – Otselic, Chenango Co., New York – July 26, 1870

June 3, 1875

Occupation – None Listed – July 26, 1870

June 3, 1875

o **Perry B. Calkins** – b. Bef. 1843 in Chenango Co., New York, d. 1843 in Chenango Co., New York

Elisha Calkins & Anna Dalrymple Descendants

Dorman Calkins (father):

Residence – Otselic, Chenango Co., New York – August 5, 1850

> *June 27, 1860*
>
> *July 26, 1870*
>
> *June 3, 1875*
>
> *June 17, 1880*

Occupation – Farmer – August 5, 1850

> *June 27, 1860*
>
> *July 26, 1870*
>
> *June 3, 1875*
>
> *June 17, 1880*

Value of Real Estate – $ 2, 000 – August 5, 1850

> *$ 4, 200 – June 27, 1860*
>
> *$ 6, 975 – July 26, 1870*

Value of Personal Estate – $ 1, 200 – June 27, 1860

> *$ 1, 600 – July 26, 1870*

Obituary –

"Much sadness was caused by the death of Dorman Calkins, an old and respected citizen of this town. The funeral occurred at Beaver Meadow, Thursday. All will deeply regret his death, while they extend the sincerest sympathies to the bereaved ones."

from The Weekly Gleaner. Thursday, January 3, 1884, De Ruyter, Madison Co., New York

Phebe Webb (mother):

Residence – Otselic, Chenango Co., New York – August 5, 1850

> *June 27, 1860*
>
> *July 26, 1870*
>
> *June 3, 1875*
>
> *June 17, 1880*

Occupation – None Listed – August 5, 1850

> *June 27, 1860*
>
> *June 3, 1875*

Keeping House – July 26, 1870

> *June 17, 1880*

Dorman Calkins

Family Photo Album (Found at an Estate Sale near Medina, Ohio)

Date of Album – 1860s

Photograph courtesy of The Hurst Family of Lake Elsinore, California

Dorman Calkins & Phebe Webb

Family Photo Album (Found at an Estate Sale near Medina, Ohio)

Date of Album – 1860s

Photographs courtesy of The Hurst Family of Lake Elsinore, California

Dorman Calkins & Phebe Webb

Photographer Credit (Left): Wick – Norwich, New York

Photographer Credit (Right): Hotchkiss – Norwich, New York

Date – 1884

Photographs courtesy of The Hurst Family of Lake Elsinore, California

Dwight Calkins & Peruda Calkins

Photographs – Tintypes

Photographs courtesy of The Hurst Family of Lake Elsinore, California

Harriet Calkins & Descendants

- **Harriet Calkins**, b. 9 Sep 1818 in Brookfield, Madison Co., New York, d. 31 Oct 1911 in Smyrna, Chenango Co., New York & **Ery W. Stokes**, b. 8 Dec 1821 in New York, d. 15 Apr 1890 in Smyrna, Chenango Co., New York – Before 1844 in Chenango Co., New York

  - **Betsy A. Stokes**, b. Jun 1844 in Chenango Co., New York & **Robert Rush Clark**, b. Apr 1835 in New York

    - **William Stokes Clark** – b. Jun 1867 in New York

William Stokes Clark (son):

Residence – Smyrna, Chenango Co., New York – June 16, 1880

Mt. Vernon, Linn Co., Iowa – 1885

Florence, Los Angeles Co., California – August 8, 1896

Occupation – At School – June 16, 1880

None listed – 1885

Real Estate – August 8, 1896

Betsey A. Stokes (daughter):

Residence – Sherburne, Chenango Co., New York – September 3, 1850

Smyrna, Chenango Co., New York – July 17, 1860

June 16, 1880

Mt. Vernon, Linn Co., Iowa – 1885

San Antonio, Los Angeles Co., California – June 27, 1900

Occupation – None Listed – September 3, 1850

July 17, 1860

1885

June 27, 1900

Keeping [House] – June 16, 1880

Robert Rush Clark (son-in-law):

Residence – Smyrna, Chenango Co., New York – June 1863

June 16, 1880

Mt. Vernon, Linn Co., Iowa – 1885

Florence, Los Angeles Co., California – August 3, 1896

San Antonio, Los Angeles Co., California – June 27, 1900

Occupation – Bar Tender – June 1863

Laborer – June 16, 1880

Farmer – 1885

August 3, 1896

U.S. Mail Carrier – June 27, 1900

○ **Olivia L. Stokes**, b. May 1849 in Chenango Co., New York & **Morrell D. Ferris**, b. 21 Apr 1852 in Smyrna, Chenango Co., New York, d. 24 Mar 1876 in Smyrna, Chenango Co., New York

▪ **Clayton Ferris** – b. 9 Aug 1873 in Smyrna, Chenango Co., New York, d. 22 Aug 1874 in Smyrna, Chenango Co., New York

▪ **Anna Ferris** – b. 6 Mar 1875 in Smyrna, Chenango Co., New York, d. 23 Mar 1876 in Smyrna, Chenango Co., New York

Olivia L. Stokes (daughter):

Residence – Sherburne, Chenango Co., New York – September 3, 1850

Smyrna, Chenango Co., New York – July 17, 1860

June 28, 1870

June 17, 1880

Manlius, Onondaga Co., New York – June 19, 1900

May 10, 1910

Occupation – None Listed – September 3, 1850

July 17, 1860

June 19, 1900

Teacher – June 28, 1870

Dressmaker – June 17, 1880

Farmer, Home Farm – May 10, 1910

○ **Isaac E. Stokes** – b. May 1847 in Smyrna, Chenango Co., New York, d. 3 Feb 1849 in Smyrna, Chenango Co., New York

○ **Charles Dever Stokes**, b. Jun 1848 in Smyrna, Chenango Co., New York & **Ella M. Nearing**, b. Jun 1846 in New York, d. Before 1897

▪ **Charles Maurice Stokes**, b. Feb 1886 in Montana & **Inez W. Warburton**, b. 31 Oct 1887 in Akron, Summit Co., Ohio

• **Jean W. Stokes** – b. 12 May 1925 in San Diego Co., California

Jean W. Stokes (daughter):

Residence – Vista, San Diego Co., California – April 3, 1930

Occupation – None – April 3, 1930

Charles Maurice Stokes (son):

 Residence – Madison, Gallatin Co., Montana – June 11ᵗʰ & 12ᵗʰ, 1900

  Pomona, Los Angeles Co., California – January 8, 1920

  Vista, San Diego Co., California – April 3, 1930

 Occupation – At School – June 11ᵗʰ & 12ᵗʰ, 1900

  Civil Engineer, General Practice – January 8, 1920

  Civil Engineer, Own Account – April 3, 1930

Inez W. Warburton (daughter-in-law):

 Residence – Vista, San Diego Co., California – April 3, 1930

 Occupation – None – April 3, 1930

Charles Dever Stokes (son):

 Residence – Smyrna, Chenango Co., New York – July 17, 1860

  June 28, 1870

  June 18, 1880

  Madison, Gallatin Co., Montana – June 11ᵗʰ & 12ᵗʰ, 1900

  Pomona, Los Angeles Co., California – April 18, 1910

  January 8, 1920

 Occupation – None Listed – July 17, 1860

  At Home – June 28, 1870

  Merchant – June 18, 1880

  Farmer – June 11ᵗʰ & 12ᵗʰ, 1900

  Clerk, Fruit Store – April 18, 1910

  Watchman, Fruit Packing House – January 8, 1920

Ella M. Nearing (daughter-in-law):

 Residence – Smyrna, Chenango Co., New York – June 18, 1880

  Madison, Gallatin Co., Montana – June 11ᵗʰ & 12ᵗʰ, 1900

  Pomona, Los Angeles Co., California – April 18, 1910

  January 8, 1920

 Occupation – Keeping House – June 18, 1880

  None Listed – June 11ᵗʰ & 12ᵗʰ, 1900

  None – April 18, 1910

  January 8, 1900

o **Ida E. Stokes**, b. 20 Aug 1851 in Smyrna, Chenango Co., New York, d. 29 Aug 1910 in Smyrna, Chenango Co., New York & **Walter A. Shepardson**, b. 23 Jun 1851 in Earlville, Chenango Co., New York, d. 21 Jan 1926 in Smyrna, Chenango Co., New York – 10 Dec 1872 in Smyrna, Chenango Co., New York

▪ **Unknown Sheparson** – b. After 1872, d. Before 1900 in New York

▪ **Ery Stokes Shepardson**, b. 7 Jan 1890 in New York, d. Aug 1981 in Smyrna, Chenango Co., New York

    & **Agnes E. Stanton**, b. about 1892 in Smyrna, Chenango Co., New York – 1 Nov 1911 in Otselic,

    Chenango Co., New York

Signature:

Signatures (Marriage):

    • **Stanton Shepardson** – b. About 1913 in Chenango Co., New York

Stanton Shepardson (son):

    Residence – Smyrna, Chenango Co., New York – April 3, 1930

    Occupation – None – April 3, 1930

    • **Stanley Shepardson** – b. About 1913 in Chenango Co., New York

Stanley Shepardson (son):

    Residence – Smyrna, Chenango Co., New York – April 3, 1930

    Occupation – None – April 3, 1930

    • **Francis G. Shepardson** – b. About 1916 in Chenango Co., New York

Francis G. Shepardson (son):

    Residence – Smyrna, Chenango Co., New York – April 3, 1930

    Occupation – None – April 3, 1930

    • **Richard A. Shepardson** – b. About 1917 in Chenango Co., New York

Richard A. Shepardson (son):

    Residence – Smyrna, Chenango Co., New York – April 3, 1930

    Occupation – None – April 3, 1930

    • **Carl John Shepardson** – b. About 1921 in Chenango Co., New York

Carl John Shepardson (son):

    Residence – Smyrna, Chenango Co., New York – April 3, 1930

    Occupation – None – April 3, 1930

Hurst

- **Mary Alice Shepardson** – b. About 1927 in Chenango Co., New York

Mary Alice Shepardson (daughter):

Residence – Smyrna, Chenango Co., New York – April 3, 1930

Occupation – None – April 3, 1930

Ery Stokes Shepardson (son):

Residence – Otselic, Chenango Co., New York – June 5, 1900

June 1, 1905

November 1, 1911

Norwich, Chenango Co., New York – April 25, 1910

Smyrna, Chenango Co., New York – June 5, 1917

January 3, 1920

April 3, 1930

Occupation – At School – June 5, 1900

June 1, 1905

None – April 25, 1910

Farmer – November 1, 1911

June 5, 1917

Farmer, Dairy Farm – January 3, 1920

Farmer, General Farm – April 3, 1930

Home Data for 1930 – Owns home, has radio set, on a farm

Agnes E. Stanton (daughter-in-law):

Residence – Otselic, Chenango Co., New York – November 1, 1911

Smyrna, Chenango Co., New York – January 3, 1920

April 3, 1930

Occupation – Domestic – November 1, 1911

None – January 3, 1920

April 3, 1920

Ida E. Stokes (daughter):

Residence – Smyrna, Chenango Co., New York – July 17, 1860

June 28, 1870

June 21, 1875

Otselic, Chenango Co., New York – June 8, 1880

June 5, 1900

June 1, 1905

Norwich, Chenango Co., New York – April 25, 1910

Occupation – None Listed – July 17, 1860

June 5, 1900

Teacher – June 28, 1870

House Keeping – June 21, 1875

Keeping House – June 8, 1880

Housework – June 1, 1905

None – April 25, 1910

Obituaries –

"*Mrs. Walter A. Shepardson, Wife of Assemblyman Died at Summer Home in Otselic. Norwich, Aug. 31 - Mrs. Walter A. Shepardson, the wife of Assemblyman Shepardson, died at their summer home at Otselic Monday night. The news came as a great shock to her friends here and elsewhere in the county. Funeral services at the home in Otselic at 1:30 to-morrow afternoon.*" *from The Utica Herald Dispatch. Wednesday Evening, August 31, 1910*

"*The many friends of Mrs. Walter A. Shepardson in this village [South Otselic] were pained to learn of her death on Monday night last. Deceased is survived by her husband, Assemblyman W. A. Shepardson, and son Stokes; also by her aged mother. We extend sympathy to the bereaved family .*" *from The De Ruyter Gleaner. De Ruyter, N. Y. Thursday, September 1, 1910*

Walter A. Shepardson (son-in-law):

Residence – Smyrna, Chenango Co., New York – June 21, 1875

Otselic, Chenango Co., New York – June 8, 1880

June 5, 1900

June 1, 1905

Norwich, Chenango Co., New York – April 25, 1910

January 5, 1920

Occupation – Staff N.Y. O M R. R. – June 21, 1875

Farmer – June 8, 1880

None Listed – June 5, 1900

County Clerk – June 1, 1905

None – January 5, 1920

Home Data for 1875 – Wood Frame, valued at $ 800

Obituaries –

"*Former Assemblyman Dead. Norwich, N.Y., Jan 21. - Walter A. Shepardson. Chenango County member of the Assembly from 1910 to 1914, and for six years prior to that time county clerk, died today. He was 75 years of age .*" *from The Auburn Citizen. Thursday, January 21, 1926*

Hurst

"Walter A. Shepardson – Walter A. Shepardson, aged 75, died at his home in Norwich, Thursday morning, January 21st. Mr. Shepardson served our county in the State Assembly for four years, elected County Clerk two terms and represented the town of Otselic on the board of supervisors for nine years, three of which he was chairman of that body, for seven years he was in the employ of the O. & W. railroad acting as station agent at Smyrna also as train dispatcher at Oswego, N. Y. Shep (as we all called him), moved to Otselic in 1879 and for several years before moving to Norwich owned and operated the large farm near Otselic Center which still bears his name. The passing of Walter A. Shepardson is a grievous loss. As a representative of our town and county he leaves a reputation of having given his constituents the best that was in him. This in turn symbolized his compassionate concern for the needy. In this direction, too his service was at all times available. This we believe is borne out by the testimony of his old neighbors in the north end of our town. Mr. Shepardson is survived by one son, Stokes, and a brother, John, both of Smyrna, N. Y." **from The De Ruyter Gleaner. Page Two Thursday, January 28, 1926**

"McDonough. Feb. 10 – Walter A. Shepardson died at his home on Hayes street, Norwich, Jan. 21. He was a director of the Chenango National Bank. He survived by a son, Stokes Shepardson, and a brother, John W. Shepardson, both of Smyrna ." **from The Binghamton Press. Wednesday Evening, February 10, 1926**

○ **Irvin Wellington Stokes**, b. Feb 1856 in Smyrna, Chenango Co., New York, & **Elizabeth E. Rinclek**, b. Oct 1856 in New York – 1876 in New York

■ **Edward Dever Stokes,** b. 10 Oct 1879 in Smyrna, Chenango Co., New York & **Nelia Pindar**, b. 10 Jul 1883 in Canastota, Madison Co., New York, d. 6 Apr 1936 in Oneida, Madison Co., New York – About 1906

Signature:

• **Iona L. Stokes**, b. About 1908 in New York & **Ernest Hilts**, b. About 1909 in New York, d. 1 Nov 1940

Iona L. Stokes (daughter):
Residence – Lenox, Madison Co., New York – April 23, 1910
Occupation – None Listed – April 23, 1910
Ernest Hilts (son-in-law):
Obituary –
"Ernest Hilts, 31, of Oneida, employed at the National Casket Company plant, was instantly killed Saturday nightwhen he was crushed between the rear of his car and a truck on Route 5 between Wampsville and Canastota ." **from The De Ruyter Gleaner. Thursday, November 7, 1940**

Elisha Calkins & Anna Dalrymple Descendants

Edward Dever Stokes (son):

Residence – Smyrna, Chenango Co., New York – June 16, 1880

Sullivan, Madison Co., New York – June 13, 1900

Lenox, Madison Co., New York – April 23, 1910

Canastota, Madison Co., New York – September 12, 1918

Occupation – None Listed – June 16, 1880

Farm Laborer – June 13, 1900

Mechanic – September 12, 1918

Boiler, Milk & Flour Plant – April 23, 1910

Nelia Pindar (daughter-in-law):

Residence – Lenox, Madison Co., New York – April 23, 1910

Canastota, Madison Co., New York – September 12, 1918

Occupation – None – April 23, 1910

Obituaries –

"Mrs. Nelia Stokes. Oneida – Mrs. Nelia Stokes, 52, patient in a local hospital since Sept. 6, 1935, died there Saturday Apr. 4, 1936. She had been in failing health for several years. Mrs. Stokes was born in Canastota July 10, 1883, daughter of Mr. and Mrs. Alvin Pindar. She made her home in the past few years with a daughter, Mrs. Ernest Hilts, Wampsville. Other survivors are another daughter, Mrs. George Winn, Oneida; two brothers, Jay Pindar and Melvin Pindar, both of Syracuse; three grand-children, Ernest, Elma and Roberts Hilts. Services will be at the funeral home of E. F. Schepp & Son, Canastota, at 3:30 p. m . Tuesday with burial in Lenox Rural Cemetery ." from The Utica Daily Press. 1936

"Oneida. Mrs. Nelia Stokes, 52, Passes Away at Hospital. Oneida. April 6 – Mrs. Nelia Stokes, 52, Wampsville, died late Saturday night at City Hospital, where she had been confined since Sept. 6, 1935. She had been in failing health several years. Mrs. Stokes was born at Canastota, July 10, 1883, a daughter of Mr. and Mrs. Alvin Pindar. She had lived in Wampsville for the last few years with a daughter, Mrs. Ernest Hilts. Surviving is another daughter, Mrs. George Winn, Oneida, and two brothers, Jay and Melvin Pindar, both of Syracuse; and three grand-children, Ernest, Alma and Robert Hilts, of Wampsville ." from The Daily Sentinel. Rome, N. Y. Monday Evening, April 6, 1936

"Mrs. Nelia Stokes – Mrs. Nelia Stokes, 52, of Oneida, sister of Jay and Melvin Pindar of Syracuse, died Saturday in the City Hospital, Oneida, after a long illness. Surviving are two daughters, Mrs. Ernest Hilts of Wampsville and Mrs. George Winn of Oneida, her brothers and three grandchildren." from The Syracuse Journal. Monday, April 6, 1936

▪ **Sarah Stokes** – b. Aug 1882 in New York

Sarah Stokes (daughter):

Residence – Sullivan, Madison Co., New York – June 13, 1900

Occupation – At School – June 13, 1900

- **Ida Stokes** – b. Feb 1885 in New York

Ida Stokes (daughter):

   Residence – Sullivan, Madison Co., New York – June 13, 1900

   Occupation – At School – June 13, 1900

- **Walter Stokes**, b. 3 Nov 1888 in Plymouth, Chenango Co., New York, d. Oct 1962 & **Alice C. Norton**, b. Apr 1893 in New York – Before 1915

Signature:

- **Walter E. Stokes** – b. About 1915 in New York

Walter E. Stokes (son):

   Residence – Manilus, Onondaga Co. New York – January 5, 1920

                                                   June 1, 1925

                                                   April 5, 1930

   Occupation – None – January 5, 1920

                          April 5, 1930

   School – June 1, 1925

- **Elizabeth Stokes** – b. About 1919 in New York

Elizabeth Stokes (daughter):

   Residence – Manilus, Onondaga Co., New York – January 5, 1920

                                                   June 1, 1925

                                                   April 5, 1930

   Occupation – None – January 5, 1920

                          April 5, 1930

   School – June 1, 1925

Walter Stokes (son):

   Residence – Sullivan, Madison Co., New York – June 13, 1900

                Madison Co., New York – June 5, 1917

                Manilus, Onondaga Co., New York – April 28, 1910

                                                   January 5, 1920

                                                   June 1, 1925

                                                   April 5, 1930

Occupation – At School – June 13, 1900

Blacksmith, Livery Barn – April 28, 1910

Automobile Garage – June 5, 1917

Proprietor, Garage – January 5, 1920

April 5, 1930

Garage Owner – June 1, 1925

Home Data for 1930 – Owns home, valued at $ 5, 000, has radio set, not on a farm

Alice C. Norton (daughter-in-law):

Residence – Manilus, Onondaga Co., New York – January 5, 1920

June 1, 1925

April 5, 1930

Occupation – None – January 5, 1920

April 5, 1930

Housework – June 1, 1925

▪ **Maud I. Stokes**, b. Mar 1891 in Oxford, Chenango Co., New York & **Harold Whitmeyer**, b. About 1892 in Roma, Oneida Co., New York – 24 Dec 1913 in Canastota, Madison Co., New York

Signatures (Marriage):

Maud Stokes (daughter):

Residence – Sullivan, Madison Co., New York – June 13, 1900

Canastota, Madison Co., New York – December 24, 1913

Occupation – At School – June 13, 1900

None – December 24, 1918

Harold Whitmeyer (son-in-law):

Residence – Canastota, Madison Co., New York – December 24, 1913

Occupation – Mechanic – December 24, 1913

▪ **Robert Stokes**, b. 11 Oct 1892 in Clockville, Madison Co., New York & **Emma Unknown**, b. About 1904 in New York – About 1910

Signature:

- **Edna B. Stokes** – b. About 1915 in New York

Edna B. Stokes (daughter):

   Residence – Lenox, Madison Co., New York – January 10, 1920

   Occupation – None – January 10, 1920

- **Evelyn A. Stokes** – b. About 1925 in New York

Evelyn A. Stokes (daughter):

   Residence – Lenox, Madison Co., New York – April 5th & 7th, 1930

   Occupation – None – April 5th & 7th, 1930

- **Robert C. Stokes** – b. About 1926 in New York

Robert C. Stokes (son):

   Residence – Lenox, Madison Co., New York – April 5th & 7th, 1930

   Occupation – None – April 5th & 7th, 1930

- **Marjorie S. Stokes** – b. About 1928 in New York

Marjorie S. Stokes (daughter):

   Residence – Lenox, Madison Co., New York – April 5th & 7th, 1930

   Occupation – None – April 5th & 7th, 1930

Robert Stokes (son):

   Residence – Sullivan, Madison Co., New York – June 13, 1900

       Lenox, Madison Co., New York – April 28th – May 5th, 1910

               January 10, 1920

               April 5th & 7th, 1930

   Occupation – None Listed – June 13, 1900

       Farm Laborer, Home Farm – April 28th – May 5th, 1910

               January 10, 1920

       Farmer – June 5, 1917

       Farming, General Farm – April 5th & 7th, 1930

Emma Unknown (daughter-in-law):

   Residence – Lenox, Madison Co., New York – April 5th & 7th, 1930

   Occupation – None – April 5th & 7th, 1930

- **Elmer Stokes** – b. Feb 1897 in New York

Elmer Stokes (son):

   Residence – Sullivan, Madison Co., New York – June 13, 1900

       Lenox, Madison Co., New York – April 28th – May 5th, 1910

       Manilus, Onondaga Co., New York – January 5, 1920

Occupation – None Listed – June 13, 1900

Farm Laborer, Home Farm – April 28th – May 5th, 1910

Repair Work, Garage – January 5, 1920

▪ **Isabella Stokes**, b. Mar 1899 in Canastota, Madison Co., New York & **Buell W. Morgan**, b. About 1897 in Rome, Oneida Co., New York – 3 Apr 1920 in Rome, Oneida Co., New York

Isabella Stokes (daughter):

Residence – Sullivan, Madison Co., New York – June 13, 1900

Lenox, Madison Co., New York – April 28th – May 5, 1910

Rome, Oneida Co., New York – April 3, 1920

Occupation – None Listed – June 13, 1900

None – April 28th – May 5th, 1910

Operator – April 3, 1920

Buell W. Morgan (son-in-law):

Residence – Rome, Oneida Co., New York – April 3, 1920

Occupation – Electrician – April 3, 1920

Irvin Wellington Stokes (son):

Residence – Smyrna, Chenango Co., New York – July 17, 1860

June 28, 1870

June 16, 1880

Sullivan, Madison Co., New York – June 13, 1900

Lenox, Madison Co., New York – April 28th – May 5th, 1910

January 10, 1920

April 5th & 7th, 1930

Manilus, Onondaga Co., New York – April 28, 1910

Occupation – None – July 17, 1860

April 5th & 7th, 1930

At Home – June 28, 1870

Laborer – June 16, 1880

Farmer – June 13, 1900

Farmer, General Farm – April 28th – May 5th – 1910

January 10, 1920

Blacksmith, General Blacksmithing – April 28, 1910

Home Data for 1930 – Owns home, has radio set, on a farm

Hurst

Elizabeth E. Rinclek (daughter-in-law):

    Residence – Smyrna, Chenango Co., New York – June 16, 1880

        Sullivan, Madison Co., New York – June 13, 1900

        Lenox, Madison Co., New York – April 28th – May 5th, 1910

            January 10, 1920

    Occupation – Keeping House – June 16, 1880

        None Listed – June 13, 1900

        None – April 28th – May 5th, 1910

        January 10, 1920

Harriet Calkins (mother):

    Residence – Sherburne, Chenango Co., New York – September 3, 1850

        Smyrna, Chenango Co., New York – July 17, 1860

            June 28, 1870

            June 17, 1880

        Otselic, Chenango Co., New York – June 5, 1900

            June 1, 1905

        Norwich, Chenango Co., New York – April 25, 1910

    Occupation – None Listed – September 3, 1850

        July 17, 1860

        June 5, 1900

        June 1, 1905

        Keeping House – June 28, 1870

        June 17, 1880

    Own Income – April 25, 1910

Obituary/Death Notice –

*"Otselic. News was received Wednesday of the death of Mrs. Harriet Stokes, who died at Norwich at W. A. Shepardson's. The funeral was held Friday; burial at Smyrna." from **The De Ruyter Gleaner. Thursday, November 9, 1911***

Ery W. Stokes (father):

Residence – Sherburne, Chenango Co., New York – September 3, 1850

Smyrna, Chenango Co., New York – July 17, 1860

July 1, 1863

June 28, 1870

June 17, 1880

Occupation – Farmer – September 3, 1850

Tavern Keeper – July 17, 1860

Inn Keeper – July 1, 1863

Flour & Feed Merchant – June 28, 1870

Farmer – June 17, 1880

Value of Real Estate – $ 2, 000 – July 17, 1860

$ 3, 000 – June 28, 1870

Value of Personal Estate – $ 1, 000 – July 17, 1863

$ 4, 000 – June 28, 1870

Obituary/Death Notice –

"Ery W. Stokes, a well known resident of Smyrna, died the 15th." from The Weekly Gleaner. Thursday, April 24, 1890, De Ruyter, Madison Co., New York

"George Finch attended the funeral of E. W. Stokes, in Smyrna, Thursday. The ceremony was conducted by the I. O. O. F., Mr. Stokes being one of the oldest in this district, having been initiated in 1847, and at the time of his death was N. G. of his lodge." from The Weekly Gleaner. Thursday, April 24, 1890, De Ruyter, Madison Co., New York

Harriet Calkins & Ery W. Stokes

Family Photo Album (Found at an Estate Sale near Medina, Ohio)

Date of Album – 1860s

Photographs courtesy of The Hurst Family of Lake Elsinore, California

Harriet Calkins

Photographer Credit: Hotchkiss – Norwich, New York

Date – 1887

Photograph courtesy of The Hurst Family of Lake Elsinore, California

Olivia L. Stokes

Photographer Credit: Hotchkiss – Norwich, New York

Date – 1888

Photograph courtesy of The Hurst Family of Lake Elsinore, California

Ida E. Stokes & Walter A. Shepardson

Photographer Credit (Left): Hotchkiss – Norwich, New York

Date – 1893

Photograph (Right) from <u>The New York Red Book</u>

Date – 1912

Photographs courtesy of The Hurst Family of Lake Elsinore, California

William Riley Calkins & Descendants

- **William Riley Calkins**, b. 7 Dec 1825 in Otselic, Chenango Co. New York, d. 16 Sep 1896 in Laurens, Otsego Co., New York & **Catharine Maria Richard**, b. About 1823 in Montgomery Co., New York, d. Before 1900 in New York – Before Aug 1849 in Otselic, Chenango Co., New York

Signatures:

- O **Perry K. Calkins** – Aug 1849 in Otselic, Chenango Co., New York, d. 26 Sep 1852 in Otselic, Chenango Co., New York

Perry K. Calkins (son):

Residence – Otselic, Chenango Co., New York – August 5, 1850

Occupation – None Listed – August 5, 1850

- O **Marion L. Calkins** – b. 1851 in Otselic, Chenango Co., New York, d. 30 Sep 1852 in Otselic, Chenango Co., New York

- O **Marjorie Calkins** – b. 1851 in Otselic, Chenango Co., New York, d. 1 Jul 1862 in Otselic, Chenango Co., New York

Marjorie Calkins (daughter):

Residence – Otselic, Chenango Co., New York – June 23, 1860

Occupation – None Listed – June 23, 1860

- O **Porter R. Calkins** – Jun 1859 in Otselic, Chenango Co., New York, d. 1 Jul 1862 in Otselic, Chenango Co., New York

Porter R. Calkins (son):

Residence – Otselic, Chenango Co., New York – June 23, 1860

Occupation – None Listed – June 23, 1860

- O **Nellie Jane Calkins** – b. About 1861 in Chenango Co., New York

Nellie Jane Calkins (adopted-daughter):

Residence – Camillus, Onondaga Co., New York – June 4, 1870

Otselic, Chenango Co., New York – June 5, 1875

Occupation – At Home – June 4, 1870

None Listed – June 5, 1875

○ **Tyler Wade Calkins**, b. May 1865 in Madison Co., New York & **Catherine L. Pickens**, b. Nov 1871 in New York, d. Before June 1, 1915 in Laurens, Otsego Co., New York – 1890 in New York

▪ **Blanche M. Calkins** – b. Nov 1893 in New York, d. 17 Feb 1911 in Oneonta, Otsego Co., New York

Blanche M. Calkins (daughter):

Residence – Laurens, Otsego Co., New York – June 22, 1900

June 1, 1905

May 13, 1910

Occupation – None Listed – June 22, 1900

At School – June 1, 1905

None – May 13, 1910

Cause of Death – Bright's Disease

Obituary –

"Miss Blanche Calkins. Miss Blanche Calkins, eldest daughter of Mr. and Mrs. Wade Calkins died at Oneonta, Sunday morning, after several months' illness, from Bright's disease, aged seventeen years, Blanche was born in Laurens and had always resided there. She attended the Laurens school. She was a member of the Christian Endeavor and the Presbyterian Sunday school. Last June her health began to fail which condition continued and in November she grew worse. Her mother took her to Oneonta where she could be with her. Since that time she has been confined to the house but was a patient sufferer until the end came. The funeral serviced were held, Tuesday at 11 o'clock in Oneonta, the Rev. E. J. Farley officiating. The body was taken to Laurens for burial on the 12:45 car, the Rev. J. J. Crane officiating at the grave. She leaves beside her parents, four sisters, Marion, Florence, Mildred and Alice, all residing at Laurens; besides many friends who sympathize with the family in their lose of a loving daughter and sister. – Our Laurens Reporter." from the Otsego Farmer. Thursday February 17, 1911, Cooperstown, Otsego Co., New York

▪ **Marion A. Calkins**, b. Feb 1896 in Laurens, Otsego Co., New York & **Ward McFee**, b. 1 Aug 1892 in Oneonta, Otsego Co., New York – 31 Dec 1914 in Oneonta, Otsego Co., New York

Signature:

Signatures (marriage):

Hurst

- **Edward F. McFee** – b. About 1916 in New York

Edward F. McFee (son):

  Residence – Oneonta, Otsego Co., New York – June 5, 1917

  January 26, 1920

  May 6, 1930

  Occupation – None – January 26, 1920

  May 6, 1930

- **Donald McFee** – b. About 1919 in New York

Donald McFee (son):

  Residence – Oneonta, Otsego Co., New York – January 26, 1920

  Occupation – None – January 26, 1920

Marian A. Calkins (daughter):

  Residence – Laurens, Otsego Co., New York – June 22, 1900

  June 1, 1905

  May 13, 1910

  Oneonta, Otsego Co., New York – December 31, 1914

  June 5, 1917

  January 26, 1920

  May 6, 1930

  Occupation – None Listed – June 22, 1900

  At School – June 1, 1905

  None – May 13, 1910

  May 6, 1930

  January 26, 1920

  Clerk – December 31, 1914

Ward McFee (son):

  Residence – Oneonta, Otsego Co., New York – December 31, 1914

  June 5, 1917

  January 26, 1920

  May 6, 1930

  Occupation – Farmer – December 31, 1914

  June 5, 1917

  Laborer, Farm – January 26, 1920

  Farmer, Diary Farm – May 6, 1930

▪ **Florence I. Calkins** – b. Dec 1897 in New York

Florence I. Calkins (daughter):

Residence – Laurens, Otsego Co., New York – June 22, 1900

June 1, 1905

May 13, 1910

Occupation – None Listed – June 22, 1900

At School – June 1, 1905

None – May 13, 1910

▪ **Mildred L. Calkins** – b. Feb 1900 in Laurens, Otsego Co., New York

Mildred L. Calkins (daughter):

Residence – Laurens, Otsego Co., New York – June 22, 1900

June 1, 1905

May 13, 1910

June 1, 1915

January 7th & 8th, 1920

Occupation – None Listed – June 22, 1900

June 1, 1905

None – May 13, 1910

School – June 1, 1915

Saleslady, Dry Goods Store – January 7th & 8th, 1920

▪ **Alice M. Calkins** – b. About 1903 in Laurens, Otsego Co., New York

Alice M. Calkins (daughter):

Residence – Laurens, Otsego Co., New York – June 1, 1905

May 13, 1910

June 1, 1915

January 7th & 8th, 1920

Occupation – None Listed – June 1, 1905

None – May 13, 1910

School – June 1, 1915

Saleslady, Dry Goods Store – January 7th & 8th, 1920

Tyler Wade Calkins (son):

    Residence – Camillus, Onondaga Co., New York – June 4, 1870

        Otselic, Chenango Co., New York – June 5, 1875

        Smyrna, Chenango Co., New York – June 14, 1880

        Laurens, Otsego Co., New York – June 22, 1900

                    June 1, 1905

                    May 13, 1910

                    June 1, 1915

                    January 7th & 8th, 1920

    Occupation – At Home – June 4, 1870

        None Listed – June 5, 1875

        At School – June 14, 1880

        House Painter – June 1, 1905

                June 1, 1915

        Farm Laborer – June 22, 1900

        Decorator, Paint & Paper – May 13, 1910

        Painter, House Painter – January 7th & 8th, 1920

Catherine L. Pickens (daughter-in-law):

    Residence – Laurens, Otsego Co., New York – June 22, 1900

                    June 1, 1905

                    May 13, 1910

    Occupation – None Listed – June 22, 1900

        Housework – June 1, 1905

        Waitress, Hotel – May 13, 1910

Elisha Calkins & Anna Dalrymple Descendants

William Riley Calkins (father):

   Residence – Otselic, Chenango Co., New York – August 5, 1850

                           June 23, 1860

                           June 5, 1875

      Camillus, Onondaga Co., New York – June 4, 1870

      Smyrna, Chenango Co., New York – June 14, 1880

   Occupation – Farmer – August 5, 1850

                   June 23, 1860

                   June 4, 1870

                   June 5, 1875

                   June 14, 1880

   Value of Real Estate – $ 1, 000

              $ 4, 000 – June 23, 1860

                    June 4, 1870

   Value of Personal Estate – $ 1, 200 – June 23, 1860

              $ 1, 000 – June 4, 1870

Catharine Maria Richard (mother):

   Residence – Otselic, Chenango Co., New York – August 5, 1850

                           June 23, 1860

                           June 5, 1875

      Camillus, Onondaga Co., New York – June 4, 1870

      Smyrna, Chenango Co., New York – June 14, 1880

   Occupation – None Listed – August 5, 1850

                   June 23, 1860

                   June 5, 1875

      Keeping House – June 4, 1870

                   June 14, 1880

William Riley Calkins & Catharine Maria Richard

Family Photo Album (Found at an Estate Sale near Medina, Ohio)

Date of Album – 1860s

Photographs courtesy of The Hurst Family of Lake Elsinore, California

William Riley Calkins & Catharine Maria Richard

Family Photo Album (Found at an Estate Sale near Medina, Ohio)

Date of Album – 1860s

Photographs courtesy of The Hurst Family of Lake Elsinore, California

William Riley Calkins

Photographer Credit: Hotchkiss – Norwich, New York

Date – 1891

Photograph courtesy of The Hurst Family of Lake Elsinore, California

Tyler Wade Calkins

Photograph courtesy of The Hurst Family of Lake Elsinore, California

Deed Transcriptions

Here follows a transcription of a deed recorded on March 12, 1847 made between Truman D. Calkins and Roana Miles:

"To all To Whom these presents shall come greeting know Y[e] that I, Truman D. Calkins of the town of Otselic in the county of Chenango State of New York for and in consideration of the sum of two hundred ninety two dollars thirty five cents lawful money of the United States of America to him in hand paid by Roana Miles of the town county and State aforesaid at on before the sealing and delivery of these presents the receipt whereof is hereby acknowledged hath remises, releases, and forever quit claims and by these presents doth remise, release, and forever quit claim unto the said Roana Miles and to her heirs and assignees forever, All those certain pieces of land lying in the town aforesaid being parts of lots No. 50, 52, 53, 54, 55, & 56, in said town being the same upon which T. D. Calkins now lives and occupies, and the same as conveyed by Solomon S. Hall & Rufus Briggs to the said Calkins on the 10th day of March 1847. Said Farm containing about one hundred and seventy four acres of land be the same more or less that part conveyed by Hall is the same as purchased by him at a Sheriff sale or an execution against the said Calkins that part conveyed by Rufus Briggs is a part of the old farm formerly occupied by Thomas Tracy now deceased to have and to hold the said released premises unto the said Roana Miles and to her heirs and to her own proper use and behoof forever In testimony whereof the said Truman D. Calkins hath hereunto set his hand and seal this twelfth day of March in the year of our Lord one thousand eighteen hundred and forty seven.

Truman D. Calkins S.S.

Sealed and delivered in presence of

F. E. Dominick

Chenango County S.S. On this 12th day of March 1847 personally appeared before me Truman D. Calkins to me known as the same person described in and who executed the same and he acknowledged that he executed the same

Recorded March 12th, 1847 1 P.M.   *F. E. Dominick Justice of the Peace*

B. B. Andersons Clerk"

Here follows a transcription of a deed recorded on June 14, 1847 between Roana Miles and Truman D. Calkins:

"To all To Whom these presents shall come greeting know Ye that I, Roana Miles of the town of Otselic in the county of Chenango State of New York for and in consideration of the sum of two hundred ninety five dollars sixty five cents lawful money of the United States of America to her in hand paid by Isaac Marsh of the town of Brookfield Madison county and State aforesaid the receipt whereof is hereby acknowledged hath remises, releases, and forever quit claims and by these presents doth remised, released, and forever quit claimed and by these presents doth remise, release and forever quit claim unto the said Isaac Marsh and to his heirs and assigns forever, All those certain pieces of land being in the town aforesaid being a part of lots No. 50, 52, 53, 54, 55, and 56, in said town being the same upon which T. D. Calkins now lives and occupies, and the same as conveyed by Solomon S. Hall and Rufus Briggs to the said Calkins on the tenth day of March 1847. Said Farm containing about one hundred and seventy four acres of land be the same more or less that part conveyed by Hall is the same as purchased by him at a Sheriff sale or an execution against said Calkins that part conveyed by Rufus Briggs

is a part of the old farm formerly occupied by Thomas Tracy now deceased reserving the cooking stove and pipe now in use on said farm for the benefit of R. Miles to have and to hold the said released premises unto the said Isaac Marsh and to his heirs and to his own proper use and behoof forever In testimony whereof the said Roana Miles hath hereunto set her hand and seal this eleventh day of June in the year eighteen hundred and forty seven.
Roana Miles S.S.

Chenango County S.S. On this eleventh day of June in the year one thousand eight hundred and forty seven personally came before me Roana Miles to me known to be the individual described in and who executed the same for the purpose therein mentioned

Recorded June 14, 1847 3/2 P.M.   *A. M. Ray Justice of the Peace of*
    the P.E. Clark Dep.   *town of Otselic in said county"*

Here follows a transcription of a deed recorded on June 14, 1847 between Truman D. Calkins and Abigail Calkins and Isaac Marsh:

"Know all men by these presents that we Truman D. Calkins and Abigail his wife of the town of Otselic County of Chenango and State of New York for and in consideration of the sum of five hundred dollars lawful money of the United States of America to them in hand paid by Isaac Marsh of the town of Brookfield Madison County & State aforesaid at or before the enssealing and delivery of these presents the receipt whereof is hereby acknowledge have remised, released, and forever quit claimed and by these presents do remise, release, and forever quit claim unto the said Isaac Marsh and to his heirs and assigns forever all those certain pieces of land lying in the town aforesaid being part of lots No. 50, 52, 52, 53, 54, 55, & 56 in said town being the same, upon which we now live and occupy and being the same, as conveyed by

Solomon S. Hall and Rufus Briggs to the said Calkins on the 10th day of March 1847 said farm containing about one hundred and sevety four acres of land be the same more or less that part conveyed by Hall is the same as purchased by him at Sheriff sale or on execution against said T. D. Calkins that part contained in the Briggs conveyance is a part of the Tracy farm To have and to hold that said released premises unto the said Isaac Marsh and his heirs and assigns to his own proper use and behoof forever In testimony whereof the said T. D. Calkins and Abigail his wife have hereunto set their hands and seals this eleventh day of June in the year of our Lord one thousand eight hundred and forty seven.

T. D. Calkins S.S.

Abigail Calkins S.S.

Chenango County S.S. On the eleventh day of June in the year of our Lord one thousand eight hundred and forty seven (Between) before me personally cam Truman D. Calkins and Abigail his wife to me known to be the individuals described in and who executed the within conveyance who acknowledged that they executed the same and that said Abigail acknowledged on a private examination by me apart from her husband that she executed the said conveyance freely and without any fear or compulsion from him. *Asher M. Ray Justice of the peace of said county*

Recorded June 14, 1847 3/2 P.M.

P. E. Clark Dept. Clerk"

Here follows a transcription of a deed recorded on September 26, 1849 made between Elisha Calkins and his son Dorman Calkins:

"This indenture made the eighth day of March in the year one thousand eight hundred and forty eight between Elisha Calkins of the town of Otselic and the county of Chenango and State of New York of the first part and Dorman Calkins son of the said Elisha Calkins of the same place of the second part witnesseth that the said party of the first part in consideration of the sum of one dollar and the natural love and affection which the said father haveth toward his said son to him duly paid before the delivery hereof hath bargained and sold and by these presents doth grant and convey to the said party of the second part his heirs and assigns forever, all that certain piece or parcel of land being the north part of lot number fifty five in subdivision number four of the seventh township town of Otselic aforesaid as surveyed and set off by Daniel Prentis and is the whole of said lot excepting so much as has heretofore been conveyed to Artemus Chapin – The part hereby conveyed or intended so to be containing according to said Prentis survey fifty acres two woods and thirty five perches be the same more or less – Also one other piece of land being a part of lot number 54 in said subdivision number four of said seventh township surveyed and set off also by said Daniel Prentis and bounded as follows, Beginning at the north west corner of lot no 55 and running thence south 10° east west four chains and 50 links to the center of the highway thence south 3° west with said highway 3 chains and 50 links thence south 10° east 15 chains and 75 links to the division of said lot, thence easy one chain and 98 links to the west line of said lot number 55 thence north 19 chains and 23 links to the place of beginning containing six acres two woods and 33 perches of land be the same more or less – the first piece more particularly described on the margin of a deed from J. J. Fenton and wife to the said Elisha dated Jan 12, 1837 and recorded in the clerk's office of Chenango Co. June 24 1837 2 P.M. No. 55 page 102 with the appearances and all the estate title and interest of the said

party of the first part therein – And the said party of the first part doth hereby convent and agree with the said party of the second part that at the time of the delivery hereof the said party of the first part is the lawful owner of the premises above granted and seized thereof in Ju simple absolute and that he will warrant and defend the above granted premises in the quiet and peaceable possession of the said party of the second part his heirs and assigns forever In witness whereof the said party of the first part hath hereunto set his hand and seal the day and year first above written

Sealed and delivered in the presence of -   *Elisha Calkins S.S.*

Chenango County S.S. On the first day of July in the year 1848 before me personally appeared Elisha Calkins to me known to be the individual described in and who executed the within conveyance and acknowledged that the executed the same for the purposes therein mentioned –

                        A. M. Ray Justice of the Peace of Otselic in said County

Recorded Sept 26, 1849 at 1 P.M.

           N Peller Clerk"

Here follows a transcription of a deed recorded on January 9, 1850 made between Elisha & Anna Calkins and their son William Riley Calkins:

"This indenture made the third day of May in the year of our Lord one thousand eight hundred and forty seven between Elisha Calkins & Anna his wife of the town of Otselic County of Chenango and state of New York of the first part and Wm R. Calkins of the town and county

aforesaid of the second part witnesseth that the said party of the first part for and in consideration of the sum of three hundred and fifty dollars lawful money of the United States of America to him in hand paid by the said party of the second part the receipt whereof is hereby confessed and acknowledged have granted aliened remised released enferffed and confirmed and by these presents do grant alien remise release enferff and confirm unto the said party of the second part and his heirs and assigns forever all that certain piece or parcel of land being the south half of the south west quarter of lot number seventy four in the town of Smyrna as surveyed by Daniel Prentis the whole of said south west quarter is bounded as follows, towit, Beginning at the south west corner of said lot number seventy four at a post marked No 73.74, thence north twenty five chains and sixty two and a half links to a basswoods tree thence east thirty chains and eighty seven and a half links to a stake and atone, thence south twenty five chains and sixty two and a half links to a stake and stone thence west thirty chains and eighty seven & a half links to the place of beginning containing seventy nine acres & eighteen perches be the same more or less – Now the piece of land hereby intended to be conveyed is the south half of the quarter of the lot above mentioned and described to be set off by a line to be run East and West parallel to the north and south bounds of said lot – Said half quarter containing thirty nine acres two woods and nine perches be the same more or less and is sold and conveyed subject to all taxes imposed thereon or any part thereof from the third day of May eighteen hundred and forty seven – Together with all and singular the hereditaments appurtenances thereunto belonging or in anywise appertaining and the reversion and reversions remainder and remainders sents issues and profits thereof and all the estate right title interest claim and demand Whatsoever of the said parties of the first part either in law or equity of in or to the above granted premises with the said hereditaments and appurtenances to have and to hold the above mentioned and described premises with the appurtenances and every part or parcel thereof to the said party of the second part his heirs assigns forever – And the said partys of the first part do herby for themselves their

356

heir executor and administrator do covenant grant bargain promise and agree to and with the said party of the second part his heirs and assigns to warrant and forever to defend the above granted premises and every part and parcel thereof now being in the quiet and peaceable possession of the said party of the second part against the said parties of the first part their heir executor administrator and assigns and against all and every other person or persons claiming or to claim the said premises or any part thereof – In witness whereof the said parties of the first part have hereunto set their hands and seals the day and year first above written –

Sealed and Delivered in the presence of Asher M. Ray –   *Elisha Calkins S.S.*

Anna Calkins S.S.

Chenango County S.S. On the first day of July 1847 personally appeared before me Elisha Calkins and Anna his wife to me known to be the same individuals described in and executed the within conveyance and acknowledged the execution of the same – And the said Anna on private examination by and before me apart from her husband acknowledged that she executed the same freely and without and fear or compulsion of him –

Asher M. ray Justice of the Peace –

Recorded Jan 9. 1850 at 1 P.M.

N Peller Clerk"

Hurst

Here follows a transcription of a deed recorded on October 12, 1850 made between

William Riley & Catherine Maria Calkins and William Riley Calkins brother Dorman Calkins:

"This indenture made the ninth day of November one thousand and eight hundred and

forty seven between William R. Calkins & Catherine Maria his wife of the town of Otselic in the

county of Chenango and state of New York of the first part and Dorman Calkins of the same

place of the second part witnesseth that the said parties of the first part for and in consideration

of the sum of two hundred and fifty dollars to them in hand paid by the said party of the second

part the receipt whereof is hereby confessed & acknowledged have remised released and quit

claimed and by these presents do grant remise release quit claim unto the said party of the

second part in his actual possession now being to his heirs and assigns forever all that certain

piece or parcel of land situated in the town of Smyrna county aforesaid being the northwest one

fourth of the southwest quarter of lot no seventy four (74) as conveyed by Jonathan Boynton and

wife to Wm R. Calkins December 25th in the year 1843 – Also one fourth of the south half of said

grantee lot no 74 to be taken from the north side of said of said south half and divided by a line

running parallel with the north and south lines of said quarter containing by estimation 29 acres

and some rods of land be the same more or less: now the land intended to be conveyed is the

northwest corner and a strip on the north side of the south half of said quarter lot – Together

with all and singular the hereditaments and appurtenances thereunto belonging or in anywise

appertaining and the reversion and reversions remainder and remainders rents issues and

forfeits there if and all the estate right titles interest claim and demand whatsoever of the said

parties of the first part either in law or equity of in and to the above bargained premises – to

have and hold the said parcel of land and every part thereof unto the said party of the second

part his heirs and assigns to the sole and only proper use of the said party of the second party his

358

heirs and assigns forever – In witness whereof the said parties of the first part had hereunto set

their hands and seal the day and year first above written –

William R. Calkins S.S.

Catherine Maria Calkins S.S.

Chenango County S.S.

On the 11th day of November in the year 1847 personally appeared before me William R. Calkins

and Catherine Maria his wife to me known to be the same individuals described in and who

executed the within conveyance and acknowledged the execution of the same and the said

Catherine Maria on a private examination by and before me apart from her husband

acknowledged that she executed the same freely and without any fear or compulsion of him –

Asher M. Ray Justice of the Peace of Otselic –

Recorded Oct. 121850 at 5 P.M.

N Peller   Clerk"

Here follows a transcription of a deed written on November 3, 1851 made between

Dorman and Phebe Calkins and Dorman Calkins brother William Riley Calkins:

"This indenture made this third day of November one thousand and eight hundred and

fifty one between Dorman Calkins and Phoebe his wife of the town of Otselic County of

Chenango and tate of New York of the first part and William R. Calkins of the same place of the

second part, Witnesseth that the said party of the first part for and in consideration of one

hundred and ninety five dollars do grant bargain sell and confirm unto the said party of the second part and to his heirs and assigns forever, All that certain piece or parcel of land situated

in the town of Otselic known as parts of lots No. 54, 55. & 56 in subdivision No 4 of said town

being a part of the farm lately owned by Thomas Tracy deceased and bounded as follows viz

Beginning at the south line of said farm in the center of the highway, thence north twenty five

degrees west 12 chains and 18 links, thence north 13° west 6 chains and 85 links, thence north

11° west 4 chains and 66 links thence east 28 chains 25 links, thence south 21 chains 88 links

thence west 19 chains and 57 links to the place of beginning containing forty three acres three

woods and ten perches of lands now the land here intended to be conveyed is thirty three acres 3

woods and 10 perches of land of the south part of said lot to be divided by an East and West line

running through said lot parallel with the North and South lines of said lot. Together with all

and singular the hereditaments and appurtenances thereunto belonging or in anywise

appertaining to have and to hold the said premises above described to the said party of the

second part his heirs and assigns forever and the said party of the first part for their heirs do

covenant, grant, promise and agree to and with the said party of the second part her heirs and

assigns the above bargain premises against all and every person or persons whatsoever lawfully

and equitably claiming or to claim the ahole or any part thereof forever to warrant and defend.

In witness whereof the said party of the first part have hereunto et their hands and seals the day

and year first above written

Dorman Calkins S.S.

Phebe Calkins S.S. "

Here follows a transcription of a deed recorded on April, 14, 1853 made between William

and Lois M. Town and Freeman Calkins concerning Lot 39:

" **This Indenture,** Made this *Fourteenth* day of *April* in the year of our Lord one

thousand eight hundred and *Fifty-three* **Between** *Wm Town & Lois M., his wife of the Town of*

Arkwright of the County of Chautauqua and State of New York of the first part, and *Freeman*

Calkins of the same place of the County of Chautauqua and State of New York of the second part:

Witnesseth, That the said party of the first part, for an in consideration of the sum of *Twelve*

hundred eighty Dollars lawful money of the United States of America, to *him* in hand paid by the

said party of the second part, the receipt whereof is hereby confessed and acknowledged, has

granted, bargained, sold, remised, released, aliened and confirmed; and by these presents do

grant, bargain, sell, remise, release, alien and confirm, unto the said party of the second part, and

to *his* heirs and assigns

forever_____ *All that Certain*

piece or parcel of Land Situate lying & being in the County of Chautauqua & State aforesaid

being the north east part of Lot number thirty nine in the fifth Township & Eleventh Range of the

Holland Land Companys survey by Joseph Ellicot Bounded South by Lot number thirty eight

forty one chains & nineteen links west by Land Deeded to Alvah Fuller nineteen chains eleven

links North by Land Deeded to Jerry Wilbur forty one chains forty three links East by Lot

number thirty one nineteen chains eleven links Containing Seventy eight & nine tenths acres be

the same more or

less_____

Together, with all and singular the hereditaments and appurtenances thereunto

belonging, or in anywise appertaining, and the reversion and reversions, remainder and

remainders, rents, issues and profits thereof, and all the estate, right, title, interest, ... *& rights of* *ones* claim or demand whatsoever, of the said party of the first part, either in Law or Equity, of

in, and to the above bargained premises, with the said hereditaments and appurtenances. **To**

Have and to Hold the said premises, as above described, with the appurtenances, unto the

said party of the second part, and to *his* heirs and assigns forever *And the said Wm Town for*

himself his heirs, executors and administrators, do*th*, covenant, grant, bargain and agree, to and

with the said party of the second part, *his* heirs, assigns, that at the time of the ensealing and

delivery of these presents, *he is* well seized of the premises above conveyed, as of a good, sure,

perfect, absolute and indefeasible estate of inheritance in the Law and Fee Simple; And that the

above bargained premises, in the quiet and peaceable possession of the said party of the second

part, *his* heirs and assigns, against all and every person or persons, lawfully claiming or to claim

the whole or any part thereof, *he* will forever **Warrant and Defend.**

In witness thereof, The said party of the first part ha*ve* hereunto set *their* hand*s* and

seal*s* the day and year first above written.

Signed, Sealed, and Delivered
In presence of}

William Town L.S.
Lois M. Town L.S.

State of New York
Chautauqua County}

On the 14ᵗʰ day of April 1853before me the subscriber personally appeared Wm Town and

Lois M. his wife, And acknowledged that they had severally executed the within instrument And

the said Lois M. his wife in a private examination apart from her husband acknowledged that she executed the within instrument freely and without any fear or compulsions of her husband, And I

further Certify that I knew the person who made the said acknowledgements to be the individuals

described in, And who executed the within instrument

A. Hinckley Justice of the Peace"

Here follows a transcription of a deed recorded on January 7, 1854 made between Freeman and Sarah Calkins and Levi Cowden concerning Lot 54:

"**This Indenture,** Made this *Seventh* day of *January* in the year of our Lord one

thousand eight hundred and *fifty four* **Between** *Freeman Calkins & Sarah his wife of the*

County of Chautauqua and State of New York of the first part, and *Levi Cowden of the County*

and State aforesaid of the second part; **Witnesseth,** That the said party of the first part, for an

in consideration of the sum of *Twelve hundred and forty eighty Dollars* lawful money of the

United States of America, to *them* in hand paid by the said party of the second part, the receipt

whereof is hereby confessed and acknowledged, have granted, bargained, sold, remised, released,

aliened and confirmed; and by these presents do grant, bargain, sell, remise, release, alien and

confirm, unto the said party of the second part, and to *his* heirs and assigns forever *All that*

certain piece or parcel of Land Situate lying & being in the Town of Arkwright being first of Lot

number fifty four in the fifth Township & eleventh Range & Bounded as follows on north by part

of Lot number fifty five sixteen chains & sixty links, On the East by a line parallel to Robert

Cowden East line sixteen chains eighty eight links thence west parallel eight ... ...of Lot

number fifty (50) four, ten chains forty links thence north sixty five degrees west six chains eighty

one links thence north parallel to Robert Cowdens east line sixteen chains to the place of beginning which is the north East corner of a certain piece of Land deeded to said Calkins by

Robert Cowden Also that other piece or parcel of Land Situate lying & being in Arkwright

aforesaid being a part of Lot number fifty four lined & Deeded as follows Viz. Beginning at the

north East corner of Land Deeded to Robert Cowden thence South Sixteen (16) chains & fifty

links to the Creek thence north seventy six degrees west eleven chains to a Stake on the South

Side of the Creek Thence north twenty eight degrees East three chains to a Stake on the north

side of the Creek thence down with the north Bank of the Creek as it winds & turns until it strikes

the west line of said Robert Cowdens Land thence north on the line between said Land & Moses

Tuckers Land to the North west side of Robert Cowdens Land thence north East on the north line

of said Lot fifty four twenty four chains and fifty eight links to the place of beginning the last

deeded parties being the ... party to F. Calkins by Robert Cowden & wife by ... deed May 25.

1832& it being the ... of this Deed, to convey the whole of said remises This conveyance which is

a Mortgage of $350. Is to this ... & one other of $260. To T. H. Wilcox & ... ... said party of

the second part to possession ... April 2nd 1854.

𝕿𝖔𝖌𝖊𝖙𝖍𝖊𝖗, with all and singular the hereditaments and appurtenances thereunto

belonging, or in anywise appertaining, and the reversion and reversions, remainder and

remainders, rents, issues and profits thereof, and all the estate, right, title, interest, _____claim

or demand whatsoever, of the said party of the first part, either in Law or Equity, of, in, and to

the above bargained premises, with the said hereditaments and appurtenances. 𝕿𝖔 𝕳𝖆𝖛𝖊 𝖆𝖓𝖉

𝖙𝖔 𝕳𝖔𝖑𝖉 the said premises, as above described, with the appurtenances, unto the said party of

the second part, and to *his* heirs and assigns forever *And the said Freeman Calkins for himself his*

heirs, executors and administrators, do*th*, covenant, grant, bargain and agree, to and with the said

party of the second part, *his* heirs, assigns, that at the time of the ensealing and delivery of these presents, *he is* well seized of the premises above conveyed, as of a good, sure, perfect, absolute and indefeasible estate of inheritance in the law in fee simple; And that the above bargained premises, in the quiet and peaceable possession of the said party of the second part, *his* heirs and assigns, against all and every person or persons, lawfully claiming or to claim the whole or any part thereof, *he* will forever 𝔚arrant and 𝔇efend.

The word ... interlined & the word ... ...entered before signing

𝔍n witness thereof, The said party of the first part ha*s* hereunto set *his* hand and seal the day and year first above written.

> Signed, Sealed, and Delivered
> In presence of}

Freeman Calkins L.S.
Sarah Calkins L.S.

State of New York
Chautauqua County}

On the eighth day of January 1854 before me the subscriber personally appeared Freeman Calkins and Sarah his wife, and acknowledged that they had severally executed the within instrument And the said Lois M. his wife in a private examination apart from her husband acknowledged that she executed the within instrument freely and without any fear or compulsions of her husband, And I further Certify that I knew the person who made the said acknowledgements to be the individuals described in, And who executed the within instrument

Nelson Gorham Justice of the Peace"

Here follows a transcription of a deed recorded on January 23, 1854 made between George H. White and Freeman and William Riley Calkins concerning Lot 38:

𝕿𝖍𝖎𝖘 𝕴𝖓𝖉𝖊𝖓𝖙𝖚𝖗𝖊, Made this *Twenty third* day of *January* in the year of our Lord one thousand eight hundred and *fifty four* 𝕭𝖊𝖙𝖜𝖊𝖊𝖓 *George H. White of the Village of*

Fredonia County of Chautauqua & State of New York of the first part, and *Freeman Calkins and William Riley Calkins of the Town of Arkwright County and State aforesaid* of the second part;

𝖂𝖎𝖙𝖓𝖊𝖘𝖘𝖊𝖙𝖍, That the said party of the first part, for an in consideration of the sum of *Fourteen hundred Dollars* lawful money of the United States of America, to *him* in hand paid by the said party of the second part, the receipt whereof is hereby confessed and acknowledged, has granted, bargained, sold, remised, released, aliened and confirmed; and by these presents do grant, bargain, sell, remise, release, alien and confirm, unto the said party of the second part, and to *their* heirs and assigns forever *All that certain piece or parcel of Land Situate lying & being in the Town of Arkwright County of Chautauqua and State of New York it being in the fifth Township and Eleventh Range as surveyed by Joseph Ellicott Bounded as follows South by Lot number thirty eight forty one chains And sixteen links West by Land Deeded to Alvah Fuller nineteen chains eleven links North to Land Deed to Jerry Wilbur forty one chains forty three links East by Lot number thirty one nineteen chains, eleven links, Containing seventy eight and nine tenths acres be the same more or less.*

𝕿𝖔𝖌𝖊𝖙𝖍𝖊𝖗, with all and singular the hereditaments and appurtenances thereunto belonging, or in anywise appertaining, and the reversion and reversions, remainder and remainders, rents, issues and profits thereof, and all the estate, right, title, interest, _____ claim or demand whatsoever, of the said party of the first part, either in Law or Equity, of, in, and to the above bargained premises, with the said hereditaments and appurtenances. 𝕿𝖔 𝕳𝖆𝖛𝖊 𝖆𝖓𝖉

𝖙𝖔 𝕳𝖔𝖑𝖉 the said premises, as above described, with the appurtenances, unto the said party of

the second part, and to *their* heirs and assigns forever *And the said George H White for himself*

his heirs, executors and administrators, do*th*, covenant, grant, bargain and agree, to and with the

said party of the second part, *their* heirs, assigns, that at the time of the ensealing and delivery of

these presents, *he is* well seized of the premises above conveyed, as of a good, sure, perfect,

absolute and indefeasible estate of inheritance in the law in fee simple; And that the above

bargained premises, in the quiet and peaceable possession of the said party of the second part,

their heirs and assigns, against all and every person or persons, lawfully claiming or to claim the

whole or any part thereof, *he* will forever 𝖂𝖆𝖗𝖗𝖆𝖓𝖙 𝖆𝖓𝖉 𝕯𝖊𝖋𝖊𝖓𝖉.

𝕴𝖓 𝖜𝖎𝖙𝖓𝖊𝖘𝖘 𝖙𝖍𝖊𝖗𝖊𝖔𝖋, The said party of the first part ha*s* hereunto set *his* hand and seal

the day and year first above written.

Signed, Sealed, and Delivered

In presence of}

George H. White L.S.

State of New York

Chautauqua County}

On the 23 day of January 1854 before me the subscriber personally appeared George H.

White to me personally known and who acknowledged that he executed the within instrument

And I Certify that I knew the person who made the said acknowledgements to be the individual

described in, And who executed the within instrument

F. S. Edward Spl. Surrogate"

Here follows a transcription of a deed recorded on August 19, 1854 made between Freeman and Sarah Calkins and their children William Riley Calkins and Fidelia L. Fuller concerning Lot 39:

This Indenture, Made this *Nineteenth* day of *August* in the year of our Lord one thousand eight hundred and fifty *four* **Between** *Freeman Calkins & Sarah Calkins his wife of the Town of Arkwright of the County of Chautauqua and State of New York* of the first part, and *William Riley Calkins & Fidelia L. Fuller of the County of Chautauqua and State of New York* of the second part; **Witnesseth,** That the said party of the first part, for an in consideration of the sum of *one thousand seven hundred thirty five Dollars eighty cents* lawful money of the United States of America, to *them* in hand paid by the said party of the second part, the receipt whereof is hereby confessed and acknowledged, ha*s* granted, bargained, sold, remised, released, aliened and confirmed; and by these presents do grant, bargain, sell, remise, release, alien and confirm, unto the said party of the second part, and to *his* heirs and assigns forever *All that certain piece or parcel of Land Situate lying & being in the County of Chautauqua and State of New York being the South East part of Lot Number thirty nine in the fifth Township and Eleventh Range of the Holland Land Companys Survey by Joseph Ellicott Bounded South by Lot Number thirty eight forty one chains and sixteen links West by Lands Deeded to Alvah Fuller nineteen chains eleven links, North by Land Deeded to Jerry Wilbur forty one chains forty three links East by Lot Number thirty one, nineteen chains, eleven links Containing Seventy eight and nine tenths acre be the same more or less.*

𝕿𝖔𝖌𝖊𝖙𝖍𝖊𝖗, with all and singular the hereditaments and appurtenances thereunto

belonging, or in anywise appertaining, and the reversion and reversions, remainder and

remainders, rents, issues and profits thereof, and all the estate, right, title, interest, *one rights of*

ones claim or demand whatsoever, of the said party of the first part, either in Law or Equity, of,

in, and to the above bargained [interlined: Subject … to a Mortgage of Eight hundred dollars]

premises, with the said hereditaments and appurtenances. 𝕿𝖔 𝕳𝖆𝖛𝖊 𝖆𝖓𝖉 𝖙𝖔 𝕳𝖔𝖑𝖉 the said

premises, as [Interlined: … of George White of Fredonia and the right then Wm Riley Calkins

has remises for] above described, with the appurtenances, unto the said party of the second part,

and to *his* heirs and assigns forever *And the said Calkins for himself his* heirs, executors and

administrators, do*th*, covenant, grant, bargain and agree, to and with the said party of the second

part, *his* heirs, assigns, that at the time of the ensealing and delivery of these presents, *he is* well

seized of the premises above conveyed, as of a good, sure, perfect, absolute and indefeasible

estate of inheritance in the Law in Fee Simple: 𝕬𝖓𝖉 𝖙𝖍𝖆𝖙 𝖙𝖍𝖊 𝖆𝖇𝖔𝖛𝖊 𝖇𝖆𝖗𝖌𝖆𝖎𝖓𝖊𝖉 𝖕𝖗𝖊𝖒𝖎𝖘𝖊𝖘, in

the quiet and peaceable possession of the said party of the second part, *his* heirs and assigns,

against all and every person or persons, lawfully claiming or to claim the whole or any part

thereof, *he* will forever 𝖂𝖆𝖗𝖗𝖆𝖓𝖙 𝖆𝖓𝖉 𝕯𝖊𝖋𝖊𝖓𝖉.

𝕴𝖓 𝖜𝖎𝖙𝖓𝖊𝖘𝖘 𝖙𝖍𝖊𝖗𝖊𝖔𝖋, the said party of the first part ha*s* hereunto set *their* hands and seal

the day and year first above written.

    Signed, Sealed, and Delivered

    In presence of}

The interline … between the eighth & ninth

line interlined before signed.

Freeman Calkins L.S.

Sarah Calkins L.S.

State of New York

Chautauqua County}

On this twenty first day of August 1854 before me the subscriber personally appeared Freeman Calkins and Sarah Calkins, his Wife And acknowledged that they severally executed the within instrument And the said Sarah Calkins in a private examination apart from her husband apart from her husband acknowledged that she executed the within instrument freely, and without any fear or compulsion of her husband And I further Certify that I know the person who made the said acknowledgements to be the individuals described in, and who executed the within instrument

Harvey Clark Justice of the Peace"

Here follows a transcription of a deed recorded on November 6, 1854 made between Fidelia L. Fuller and her brother William Riley Calkins concerning Lot 39:

`This Indenture,` Made this *Sixth* day of *November* in the year of our Lord one thousand eight hundred and *fifty four* **Between** *Fidelia L. Fuller of the Town of Arkwright of the County of Chautauqua and State of New York* of the first part, and *William Riley Calkins of Town of Arkwright of the County of Chautauqua and State of New York* of the second part;

Witnesseth, That the said party of the first part, for an in consideration of the sum of *Fifty Dollars* lawful money of the United States of America, to *me* in hand paid by the said party of the second part, the receipt whereof is hereby confessed and acknowledged, has granted, bargained, sold, remised, released, aliened and confirmed; and by these presents do grant, bargain, sell, remise, release, alien and confirm, unto the said party of the second part, and to *his* heirs and assigns forever *All of my interest to all that certain piece or parcel of Land Situate lying & being in the Town of Arkwright County of Chautauqua and State of New York lined & Bounded as follows to wit it is the South East part of Lot No. thirty nine in fifth Township & Eleventh Range of the Holland Land Company's Survey by Joseph Ellicott Bounded South by Lot No. thirty eight forty one chains & sixteen links West by Lands Deeded to Alvah Fuller nineteen chains & eleven links North by Land Deeded to Jerry Wilbur forty one chains & forty three links East by Lot No. thirty one nineteen chains & eleven links, Containing eight and nine tenths of an acre be the same more or less_____ The Land hereby conveyed is the same thus one Freeman Calkins and William Riley Calkins Bought of George H. White on or about the twenty third day of January eighteen hundred fifty four & the same thus William R. Calkins and Fidelia L. Fuller Bought of the said Freeman Calkins is his interest whatever it might be at the time.*

𝕿𝖔𝖌𝖊𝖙𝖍𝖊𝖗, with all and singular the hereditaments and appurtenances thereunto belonging, or in anywise appertaining, and the reversion and reversions, remainder and remainders, rents, issues and profits thereof, and all the estate, right, title, interest, claim or demand whatsoever, of the said party of the first part, either in Law or equity, of, in, and to the above bargained premises, with the said hereditaments and appurtenances. 𝕿𝖔 𝕳𝖆𝖛𝖊 𝖆𝖓𝖉 𝖙𝖔 𝕳𝖔𝖑𝖉 the said premises, as above described, with the appurtenances, unto the said party of the second part, and to *his* heirs and assigns forever *And the said Fidelia L. Fuller for herself hers* heirs, executors and administrators, do*th*, covenant, grant, bargain and agree, to and with the said party of the second part, *his* heirs, assigns, that at the time of the ensealing and delivery of these presents, *that she was* well seized of the premises above conveyed, as of a good, sure, perfect, absolute and indefeasible estate of inheritance in the Law in Fee Simple: And that the above bargained premises, in the quiet and peaceable possession of the said party of the second part, *his* heirs and assigns, against all and every person or persons, lawfully claiming or to claim the whole or any part thereof,   will forever 𝔚𝔞𝔯𝔯𝔞𝔫𝔱 𝔞𝔫𝔡 𝔇𝔢𝔣𝔢𝔫𝔡.

𝔍𝔫 𝔴𝔦𝔱𝔫𝔢𝔰𝔰 𝔱𝔥𝔢𝔯𝔢𝔬𝔣, The said party of the first part has hereunto set *her* hand and seal the day and year first above written.

Signed, Sealed, and Delivered

In presence of}

F. Calkins, the words of my interest to between lines nine &
Ten was interlined before signing.

Fidelia L. Fuller L.S.

Chautauqua County}

On this fourteenth day of January eighteen hundred and fifty six before me personally appeared Freeman Calkins subscribing ... to the within conveyance to me known who being ... ... did depose and say that he resided in the town of Arkwright in said County that he knew Fidelia L. Fuller the individual described in and who executed the said conveyance that he was present and saw the said Fidelia L. Fuller sign seal and deliver the same as and for her act and Deed and that the said Fidelia L. Fuller acknowledge the execution thereof where upon the said Freeman Calkins became the subscribing ... thereto

Nelson Gorham Justice of the Peace"

Here follows a transcription of a deed recorded on January 14, 1856made between William Riley Calkins and Joel R. Parker, a resident of the town of Pomfret in Chautauqua County in the state of New York, concerning Lot 39:

This Indenture, Made this *fourteenth* day of *January* in the year of our Lord one thousand eight hundred and *fifty six* **Between** *William Riley Calkins of the Town of Arkwright of the County of Chautauqua and State of New York* of the first part, and *Joel R. Parker of Town of Pomfret of the County of Chautauqua and State of New York* of the second part;

Witnesseth, That the said party of the first part, for an in consideration of the sum of *Seventeen hundred and fifty one Dollars* lawful money of the United States of America, to *him* in hand paid by the said party of the second part, the receipt whereof is hereby confessed and acknowledged, ha*s* granted, bargained, sold, remised, released, aliened and confirmed; and by these presents do grant, bargain, sell, remise, release, alien and confirm, unto the said party of the second part, and to *his* heirs and assigns forever *All that certain piece or parcel of Land Situate lying & being in the Town of Arkwright County and State aforesaid and being in the fifth Township and eleventh Range as surveyed Joseph Ellicott Bounded as follows, South by Lot number thirty eight forty one chains and sixteen links West by Land Deeded to Alvah Fuller nineteen chains eleven links North by Land Deeded to Jerry Wilbur forty one chains forty three links East by Lot Number thirty one nineteen chains eleven links Containing seventy eight and nine tenths acres be the same more or less to a mortgage executed by Freeman Calkins and William Riley Calkins for the Sum of eight hundred and seventy one dollars to George H. White of Fredonia in the County aforesaid and upon which Mortgage there was due the sum of eight hundred Dollars on the twenty third day of January 1855 the said eight hundred dollars falling due in four annual payments for said 23 day of January 1855.*

𝕿𝖔𝖌𝖊𝖙𝖍𝖊𝖗, with all and singular the hereditaments and appurtenances thereunto belonging, or in anywise appertaining, and the reversion and reversions, remainder and remainders, rents, issues and profits thereof, and all the estate, right, title, interest, claim or demand whatsoever, of the said party of the first part, either in Law or equity, of, in, and to the above bargained premises, with the said hereditaments and appurtenances. 𝕿𝖔 𝕳𝖆𝖛𝖊 𝖆𝖓𝖉 𝖙𝖔

𝕳𝖔𝖑𝖉 the said premises, as above described, with the appurtenances, unto the said party of the second part, and to heirs and assigns forever *And the said William Riley Calkins for himself* heirs, executors and administrators, do covenant, grant, bargain and agree, to and with the said party of the second part, *his* heirs, assigns, that at the time of the ensealing and delivery of these presents, *he is* well seized of the premises above conveyed, as of a good, sure, perfect, absolute and indefeasible estate of inheritance in the Law in Fee Simple: And that the above bargained premises, in the quiet and peaceable possession of the said party of the second part, *his* heirs and assigns, against all and every person or persons, lawfully claiming or to claim the whole or any part thereof, *he* will forever 𝖂𝖆𝖗𝖗𝖆𝖓𝖙 𝖆𝖓𝖉 𝕯𝖊𝖋𝖊𝖓𝖉.

𝕵𝖓 𝖜𝖎𝖙𝖓𝖊𝖘𝖘 𝖙𝖍𝖊𝖗𝖊𝖔𝖋, The said party of the first part has hereunto set *his* hand and seal the day and year first above written.

Signed, Sealed, and Delivered
In presence of}

William Riley Calkins L.S.

State of New York

Chautauqua County}

On this 14th day of January 1856 before the subscriber personally appeared William Riley Calkins who acknowledged that he executed the within instrument, And I certify that I know the person who made the said acknowledgement to be the individual described in and who executed the within instrument

Nelson Gorham Justice of the Peace"

Western Half of Arkwright, Chautauqua Co., New York 1854

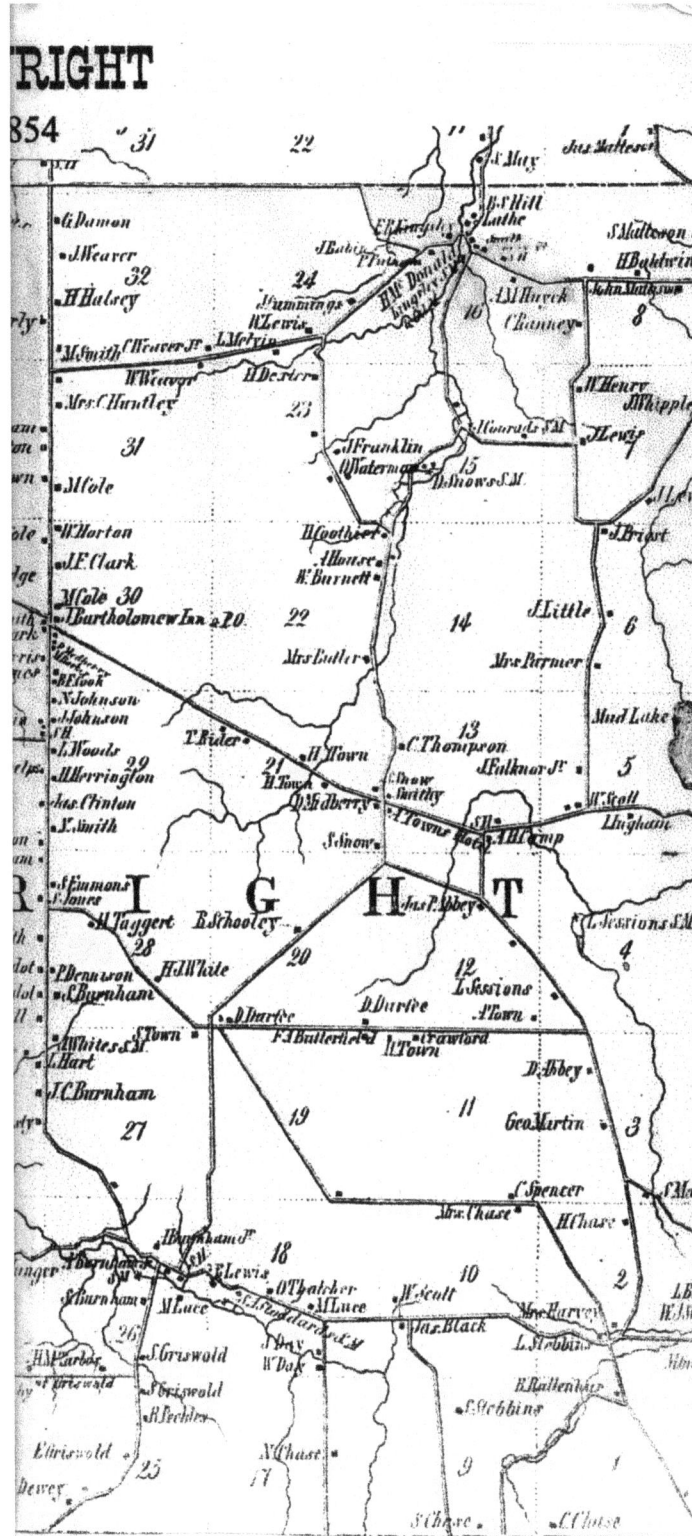

Eastern Half of Arkwright, Chautauqua Co., New York 1854

377

Farm Descriptions

Truman D. Calkins

LOCATION – LEBANON, MADISON CO., NEW YORK – JULY 18TH – 24TH, 1860

ACRES OF LAND – 200 (IMPROVED)

                     0 (UNIMPROVED)

CASH VALUE OF FARM – $7,000

VALUE OF FARMING IMPLEMENTS & MACHINERY – $250

LIVESTOCK, JUNE 1, 1860 – 3 HORSES

                     32 MILK COWS

                     1 OTHER CATTLE

                     6 SWINE

VALUE OF LIVESTOCK – $1,592

PRODUCE DURING THE YEAR ENDING JUNE 1, 1860 – 16 WHEAT (BUSHELS OF)

                     150 INDIAN CORN (BUSHELS OF)

                     250 OATS (BUSHELS OF)

                     50 PEAS AND BEANS (BUSHELS OF)

                     120 IRISH POTATOES (BUSHELS OF)

                     18 BUCKWHEAT (BUSHELS OF)

VALUE OF ORCHARD PRODUCTS – $25

                     1,400 BUTTER (LBS. OF)

                     7,000 CHEESE (LBS. OF)

                     35 HAY (TONS OF)

                     180 MAPLE SUGAR (LBS. OF)

VALUE OF HOMEMADE MANUFACTURES – $15

VALUE OF ANIMALS SLAUGHTERED – $147

Jacob Walradt

LOCATION — LEBANON, MADISON CO., NEW YORK — JUNE 10, 1875

ACRES OF LAND — 130 (IMPROVED)

       50 (UNIMPROVED, TOTAL)

       50 (UNIMPROVED, IN WOOD & TIMBER LAND)

CASH VALUE — OF FARM — $ 6, 300

       OF FARM BUILDINGS OTHER THAN DWELLINGS — $ 1, 200

       OF STOCK — $ 1, 545

       OF TOOLS & IMPLEMENTS — $ 500

       OF GROSS SALES FROM FARMS IN 1874 — $ 1, 000

ACRES PLOWED — IN 1874 — 17

       IN 1875 — 16

GRASS LANDS — ACRES IN PASTURE (IN 1874) — 78

       ACRES IN PASTURE (IN 1875) — 78

       MEADOW (ACRES, 1874) — 35

       MEADOW (ACRES, 1875) — 36

       MEADOW (TONS OF HAY, 1874) — 50

OATS — ACRES SOWN (1874) — 13

       ACRES SOWN (1875) — 10

       BUSHELS HARVESTED, 1874 — 460

SPRING BARLEY — ACRES SOWN (1874) — 2

       ACRES SOWN (1875) — 1

       BUSHELS HARVESTED, 1874 — 40

INDIAN CORN — FOR THE GRAIN (ACRES PLANTED, 1874) — ½

       (ACRES PLANTED, 1875) — 1

       BUSHELS HARVESTED, 1874 — 75

       ACRES SOWN FOR FODDER (1874) — ½

POTATOES — ACRES PLANTED (1874) — 2 ½

       ACRES PLANTED (1875) — 2

       BUSHELS HARVESTED, 1874 — 425

HOPS – ACRES IN CROP, 1875 – 3

ORCHARDS – KIND OF TREES – APPLES

      NUMBER OF TREES – 75

      BUSHELS OF FRUIT, HARVESTED IN 1874 – 140

      BARRELS OF CIDER, MADE IN 1874 – 3

POUNDS OF MAPLE SUGAR, MADE IN 1874 – 650

GALLONS OF MAPLE MOLASSES, MADE IN 1874 – 7

UNENUMERATED ARTICLES OF FARM PRODUCE, 1874 – KIND – WOOD

      QUANTITY – 29 CORD

      VALUE – $ 48

NEAT CATTLE – HEIFER CALVES (SEASON OF 1873) – 3

      (SEASON OF 1874) – 2

      (SEASON OF 1875) – 4

      BULLS OF ALL AGES – 3

      MILK COWS (AVERAGE NO. 1874) – 18

      (TOTAL NO. 1875) – 20

      (MILK SENT TO FACTORY, 1874) – 18

      CATTLE KILLED FOR BEEF, 1874 – 2

BUTTER (POUNDS MADE BY FAMILIES, 1874) – 1,550

HORSES (TWO YEARS OLD AND OVER, OWNED IN 1875) – 4

SWINE – PIGS OF 1873 – 3

      SEASON OF 1874 AND OLDER – 3

      NUMBER SLAUGHTERED IN 1874 – 3

      POUNDS OF PORK MADE, 1874 – 750

SHEEP – SHORN IN 1874 – 6

      SHORN IN 1875 – 5

      LAMBS RAISED IN 1874 – 7

      LAMBS RAISED IN 1875 – 3

      POUNDS OF WOOL SHORN IN 1874 – 30

      POUNDS OF WOOL SHORN IN 1875 – 25

POULTRY — VALUE OWNED, 1875 — 20

VALUE SOLD, 1874 — 7

VALUE OF EGGS SOLD, 1874 — 12

Edwin Humphrey

LOCATION — GEORGETOWN, MADISON CO., NEW YORK — AUGUST 15, 1870

ACRES OF LAND — 60 (IMPROVED)

15 (UNIMPROVED)

CASH VALUE OF FARM — $ 3, 000

VALUE OF FARMING IMPLEMENTS & MACHINERY — $ 100

TOTAL AMOUNT OF WAGES PAID DURING THE YEAR — $ 50

LIVESTOCK, JUNE 1, 1870 — 4 HORSES

9 MILK COWS

5 OTHER CATTLE

5 SHEEP

1 SWINE

VALUE OF LIVESTOCK — $ 600

PRODUCE DURING THE YEAR ENDING JUNE 1, 1870 — 4 INDIAN CORN (BUSHELS OF)

75 OATS (BUSHELS OF)

35 BARLEY (BUSHELS OF)

50 IRISH POTATOES (BUSHELS OF)

ORCHARD PRODUCTS — $ 5

600 BUTTER (LBS. OF)

30 HAY (TONS OF)

1 GRASS SEED (BUSHEL OF)

50 MAPLE SUGAR (LBS. OF)

VALUE OF ANIMALS SLAUGHTERED — $ 51

VALUE OF ALL FARM PRODUCTIONS — $ 501

Edwin Humphrey

LOCATION – GEORGETOWN, MADISON CO., NEW YORK – JUNE 3, 1880

ACRES OF LAND – IMPROVED, TILLED – 60

IMPROVED, PERMANENT MEADOWS, PASTURES,

ORCHARDS, VINEYARDS – 1

UNIMPROVED, WOODLAND & FOREST – 10

FARM VALUES – OF FARM – $ 2, 000

OF FARMING IMPLEMENTS & MACHINERY – $ 150

OF LIVESTOCK – $ 400

FENCES – COST OF BUILDING & REPAIRING IN 1879 – $ 10

LABOR – AMOUNT PAID FOR WAGES – $ 200

WEEKS HIRED LABOR FOR 1879 – 40

ESTIMATED VALUE OF ALL FARM PRODUCTIONS – $ 807

GRASS LANDS – ACRES MOWN (IN 1879) – 20

ACRES NOT MOWN (IN 1879) – 26

TONS OF HAY, HARVESTED IN 1879 – 30

HORSES OFF ALL AGES ON HAND JUNE 1, 1880 – 2

NEAT CATTLE AND THEIR PRODUCTS – ON HAND JUNE 1, 1880 – MILK COWS – 10

CALVES DROPPED – 14

PURCHASED – 3

SOLD LIVING – 2

MILK SOLD OR SENT TO BUTTER & CHEESE FACTORIES IN 1879 – 6, 225 GALLONS

BUTTER MADE ON THE FARM IN 1879 – 400 LBS.

SHEEP – LAMBS DROPPED – 10

SOLD LIVING – 20

SWINE – ON HAND JUNE 1, 1880 – 4

POULTRY – ON HAND JUNE 1, 1880 (BARNYARD) – 20

EGGS PRODUCED IN 1879 – 50

INDIAN CORN, 1879 – ACRES – 2

CROP, BUSHEL – 30

OATS, 1879 – ACRES – 7

CROP, BUSHEL – 243

MAPLE, 1879 – SUGAR – 125 LBS.

MOLASSES – 2 GALLONS

HOPS, 1879 – ACRES – 4

CROP, BUSHEL – 500

POTATOES (IRISH) – ACRES – 1

CROP, BUSHEL – 200

ORCHARDS, 1879 (APPLE) – ACRE – 1

BEARING TREES – 30

BUSHELS, 1879 – 100

TOTAL VALUE OF ORCHARD PRODUCTS – $ 15

FOREST PRODUCTS – AMOUNT OF WOOD CUT IN 1879 – 40 CORDS

VALUE OF ALL FOREST PRODUCTS – $ 20

Weaver Wilson Calkins

LOCATION – OTSELIC, CHENANGO CO., NEW YORK – JULY 28TH – 29TH, 1870

ACRES OF LAND – 20 (IMPROVED)

        2 (UNIMPROVED)

CASH VALUE OF FARM – $ 1,500

VALUE OF FARMING IMPLEMENTS & MACHINERY – $ 800

LIVESTOCK, JUNE 1, 1870 – 2 HORSES

        2 MILK COWS

        6 SHEEP

        2 SWINE

VALUE OF LIVESTOCK – $ 554

PRODUCE DURING THE YEAR ENDING JUNE 1, 1870 – 100 OATS (BUSHELS OF)

        25 WOOL (LBS. OF)

        50 IRISH POTATOES (BUSHELS OF)

        200 BUTTER (LBS. OF)

        4 HAY (TONS OF)

        700 HOPS (LBS. OF)

VALUE OF ALL FARM PRODUCTIONS – $ 300

Ensign Briggs

LOCATION – SMYRNA, CHENANGO CO., NEW YORK – JUNE 4, 1875

ACRES OF LAND – 60 (IMPROVED)

        53 (UNIMPROVED, TOTAL)

        40 (UNIMPROVED, IN WOOD & TIMBER LAND)

CASH VALUE – OF FARM – $ 2,000

        OF FARM BUILDINGS OTHER THAN DWELLINGS – $ 300

        OF STOCK – $ 600

        OF TOOLS & IMPLEMENTS – $ 100

        OF GROSS SALES FROM FARMS IN 1874 – $ 350

Acres Plowed – in 1874 – 12

in 1875 – 12

Grass Lands – Acres in Pasture (in 1874) – 30

Acres in Pasture (in 1875) – 30

Meadow (Acres, 1874) – 18

Meadow (Acres, 1875) – 18

Meadow (Tons of Hay, 1874) – 15

Meadow (Bushels of Grass Seed, 1874) – 1 ½

Winter Wheat – Acres Sown (1873) – 2

Acres Sown (1874) – 2

Bushels Harvested, 1874 – 28

Oats – Acres Sown (1874) – 7

Acres Sown (1875) – 5

Bushels Harvested, 1874 – 200

Indian Corn – For the Grain (Acres Planted, 1874) – 2

(Acres Planted, 1875) – 3

Bushels Harvested, 1874 – 50

Acres Sown for Fodder (1874) – 1

Potatoes – Acres Planted (1874) – 1 ½

Acres Planted (1875) – 1

Bushels Harvested, 1874 – 150

Orchards – Kind of Trees – Apples

Number of Trees – 60

Bushels of Fruit, Harvested in 1874 – 70

Barrels of Cider, Made in 1874 – Blank

Pounds of Maple Sugar, made in 1874 – 100

Gallons of Maple Molasses, made in 1874 – 2

Unenumerated articles of Farm Produce, 1874 – Kind – Stove Wood

Quantity – 30 Cords

Value – $ 45

NEAT CATTLE – HEIFER CALVES (SEASON OF 1873) – BLANK

(SEASON OF 1874) – 1

(SEASON OF 1875) – 5

BULLS OF ALL AGES – 2

MILK COWS (AVERAGE NO. 1874) – 12

(TOTAL NO. 1875) – 9

(MILK SENT TO FACTORY, 1874) – 12

CATTLE KILLED FOR BEEF, 1874 – 2

HORSES – COLTS OF 1875 – 2

TWO YEARS OLD AND OVER, OWNED IN 1875 – 2

SWINE – PIGS OF 1873 – 2

SEASON OF 1874 AND OLDER – 1

NUMBER SLAUGHTERED IN 1874 – 2

POUNDS OF PORK MADE, 1874 – 300

SHEEP – SHORN IN 1874 – 1

SHORN IN 1875 – BLANK

LAMBS RAISED IN 1874 – BLANK

LAMBS RAISED IN 1875 – BLANK

POUNDS OF WOOL SHORN IN 1874 – 6

POUNDS OF WOOL SHORN IN 1875 – BLANK

SHEEP SLAUGHTERED IN 1874 – 1

POULTRY – VALUE OWNED, 1875 – $ 10

VALUE SOLD, 1874 – BLANK

VALUE OF EGGS SOLD, 1874 – $ 15

Ensign Briggs

LOCATION – SMYRNA, CHENANGO CO., NEW YORK – JUNE 8, 1880

ACRES OF LAND – IMPROVED, TILLED – 37

IMPROVED, PERMANENT MEADOWS, PASTURES,

ORCHARDS, VINEYARDS – 38

UNIMPROVED, WOODLAND & FOREST – 40

FARM VALUES – OF FARM – $ 3,000

OF FARMING IMPLEMENTS & MACHINERY – $ 100

OF LIVESTOCK – $ 495

FENCES – COST OF BUILDING & REPAIRING IN 1879 – $ 30

LABOR – AMOUNT PAID FOR WAGES – $ 55

WEEKS HIRED LABOR FOR 1879 – 6

ESTIMATED VALUE OF ALL FARM PRODUCTIONS – $ 350

GRASS LANDS – ACRES MOWN (IN 1879) – 15

ACRES NOT MOWN (IN 1879) – 40

TONS OF HAY, HARVESTED IN 1879 – 15

HORSES OFF ALL AGES ON HAND JUNE 1, 1880 – 4

NEAT CATTLE AND THEIR PRODUCTS – ON HAND JUNE 1, 1880 – OTHER – 8

CALVES DROPPED – 8

PURCHASED – 2

SLAUGHTERED – 2

DIED, STRAYED, OR UNRECOVERED – 1

MILK SOLD OR SENT TO BUTTER & CHEESE FACTORIES IN 1879 – 3,000 GALLONS

BUTTER MADE ON THE FARM IN 1879 – 400 LBS.

SHEEP – SOLD LIVING – 22

DIED OF STRESS OR WEATHER – 2

SWINE – ON HAND JUNE 1, 1880 – 2

POULTRY – ON HAND JUNE 1, 1880 (BARNYARD) – 24

EGGS PRODUCED IN 1879 – 135

INDIAN CORN, 1879 – ACRES – 1

CROP, BUSHEL – 25

OATS, 1879 – ACRES – 3

CROP, BUSHEL – 100

WHEAT, 1879 – ACRES – 1

CROP, BUSHELS – 13

MAPLE, 1879 – SUGAR – 150 LBS.

MOLASSES – 5 GALLONS

POTATOES (IRISH) – ACRES – 1

CROP, BUSHEL – 50

ORCHARDS, 1879 (APPLE) – ACRE – 1

BEARING TREES – 50

BUSHELS, 1879 – 100

TOTAL VALUE OF ORCHARD PRODUCTS – $ 10

BEES, 1879 – HONEY – 100 LBS.

WAX – 7 LBS.

FOREST PRODUCTS – AMOUNT OF WOOD CUT IN 1879 – 25 CORDS

VALUE OF ALL FOREST PRODUCTS – $ 12

Alexander Butts

LOCATION – OTSELIC, CHENANGO CO., NEW YORK – JUNE 1, 1850

ACRES OF LAND – 80 (IMPROVED)

35 (UNIMPROVED)

CASH VALUE OF FARM – $ 1, 800

VALUE OF FARMING IMPLEMENTS & MACHINERY – $ 40

LIVESTOCK, JUNE 1, 1850 – 2 HORSES

4 MILK COWS

2 OTHER CATTLE

10 SHEEP

1 SWINE

388

VALUE OF LIVESTOCK – $ 150

PRODUCE DURING THE YEAR ENDING JUNE 1, 1850 – 25 WHEAT (BUSHELS OF)

25 INDIAN CORN (BUSHELS OF)

500 OATS (BUSHELS OF)

30 WOOL (LBS. OF)

25 IRISH POTATOES (BUSHELS OF)

15 BARLEY (BUSHELS OF)

200 BUTTER (LBS. OF)

10 HAY (TONS OF)

104 FLAX (LBS. OF)

3 FLAXSEED (BUSHELS OF)

VALUE OF ANIMALS SLAUGHTERED – $ 20

Alexander Butts

LOCATION – OTSELIC, CHENANGO CO., NEW YORK – JULY 25TH – 26TH, 1870

ACRES OF LAND – 20 (IMPROVED)

CASH VALUE OF FARM – $ 1, 200

VALUE OF FARMING IMPLEMENTS & MACHINERY – $ 10

LIVESTOCK, JUNE 1, 1870 – 1 HORSES

2 MILK COWS

VALUE OF LIVESTOCK – $ 250

PRODUCE DURING THE YEAR ENDING JUNE 1, 1870 – 15 HAY (TONS OF)

800 HOPS (LBS. OF)

80 MAPLE SUGAR (LBS. OF)

VALUE OF ANIMALS SLAUGHTERED – $ 20

VALUE OF ALL FARM PRODUCTIONS – $ 175

Philander Butts

LOCATION – OTSELIC, CHENANGO CO., NEW YORK – JULY 25TH – 26TH, 1870

ACRES OF LAND – 45 (IMPROVED)

15 (UNIMPROVED)

CASH VALUE OF FARM – $ 4, 000

VALUE OF FARMING IMPLEMENTS & MACHINERY – $ 100

LIVESTOCK, JUNE 1, 1870 – 2 HORSES

2 MILK COWS

1 SWINE

VALUE OF LIVESTOCK – $ 365

PRODUCE DURING THE YEAR ENDING JUNE 1, 1870 – 50 BUCKWHEAT (BUSHELS OF)

100 BUTTER (LBS. OF)

1, 875 MILK SOLD (GALLONS OF)

8 HAY (TONS OF)

FOREST PRODUCTS – $ 15

VALUE OF ALL FARM PRODUCTIONS – $ 372

William Riley Calkins, son of Freeman Calkins

LOCATION – ARKWRIGHT, CHAUTAUQUA CO., NEW YORK – AUGUST 26, 1850

ACRES OF LAND – 35 (IMPROVED)

18 (UNIMPROVED)

CASH VALUE OF FARM – $ 1,000

VALUE OF FARMING IMPLEMENTS & MACHINERY – $ 110

LIVESTOCK, JUNE 1, 1850 – 4 HORSES

6 MILK COWS

2 WORKING OXEN

4 OTHER CATTLE

8 SHEEP

1 SWINE

VALUE OF LIVESTOCK – $ 389

Elisha Calkins & Anna Dalrymple Descendants

PRODUCE DURING THE YEAR ENDING JUNE 1, 1850 — 20 WHEAT (BUSHELS OF)

                                        35 INDIAN CORN (BUSHELS OF)

                                        170 OATS (BUSHELS OF)

                                        20 WOOL (LBS. OF)

                                        20 POTATOES, IRISH (BUSHELS OF)

                                        500 BUTTER (LBS. OF)

                                        12 HAY (TONS OF)

VALUE OF HOME-MADE MANUFACTURES — $ 10

VALUE OF ANIMALS SLAUGHTERED — $ 32

William Riley Calkins, son of Freeman Calkins

LOCATION — GREEN, IOWA CO., IOWA — JUNE 6, 1860

ACRES OF LAND — 100 (IMPROVED)

                217 (UNIMPROVED)

CASH VALUE OF FARM — $ 5,000

VALUE OF FARMING IMPLEMENTS & MACHINERY — $ 100

LIVESTOCK, JUNE 1, 1860 — 6 HORSES

                5 MILK COWS

                20 SHEEP

                45 SWINE

VALUE OF LIVESTOCK — $ 615

PRODUCE DURING THE YEAR ENDING JUNE 1, 1860 — 356 WHEAT (BUSHELS OF)

                            2,000 INDIAN CORN (BUSHELS OF)

                            100 OATS (BUSHELS OF)

                            30 POTATOES, IRISH (BUSHELS OF)

                            500 BUTTER (LBS. OF)

                            20 HAY (TONS OF)

                100 MOLASSES FROM SYRUP (GALLONS OF, AND FROM WHAT MADE)

VALUE OF HOME-MADE MANUFACTURES — $ 120

VALUE OF ANIMALS SLAUGHTERED — $ 119

William Riley Calkins, son of Freeman Calkins

LOCATION – ELGIN, WABASHA CO., MINNESOTA – JULY 6, 1870

ACRES OF LAND – 80 (IMPROVED)

CASH VALUE OF FARM – $ 2,500

VALUE OF FARMING IMPLEMENTS & MACHINERY – $ 200

TOTAL AMOUNT OF WAGES PAID DURING THE YEAR – $ 100

LIVESTOCK, JUNE 1, 1870 – 2 HORSES

2 MILK COWS

2 OTHER CATTLE

6 SHEEP

3 SWINE

VALUE OF LIVESTOCK – $ 340

PRODUCE DURING THE YEAR ENDING JUNE 1, 1870 – 600 SPRING WHEAT (BUSHELS OF)

20 INDIAN CORN (BUSHELS OF)

300 OATS (BUSHELS OF)

84 BARLEY (BUSHELS OF)

60 WOOL (LBS. OF)

200 BUTTER (LBS. OF)

VALUE OF ANIMALS SLAUGHTERED OR SOLD FOR SLAUGHTER – $ 40

ESTIMATED VALUE OF ALL FARM PRODUCTIONS – $ 690

William Riley Calkins, son of Freeman Calkins

LOCATION – PEBBLE PRECINCT, DODGE CO., NEBRASKA – JUNE 1880

ACRES OF LAND – 60 (IMPROVED)

VALUE OF FARM, INCLUDING LAND, FENCES, & BUILDINGS – $ 600

ESTIMATED VALUE OF ALL FARM PRODUCTIONS FOR 1879 – $ 540

CEREALS – INDIAN CORN, 1879 – ACRES – 60

CROP, BUSHEL – 2, 700

William Riley Calkins, son of Freeman Calkins

LOCATION – McClure Precinct, Holt Co., Nebraska – June 23, 1880

ACRES OF LAND – 72 (improved)

VALUE OF FARM, including land, fences, & buildings – $ 8

VALUE OF FARMING IMPLEMENTS & MACHINERY – $ 80

VALUE OF LIVESTOCK – $ 250

GRASSLANDS – Acre – 1 (not mown)

HORSES OF ALL AGES ON HAND JUNE 1, 1885 – 6

NEAT CATTLE AND THEIR PRODUCTS, ON HAND JUNE 1, 1885 – 5 Milk Cows

1 Other

2 Calves Dropped

? (0 or 6) Purchased

William Towne

LOCATION – Elgin, Wabasha Co., Minnesota – July 6, 1870

ACRES OF LAND – 160 (improved)

O (unimproved)

CASH VALUE OF FARM – $ 4,500

VALUE OF FARMING IMPLEMENTS & MACHINERY – $ 400

TOTAL AMOUNT OF WAGES PAID DURING THE YEAR – $ 450

LIVESTOCK, JUNE 1, 1870 – 2 Horses

12 Milk Cows

2 Working Oxen

10 Other Cattle

8 Swine

VALUE OF LIVESTOCK – $ 780

PRODUCE DURING THE YEAR ENDING JUNE 1, 1870 – 1, 960 Spring Wheat (bushels of)

200 Indian Corn (bushels of)

950 Oats (bushels of)

75 Barley (bushels of)

25 POTATOES, IRISH (BUSHELS OF)

200 BUTTER (LBS. OF)

3 HAY (TONS OF)

ESTIMATED VALUE OF ALL FARM PRODUCTIONS – $ 2, 130

Heman Calkins

LOCATION – OTSELIC, CHENANGO CO., NEW YORK – JUNE 1, 1850

ACRES OF LAND – 70 (IMPROVED)

30 (UNIMPROVED)

CASH VALUE OF FARM – $ 1,200

VALUE OF FARMING IMPLEMENTS & MACHINERY – $ 40

LIVESTOCK, JUNE 1, 1850 – 1 HORSES

2 MILK COWS

4 WORKING OXEN

5 OTHER CATTLE

14 SHEEP

2 SWINE

VALUE OF LIVESTOCK – $ 220

PRODUCE DURING THE YEAR ENDING JUNE 1, 1850 – 40 INDIAN CORN (BUSHELS OF)

300 OATS (BUSHELS OF)

30 WOOL (LBS. OF)

30 IRISH POTATOES (BUSHELS OF)

20 BUCKWHEAT (BUSHELS OF)

200 BUTTER (LBS. OF)

2 HAY (TONS OF)

3 OTHER GRASS SEEDS (BUSHELS OF)

VALUE OF HOME-MADE MANUFACTURES – $ 15

VALUE OF ANIMALS SLAUGHTERED – $ 20

Elisha Calkins & Anna Dalrymple Descendants

Heman Calkins

LOCATION – OTSELIC, CHENANGO CO., NEW YORK – JULY 25TH – 26TH, 1870

ACRES OF LAND – 80 (IMPROVED)

20 (UNIMPROVED)

CASH VALUE OF FARM – $ 4, 500

VALUE OF FARMING IMPLEMENTS & MACHINERY – $ 250

TOTAL AMOUNT OF WAGES PAID DURING THE YEAR – $ 50

LIVESTOCK, JUNE 1, 1870 – 4 HORSES

12 MILK COWS

3 SWINE

VALUE OF LIVESTOCK – $ 1, 300

PRODUCE DURING THE YEAR ENDING JUNE 1, 1870 – 100 OATS (BUSHELS OF)

100 IRISH POTATOES (BUSHELS OF)

1, 200 BUTTER (LBS. OF)

1, 268 CHEESE (LBS. OF)

40 HAY (TONS OF)

800 HOPS (LBS. OF)

80 MAPLE SUGAR (LBS. OF)

VALUE OF HOME MANUFACTURES – $ 47

VALUE OF ANIMALS SLAUGHTERED – $ 129

VALUE OF ALL FARM PRODUCTIONS – $ 1, 312

Sidney M. Calkins

LOCATION– OTSELIC, CHENANGO CO., NEW YORK – JULY 25TH – 26TH, 1870

ACRES OF LAND– 12 (IMPROVED)

3 (UNIMPROVED)

CASH VALUE OF FARM– $ 1,000

VALUE OF FARMING IMPLEMENTS & MACHINERY– $ 10

LIVESTOCK, JUNE 1, 1870– 1 MILK COWS

VALUE OF LIVESTOCK– $ 50

PRODUCE DURING THE YEAR ENDING JUNE 1, 1870 – 150 OATS (BUSHELS OF)

30 IRISH POTATOES (BUSHELS OF)

100 BUTTER (LBS. OF)

5 HAY (TONS OF)

VALUE OF ANIMALS SLAUGHTERED– $ 20

VALUE OF ALL FARM PRODUCTIONS– $ 195

Sidney M. Calkins

LOCATION– OTSELIC, CHENANGO CO., NEW YORK – JUNE 1, 1875

ACRES OF LAND– 100 (IMPROVED)

15 (UNIMPROVED, TOTAL)

15 (UNIMPROVED, IN WOOD & TIMBER LAND)

CASH VALUE– OF FARM – $ 2,500

OF FARM BUILDINGS OTHER THAN DWELLINGS – $ 400

OF STOCK – $ 500

OF TOOLS & IMPLEMENTS – $ 100

OF GROSS SALES FROM FARMS IN 1874 – $ 300

ACRES PLOWED– IN 1874 – 14

IN 1875 – 15

GRASS LANDS– ACRES IN PASTURE (IN 1874) – 56

ACRES IN PASTURE (IN 1875) – 55

MEADOW (ACRES, 1874) – 30

Elisha Calkins & Anna Dalrymple Descendants

MEADOW (ACRES, 1875) – 30

MEADOW (TONS OF HAY, 1874) – 40

OATS – ACRES SOWN (1874) – 9

ACRES SOWN (1875) – 9

BUSHELS HARVESTED, 1874 – 300

BUCKWHEAT – ACRES SOWN (1874) – 1

ACRES SOWN (1875) – 1

BUSHELS HARVESTED, 1874 – 20

POTATOES – ACRES PLANTED (1874) – 3

ACRES PLANTED (1875) – 2

BUSHELS HARVESTED, 1874 – 450

ORCHARDS – KIND OF TREES – APPLE

NUMBER OF TREES – 75

NEAT CATTLE – MILK COWS (TOTAL NO. 1875) – 1

HORSES – TWO YEARS OLD AND OVER, OWNED IN 1875 – 4

SWINE – SEASON OF 1874 AND OLDER – 1

NUMBER SLAUGHTERED IN 1874 – 2

POUNDS OF PORK MADE, 1874 – 300

SHEEP – SHORN IN 1874 – 4

SHORN IN 1875 – 4

LAMBS RAISED IN 1874 – 3

LAMBS RAISED IN 1875 – 5

POUNDS OF WOOL SHORN IN 1874 – 20

POUNDS OF WOOL SHORN IN 1875 – 20

POULTRY – VALUE OWNED, 1875 – $ 10

VALUE SOLD, 1874 – $ 6

VALUE OF EGGS SOLD, 1874 – $ 6

Leman Calkins

LOCATION– SMYRNA, CHENANGO CO., NEW YORK – JULY 23, 1860

ACRES OF LAND– 40 (IMPROVED)

10 (UNIMPROVED)

CASH VALUE OF FARM– $ 1, 200

VALUE OF FARMING IMPLEMENTS & MACHINERY– $ 30

LIVESTOCK, JUNE 1, 1860– 1 MILK COWS

2 WORKING OXEN

1 OTHER CATTLE

6 SWINE

VALUE OF LIVESTOCK– $ 147

PRODUCE DURING THE YEAR ENDING JUNE 1, 1860 – 50 OATS (BUSHELS OF)

Daniel B. Rider

LOCATION– OTSELIC, CHENANGO CO., NEW YORK – JULY 28TH – 29TH, 1870

ACRES OF LAND– 24 (IMPROVED)

5 (UNIMPROVED)

CASH VALUE OF FARM– $ 1, 100

VALUE OF FARMING IMPLEMENTS & MACHINERY– $ 40

LIVESTOCK, JUNE 1, 1870– 2 MILK COWS

1 OTHER CATTLE

VALUE OF LIVESTOCK– $ 140

PRODUCE DURING THE YEAR ENDING JUNE 1, 1870 – 10 OATS (BUSHELS OF)

30 IRISH POTATOES (BUSHELS OF)

250 BUTTER (LBS. OF)

12 HAY (TONS OF)

VALUE OF ANIMALS SLAUGHTERED– $ 38

VALUE OF ALL FARM PRODUCTIONS– $ 233

Daniel B. Rider

LOCATION — OTSELIC, CHENANGO CO., NEW YORK — JUNE 1, 1875

ACRES OF LAND — 18 (IMPROVED)

CASH VALUE — OF FARM — $ 1,200

      OF FARM BUILDINGS OTHER THAN DWELLINGS — $ 500

      OF STOCK — $ 50

      OF TOOLS & IMPLEMENTS — $ 20

      OF GROSS SALES FROM FARMS IN 1874 — $ 100

ACRES PLOWED — IN 1874 — ½

      IN 1875 — ½

GRASS LANDS — ACRES IN PASTURE (IN 1874) — 2

      ACRES IN PASTURE (IN 1875) — 2

      MEADOW (ACRES, 1874) — 15

      MEADOW (ACRES, 1875) — 15

      MEADOW (TONS OF HAY, 1874) — 15

INDIAN CORN — FOR THE GRAIN (ACRES PLANTED, 1875) — ½

      ACRES SOWN FOR FODDER (1875) — ½

POTATOES — ACRES PLANTED (1875) — ½

ORCHARDS — KIND OF TREES — APPLE

      NUMBER OF TREES — 25

      BUSHELS OF FRUIT, HARVESTED IN 1874 — 50

NEAT CATTLE — HEIFER CALVES (SEASON OF 1873) — 1

      (SEASON OF 1875) — 1

      MILK COWS (TOTAL NO. 1875) — 1

SWINE — PIGS OF 1873 — 1

POULTRY — VALUE OWNED, 1875 — 8

OTHER ARTICLE OF DOMESTIC MANUFACTURE — DRIED BERRIES — QUANTITY — 72 QTS.

      VALUE — $ 9

Dorman Calkins

LOCATION— OTSELIC, CHENANGO CO., NEW YORK — JUNE 1, 1850

ACRES OF LAND— 80 (IMPROVED)

            30 (UNIMPROVED)

CASH VALUE OF FARM— $ 2,000

VALUE OF FARMING IMPLEMENTS & MACHINERY— $ 150

LIVESTOCK, JUNE 1, 1850— 2 HORSES

           11 MILK COWS

           4 OTHER CATTLE

           36 SHEEP

           5 SWINE

VALUE OF LIVESTOCK— $ 400

PRODUCE DURING THE YEAR ENDING JUNE 1, 1850— 25 INDIAN CORN (BUSHELS OF)

           150 OATS (BUSHELS OF)

           110 WOOL (LBS. OF)

           75 GINNED COTTON (BALES OF 400 LB. EACH)

           35 POTATOES, IRISH (BUSHELS OF)

           25 BARLEY (BUSHELS OF)

           6 BUCKWHEAT (BUSHELS OF)

           600 BUTTER (LBS. OF)

           200 CHEESE (LBS. OF)

           40 HAY (TONS OF)

           4 OTHER GRASS SEEDS (BUSHELS OF)

           50 FLAX (LBS. OF)

           3 FLAXSEED (BUSHELS OF)

           50 MAPLE SUGAR (LBS. OF)

           5 BEESWAX AND HONEY (LBS. OF)

VALUE OF HOME-MADE MANUFACTURES— $ 5

VALUE OF ANIMALS SLAUGHTERED— $ 35

Dorman Calkins

LOCATION – OTSELIC, CHENANGO CO., NEW YORK – JUNE, 1860

ACRES OF LAND – 120 (IMPROVED)

30 (UNIMPROVED)

CASH VALUE OF FARM – $ 4, 200

VALUE OF FARMING IMPLEMENTS & MACHINERY – $ 250

LIVESTOCK, JUNE 1, 1860 – 2 HORSES

11 MILK COWS

7 OTHER CATTLE

29 SHEEP

2 SWINE

VALUE OF LIVESTOCK – $ 750

PRODUCE DURING THE YEAR ENDING JUNE 1, 1860 – 37 WHEAT (BUSHELS OF)

150 OATS (BUSHELS OF)

110 WOOL (LBS. OF)

Dorman Calkins

LOCATION – OTSELIC, CHENANGO CO., NEW YORK – JULY 25TH – 26TH, 1870

ACRES OF LAND – 130 (IMPROVED)

25 (UNIMPROVED)

CASH VALUE OF FARM – $ 6, 975

VALUE OF FARMING IMPLEMENTS & MACHINERY – $ 200

LIVESTOCK, JUNE 1, 1870 – 3 HORSES

15 MILK COWS

6 OTHER CATTLE

4 SHEEP

2 SWINE

VALUE OF LIVESTOCK – $ 1, 325

Hurst

Produce during the Year ending June 1, 1870 – 15 Indian Corn (bushels of)

40 Oats (bushels of)

70 Buckwheat (bushels of)

200 Irish Potatoes (bushels of)

Orchard Products – $ 5

1, 650 Butter (lbs. of)

190 Cheese (lbs. of)

60 Hay (tons of)

530 Hops (lbs. of)

Value of animals slaughtered – $ 90

Value of all Farm Productions – $ 1, 627

Dorman Calkins

Location – Otselic, Chenango Co., New York – June 1, 1875

Acres of Land – 85 (improved)

15 (unimproved)

Cash Value – of Farm – $ 3, 500

of Farm Buildings other than Dwellings – $ 1, 000

of Stock – $ 700

of Tools & Implements – $ 100

of Gross Sales from Farms in 1874 – $ 700

Acres Plowed – in 1874 – 10

in 1875 – 15

Grass Lands – Acres in Pasture (in 1874) – 55

Acres in Pasture (in 1875) – 30

Meadow (Acres, 1874) – 44

Meadow (Acres, 1875) – 55

Meadow (Tons of Hay, 1874) – 35

OATS – ACRES SOWN (1874) – 7

ACRES SOWN (1875) – 7

BUSHELS HARVESTED, 1874 – 135

BUCKWHEAT – ACRES SOWN (1874) – 1

ACRES SOWN (1875) – 2

BUSHELS HARVESTED, 1874 – 15

INDIAN CORN – FOR THE GRAIN (ACRES PLANTED, 1875) – 1

ACRES SOWN FOR FODDER (1874) – $\frac{1}{2}$

ACRES SOWN FOR FODDER (1875) – $\frac{1}{2}$

POTATOES – ACRES PLANTED (1874) – 2

ACRES PLANTED (1875) – 2

BUSHELS HARVESTED, 1874 – 400

BEANS – ACRES PLANTED (1875) – $\frac{1}{2}$

HOPS – ACRES IN CROP (1874) – 1

ACRES IN CROP (1875) – 3

POUNDS HARVESTED, 1874 – 600

ORCHARDS – KIND OF TREES – APPLE

NUMBER OF TREES – 200

BUSHELS OF FRUIT, HARVESTED IN 1874 – 150

BARRELS OF CIDER MADE, 1874 – 3

POUNDS OF MAPLE SUGAR MADE, 1875 – 50

GALLONS OF MAPLE MOLASSES MADE, 1875 – 3

NEAT CATTLE – HEIFER CALVES (SEASON OF 1873) – 1

(SEASON OF 1874) – 2

(SEASON OF 1875) – 1

BULLS OF ALL AGES – 1

MILK COWS (AVERAGE NO. 1874) – 10

(TOTAL NO. 1875) – 4

BUTTER (POUNDS MADE BY FAMILIES, 1874) – 1,500

HORSES – COLTS OF 1874 – 1

TWO YEARS OLD AND OVER, OWNED IN 1875 – 3

SWINE – PIGS OF 1873 – 9

SEASON OF 1874 AND OLDER – 1

NUMBER SLAUGHTERED IN 1874 – 2

POUNDS OG PORK MADE, 1874 – 400

POULTRY – VALUE OWNED, 1875 – $ 21

VALUE SOLD, 1874 – $ 45

VALUE OF EGGS SOLD, 1874 – $ 25

OTHER ARTICLE OF DOMESTIC MANUFACTURE – DRIED APPLES – QUANTITY – 300

VALUE – $ 33

Noyes Robbins

LOCATION – OTSELIC, CHENANGO CO., NEW YORK – JULY 28ᵀᴴ – 29ᵀᴴ, 1870

ACRES OF LAND – 106 (IMPROVED)

25 (UNIMPROVED)

CASH VALUE OF FARM – $ 1, 500

VALUE OF FARMING IMPLEMENTS & MACHINERY – $ 200

TOTAL AMOUNT OF WAGES PAID DURING THE YEAR – $ 100

LIVESTOCK, JUNE 1, 1870 – 3 HORSES

12 MILK COWS

3 OTHER CATTLE

6 SHEEP

2 SWINE

VALUE OF LIVESTOCK – $ 1, 170

PRODUCE DURING THE YEAR ENDING JUNE 1, 1870 – 30 INDIAN CORN (BUSHELS OF)

80 OATS (BUSHELS OF)

15 BUCKWHEAT (BUSHELS OF)

42 WOOL (LBS. OF)

70 IRISH POTATOES (BUSHELS OF)

1, 800 BUTTER (LBS. OF)

40 HAY (TONS OF)

4 Bees Wax (lbs. of)

100 Honey (lbs. of)

Value of animals slaughtered – $ 91

Value of all Farm Productions – $ 1,283

Ery W. Stokes

Location – Smyrna, Chenango Co., New York – June, 1870

Acres of Land – 7 (improved)

Cash Value of Farm – $ 3,000

Value of Farming Implements & Machinery – $ 175

Total amount of wages paid during the year – $ 150

Livestock, June 1, 1860 – 2 Horses

1 Milk Cows

2 Other Cattle

1 Swine

Value of Livestock – $ 575

Produce during the Year ending June 1, 1860 – 65 Oats (bushels of)

William Riley Calkins

Location – Otselic, Chenango Co., New York – June 1, 1850

Acres of Land – 40 (improved)

23 (unimproved)

Cash Value of Farm – $ 1,000

Value of Farming Implements & Machinery – $ 40

Livestock, June 1, 1850 – 1 Horses

2 Milk Cows

2 Other Cattle

14 Sheep

2 Swine

Value of Livestock – $ 250

Hurst

PRODUCE DURING THE YEAR ENDING JUNE 1, 1850 — 12 WHEAT (BUSHELS OF)

10 INDIAN CORN (BUSHELS OF)

200 OATS (BUSHELS OF)

44 WOOL (LBS. OF)

30 POTATOES, IRISH (BUSHELS OF)

3 BUCKWHEAT (BUSHELS OF)

300 BUTTER (LBS. OF)

10 HAY (TONS OF)

3 OTHER GRASS SEEDS (BUSHELS OF)

64 FLAX (LBS. OF)

3 FLAXSEED (BUSHELS OF)

100 MAPLE SUGAR (LBS. OF)

30 BEESWAX AND HONEY (LBS. OF)

VALUE OF HOME-MADE MANUFACTURES — $ 5

VALUE OF ANIMALS SLAUGHTERED — $ 10

William Riley Calkins

LOCATION — OTSELIC, CHENANGO CO., NEW YORK — JUNE 3, 1875

ACRES OF LAND — 180 (IMPROVED)

55 (UNIMPROVED)

CASH VALUE — OF FARM — $ 9, 250

OF FARM BUILDINGS OTHER THAN DWELLINGS — $ 1, 200

OF STOCK — $ 1, 500

OF TOOLS & IMPLEMENTS — $ 200

OF GROSS SALES FROM FARMS IN 1874 — $ 700

ACRES PLOWED — IN 1874 — 10

IN 1875 — 10

GRASS LANDS — ACRES IN PASTURE (IN 1874) — 65

ACRES IN PASTURE (IN 1875) — 65

MEADOW (ACRES, 1874) — 50

MEADOW (ACRES, 1875) — 50

MEADOW (TONS OF HAY, 1874) — 70

OATS — ACRES SOWN (1874) — 7

ACRES SOWN (1875) — 7

BUSHELS HARVESTED, 1874 — 240

BUCKWHEAT — ACRES SOWN (1874) — 1

BUSHELS HARVESTED, 1874 — 20

INDIAN CORN — FOR THE GRAIN (ACRES PLANTED, 1875) — ½

ACRES SOWN FOR FODDER (1874) — 1

ACRES SOWN FOR FODDER (1875) — 1

POTATOES — ACRES PLANTED (1874) — 1

ACRES PLANTED (1875) — 1

BUSHELS HARVESTED, 1874 — 250

ORCHARDS — KIND OF TREES — APPLE

NUMBER OF TREES — 50

BUSHELS OF FRUIT, HARVESTED IN 1874 — 50

NEAT CATTLE — HEIFER CALVES (SEASON OF 1874) — 5

(SEASON OF 1875) — 5

BULLS OF ALL AGES — 2

MILK COWS (AVERAGE NO. 1874) — 20

(TOTAL NO. 1875) — 18

(MILK SENT TO FACTORY, 1874) — 20

(CATTLE KILLED FOR BEEF, 1874) — 1

BUTTER (POUNDS MADE BY FAMILIES, 1874) — 250

HORSES — TWO YEARS OLD AND OVER, OWNED IN 1875 — 2

SWINE — PIGS OF 1873 — 2

SEASON OF 1874 AND OLDER — 2

NUMBER SLAUGHTERED IN 1874 — 2

POUNDS OG PORK MADE, 1874 — 500

SHEEP – SHORN, 1875 – 2

      LAMBS RAISED IN 1875 – 2

      POUNDS OF WOOL SHORN IN 1875 – 13

POULTRY – VALUE OWNED, 1875 – $ 40

      VALUE OF EGGS SOLD, 1874 – $ 10

Civil War Soldiers

Conrad M. Folts at age 21 enlisted on August 29, 1862 at Hamilton, Madison Co., New York to serve three years of service. He was mustered in as private in Company G of the 157th New York Infantry on September 19, 1862. He was discharged on October 29, 1863 for a disability from the hospital in Philadelphia, Pennsylvania.

Lyman Miller at age 30 enlisted on August 21, 1862 at Smyrna, Chenango Co., New York to serve three years of service. He was mustered in as private in Company F of the 157th New York Infantry on September 19, 1862. He was discharged on June 8, 1865 from the hospital at Hilton Head, South Carolina.

Alexander Butts at age 30 enlisted on January 9, 1864 at Smyrna, Chenango Co., New York to serve three years. He was mustered in as a private who was unassigned in the 9th Artillery. No further record on his service.

Lysander Butts at age 21 enlisted on August 11, 1862 at Otselic, Chenango Co., New York to serve three years of service. He was mustered in as a musician in Company I of the 114th New York Volunteer Infantry on August 14, 1862. He died from consumption on December 18, 1864 at McKim's Mansion Hospital in Baltimore, Maryland.

Samuel Calkins Butts at age 39 enlisted on August 11, 1862 at Norwich, Chenango Co., New York to serve three years of service. He was mustered in as a musician to Company K of the 114th New York Volunteer Infantry on August 15, 1862. He was mustered out with company on June 8, 1865 at Washington, D.C.

William Henry Calkins at age 21 enlisted on August 11, 1862 at Otselic, Chenango Co., New York to serve three years of service. He was mustered in as a sergeant to Company I of the 114th New York Volunteer Infantry on August 14, 1862. He died of Typhoid fever on August 16, 1863 at Thibodeaux, Lafourche Parish, Louisiana.

Physical Descriptions

(In order of appearance in the book)

George La Fayette Stowell – tall, medium build, gray eyes, brown hair – (18 years of age)

Bryan Jennings Stone – medium, medium build, gray eyes, dark brown hair –

(18 years of age)

Lionell Mayne Kinney – medium, slender build, gray eyes, dark brown hair – (21 years of age)

Glenn Stone – medium, slender build, brown eyes, brown hair (not bald) – (21 years of age)

Fred Truman Walradt – medium, medium build, blue eyes, brown hair – (40 years of age)

Frank Jacob Walradt – medium, medium build, light blue eyes, light brown hair –

(39 years of age)

Earl Samuel Walradt – medium, medium build, blue eyes, gray hair – (37 years of age)

Olin Irving Walradt – medium, medium build, light blue eyes, dark brown hair –

(34 years of age)

Windsor Charles Brown – tall, slender build, gray eyes, dark brown hair – (32 years of age)

Charles Arthur Waggoner – medium, medium build, blue eyes, brown hair (not bald) –

(26 years of age)

Herbert Isaac Coy – medium, medium build, blue eyes, black hair (bald) – (38 years of age)

Milton Adellon Walradt – tall, slender build, blue eyes, brown hair (not bald) –

(28 years of age)

Howard Millard Greene – short, medium build, blue eyes, dark hair (not bald) –

(24 years of age)

Harvey L. Jackson – medium, medium build, blue eyes, brown hair (not bald) –

(21 years of age)

Samuel Leroy Jackson – medium, medium build, blue eyes, light hair – (20 years of age)

Ernest F. Tabor – medium, stout build, light blue eyes, light brown hair – (24 years of age)

Harold J. Tabor – medium, slender build, brown eyes, brown hair (not bald) – (21 years of age)

Willard Leigh Sudenga – medium, slender build, gray eyes, brown hair – (19 years of age)

Peter Edward Thimineur – medium, slender build, brown eyes, black hair – (22 years of age)

Weaver Lamont Northrup – medium, medium build, blue eyes, brown hair – (21 years of age)

Harry Banks Briggs – medium, slender build, grey eyes, light hair – (45 years of age)

Frederick Plumb Briggs – medium, medium build, blue eyes, gray hair – (42 years of age)

William Wallace Huntley – medium, slender build, dark brown eyes, dark brown hair –

(32 years of age)

Jerome Francis Briggs – short, medium build, brown eyes, brown hair (not bald) –

(23 years of age)

– 5', 2", 116 lbs., blue eyes, gray hair, ruddy complexion,

scar on index finger of right hand – (48 years of age)

Walter Niles Butts – medium, medium build, brown eyes, black hair – (40 years of age)

Hubert William Butts – medium, medium build, brown eyes, black hair (not bald) –

(22 years of age)

Alexander Butts – 5', 10", blue eyes, brown hair, fair complexion – (30 years of age)

Lysander Butts – 5', 8", blue eyes, brown hair, dark complexion – (21 years of age)

Dexter Florello Woods – 5', 7 ½", gray eyes, dark hair, light complexion, blind in right eye –

(64 years of age)

Clayton Forest Woods – 5', 8", blue eyes, brown hair, light complexion – (38 years of age)

– 5', 7 ¾", blue eyes, light brown hair, light complexion –

(41 years of age)

Victor Wayne Newman – 5' 11 ½", 180 lbs., blue eyes, gray hair, ruddy complexion,

tattoo on right forearm – (54 years of age)

Jay Lemar Newman – medium, medium build, dark blue eyes, light brown hair –

(19 years of age)

Embert Morelle Brown – medium, medium build, blue eyes, light hair – (43 years of age)

Elisha Calkins & Anna Dalrymple Descendants

Luther Garrett Bean – 5', 9", 160 lbs., brown eyes, brown hair, light complexion,

disfigures thumb on left hand – (35 years of age)

Theron Eugene Eldred – tall, slender build, brown eyes, bald – (43 years of age)

Alvah Devillo Jones – tall, slender build, light blue eyes, bark brown hair, badly crippled –

(33 years of age)

Ray Ottaway Jones – tall, slender build, blue eyes, dark brown hair – (29 years of age)

David Zach Kerr – 6', 2", 220 lbs., brown eyes, gray hair, light complexion – (62 years of age)

Alpha Jefferson Kerr – medium, medium build, gray eyes, brown hair – (34 years of age)

– 5', 6", 170 lbs., blue eyes, brown hair, light complexion –

(58 years of age)

Friend Ellsworth Kerr – medium, medium build, light brown eyes, light brown hair –

(27 years of age)

– 5', 6 ½", 190 lbs., blue eyes, gray hair, light complexion,

a [hard to read] right leg – (51 years of age)

Worth David Alcorn – medium, slender build, blue eyes, red hair (not bald) – (23 years of age)

– 5', 6", 145 lbs., blue eyes, blond hair, ruddy complexion –

(48 years of age)

Vincent James Galloway – medium, medium build, blue eyes, light hair (not bald) –

(22 years of age)

Clifford Le Roy Harmelink – tall, slender build, gray eyed, brown hair – (21 years of age)

Jule P. Aikens – medium, medium build, blue eyes, brown hair – (34 years of age)

– 5', 6", 155 lbs., blue eyes, gray hair, ruddy complexion, two crooked

fingers on left hand – (58 years of age)

Paul D. Aikens – medium, medium build, blue eyes, brown hair (not bald), 2 ruptures –

(28 years of age)

– 5', 10", 155 lbs., blue eyes, black hair, light complexion, bunch on left wrist

(53 years of age)

Albert Davilla Woods – 5', 9", hazel eyes, dark hair, dark complexion – (24 years of age)

413

Hurst

Wayne Waverly Barnett – short, slender build, blue eyes, brown hair (not bald) –

(21 years of age)

Charles Albert Woods – medium, medium build, blue eyes, brown hair – (34 years of age)

Alvin Hall James – tall, slender build, graying eyes, black hair – (36 years of age)

Leon Raymond Dodd – medium, medium build, hazel eyes, dark brown hair – (38 years of age)

Nathan Elton Dodd – tall, medium build, blue eyes, brown hair (not bald) – (30 years of age)

– 5' 7", 160 lbs., brown eyes, black & gray hair, dark brown complexion

(he was listed as Negro), scars on both cheeks – (55 years of age)

Nelson Wickwire Trisket – medium, medium build, black eyes, black hair – (29 years of age)

– 6', 160 lbs., blue eyes, brown hair, light complexion –

(54 years of age)

Frank Leslie Dodd – 5', 4", 165 lbs., hazel eyes, gray hair, ruddy complexion – (49 years of age)

Merton Charles Day – tall, medium build, brown eyes, dark hair – (32 years of age)

Sears Seth Day – tall, medium build, blue eyes, light hair (not bald) – (28 years of age)

Lester Alvah Fuller – 5', 10", 160lbs., blue eyes, gray hair, light complexion – (52 years of age)

Clifford Alva Fuller – medium, medium build, blue eyes, light hair (not bald),

ruptured -- poor eyes – (24 years of age)

Leland Raymond Fuller – 5', 11", 160 lbs., blue eyes, brown hair, light complexion,

scar on instep of left foot, scar on lid of right eye – (46 years of age)

Otto Marcelius Johnson – tall, stout build, light blue eyes, light brown hair (not bald) –

(28 years of age)

Carlton Lewis Fuller – short, stout build, gray eyes, dark brown hair – (35 years of age)

Wilton John Lord – medium, medium build, gray eyes, light hair – (41 years of age)

– 5', 9", 145 lbs., hazel eyes, brown hair, light complexion, small scar

left side on nose – (64 years of age)

Earl Vincent Fuller – tall, stout build, gray eyes, black hair (not bald) – (29 years of age)

Simon Stanley McMahon – medium, medium build, gray eyes, auburn hair (not bald) –

(30 years of age)

– 5', 8", 153 lbs., blue eyes, red hair, light complexion,

6 inch scar on right forearm – (55 years of age)

Leslie Donald Cowie – medium, medium build, blue eyes, brown hair – (32 years of age)

Andrew Jackson Caldwell – tall, slender build, blue eyes, light brown hair – (27 years of age)

Robert Sheldon Cowie – medium, medium build, gray eyes, black hair (not bald) –

(27 years of age)

George Carlton Cowie – medium, medium build, blue eyes, brown hair (not bald) –

(25 years of age)

Albert Burr Morris – short, slender build, light brown eyes, light brown hair – (18 years of age)

Julius Oscar Thone – tall, medium build, gray eyes, dark hair – (44 years of age)

James Werdna Calkins – tall, medium build, brown eyes, brown (balding) – (38 years of age)

Floyd Elisha Calkins – medium, medium build, light eyes, light hair – (33 years of age)

William Arthur Calkins – short, medium build, dark hue eyes, black hair – (30 years of age)

George Leland Morgan – tall, medium build, gray eyes, dark brown hair (not bald) –

(23 years of age)

Lyle Hurst Badgley – 5', 10", 120 lbs., gray eyes, gray hair, light complexion – (61 years of age)

Archie Lamont McDonald – medium, slender build, blue eyes, dark hair (not bald) –

(28 years of age)

James Donald McDonald – tall, medium build, blue eyes, dark brown hair (not bald) –

(24 years of age)

Gerald John McDonald – brown eyes, black brown hair – (22 years of age)

Earle Denton Calkins – medium, medium build, brown eyes, brown hair (not bald) –

(22 years of age)

– 5', 9", 150 lbs., brown eyes, gray hair, ruddy complexion –

(47 years of age)

Arcus Riley Calkins – 5', 8", 160lbs., blue eyes, gray hair, ruddy complexion – (45 years of age)

Ralph Mason Calkins – medium, medium build, brown eyes, dark brown hair,

has lost sight of left eye – (20 years of age)

Arthur Riley Calkins – medium, medium build, blue eyes, brown hair – (41 years of age)

Albert Stanley Persons – short, medium build, blue eyes, brown hair – (38 years of age)

Nathan Orson Calkins – 5', 8", blue eyes, auburn hair, light complexion – (55 years of age)

Lyman Oral Calkins – medium, medium build, gray eyes, brown hair – (41 years of age)

Rueben Roy Calkins – medium, medium build, brown eyes, dark brown hair –

(38 years of age)

Oel Leo Calkikns – tall, slender build, gray eyes, dark brown hair – (36 years of age)

Bert Eugene Ingalls – medium, medium, brown eyes, dark hair – (35 years of age)

Randall Branch Calkins – medium, medium build, gray eyes, dark hair – (37 years of age)

William Luther Shepard – medium, medium build, brown eyes, brown hair – (42 years of age)

Frank Vernon Randall – tall, slender build, blue eyes, brown hair – (33 years of age)

George McKinley Fosdick – 5', 3", stout build, blue eyes, light hair (not bald) –

(25 years of age)

Charles Abner Tucker – medium, medium build, light blue eyes, light brown hair (not bald)

(28 years of age)

Leon Wallace Sherwood – medium, stout build, gray eyes, black hair – (32 years of age)

Myrl La Fayette Sherwood – medium, medium build, light brown eyes, dark brown hair –

(20 years of age)

William Henry Calkins – 5', 7", blue eyes, brown hair, fair complexion – (21 years of age)

Charles Calkins – medium, medium build, black eyes, black hair – (39 years of age)

Clyde Calkins – medium, medium build, dark brown eyes, dark brown hair (not bald) –

(26 years of age)

Irving Washington Dutcher – medium, slender build, blue eyes, brown hair – (39 years of age)

Robert Rush Clark – 6', brown eyes, gray hair, dark complexion – (61 years of age)

William Stokes Clark – 5', 10", blue eyes, black hair, dark complexion – (30 years of age)

Ery Stokes Shepardson – medium, medium build, light brown eyes, black hair (not bald) –

(27 years of age)

Edward Dever Stokes – medium, medium build, blue eyes, brown hair – (39 years of age)

Walter Stokes – short, medium build, blue eyes, brown hair (not bald) – (29 years of age)

Ward McFee – medium, medium build, light blue eyes, brown hair (not bald) – (25 years of age)

References

Andreas, A. T. (1874) . <u>An Illustrated Historical Atlas of the state of Minnesota</u>. Chicago: Lakeside Building.

<u>Biographical Souvenir of the counties of Buffalo, Kearney, Phelps, Harlan, and Franklin Nebraska</u> (1890) . Chicago: F. A. Battey & Company

Burton, W. R. (1916) . <u>Past and Present of Adams County Nebraska</u> (vol. II). Chicago: The S. J. Clarke Publishing Company

Calkins, W. W. (1903) . <u>The Calkins memorial military roster</u>. Chicago: M. A. Donohue & Company.

Cutter, W. R. (1913) . <u>New England Families: Genealogical and Memorial</u> (vol. II). New York: Lewis Historical Publishing Company

Guinn, J. M. (1907). <u>A History of California and an Extended History of Its Southern Coast Counties</u> (vol. II). Los Angles: Historic Record Company

<u>History of Grant County Wisconsin</u> (1881) . Chicago: Western Historical Company

<u>Portrait and Biographical Album of Jackson, Jefferson and Pottawatomie Counties, Kansas</u> (1890) . Chicago: Chapman Bros.

Skinner, Dolphus & A. B. Grosh (Eds.). (1832) . <u>Evangelical Magazine and Gospel Advocate</u>. Utica: A. B. Grosh, Printer, Canal Buildings, corner of Seneca and Liberty Streets.

Towne, E. E. (1901) . <u>The Descendants of William Towne</u>. Newtonville, Massachusetts: Published by the author.

Index

Hurst

ABOUT THE AUTHOR

Donovan Hurst graduated from San Diego State University with a Bachelor of Arts in the major field of studies of History and a minor in the field of studies of Anthropology. He is a current member of The General Society of Mayflower Descendants and has been conducting genealogical research for over 10 years tracing back his ancestors to their ancestral homelands in Denmark, England, France, Germany, Ireland, Norway, and Scotland.

www.ingramcontent.com/pod-product-compliance
Lightning Source LLC
Chambersburg PA
CBHW080810280326
41926CB00091B/4138